I said this in the magazine's comment section, but I broke my phone and all of my contacts are gone. If you need to reach me, please send me an email. Here's *World Trigger* volume 17.

—Daisuke Ashihara, 2016

Daisuke Ashihara began his manga career at the age of 27 when his manga *Room 303* won second place in the 75th Tezuka Awards. His first series, *Super Dog Rilienthal*, began serialization in *Weekly Shonen Jump* in 2009. *World Trigger* is his second serialized work in *Weekly Shonen Jump*. He is also the author of several shorter works, including the one-shots *Super Dog Rilienthal*, *Trigger Keeper* and *Elite Agent Jin*.

WORLD TRIGGER VOL. 17
SHONEN JUMP Manga Edition

STORY AND ART BY DAISUKE ASHIHARA

Translation/Toshikazu Aizawa
Touch-Up Art & Lettering/Annaliese Christman
Design/Julian [JR] Robinson
Editor/Marlene First

WORLD TRIGGER © 2013 by Daisuke Ashihara/SHUEISHA Inc.
All rights reserved.
First published in Japan in 2013 by SHUEISHA Inc., Tokyo.
English translation rights arranged by SHUEISHA Inc.

The stories, characters and incidents mentioned
in this publication are entirely fictional.

Printed in the U.S.A.

Published by VIZ Media, LLC
P.O. Box 77010
San Francisco, CA 94107

10 9 8 7 6 5 4 3 2 1
First printing, October 2017

WORLD TRIGGER

DAISUKE ASHIHARA

17

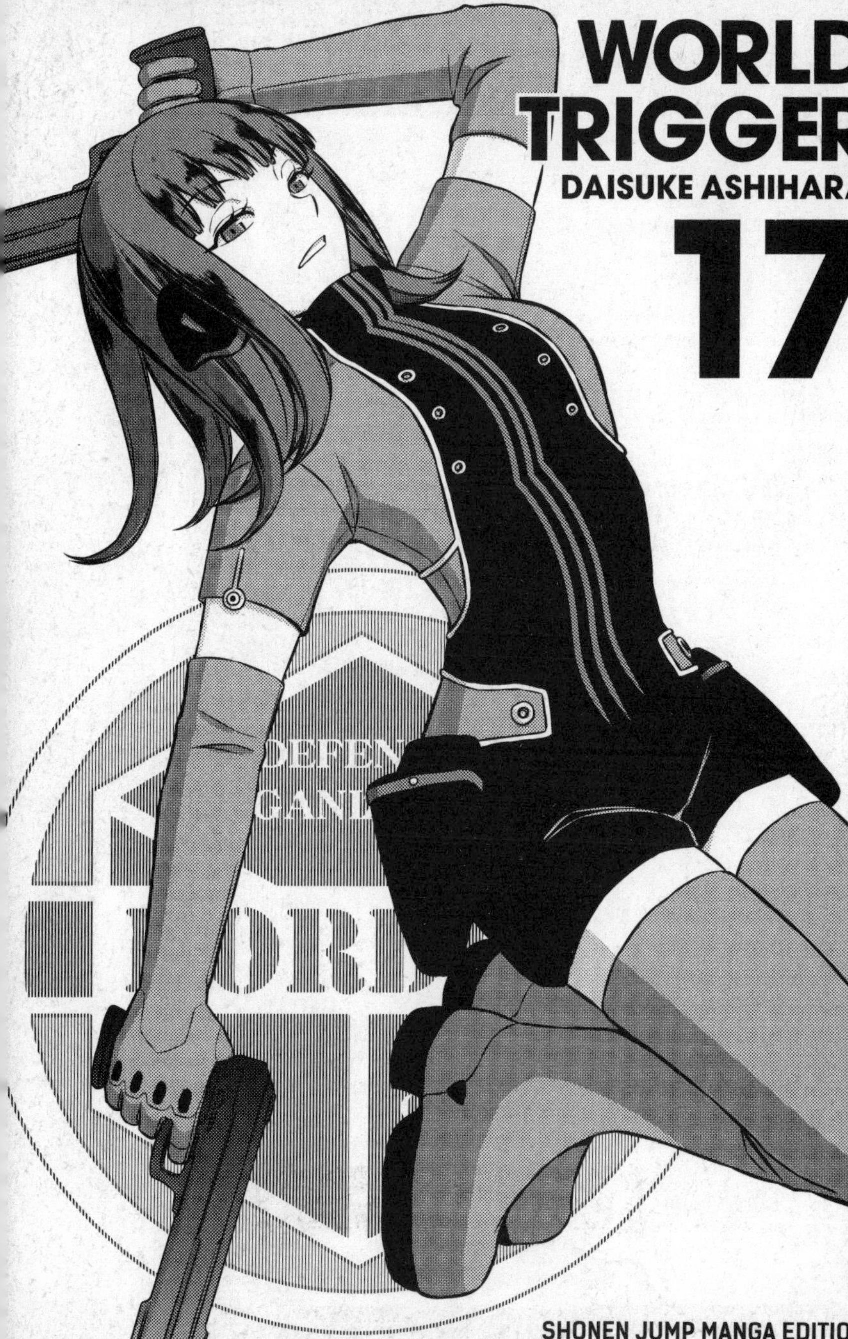

SHONEN JUMP MANGA EDITION

WORLD TRIGGER DATA BASE

BORDER

An agency founded to protect the city's peace from Neighbors.

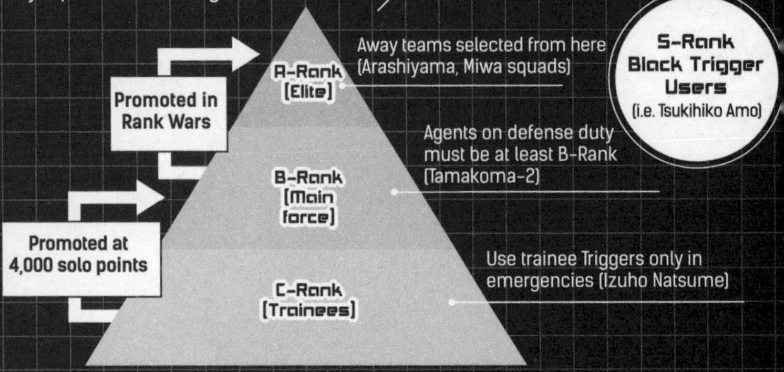

S-Rank Black Trigger Users (i.e. Tsukihiko Amo)
A-Rank [Elite]
Away teams selected from here (Arashiyama, Miwa squads)
Promoted in Rank Wars
B-Rank [Main force]
Agents on defense duty must be at least B-Rank (Tamakoma-2)
Promoted at 4,000 solo points
C-Rank [Trainees]
Use trainee Triggers only in emergencies (Izuho Natsume)

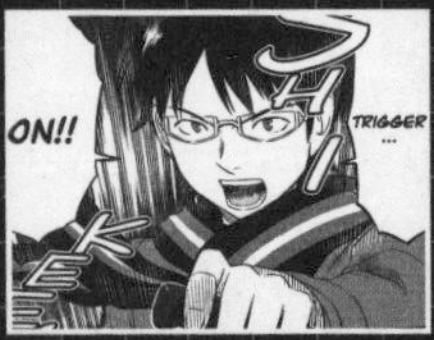

TRIGGER...
ON!!

TRIGGER

A technology created by Neighbors to manipulate Trion. Used mainly as weapons, Triggers come in various types.

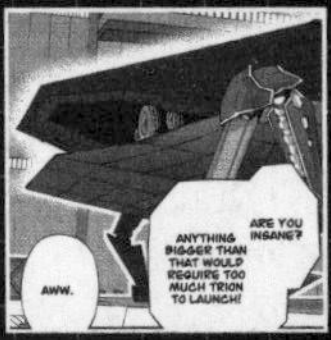

ARE YOU INSANE?
ANYTHING BIGGER THAN THAT WOULD REQUIRE TOO MUCH TRION TO LAUNCH!
AWW.

◀ A
miss
ships
also
run
Trion

POSITIONS

Border classifies them into three groups: Attacker, Gunner and Sniper.

Attacker

Close-range attacks. Weapons include: close-range Scorpions that are good for surprise attacks, the balanced Kogetsu sword, and the defense-heavy Raygust.

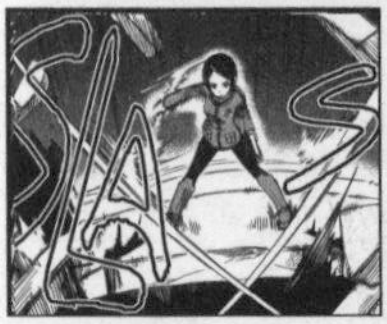

Gunner

Shoots from mid-range. There are several types of bullets, including multipurpose Asteroids, twisting Vipers, exploding Meteors, and tracking Hounds. People who don't use gun-shaped Triggers are called Shooters.

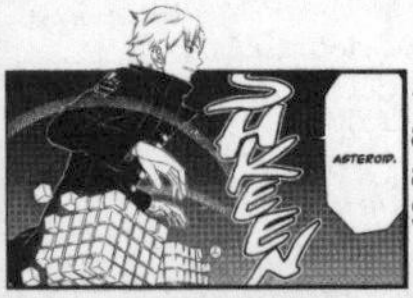

ASTEROID.

◀ Osamu and Izumi are Shooters.

Sniper

Fires from a long distance. There are three sniping rifles: the well-balanced Egret, the light and easy Lightning, and the powerful but unwieldy Ibis.

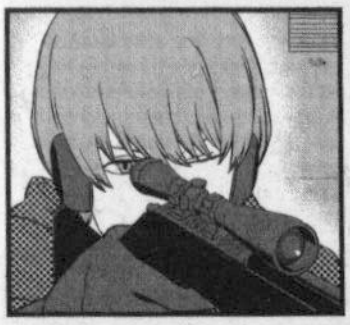

Operator

Supports combatants by relaying information such as enemy positions and abilities.

RANK WARS

Practice matches between Border agents. Promotions in Border are based on good results in the Rank Wars and defense duty achievements.

B-Rank agents are split into top, middle, and bottom groups. Three to four teams fight in a melee battle. Defeating an opposing squad member earns you one point and surviving to the end nets two points. Top teams from the previous season get a bonus.

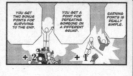

EARNING POINTS IS REALLY SIMPLE.
YOU GET A POINT FOR DEFEATING SOMEONE ON A DIFFERENT SQUAD.
YOU GET TWO BONUS POINTS FOR SURVIVING TO THE END.
+1
+2

THE TOP GROUP IS MOSTLY SO-SO.
EACH SQUAD HAS AN A-LEVEL ACE.
B-002
003
B-004
B-005
B-006
B-007

B-Rank middle groups have set strategies. Top groups all have an A-Rank level ace.

The lowest-ranked team in each match gets to pick the stage.

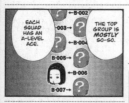

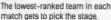

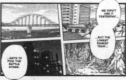

WE DIDN'T USE IT YESTERDAY...
...BUT THE LOWEST RANKED TEAM...
...GETS TO PICK THE BATTLE STAGE.

A-Rank

Top two B-Rank squads get to challenge A-Rank.

B-Rank

Agents ▶ (B-Rank and above) can't fight trainees (C-Rank) for points.

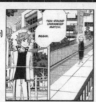

TEN-ROUND UNRANKED MATCH.
BEGIN.

C-Rank Wars are fought through solo matches. Beating someone with more points than you gets you a lot of points. On the other hand, beating someone with fewer points doesn't get you as many.

C-Rank

STORY

About four years ago, a Gate connecting to another dimension opened in Mikado City, leading to the appearance of invaders called Neighbors. After the establishment of the Border Defence Agency, people were able to return to their normal lives.

Osamu Mikumo is a junior high student who meets Yuma Kuga, a Neighbor. Yuma is targeted for capture by Border, but Tamakoma branch agent Yuichi Jin steps in to help. He convinces Yuma to join Border instead, then gives his Black Trigger to HQ in exchange for Yuma's enlistment. Now Osamu, Yuma and Osamu's friend Chika work toward making A-Rank together.

Aftokrator, the largest military nation in the Neighborhood, begins another large-scale invasion! Border succeeds in driving them back, but over 30 C-Rank trainees are kidnapped in the process. Border implements more plans for away missions to retrieve the missing Agents.

Osamu's squad, Tamakoma-2, enters the Rank Wars for a chance to be chosen for away missions. The fifth round is about to begin when Border HQ comes under attack by Galopoula, Aftokrator's subordinate nation. As the battle is coming to a close, Hyuse meets up with Reghindetz and defeats him. The Rank Wars Round 5 starts and Tamakoma-2 faces off against Kakizaki and Katori Squads using a brand new wire technique!

WORLD TRIGGER CHARACTERS

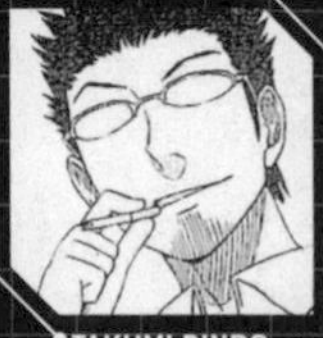

TAKUMI RINDO

Tamakoma Branch Director.

TAMAKOMA BRANCH

Understanding toward Neighbors. Considered divergent from Border's main philosophy.

TAMAKOMA-2

Tamakoma's B-Rank squad, aiming to get promoted to A-Rank.

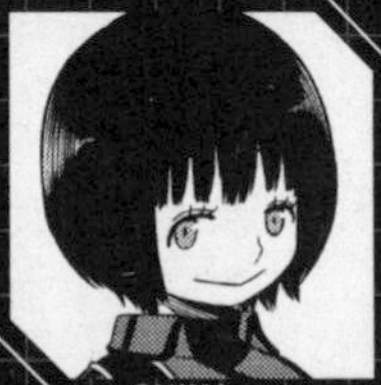

CHIKA AMATORI

Osamu's childhood friend. She has high Trion levels.

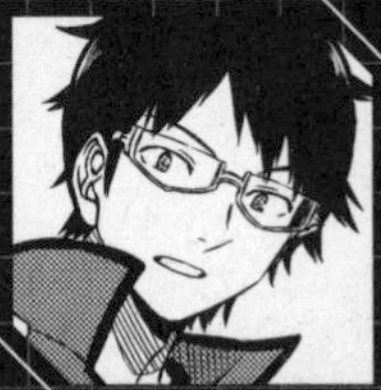

OSAMU MIKUMO

Ninth-grader who's compelled to help those in trouble. Captain of Tamakoma-2 (Mikumo squad).

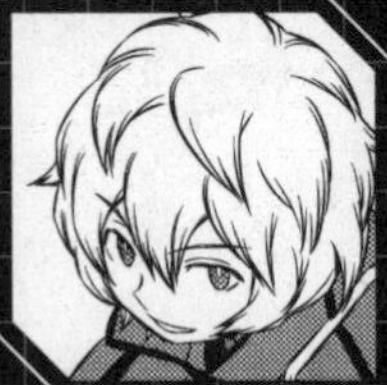

YUMA KUGA

A Neighbor who carries a Black Trigger.

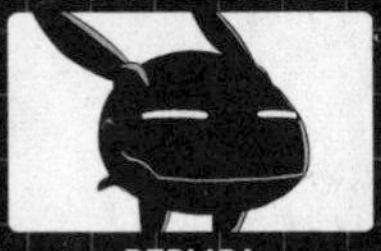

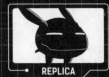

REPLICA

Yuma's chaperone. Missing after recent invasion.

TAMAKOMA-1

Tamakoma's A-Rank squad.

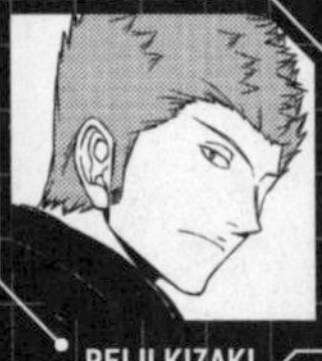

REIJI KIZAKI

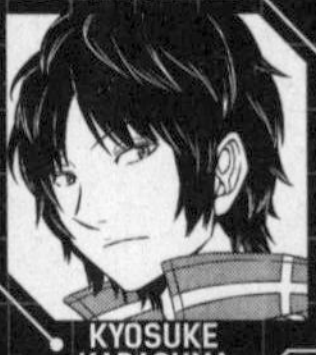

KYOSUKE KARASUMA

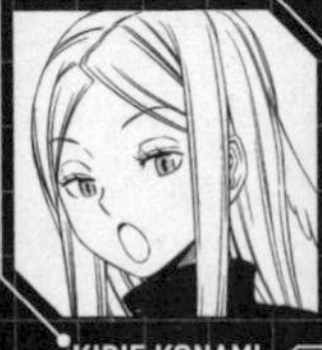

KIRIE KONAMI

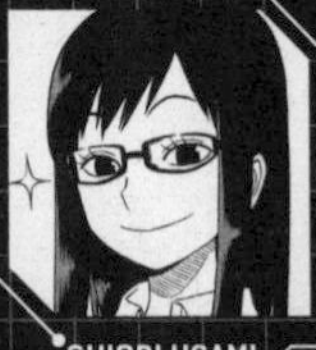

SHIORI USAMI

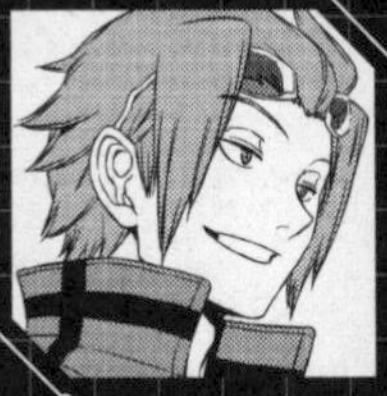

YUICHI JIN

Former S-Rank Black Trigger user. His Side Effect lets him see the future.

KATORI SQUAD

B-Rank #9 Squad operating out of Border HQ.

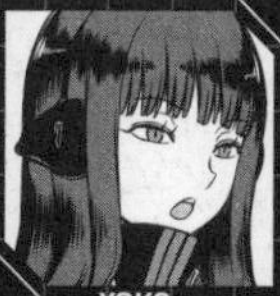
YOKO KATORI

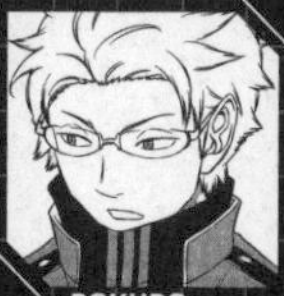
ROKURO WAKAMURA

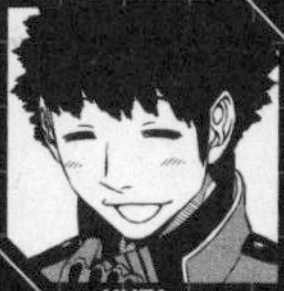
YUTA MIURA

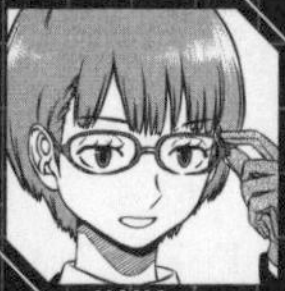
HANA SOMEI

KAKIZAKI SQUAD

B-Rank #13 Squad operating out of Border HQ. Squad has two all-rounders.

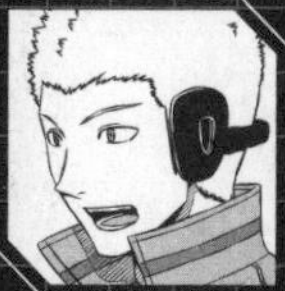
KUNIHARU KAKIZAKI

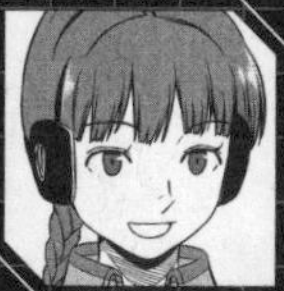
FUMIKA TERUYA

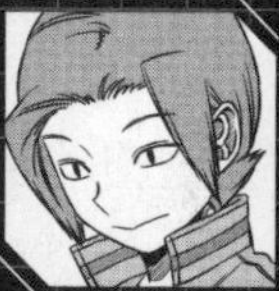
KOTARO TOMOE

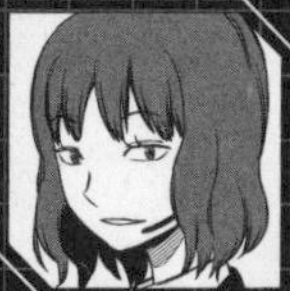
MADOKA UI

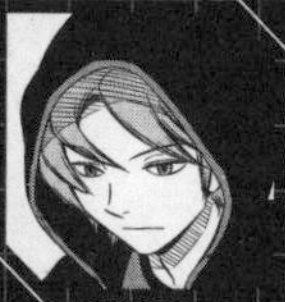
HYUSE

Neighbor from Aftokrator left behind in the invasion.

B-RANK AGENTS

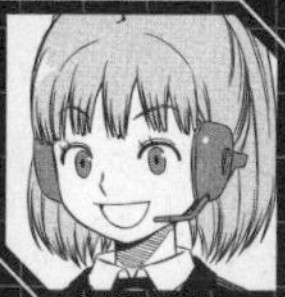
SAKURAKO TAKETOMI

Operator for B-Rank #16 Ebina Squad.

A-RANK AGENTS

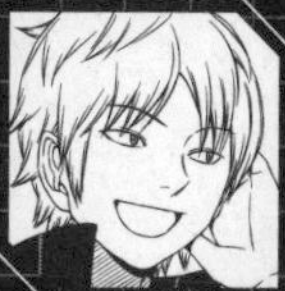
KOHEI IZUMI

Shooter from A-Rank #1 Tachikawa Squad.

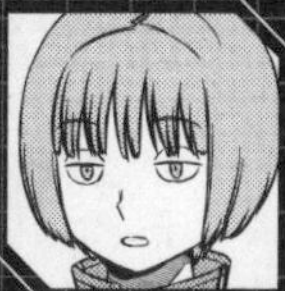
MITSURU TOKIEDA

All-Rounder from A-Rank #5 Arashiyama Squad.

BORDER HQ

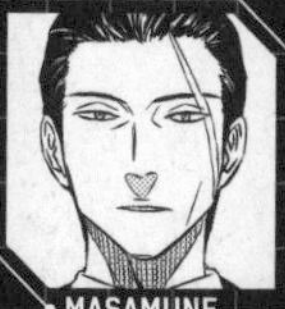
MASAMUNE KIDO

HQ Commander

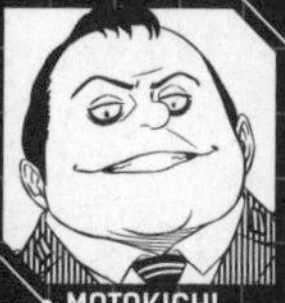
MOTOKICHI KINUTA

R&D Director

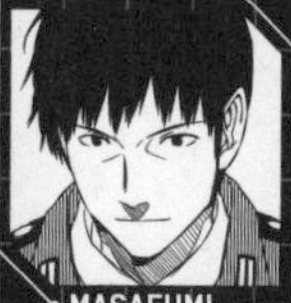
MASAFUMI SHINODA

HQ Director and Defense commander.

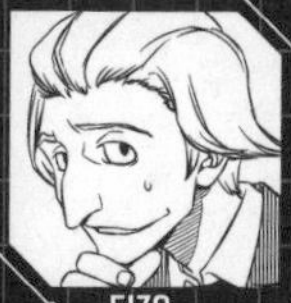
EIZO NETSUKI

PR Director

WORLD TRIGGER

CONTENTS

11

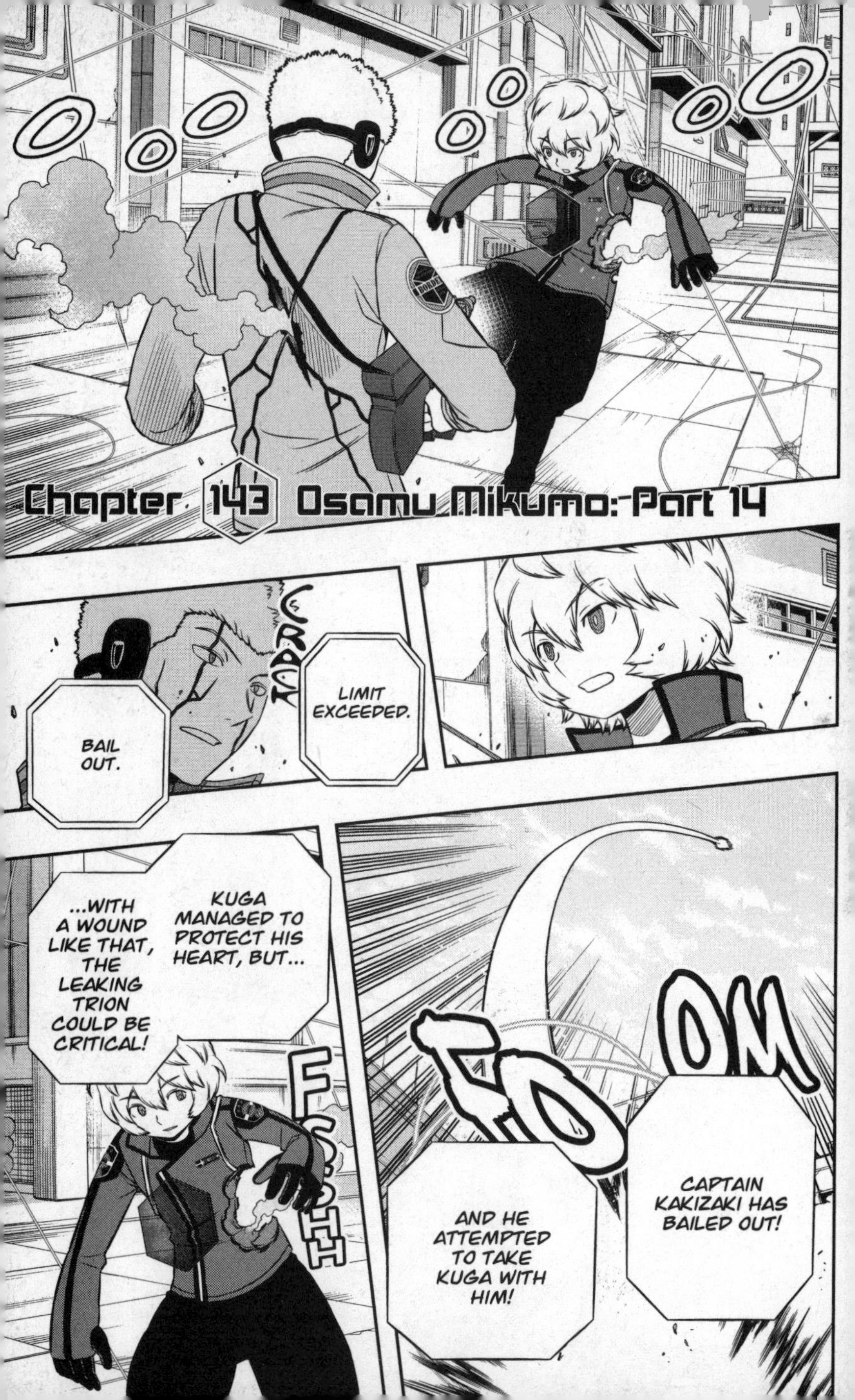
Chapter 143 Osamu Mikumo: Part 14
LIMIT EXCEEDED.
BAIL OUT.
CAPTAIN KAKIZAKI HAS BAILED OUT!
AND HE ATTEMPTED TO TAKE KUGA WITH HIM!
KUGA MANAGED TO PROTECT HIS HEART, BUT...
...WITH A WOUND LIKE THAT, THE LEAKING TRION COULD BE CRITICAL!

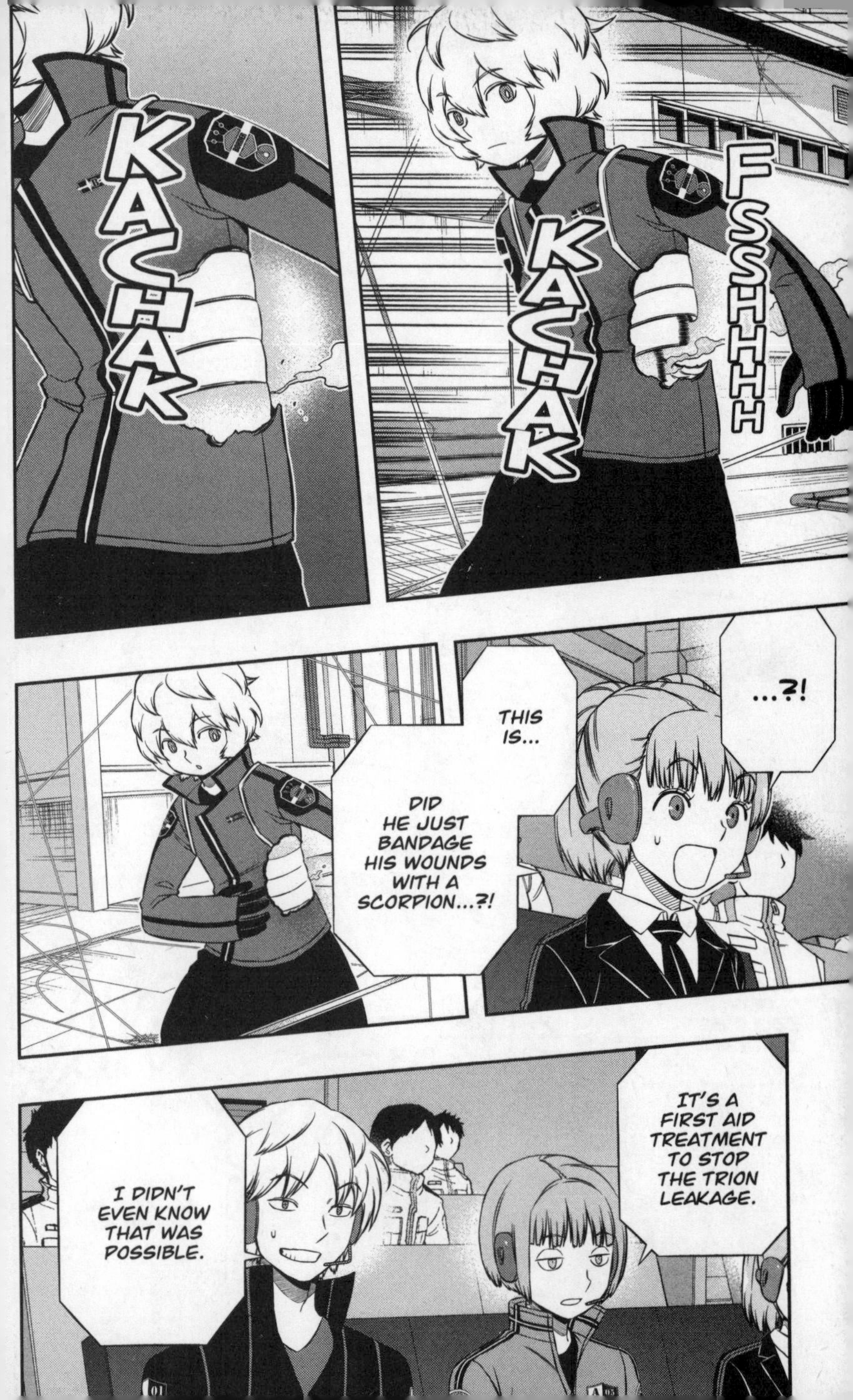
FSSHHHH
KACHAK
KACHAK
...?!
THIS IS...
DID HE JUST BANDAGE HIS WOUNDS WITH A SCORPION...?!
IT'S A FIRST AID TREATMENT TO STOP THE TRION LEAKAGE.
I DIDN'T EVEN KNOW THAT WAS POSSIBLE.

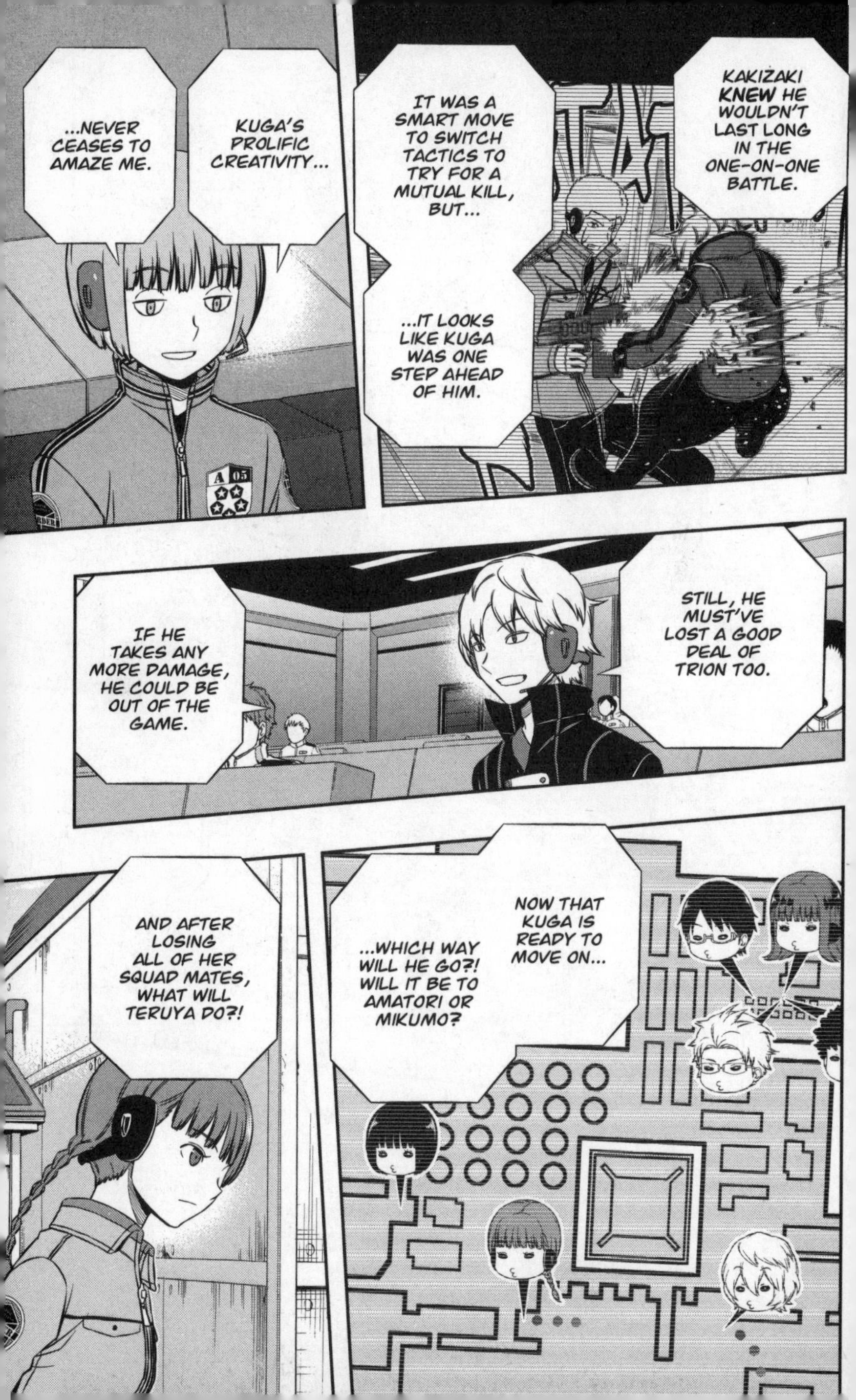
KAKIZAKI KNEW HE WOULDN'T LAST LONG IN THE ONE-ON-ONE BATTLE.
IT WAS A SMART MOVE TO SWITCH TACTICS TO TRY FOR A MUTUAL KILL, BUT...
...IT LOOKS LIKE KUGA WAS ONE STEP AHEAD OF HIM.
KUGA'S PROLIFIC CREATIVITY...
...NEVER CEASES TO AMAZE ME.
STILL, HE MUST'VE LOST A GOOD DEAL OF TRION TOO.
IF HE TAKES ANY MORE DAMAGE, HE COULD BE OUT OF THE GAME.
NOW THAT KUGA IS READY TO MOVE ON...
...WHICH WAY WILL HE GO?! WILL IT BE TO AMATORI OR MIKUMO?
AND AFTER LOSING ALL OF HER SQUAD MATES, WHAT WILL TERUYA DO?!

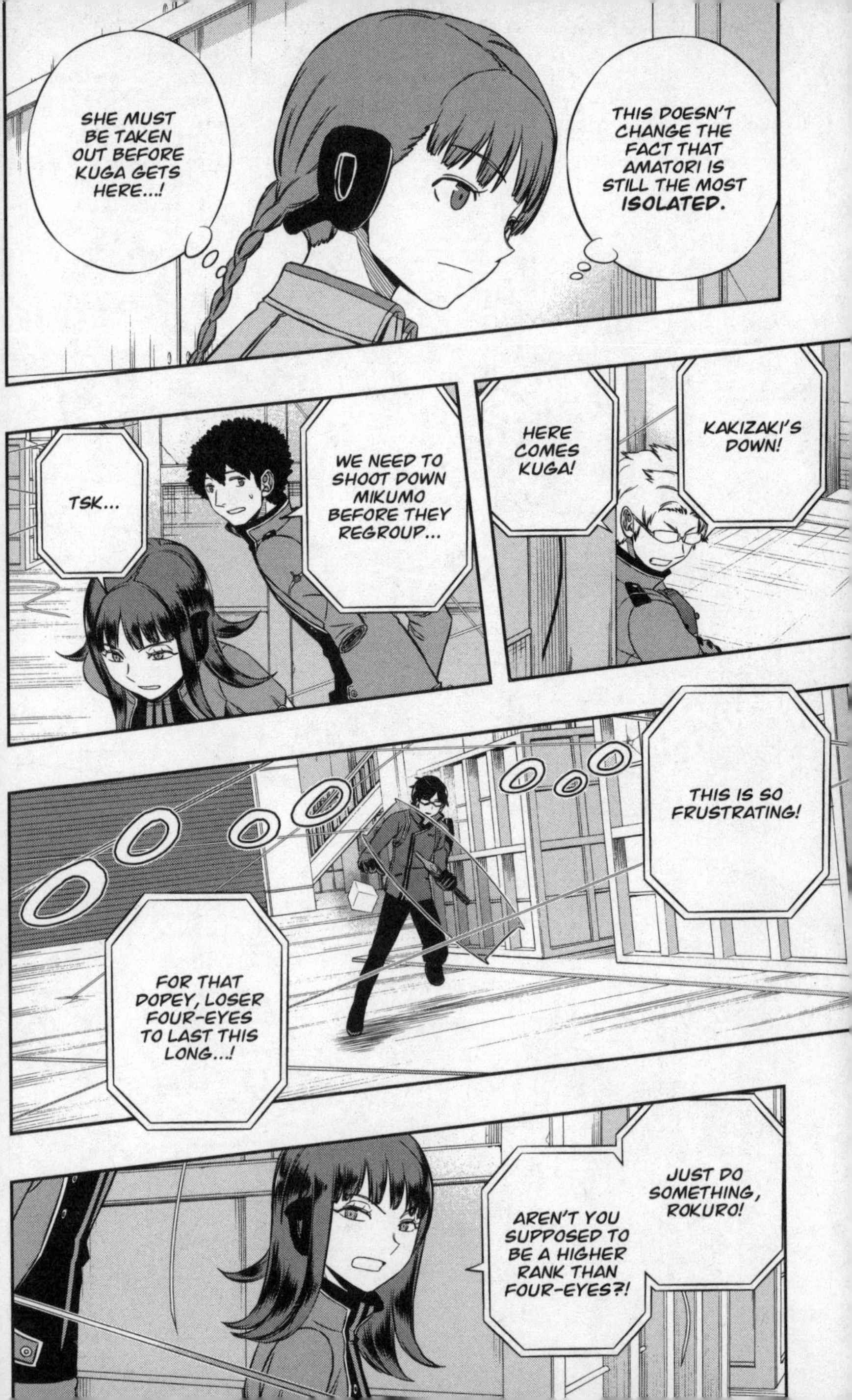
THIS DOESN'T CHANGE THE FACT THAT AMATORI IS STILL THE MOST ISOLATED.
SHE MUST BE TAKEN OUT BEFORE KUGA GETS HERE...!
KAKIZAKI'S DOWN!
HERE COMES KUGA!
WE NEED TO SHOOT DOWN MIKUMO BEFORE THEY REGROUP...
TSK...
THIS IS SO FRUSTRATING!
FOR THAT DOPEY, LOSER FOUR-EYES TO LAST THIS LONG...!
JUST DO SOMETHING, ROKURO!
AREN'T YOU SUPPOSED TO BE A HIGHER RANK THAN FOUR-EYES?!

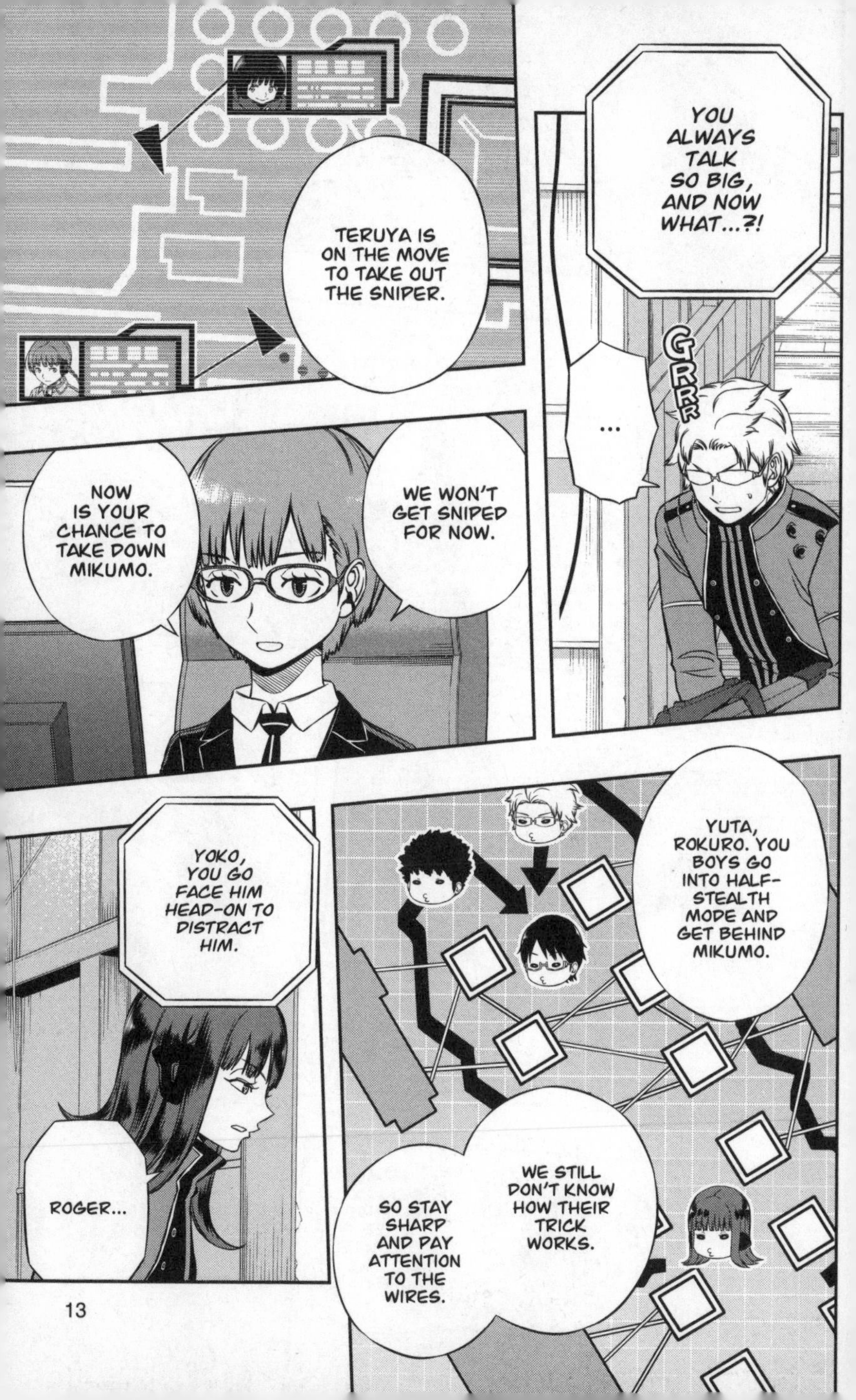
TERUYA IS ON THE MOVE TO TAKE OUT THE SNIPER.
WE WON'T GET SNIPED FOR NOW.
NOW IS YOUR CHANCE TO TAKE DOWN MIKUMO.
YOU ALWAYS TALK SO BIG, AND NOW WHAT...?!
GRRR
...
YUTA, ROKURO. YOU BOYS GO INTO HALF-STEALTH MODE AND GET BEHIND MIKUMO.
WE STILL DON'T KNOW HOW THEIR TRICK WORKS.
SO STAY SHARP AND PAY ATTENTION TO THE WIRES.
YOKO, YOU GO FACE HIM HEAD-ON TO DISTRACT HIM.
ROGER...

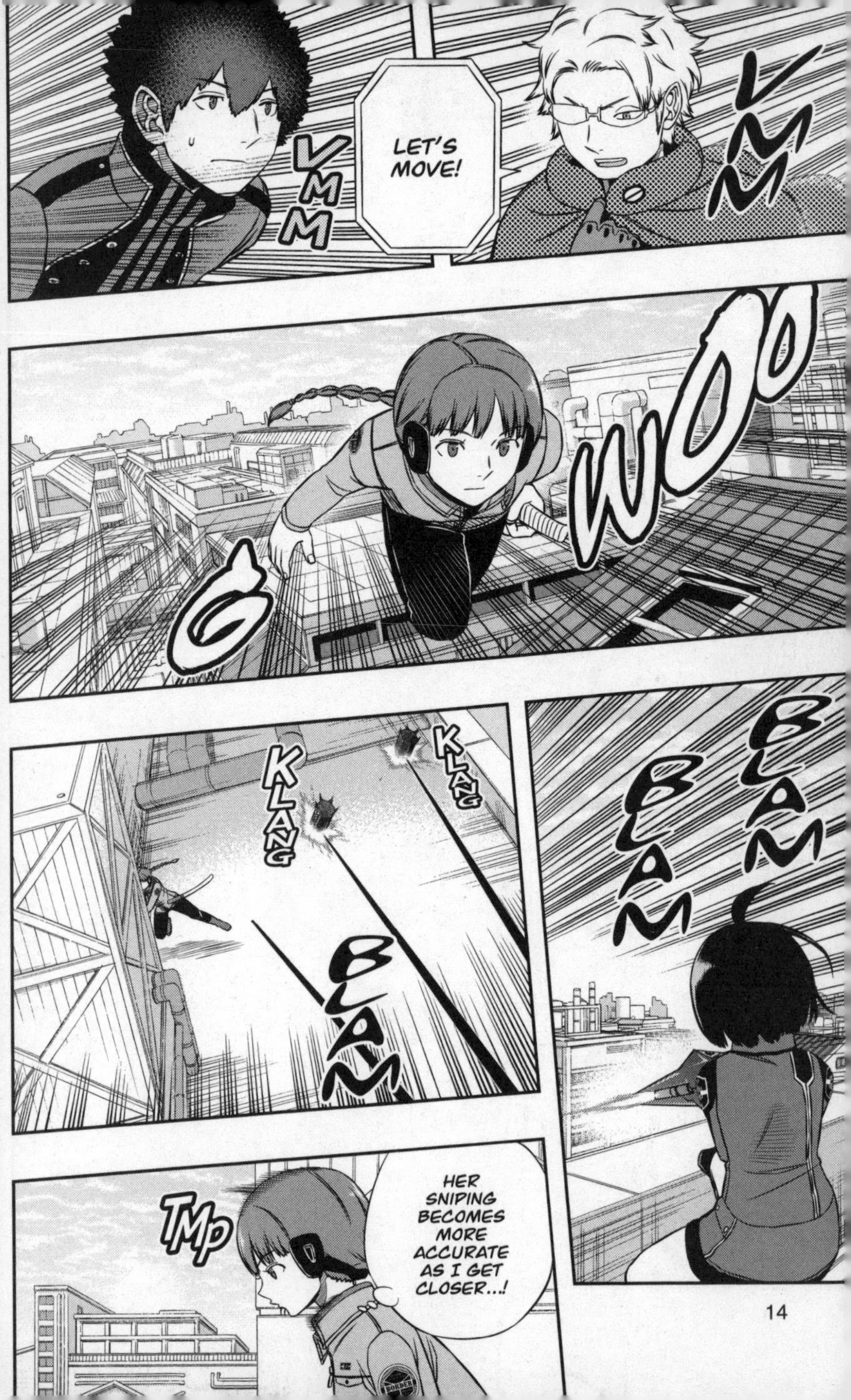
VMM
LET'S MOVE!
VMM
GWOOO
BLAM
BLAM
KLANG
KLANG
BLAM
TMP
HER SNIPING BECOMES MORE ACCURATE AS I GET CLOSER...!

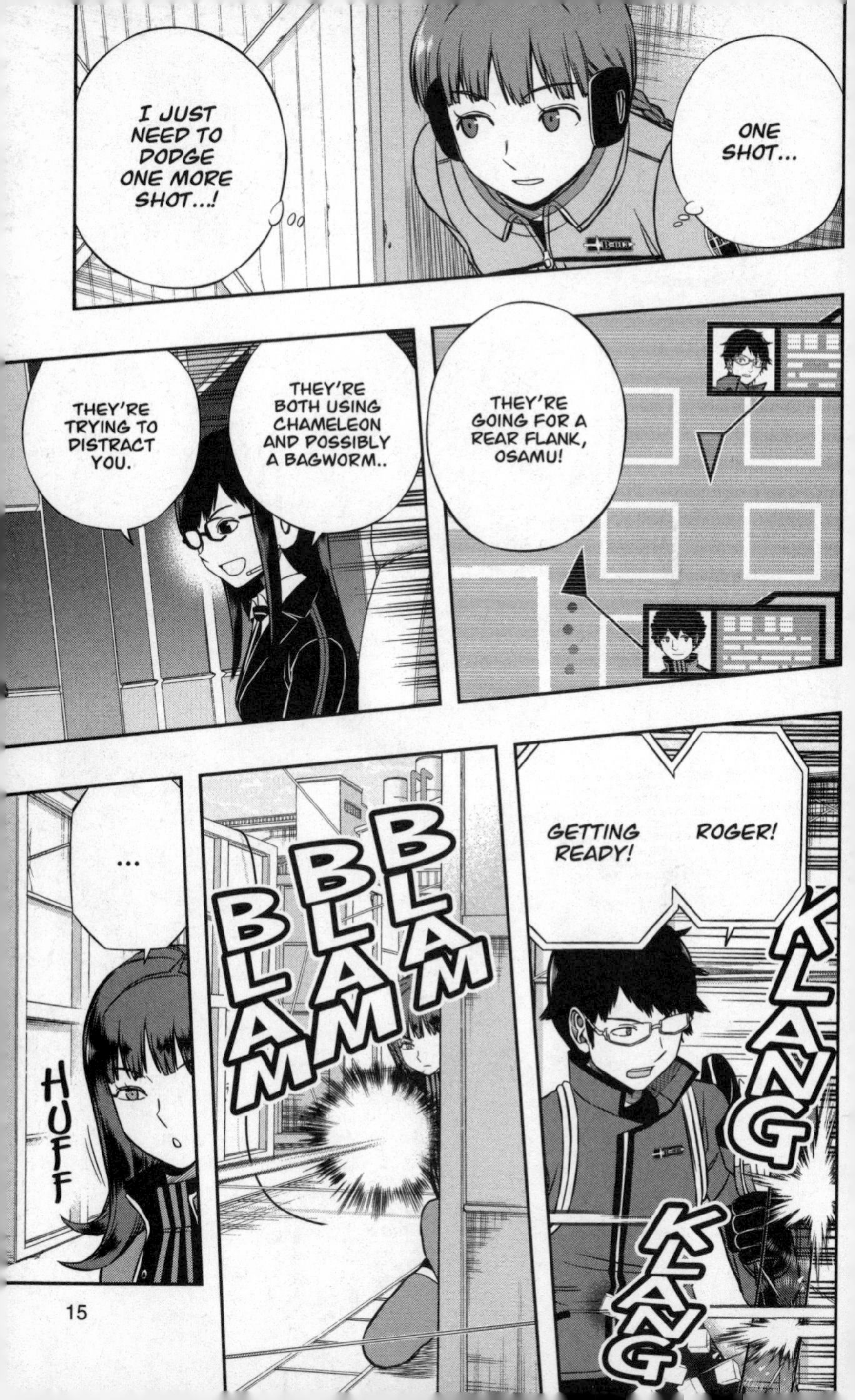
ONE SHOT...
I JUST NEED TO DODGE ONE MORE SHOT...!
THEY'RE GOING FOR A REAR FLANK, OSAMU!
THEY'RE BOTH USING CHAMELEON AND POSSIBLY A BAGWORM..
THEY'RE TRYING TO DISTRACT YOU.
ROGER!
GETTING READY!
KLANG
KLANG
BLAM
BLAM
BLAM
...
HUFF

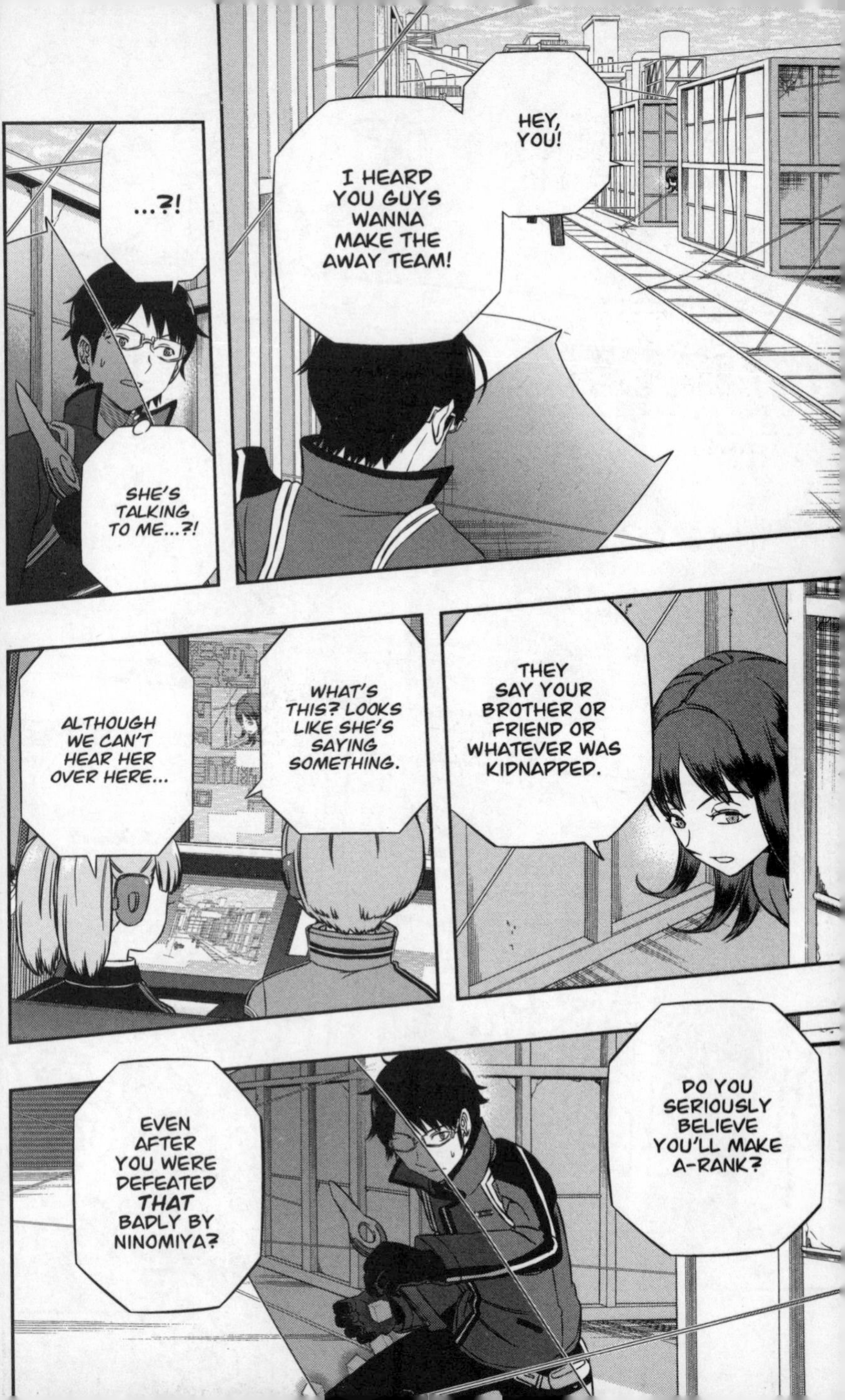
HEY, YOU!
I HEARD YOU GUYS WANNA MAKE THE AWAY TEAM!
...?!
SHE'S TALKING TO ME...?!
THEY SAY YOUR BROTHER OR FRIEND OR WHATEVER WAS KIDNAPPED.
WHAT'S THIS? LOOKS LIKE SHE'S SAYING SOMETHING.
ALTHOUGH WE CAN'T HEAR HER OVER HERE...
DO YOU SERIOUSLY BELIEVE YOU'LL MAKE A-RANK?
EVEN AFTER YOU WERE DEFEATED THAT BADLY BY NINOMIYA?

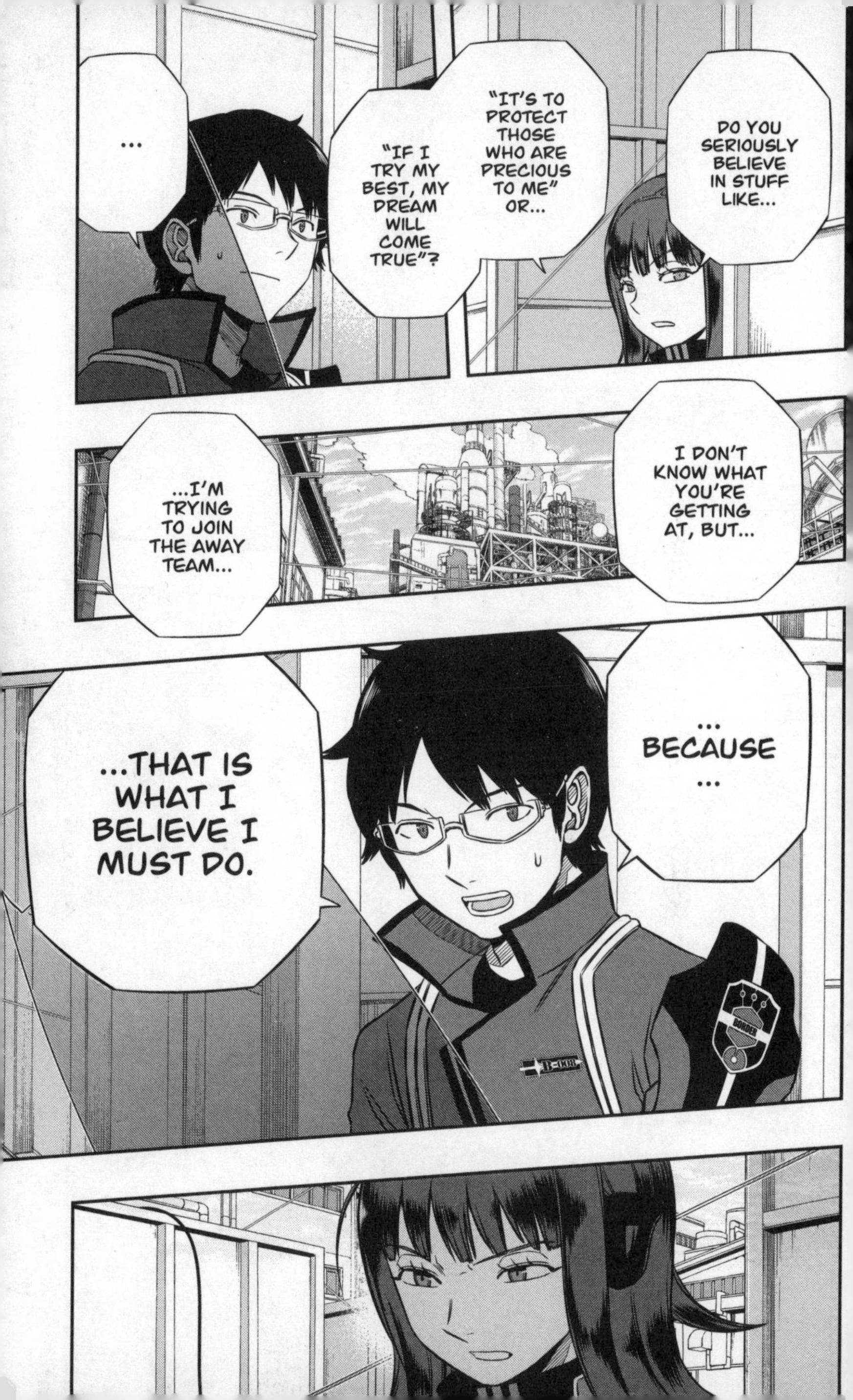
DO YOU SERIOUSLY BELIEVE IN STUFF LIKE...
"IT'S TO PROTECT THOSE WHO ARE PRECIOUS TO ME" OR...
"IF I TRY MY BEST, MY DREAM WILL COME TRUE"?
...
I DON'T KNOW WHAT YOU'RE GETTING AT, BUT...
...I'M TRYING TO JOIN THE AWAY TEAM...
... BECAUSE ...
...THAT IS WHAT I BELIEVE I MUST DO.

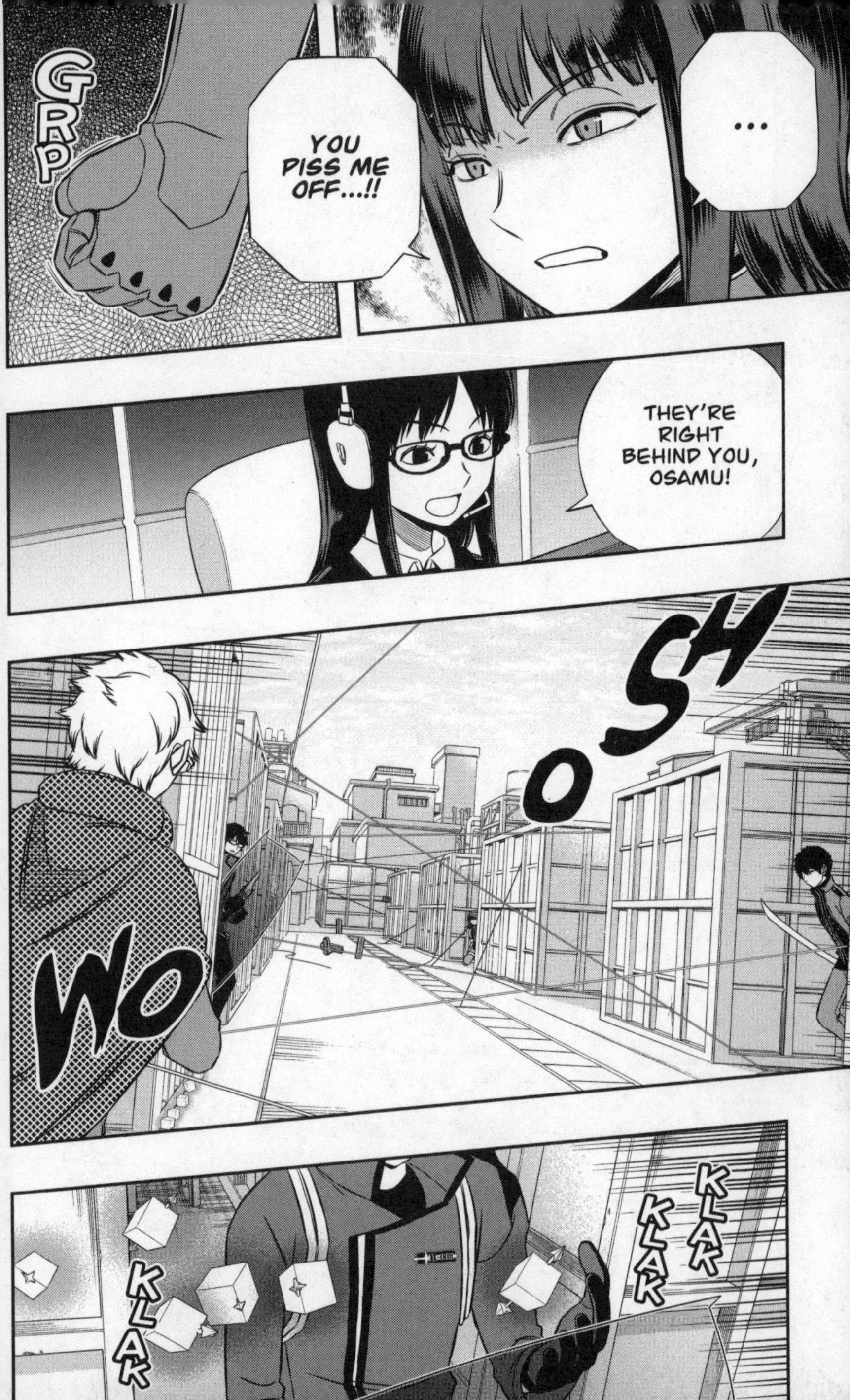
...
YOU PISS ME OFF...!!
GRP
THEY'RE RIGHT BEHIND YOU, OSAMU!
WOOSH
KLAK KLAK
KLAK

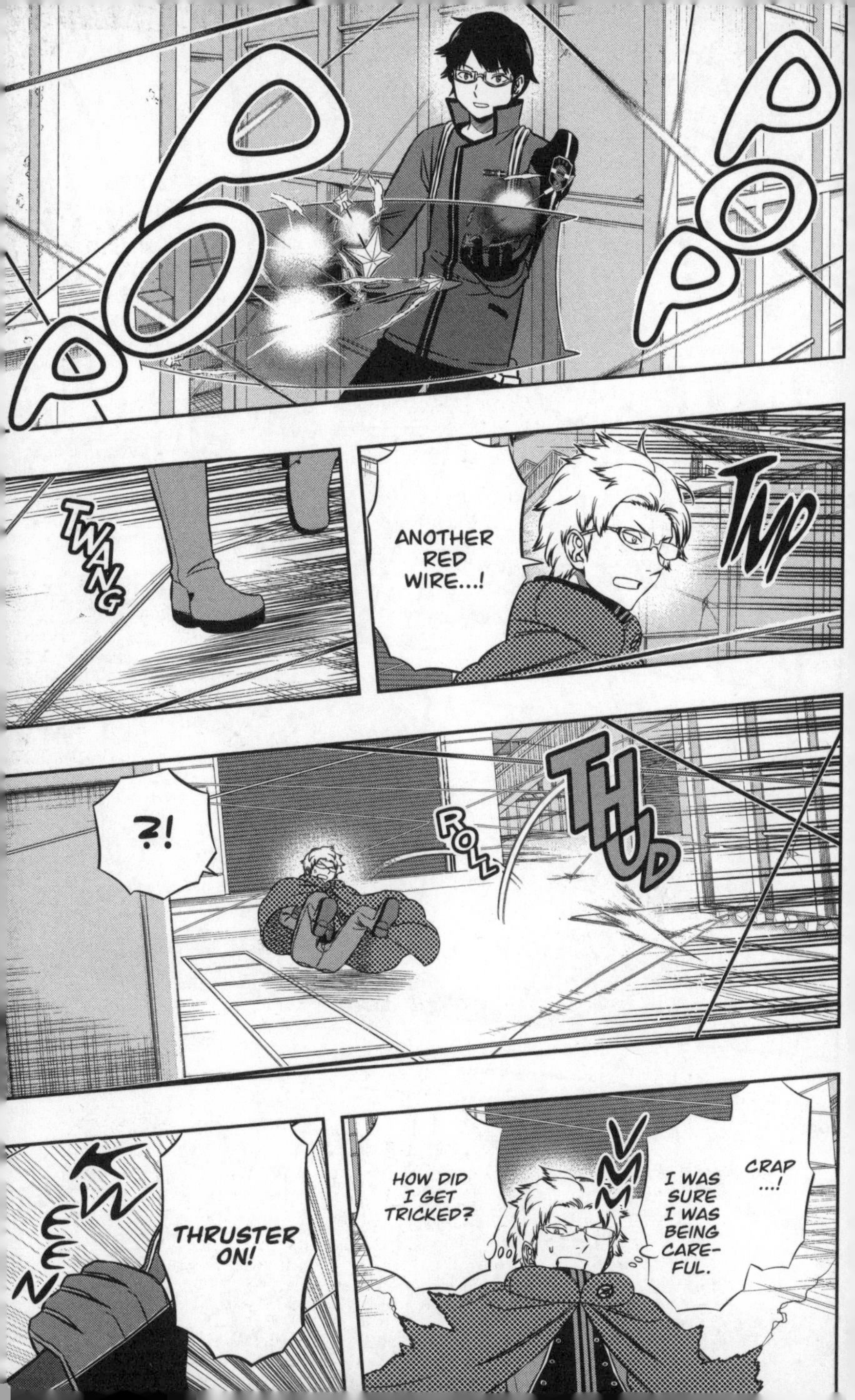
POP POP
POP POP
TMP
ANOTHER RED WIRE...!
TWANG
THUD
ROLL
?!
CRAP...!
I WAS SURE I WAS BEING CAREFUL.
VMM
HOW DID I GET TRICKED?
THRUSTER ON!
KWEEN

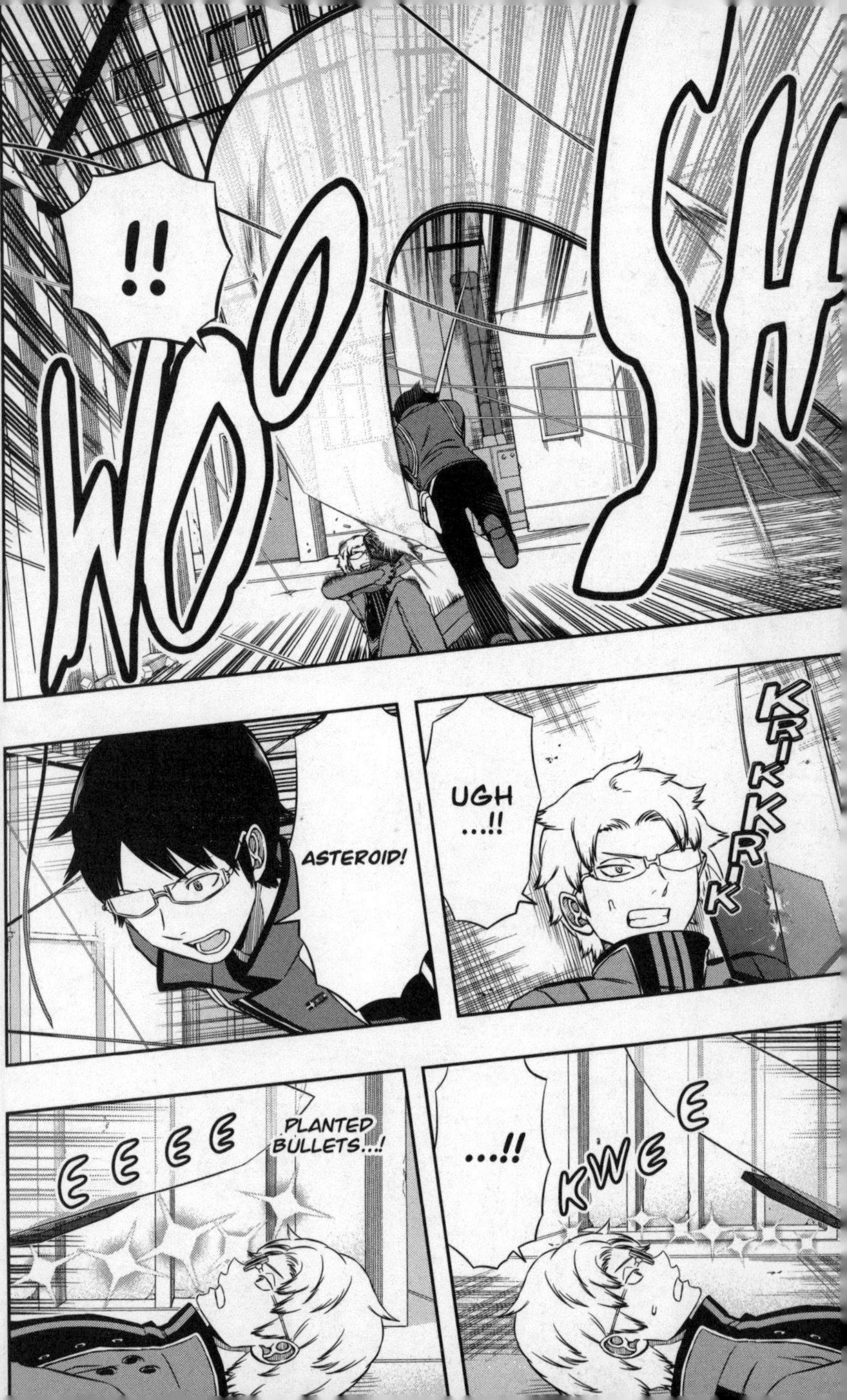
WHOOSH
!!
KRIKKRIK
UGH ...!!
ASTEROID!
KWEE
...!!
EEEE
PLANTED BULLETS...!

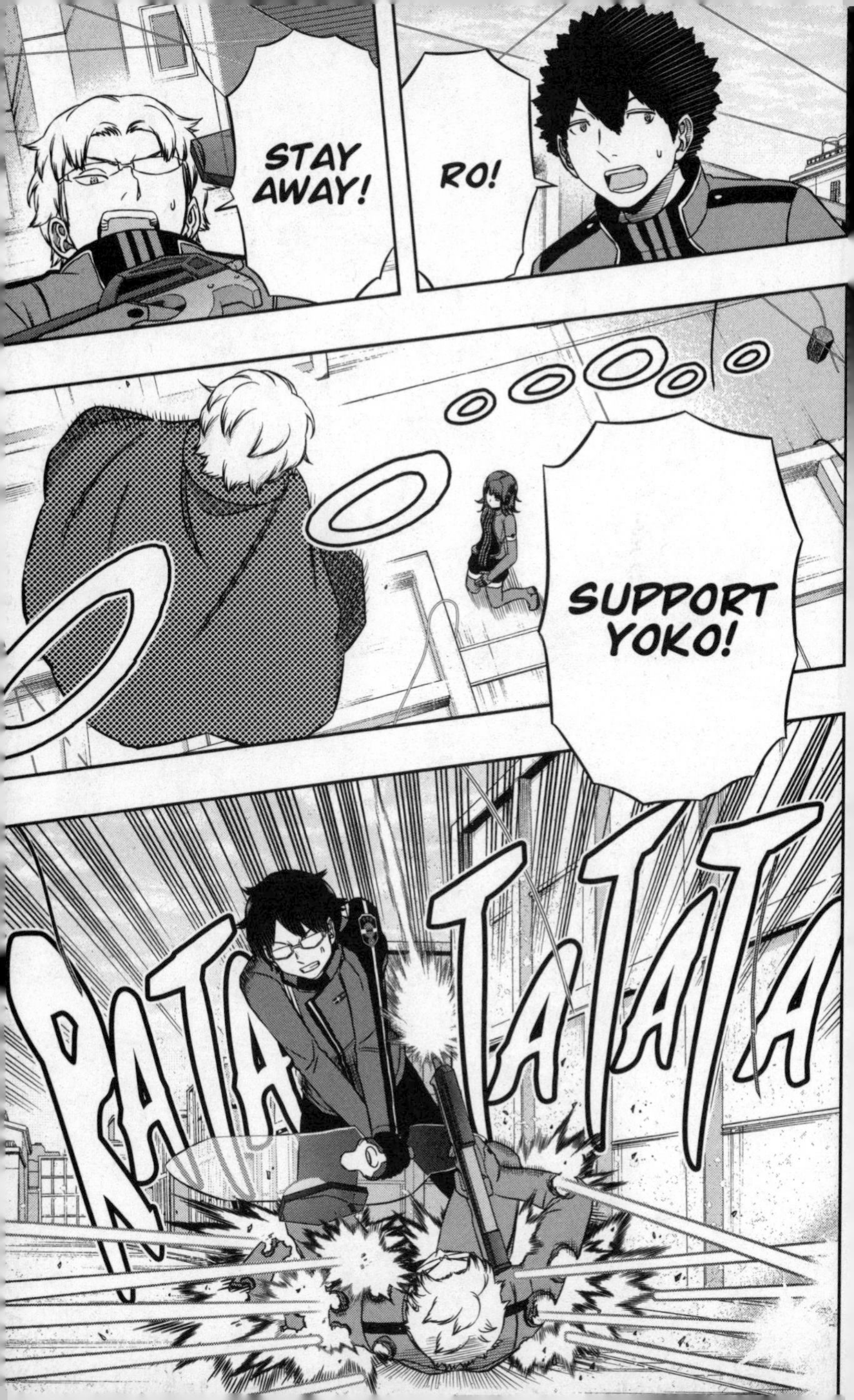
RO!
STAY AWAY!
SUPPORT YOKO!
RATATATATA

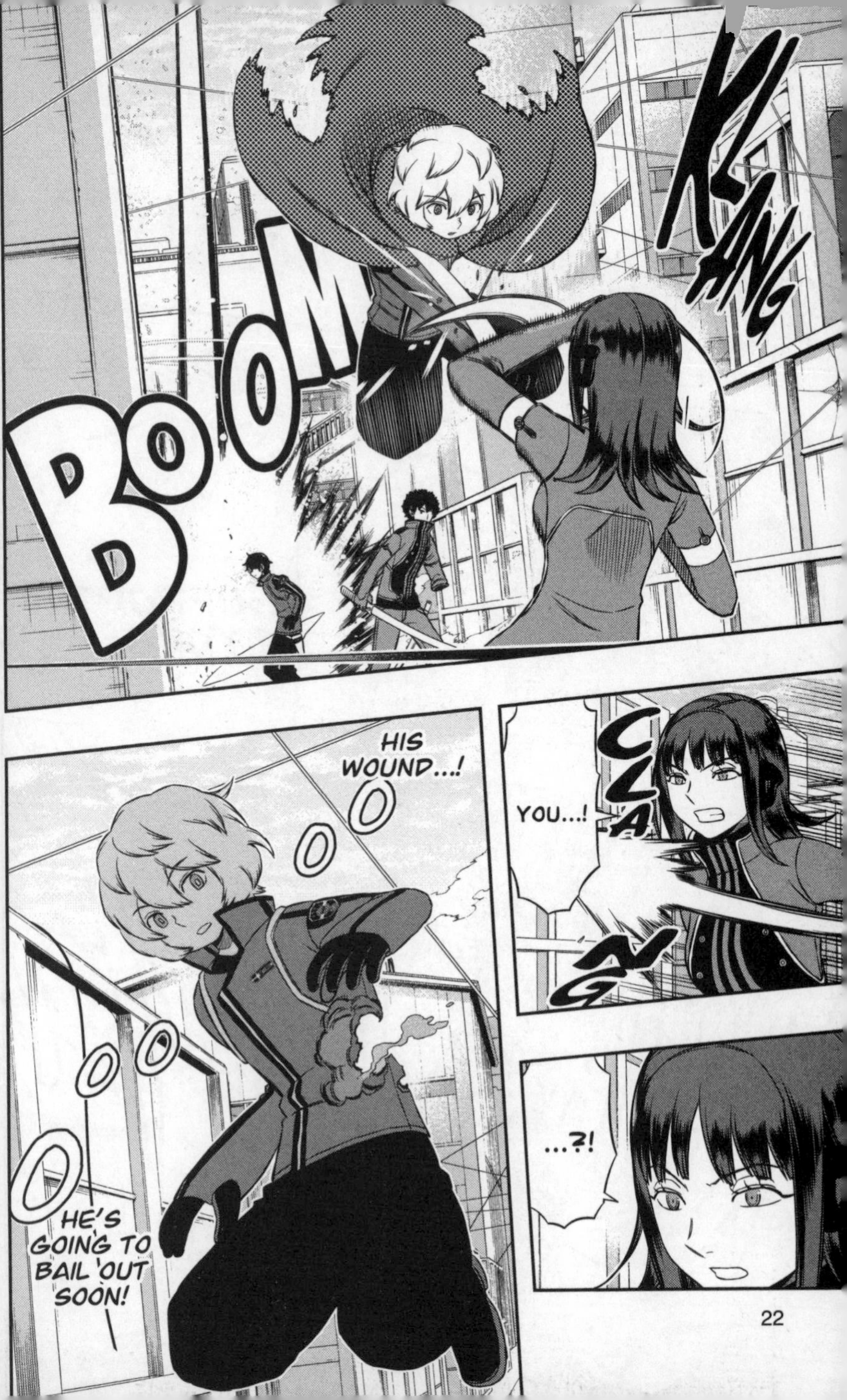
KLANG
BOOM
YOU...!
CLANG
...?!
HIS WOUND...!
HE'S GOING TO BAIL OUT SOON!

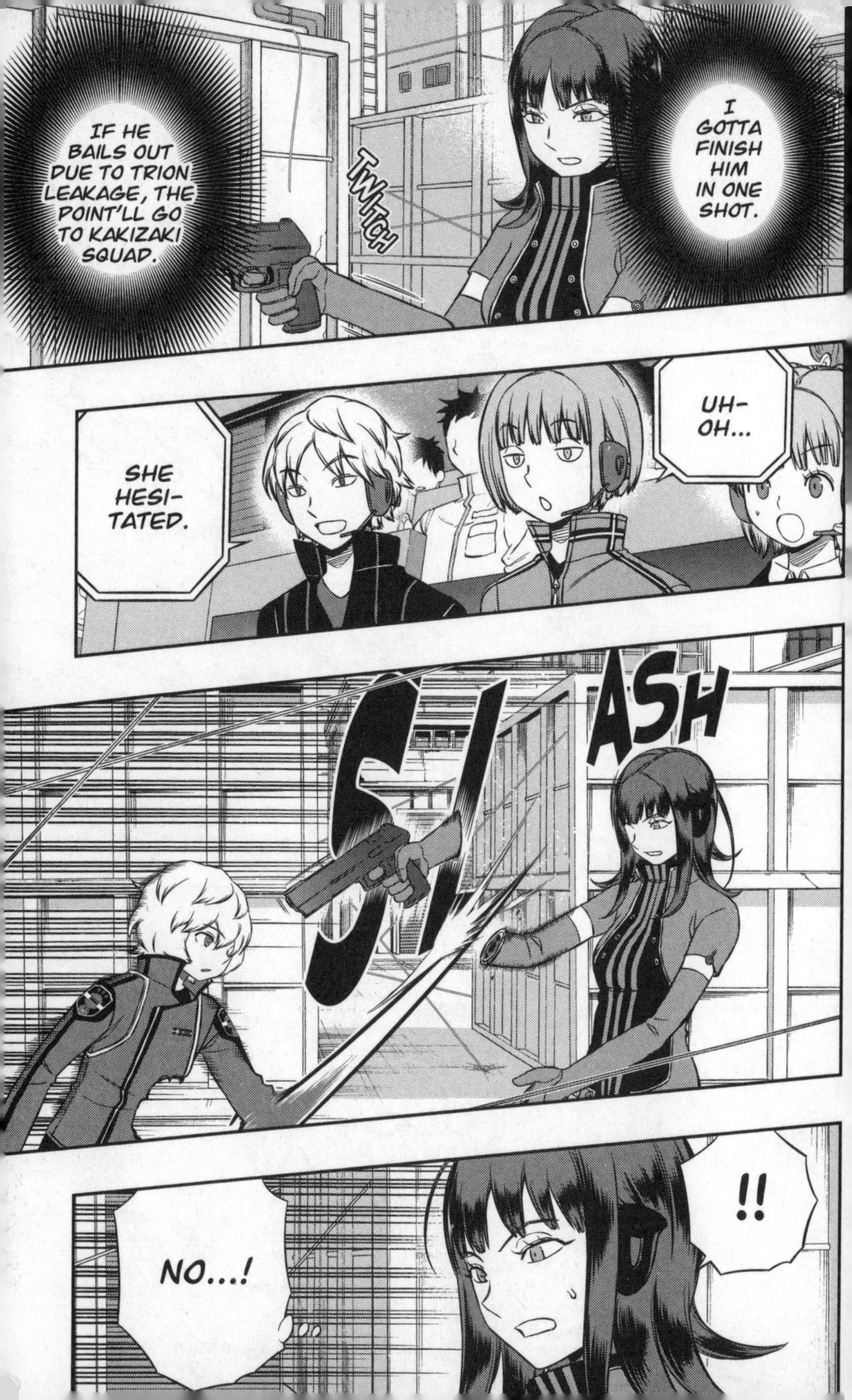
I GOTTA FINISH HIM IN ONE SHOT.
TWITCH
IF HE BAILS OUT DUE TO TRION LEAKAGE, THE POINT'LL GO TO KAKIZAKI SQUAD.
UH-OH...
SHE HESI-TATED.
SHASH
!!
NO...!

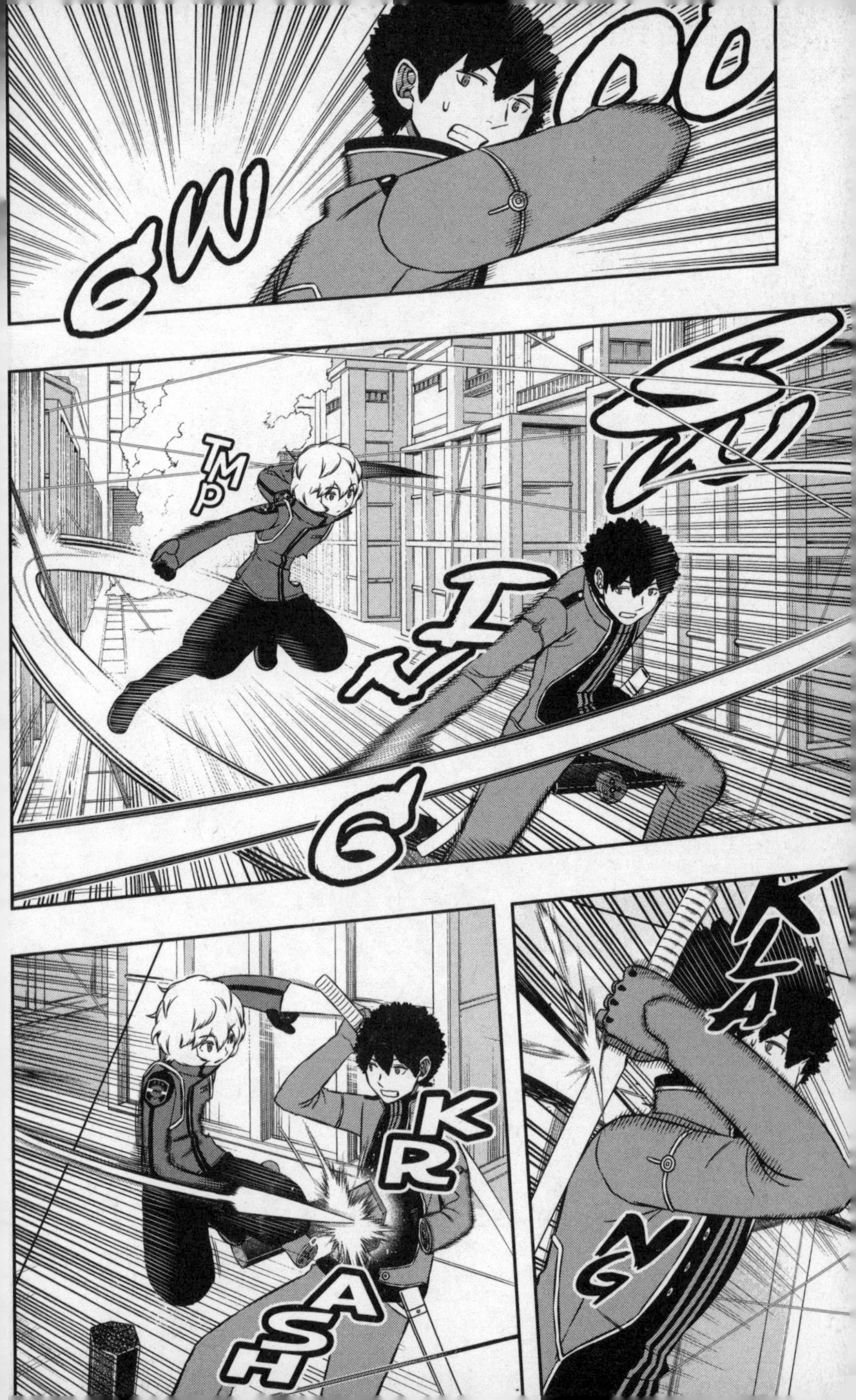
GWOO
SWING
TMP
KLANG
KRASH

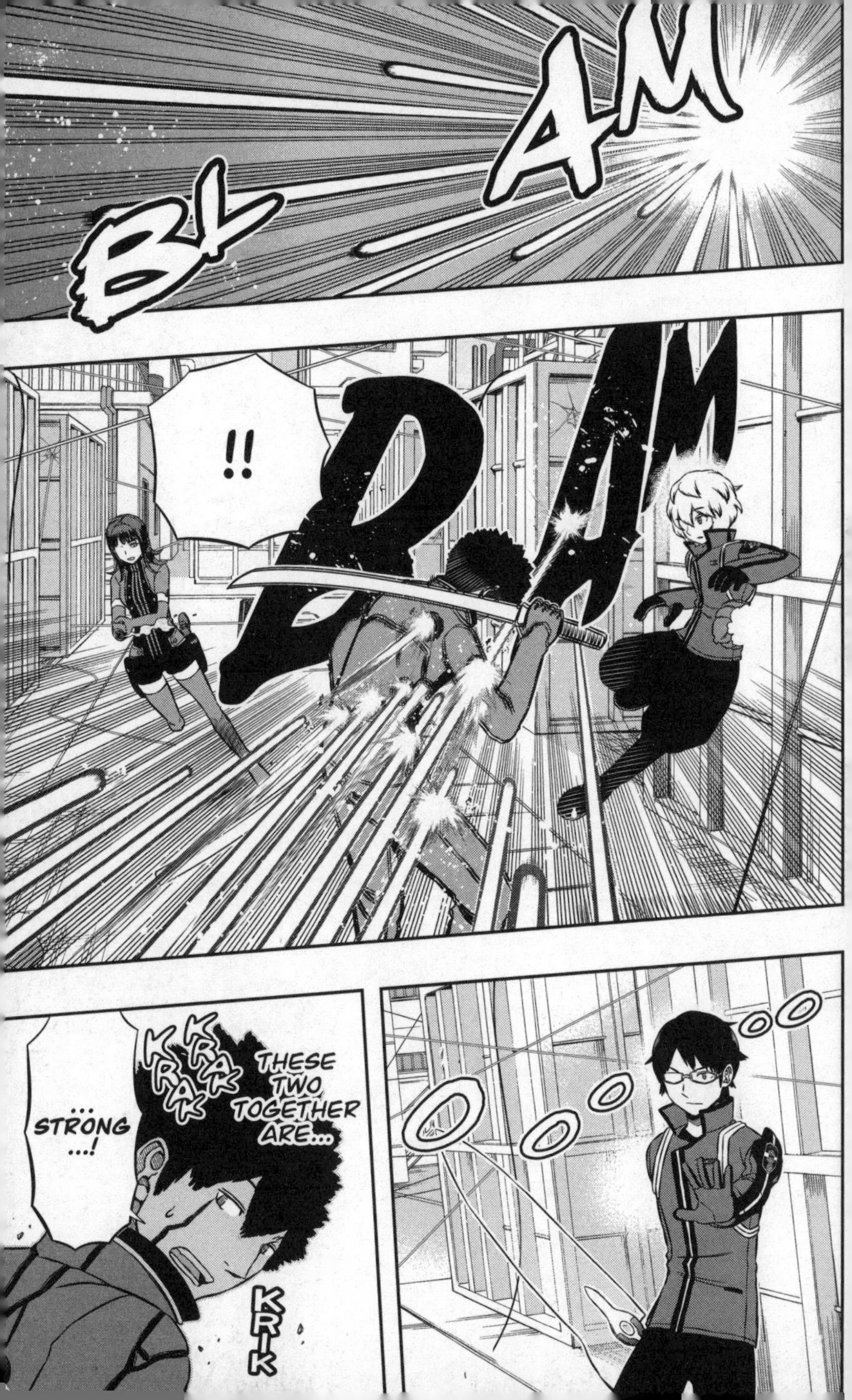
BLAM
!!
THESE TWO TOGETHER ARE...
KRAK KRAK
...STRONG...!
KRIK

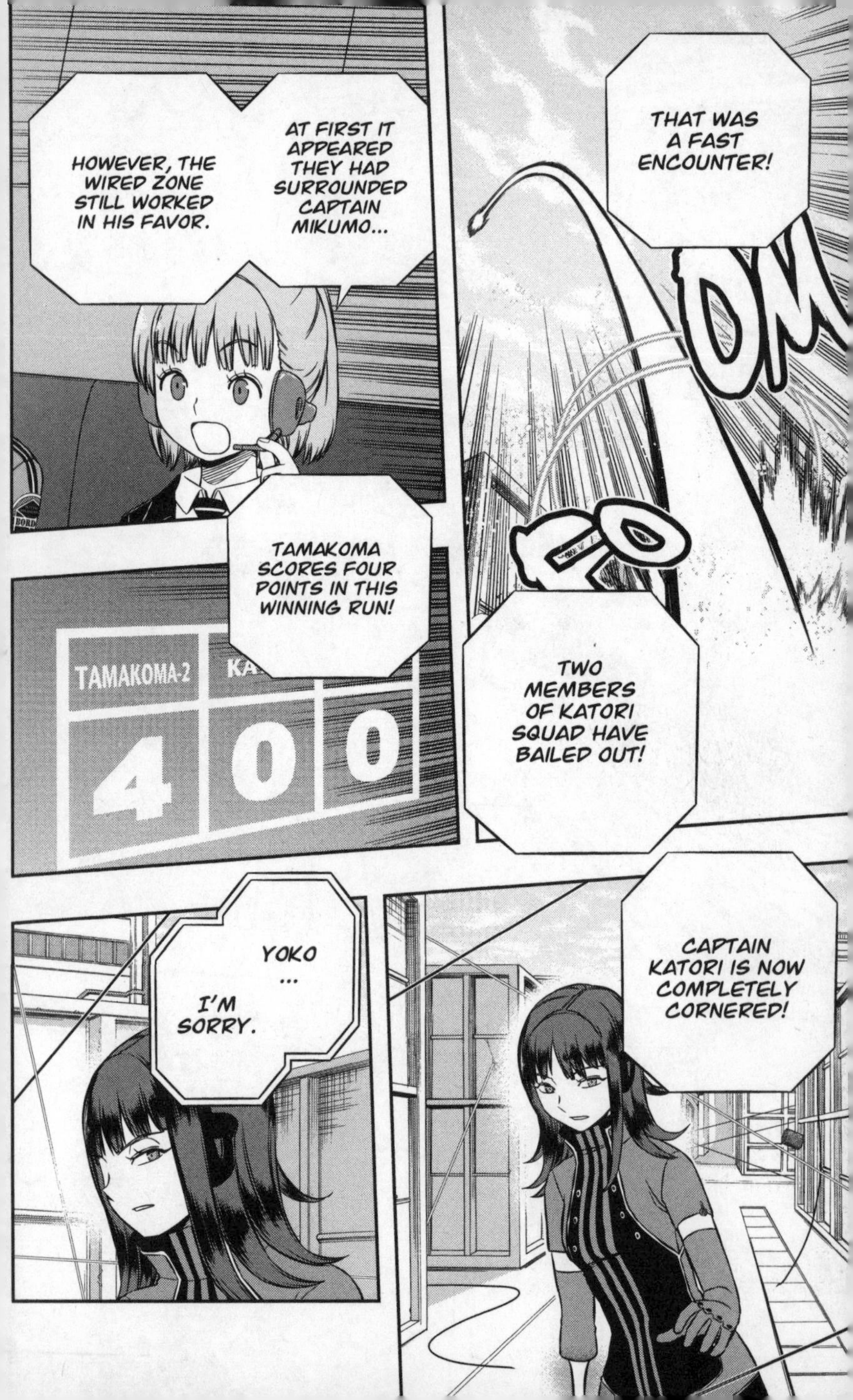
THAT WAS A FAST ENCOUNTER!
TWO MEMBERS OF KATORI SQUAD HAVE BAILED OUT!
AT FIRST IT APPEARED THEY HAD SURROUNDED CAPTAIN MIKUMO...
HOWEVER, THE WIRED ZONE STILL WORKED IN HIS FAVOR.
TAMAKOMA SCORES FOUR POINTS IN THIS WINNING RUN!
TAMAKOMA-2
4 0 0
CAPTAIN KATORI IS NOW COMPLETELY CORNERED!
YOKO ... I'M SORRY.

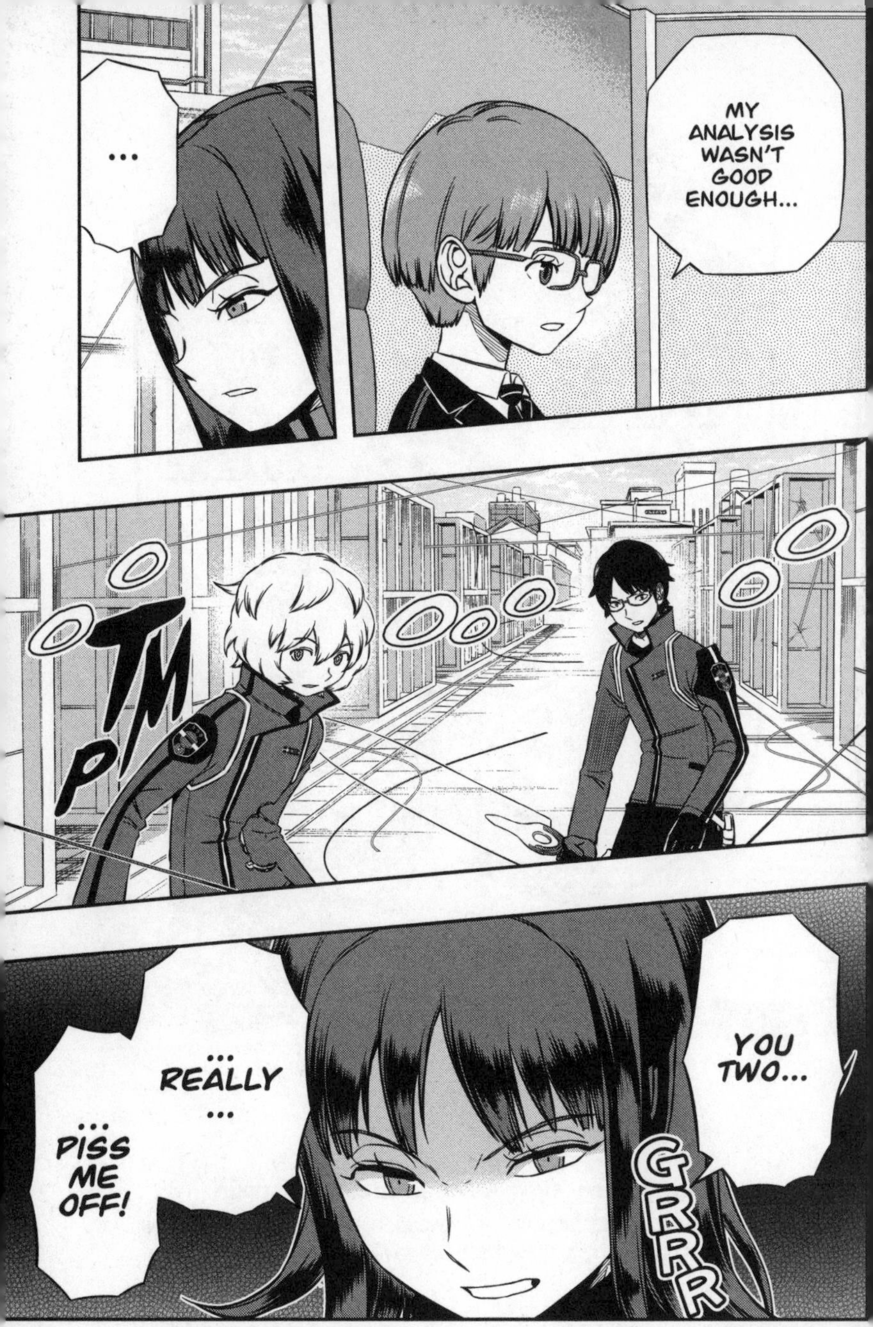
MY ANALYSIS WASN'T GOOD ENOUGH...
...
TMP
YOU TWO...
GRRR
...REALLY...
...PISS ME OFF!

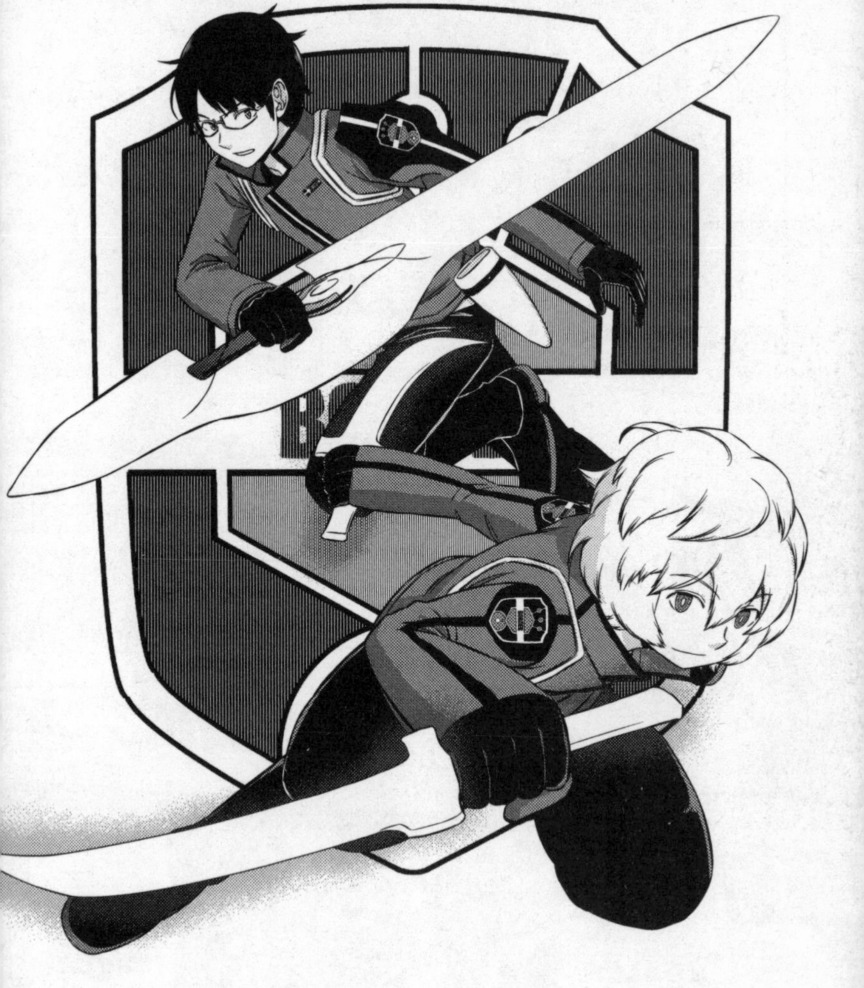

■ 2016 *Weekly Shonen Jump* issue 21 Cover Illustration

Yuma and Osamu crossing paths with their weapons! The designer told me what to do and I drew it. Only having to draw these two saved me a lot of time!

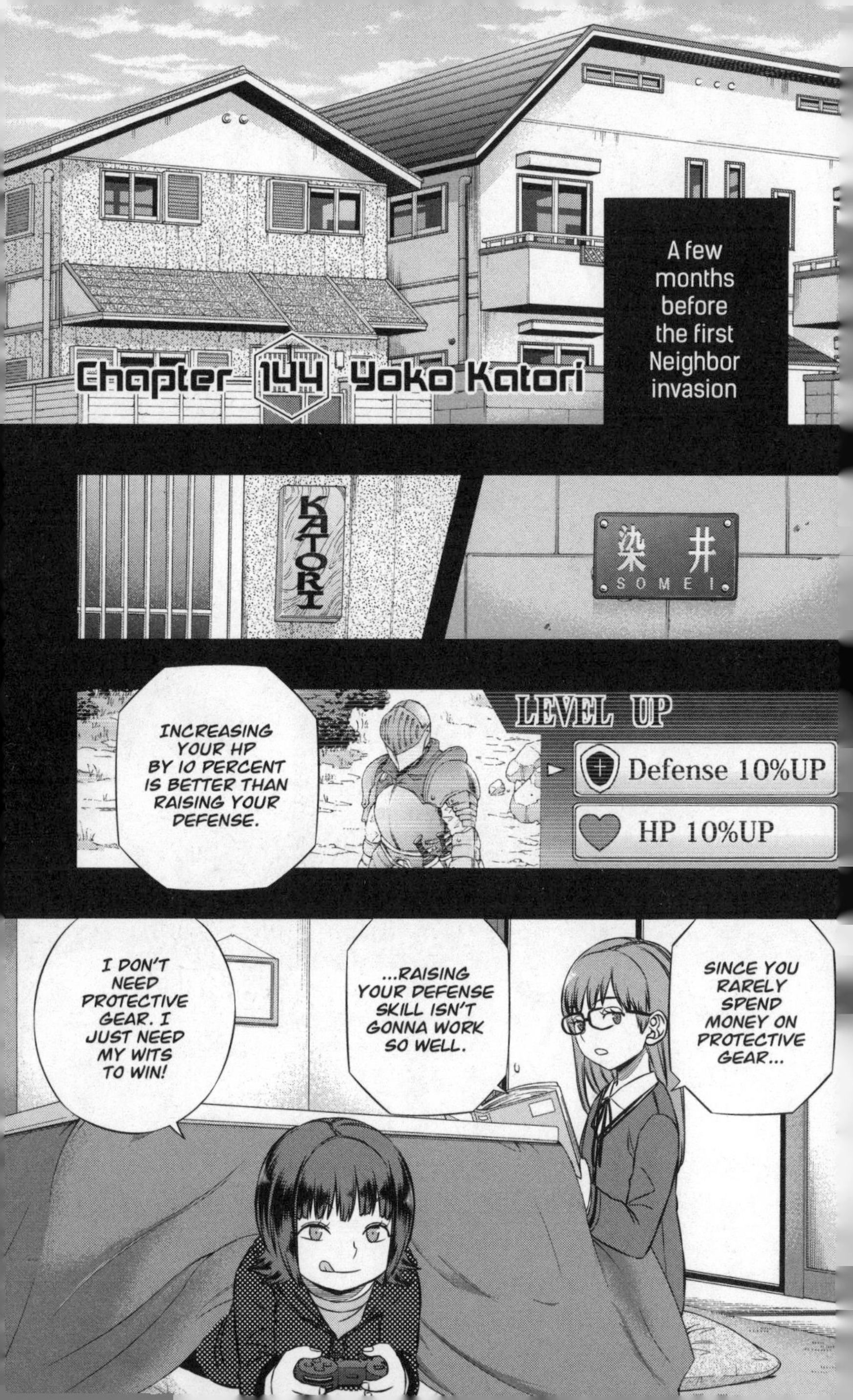
A few months before the first Neighbor invasion
Chapter 144 Yoko Katori
染井 SOMEI
KATORI
LEVEL UP
Defense 10%UP
HP 10%UP
INCREASING YOUR HP BY 10 PERCENT IS BETTER THAN RAISING YOUR DEFENSE.
SINCE YOU RARELY SPEND MONEY ON PROTECTIVE GEAR...
...RAISING YOUR DEFENSE SKILL ISN'T GONNA WORK SO WELL.
I DON'T NEED PROTECTIVE GEAR. I JUST NEED MY WITS TO WIN!

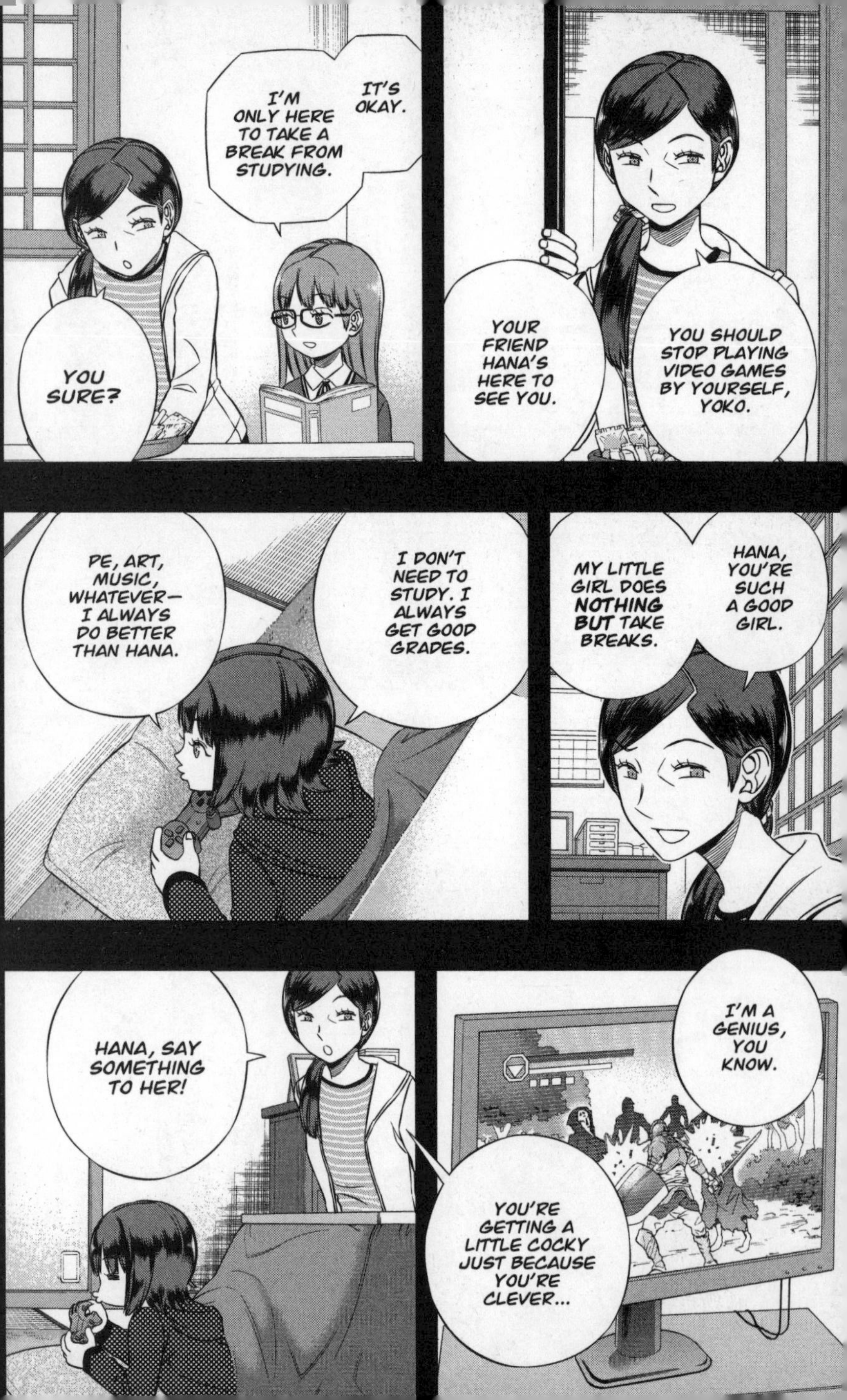
YOU SHOULD STOP PLAYING VIDEO GAMES BY YOURSELF, YOKO.
YOUR FRIEND HANA'S HERE TO SEE YOU.
IT'S OKAY.
I'M ONLY HERE TO TAKE A BREAK FROM STUDYING.
YOU SURE?
HANA, YOU'RE SUCH A GOOD GIRL.
MY LITTLE GIRL DOES NOTHING BUT TAKE BREAKS.
I DON'T NEED TO STUDY. I ALWAYS GET GOOD GRADES.
PE, ART, MUSIC, WHATEVER— I ALWAYS DO BETTER THAN HANA.
I'M A GENIUS, YOU KNOW.
YOU'RE GETTING A LITTLE COCKY JUST BECAUSE YOU'RE CLEVER...
HANA, SAY SOMETHING TO HER!

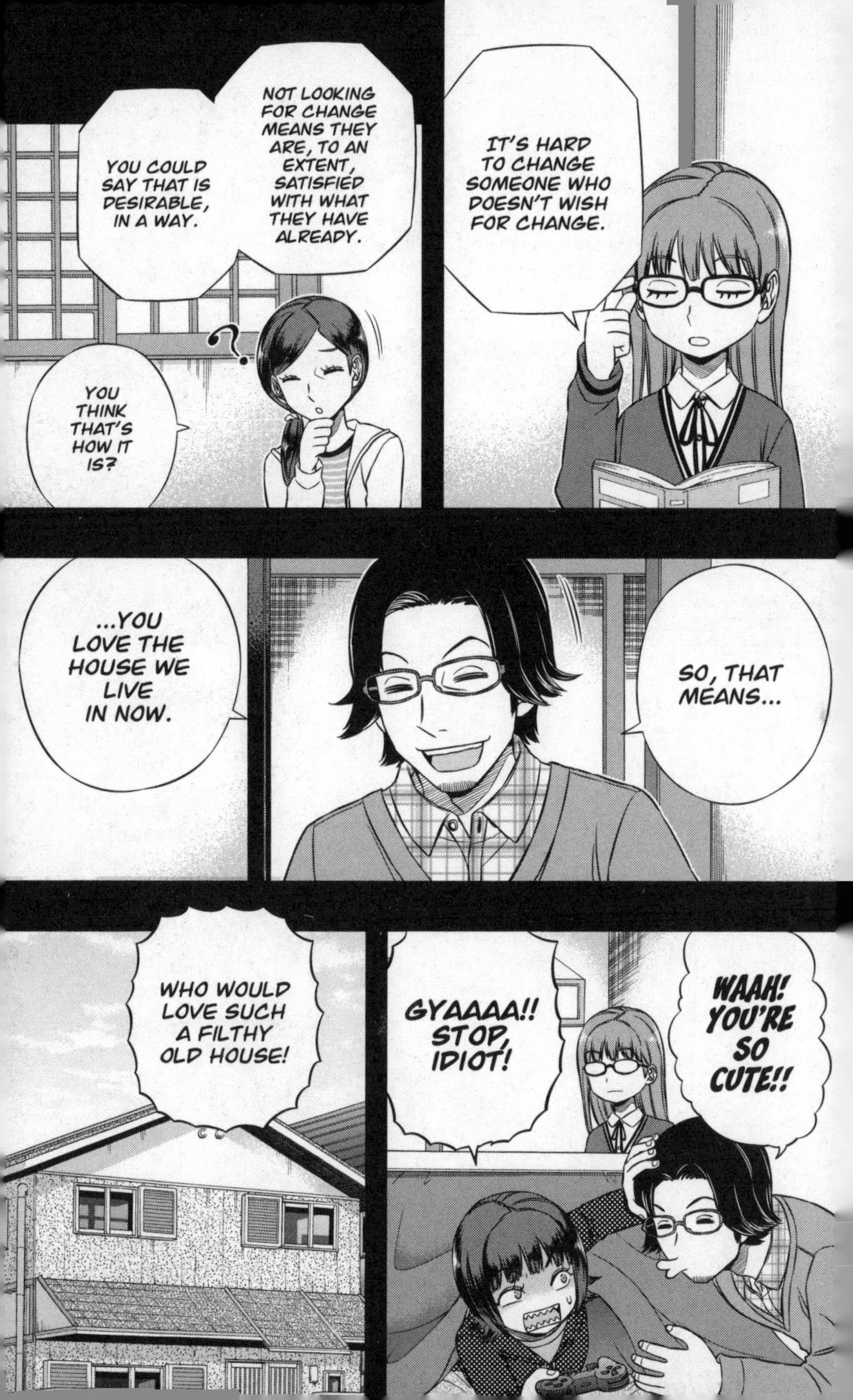
IT'S HARD TO CHANGE SOMEONE WHO DOESN'T WISH FOR CHANGE.
NOT LOOKING FOR CHANGE MEANS THEY ARE, TO AN EXTENT, SATISFIED WITH WHAT THEY HAVE ALREADY.
YOU COULD SAY THAT IS DESIRABLE, IN A WAY.
YOU THINK THAT'S HOW IT IS?
SO, THAT MEANS...
...YOU LOVE THE HOUSE WE LIVE IN NOW.
WAAH! YOU'RE SO CUTE!!
GYAAAA!! STOP, IDIOT!
WHO WOULD LOVE SUCH A FILTHY OLD HOUSE!

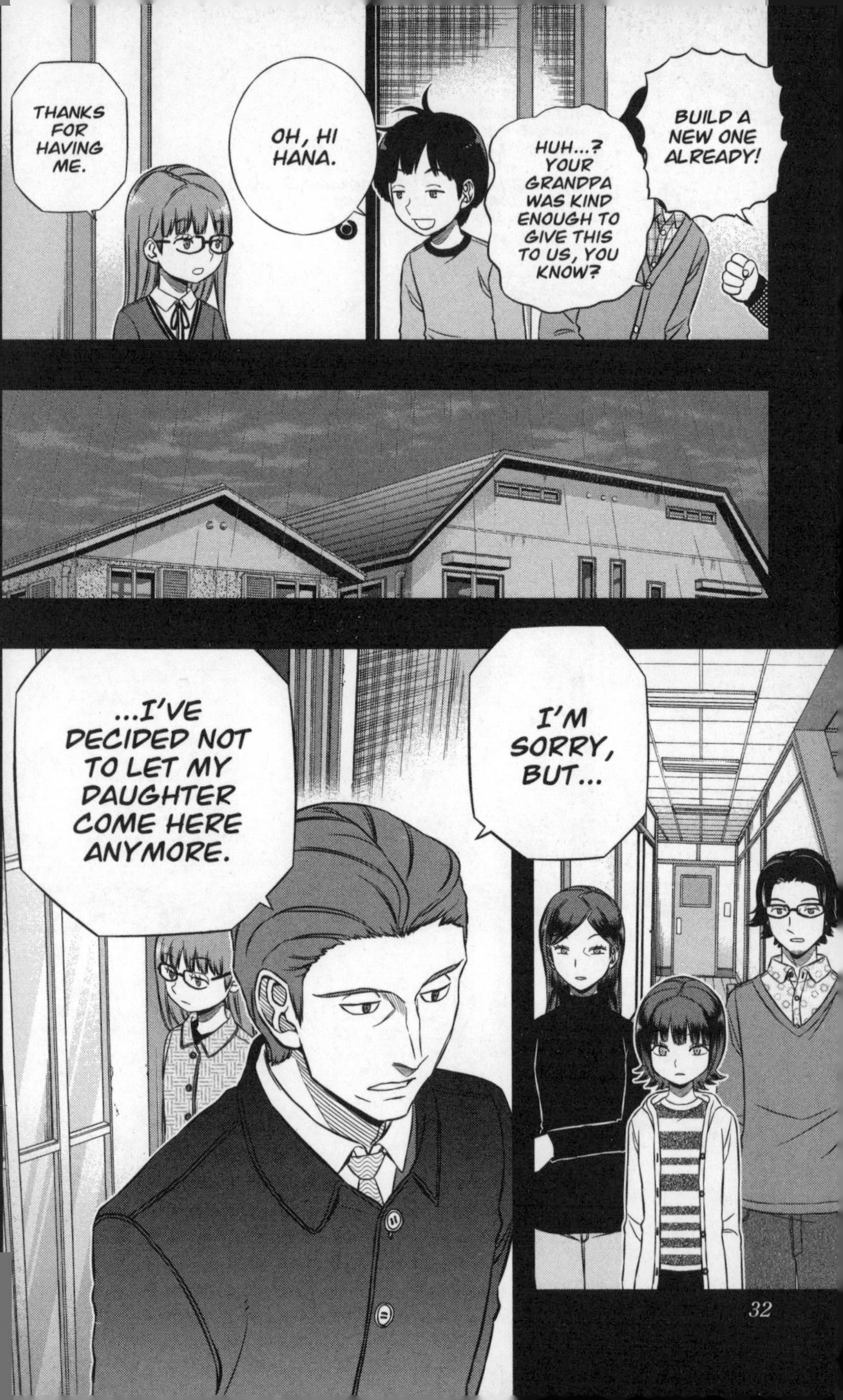

BUILD A NEW ONE ALREADY!
HUH...? YOUR GRANDPA WAS KIND ENOUGH TO GIVE THIS TO US, YOU KNOW?
OH, HI HANA.
THANKS FOR HAVING ME.
I'M SORRY, BUT...
...I'VE DECIDED NOT TO LET MY DAUGHTER COME HERE ANYMORE.

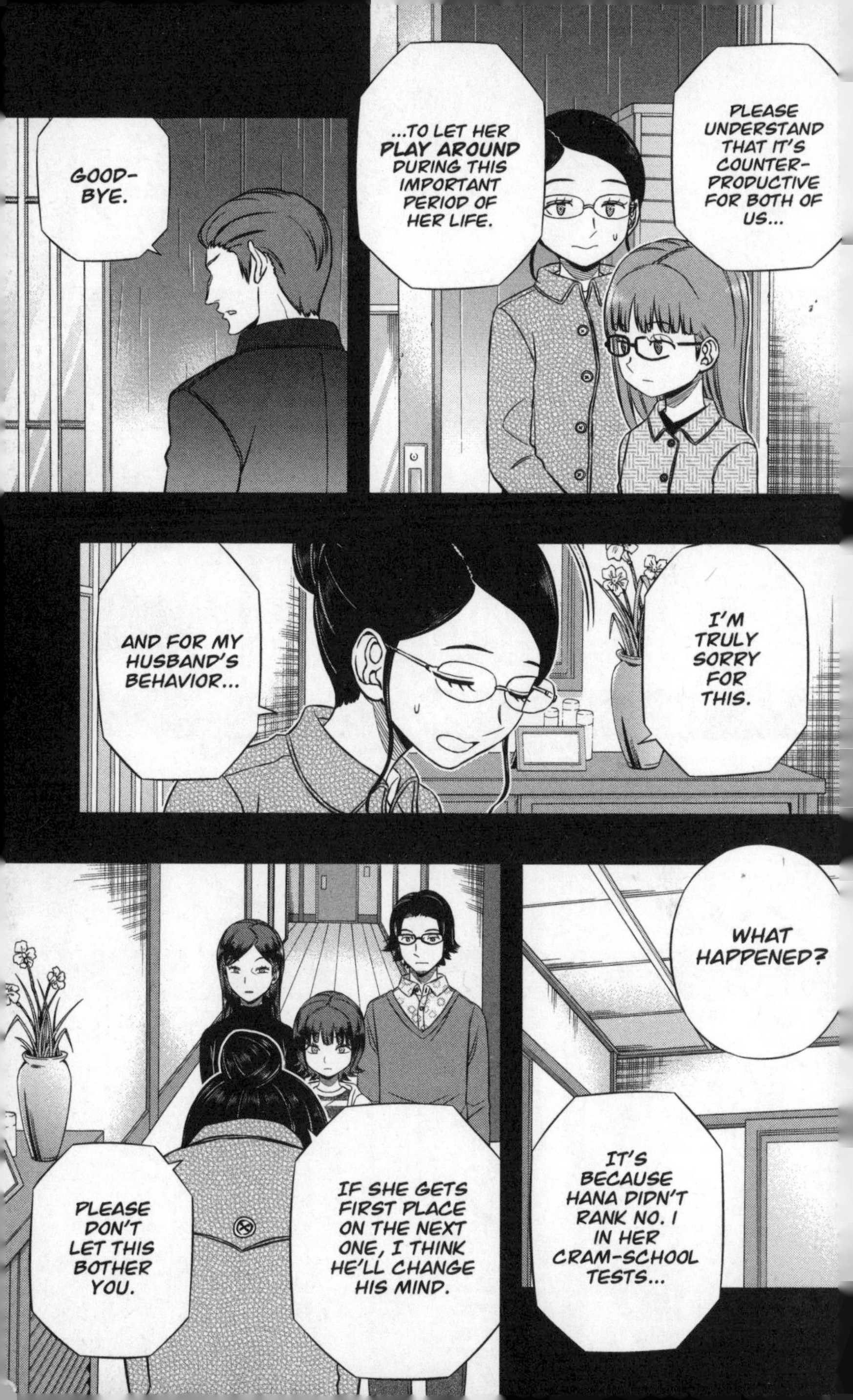
PLEASE UNDERSTAND THAT IT'S COUNTER-PRODUCTIVE FOR BOTH OF US...
...TO LET HER PLAY AROUND DURING THIS IMPORTANT PERIOD OF HER LIFE.
GOOD-BYE.
I'M TRULY SORRY FOR THIS.
AND FOR MY HUSBAND'S BEHAVIOR...
WHAT HAPPENED?
IT'S BECAUSE HANA DIDN'T RANK NO. 1 IN HER CRAM-SCHOOL TESTS...
IF SHE GETS FIRST PLACE ON THE NEXT ONE, I THINK HE'LL CHANGE HIS MIND.
PLEASE DON'T LET THIS BOTHER YOU.

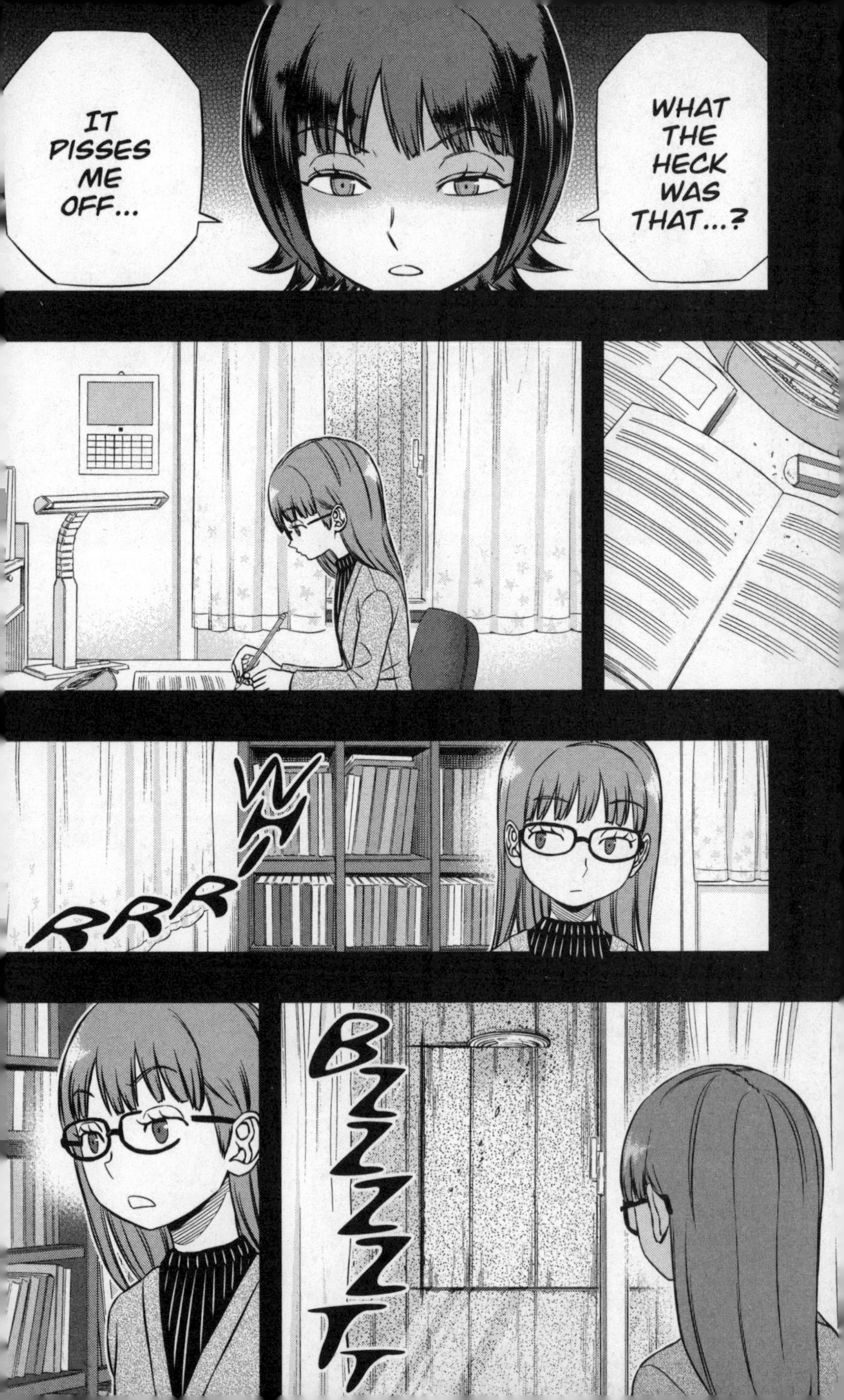
WHAT THE HECK WAS THAT...?
IT PISSES ME OFF...
WHIRRR
BZZZZTT

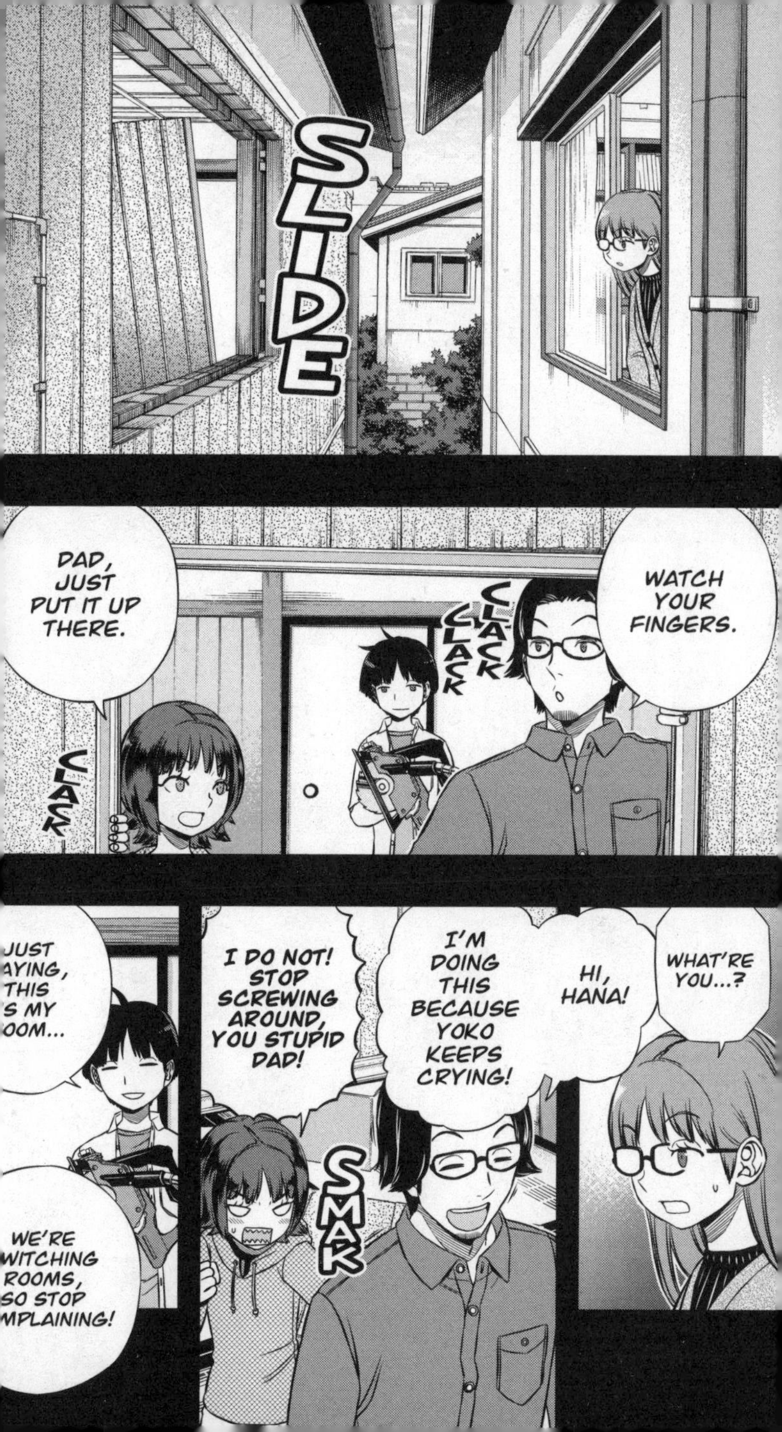
SLIDE
WATCH YOUR FINGERS.
CLACK CLACK
DAD, JUST PUT IT UP THERE.
CLACK
WHAT'RE YOU...?
HI, HANA!
I'M DOING THIS BECAUSE YOKO KEEPS CRYING!
I DO NOT! STOP SCREWING AROUND, YOU STUPID DAD!
SMAK
JUST AYING, THIS S MY OOM...
WE'RE WITCHING ROOMS, SO STOP MPLAINING!

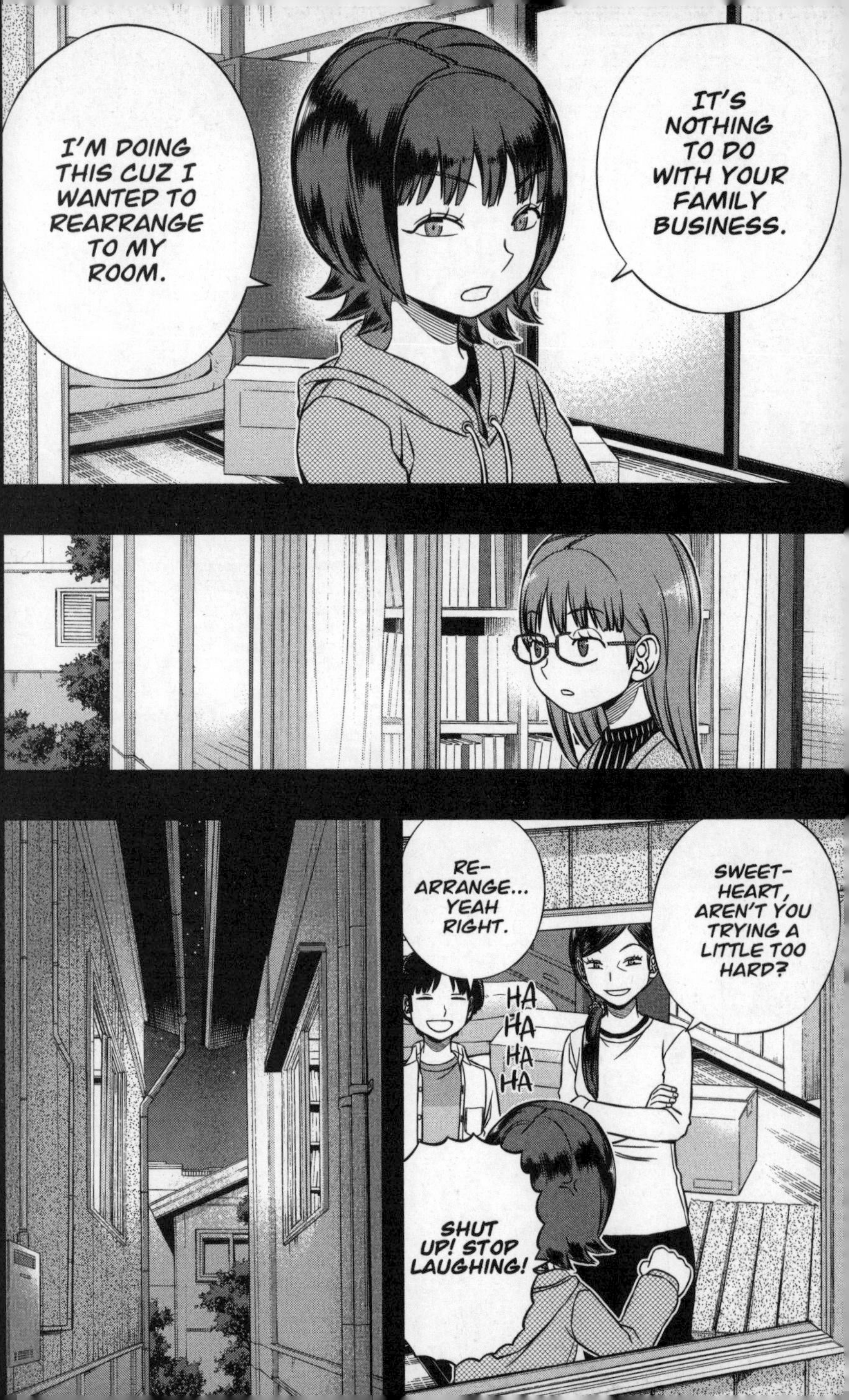
IT'S NOTHING TO DO WITH YOUR FAMILY BUSINESS.
I'M DOING THIS CUZ I WANTED TO REARRANGE TO MY ROOM.
SWEET-HEART, AREN'T YOU TRYING A LITTLE TOO HARD?
RE-ARRANGE... YEAH RIGHT.
HA HA HA HA
SHUT UP! STOP LAUGHING!

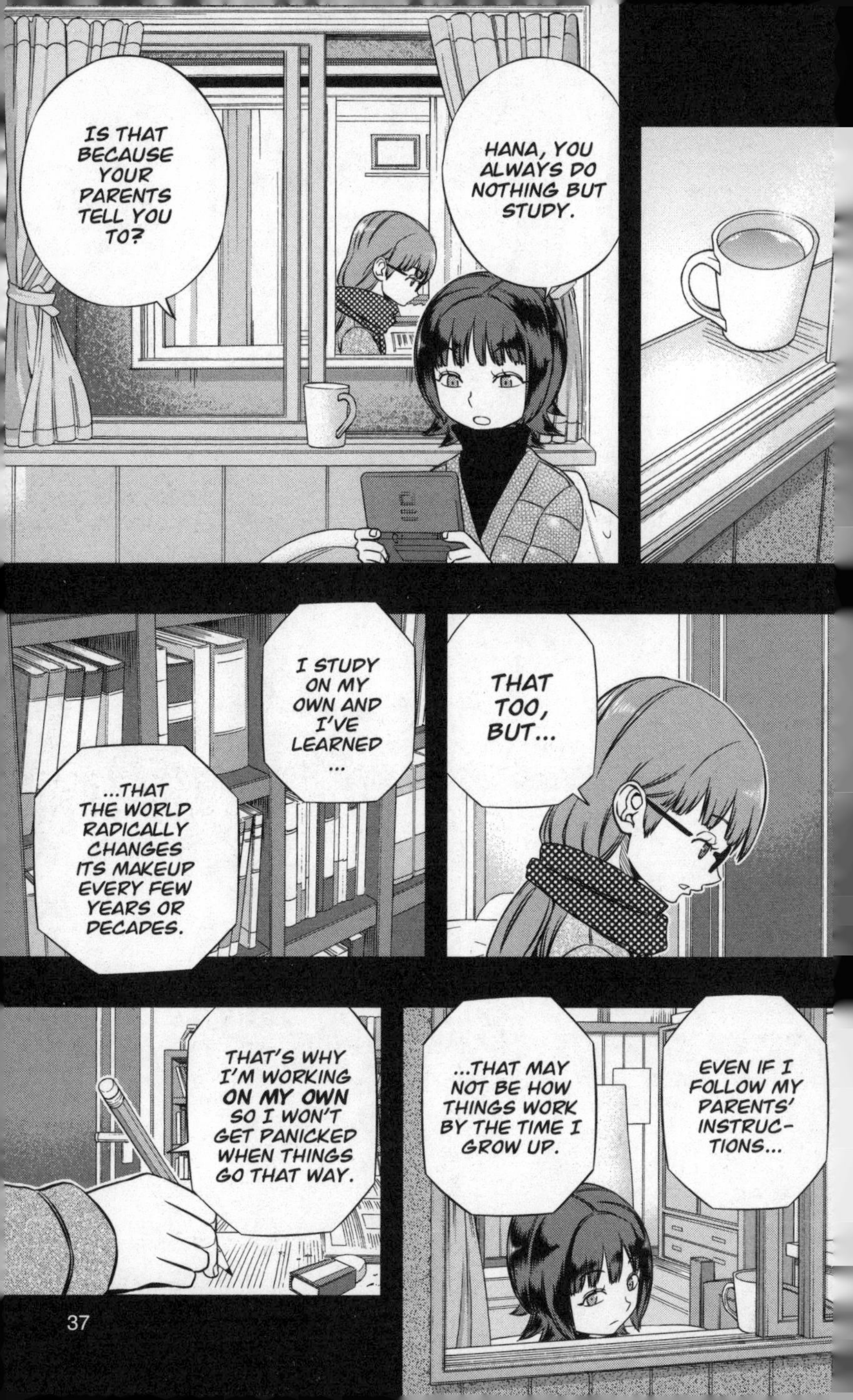
HANA, YOU ALWAYS DO NOTHING BUT STUDY.
IS THAT BECAUSE YOUR PARENTS TELL YOU TO?
THAT TOO, BUT...
I STUDY ON MY OWN AND I'VE LEARNED...
...THAT THE WORLD RADICALLY CHANGES ITS MAKEUP EVERY FEW YEARS OR DECADES.
EVEN IF I FOLLOW MY PARENTS' INSTRUCTIONS...
...THAT MAY NOT BE HOW THINGS WORK BY THE TIME I GROW UP.
THAT'S WHY I'M WORKING **ON MY OWN** SO I WON'T GET PANICKED WHEN THINGS GO THAT WAY.

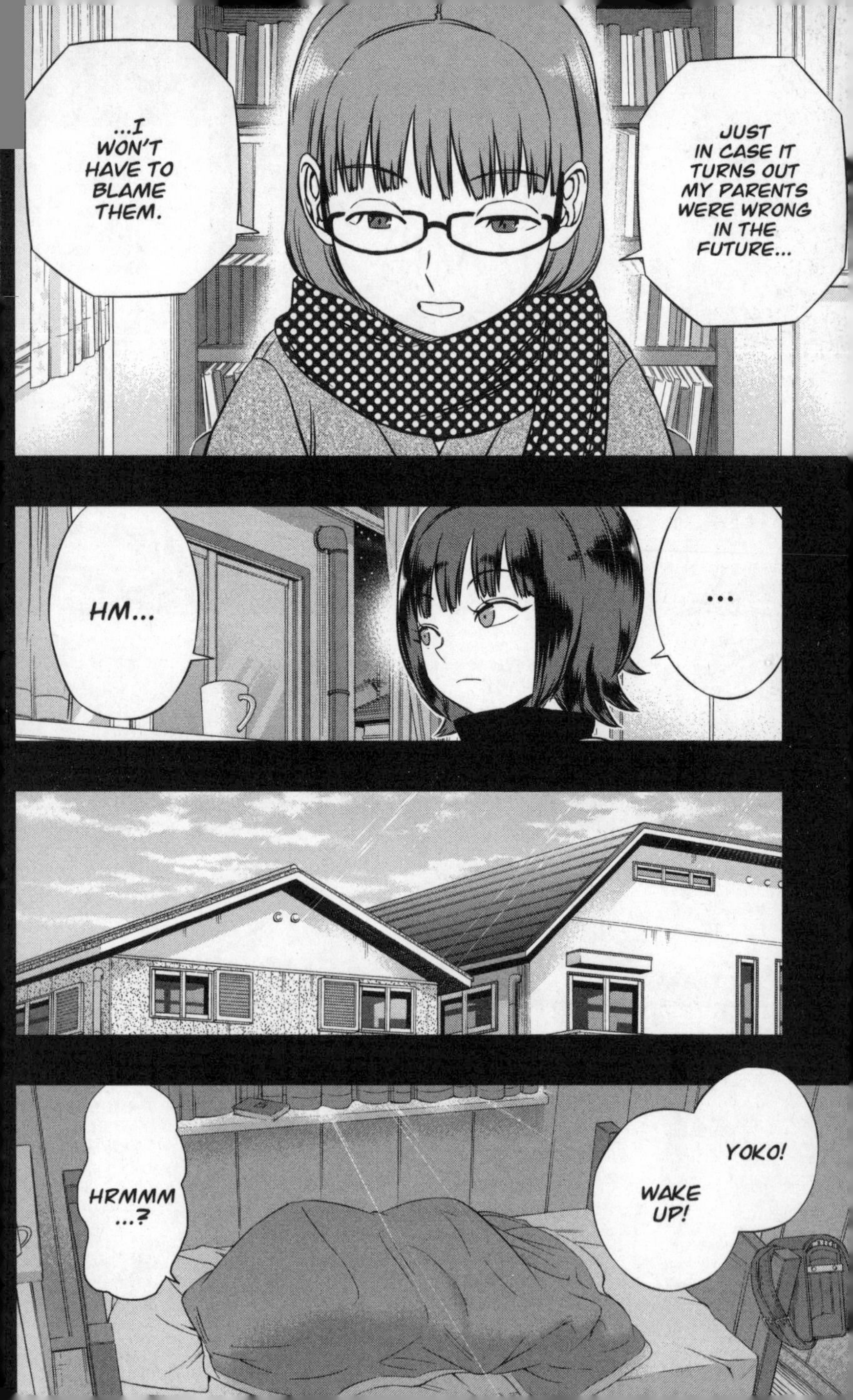
JUST IN CASE IT TURNS OUT MY PARENTS WERE WRONG IN THE FUTURE...
...I WON'T HAVE TO BLAME THEM.
...
HM...
YOKO!
WAKE UP!
HRMMM ...?

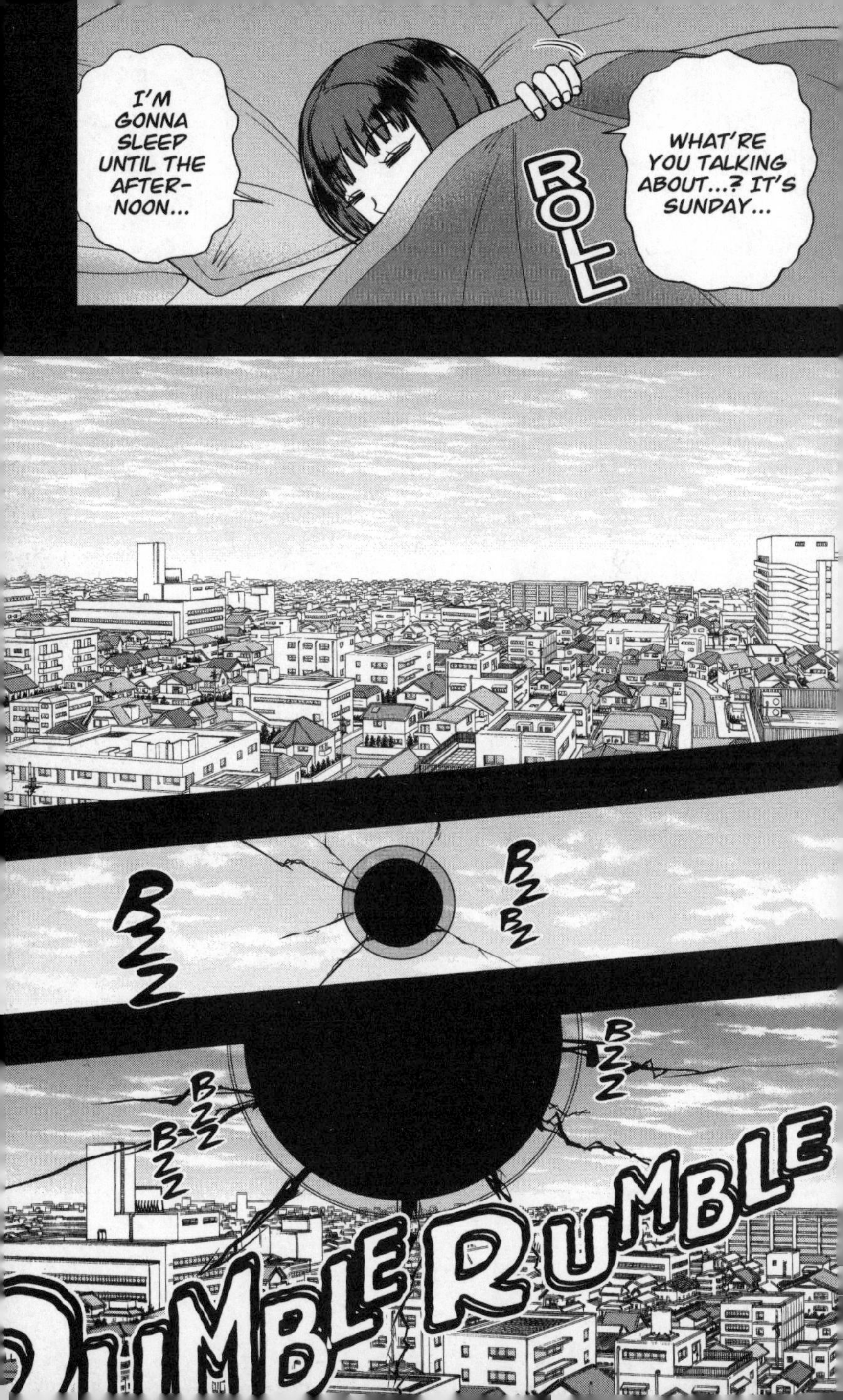
WHAT'RE YOU TALKING ABOUT...? IT'S SUNDAY...
ROLL
I'M GONNA SLEEP UNTIL THE AFTER-NOON...
BZZ BZZ
BZZZ
BZZ
B-ZZ
B-ZZ
UMBLE RUMBLE

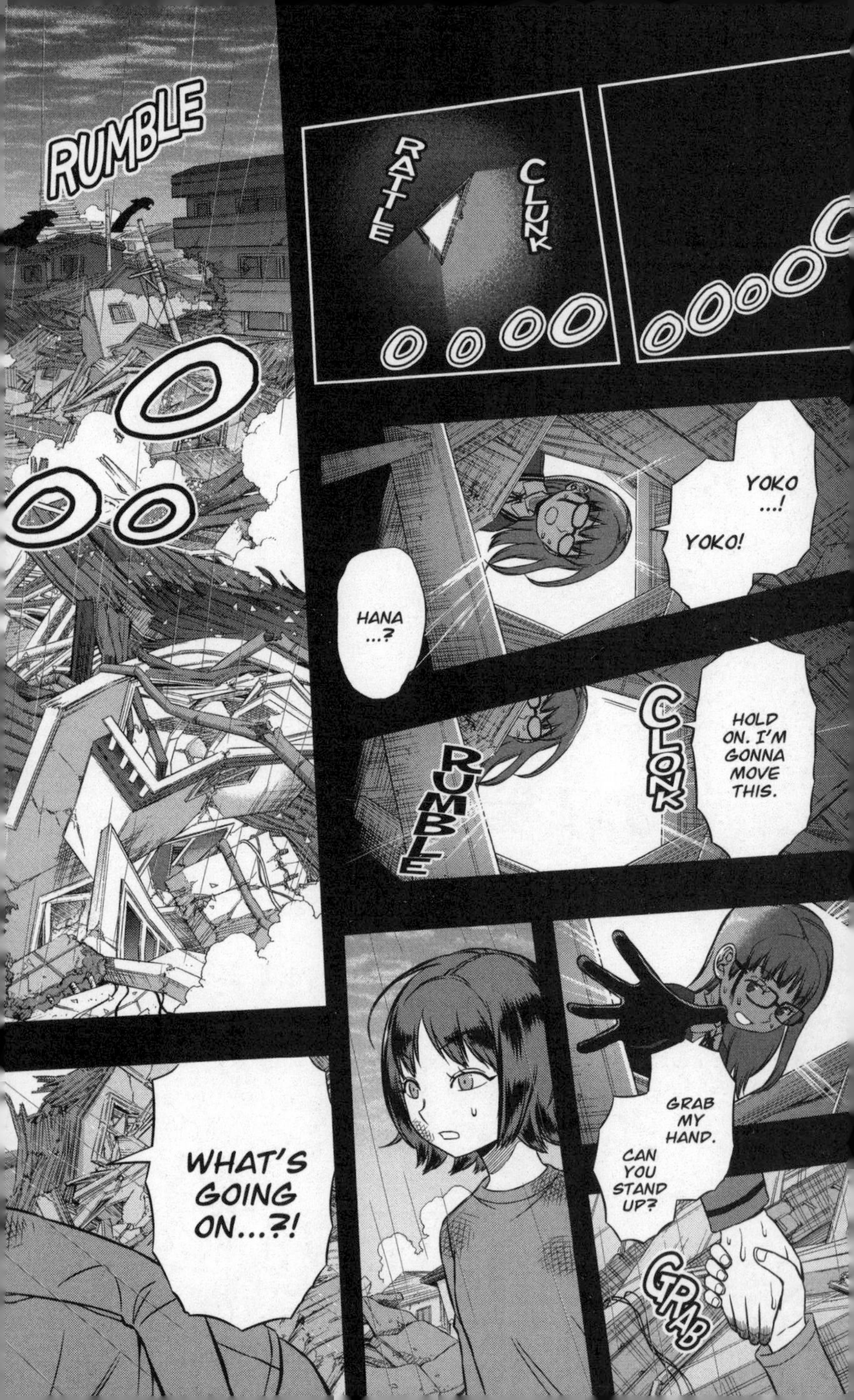
OOOOOO
RATTLE
CLUNK
OOOO
YOKO ...!
YOKO!
HANA ...?
HOLD ON. I'M GONNA MOVE THIS.
CLONK
RUMBLE
RUMBLE
OOOO
GRAB MY HAND.
CAN YOU STAND UP?
GRAB
WHAT'S GOING ON...?!

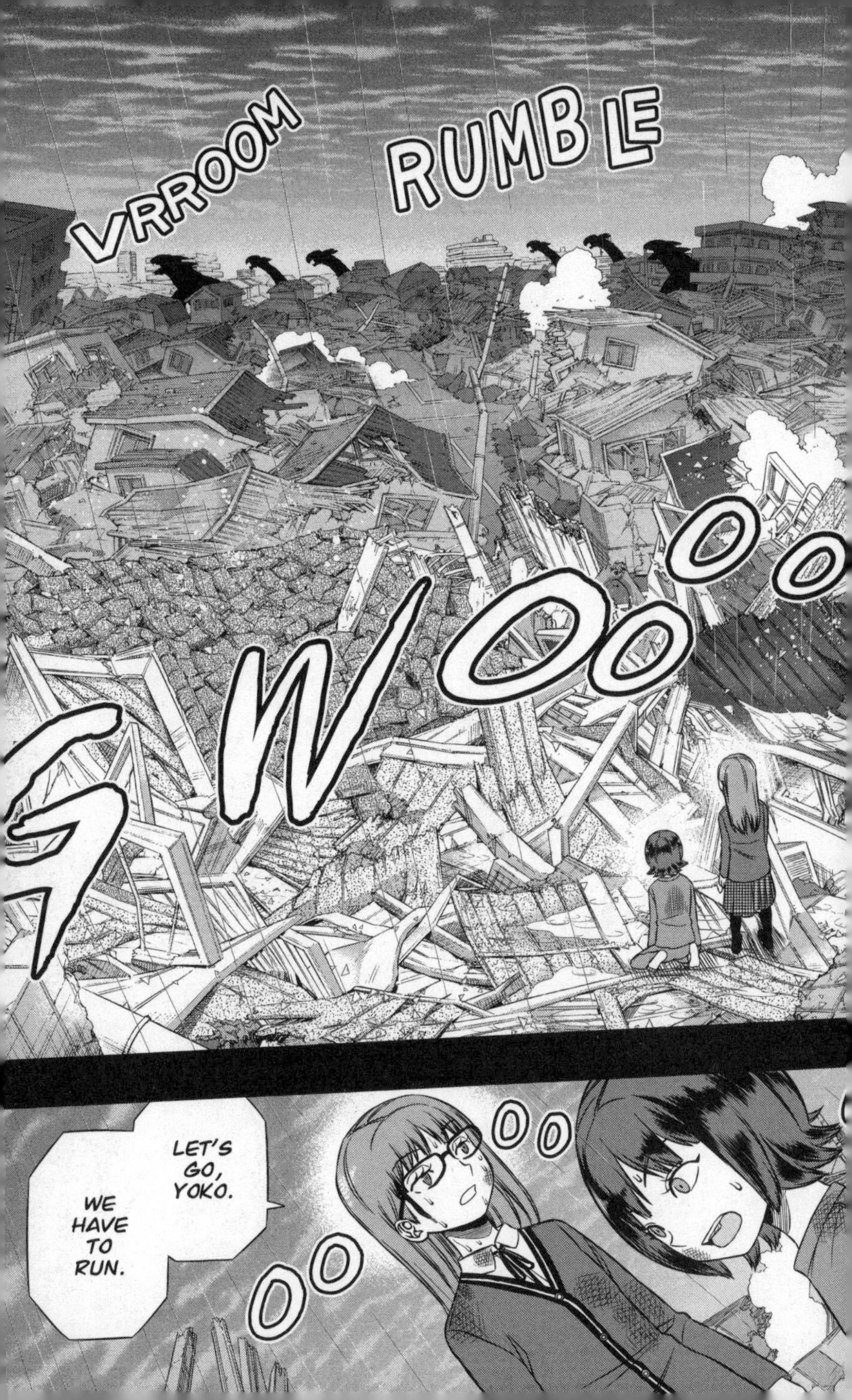

RUMBLE
VRROOM
SWOOOOO
OOOO
LET'S GO, YOKO.
WE HAVE TO RUN.

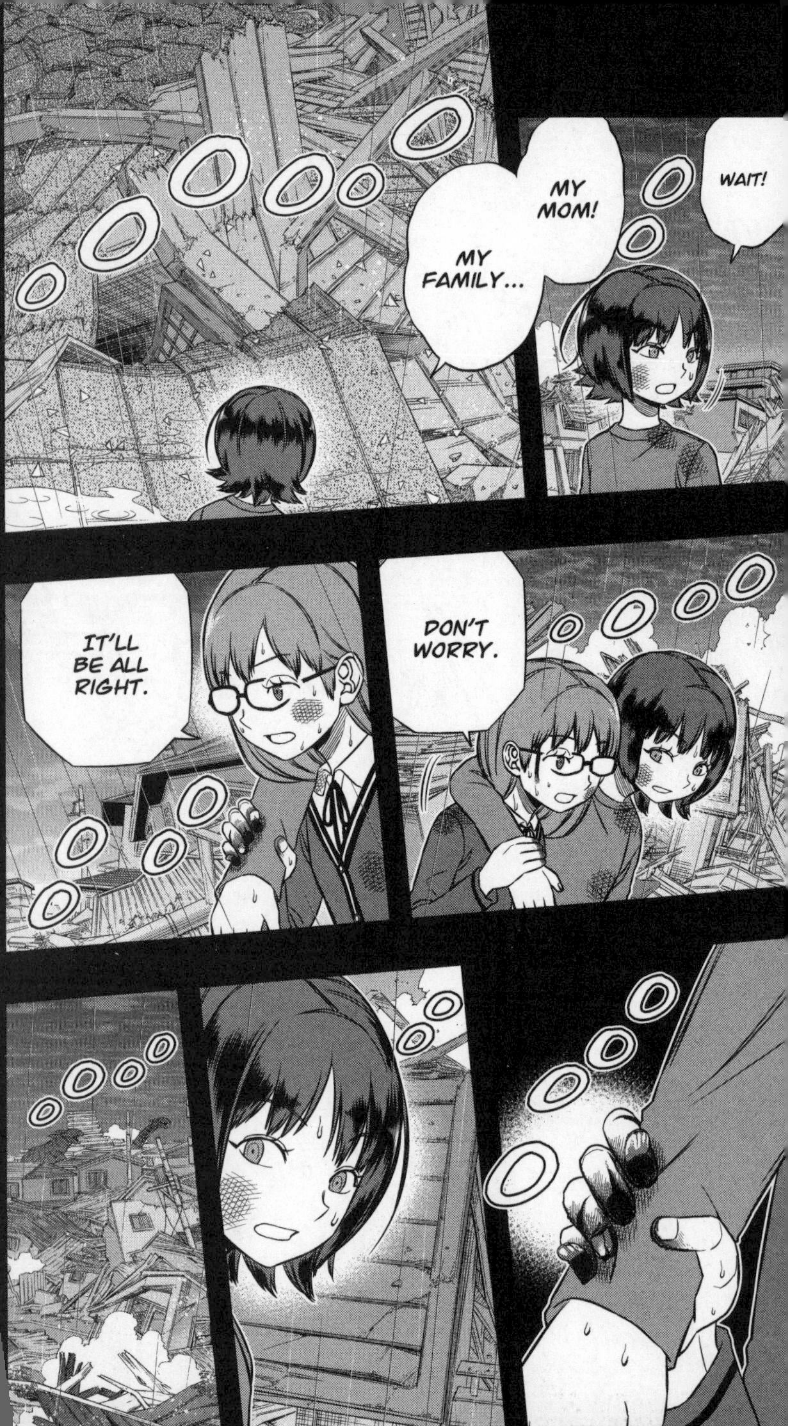
WAIT!
MY MOM!
MY FAMILY...
DON'T WORRY.
IT'LL BE ALL RIGHT.

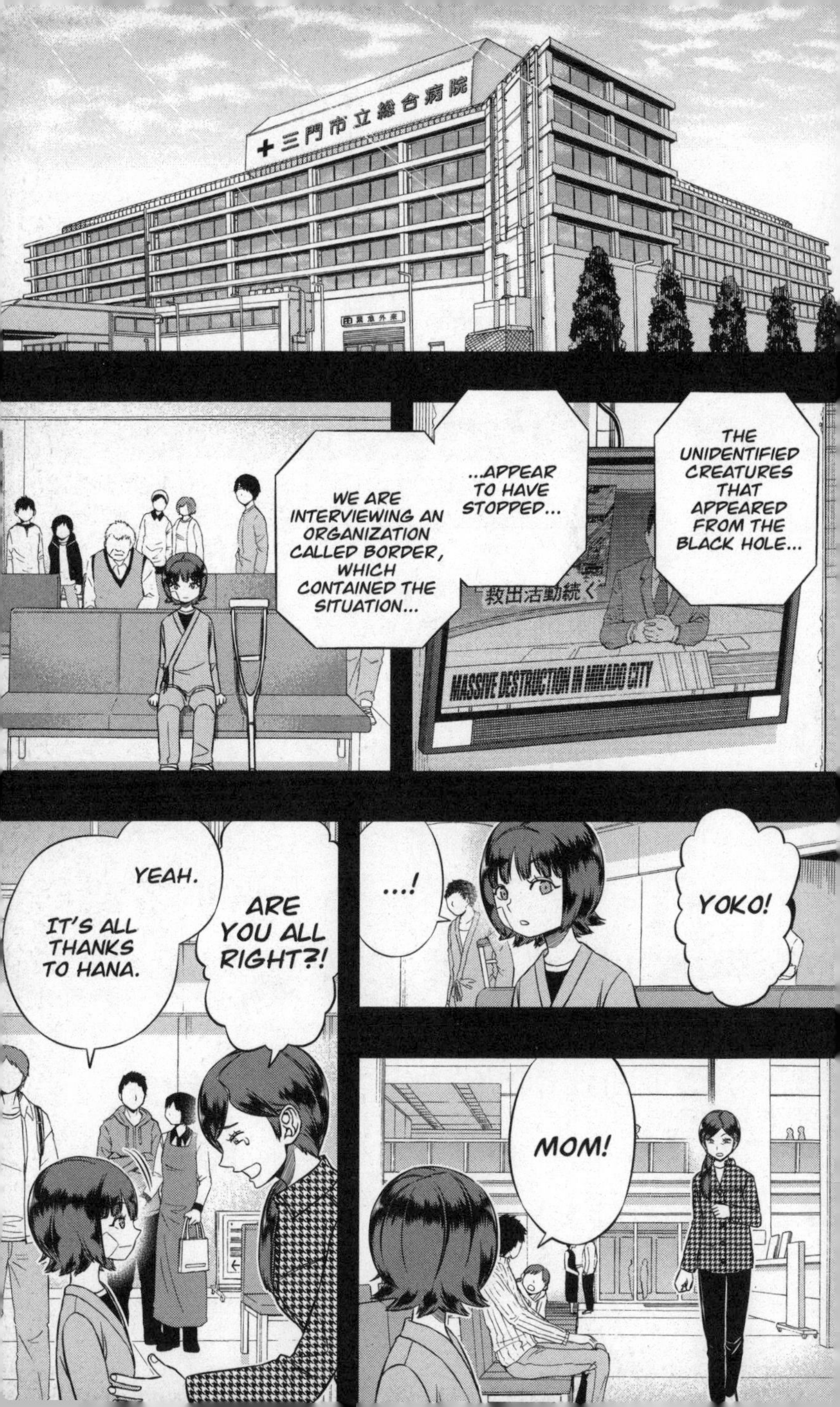
三門市立総合病院
救急外来
THE UNIDENTIFIED CREATURES THAT APPEARED FROM THE BLACK HOLE...
...APPEAR TO HAVE STOPPED...
WE ARE INTERVIEWING AN ORGANIZATION CALLED BORDER, WHICH CONTAINED THE SITUATION...
救出活動続く
MASSIVE DESTRUCTION IN MIKADO CITY
YOKO!
...!
MOM!
ARE YOU ALL RIGHT?!
YEAH.
IT'S ALL THANKS TO HANA.

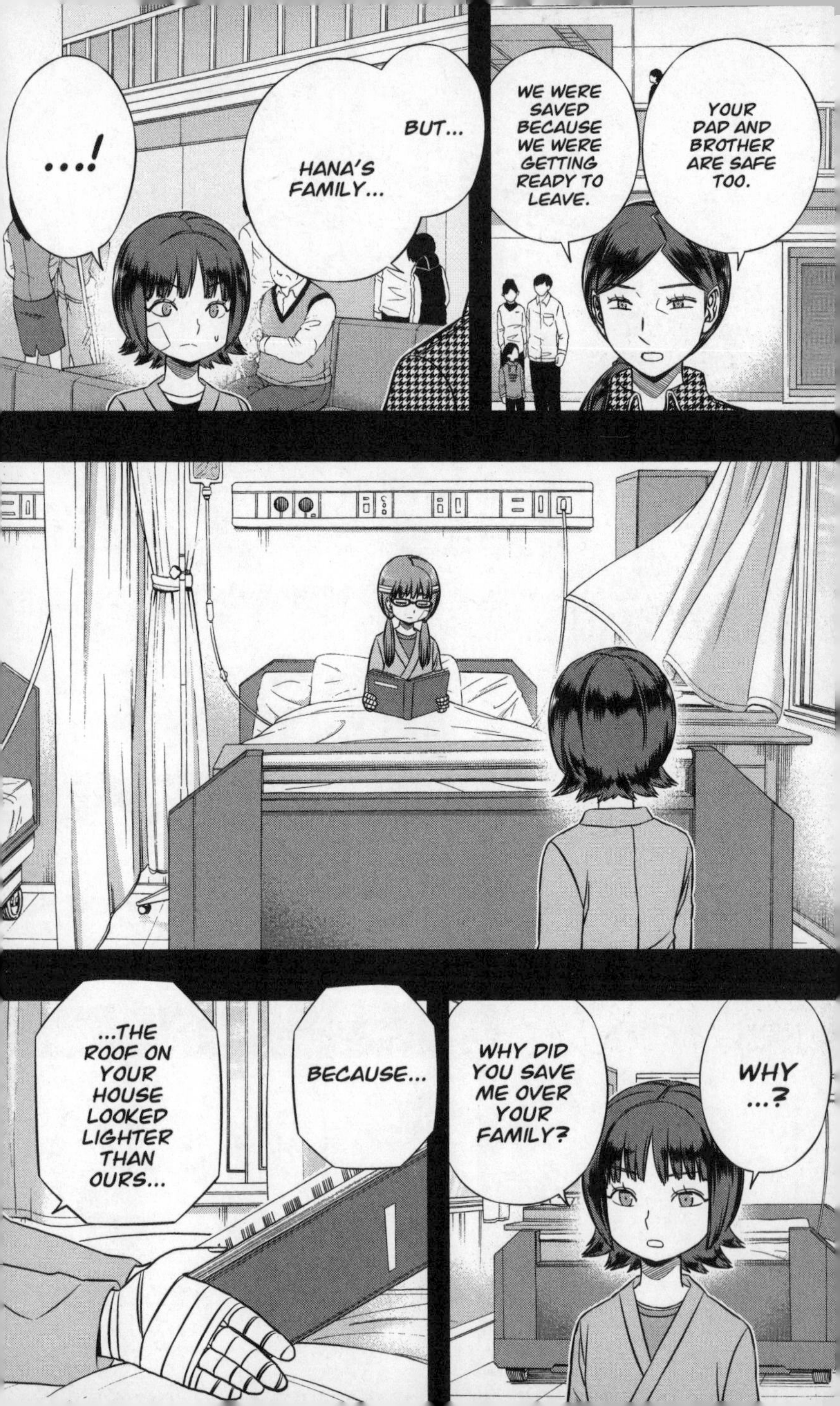
YOUR DAD AND BROTHER ARE SAFE TOO.
WE WERE SAVED BECAUSE WE WERE GETTING READY TO LEAVE.
BUT... HANA'S FAMILY...
...!
WHY ...?
WHY DID YOU SAVE ME OVER YOUR FAMILY?
BECAUSE...
...THE ROOF ON YOUR HOUSE LOOKED LIGHTER THAN OURS...

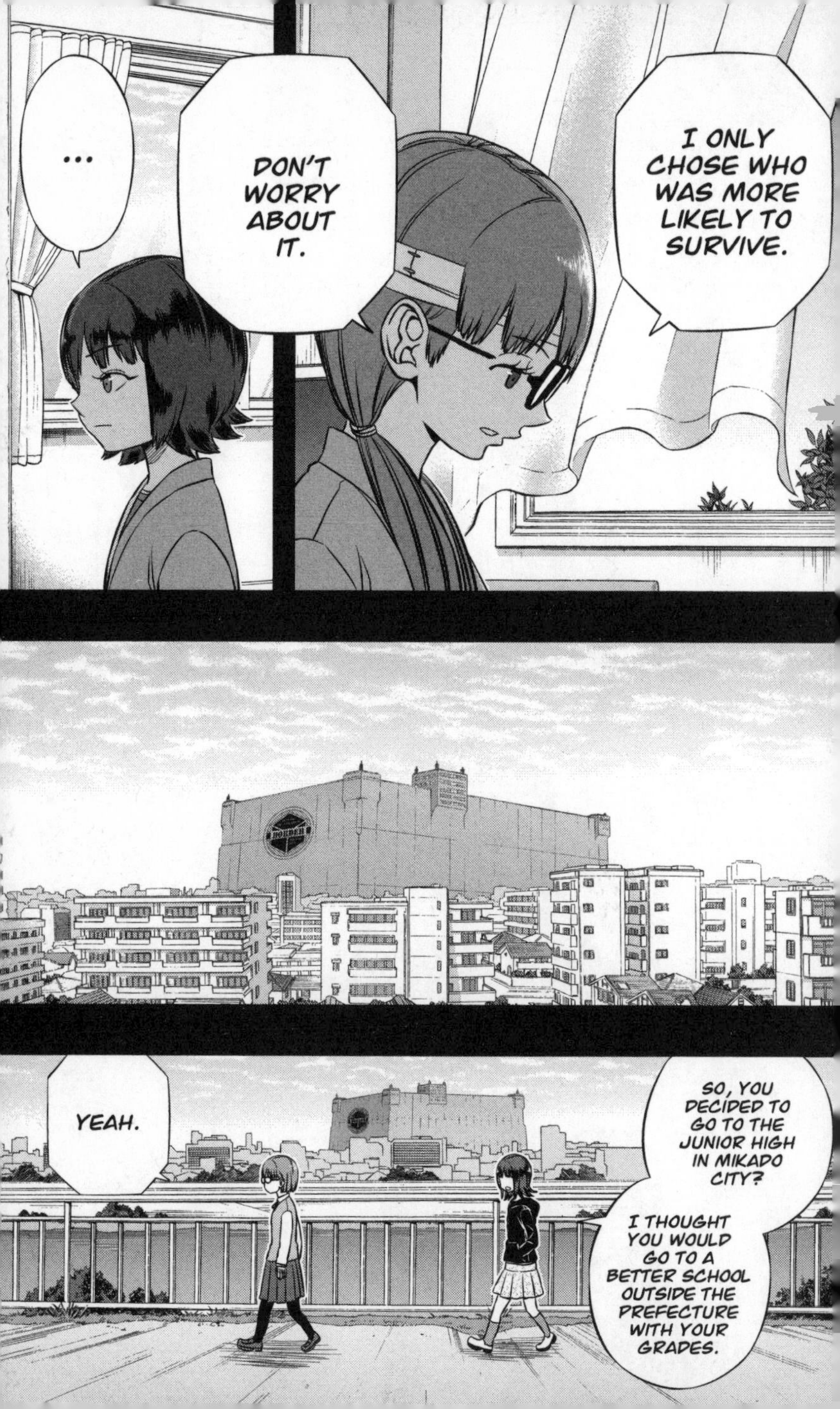
I ONLY CHOSE WHO WAS MORE LIKELY TO SURVIVE.
DON'T WORRY ABOUT IT.
...
SO, YOU DECIDED TO GO TO THE JUNIOR HIGH IN MIKADO CITY?
I THOUGHT YOU WOULD GO TO A BETTER SCHOOL OUTSIDE THE PREFECTURE WITH YOUR GRADES.
YEAH.

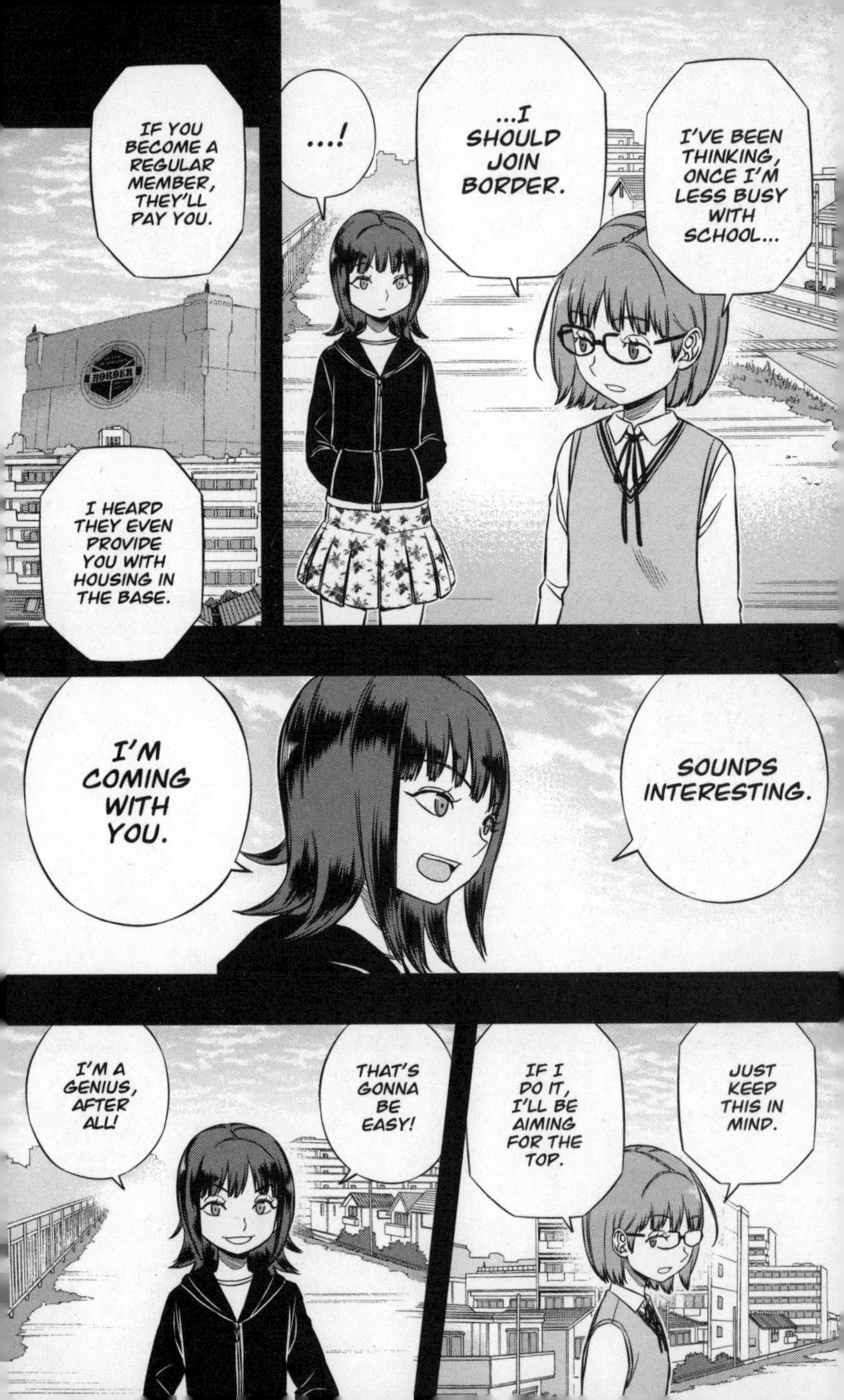
I'VE BEEN THINKING, ONCE I'M LESS BUSY WITH SCHOOL...
...I SHOULD JOIN BORDER.
...!
IF YOU BECOME A REGULAR MEMBER, THEY'LL PAY YOU.
I HEARD THEY EVEN PROVIDE YOU WITH HOUSING IN THE BASE.
SOUNDS INTERESTING.
I'M COMING WITH YOU.
JUST KEEP THIS IN MIND.
IF I DO IT, I'LL BE AIMING FOR THE TOP.
THAT'S GONNA BE EASY!
I'M A GENIUS, AFTER ALL!

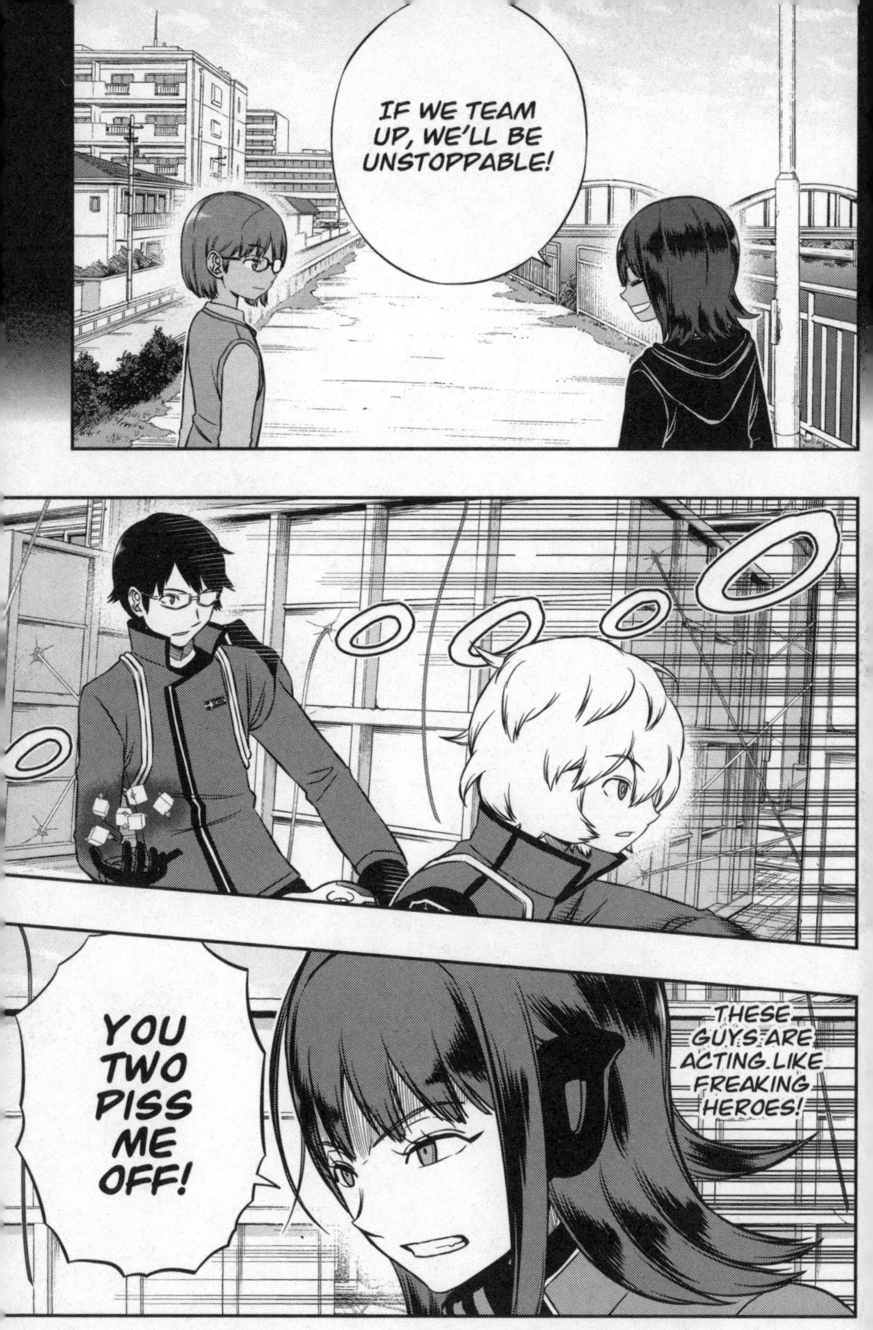
IF WE TEAM UP, WE'LL BE UNSTOPPABLE!
THESE GUYS ARE ACTING LIKE FREAKING HEROES!
YOU TWO PISS ME OFF!

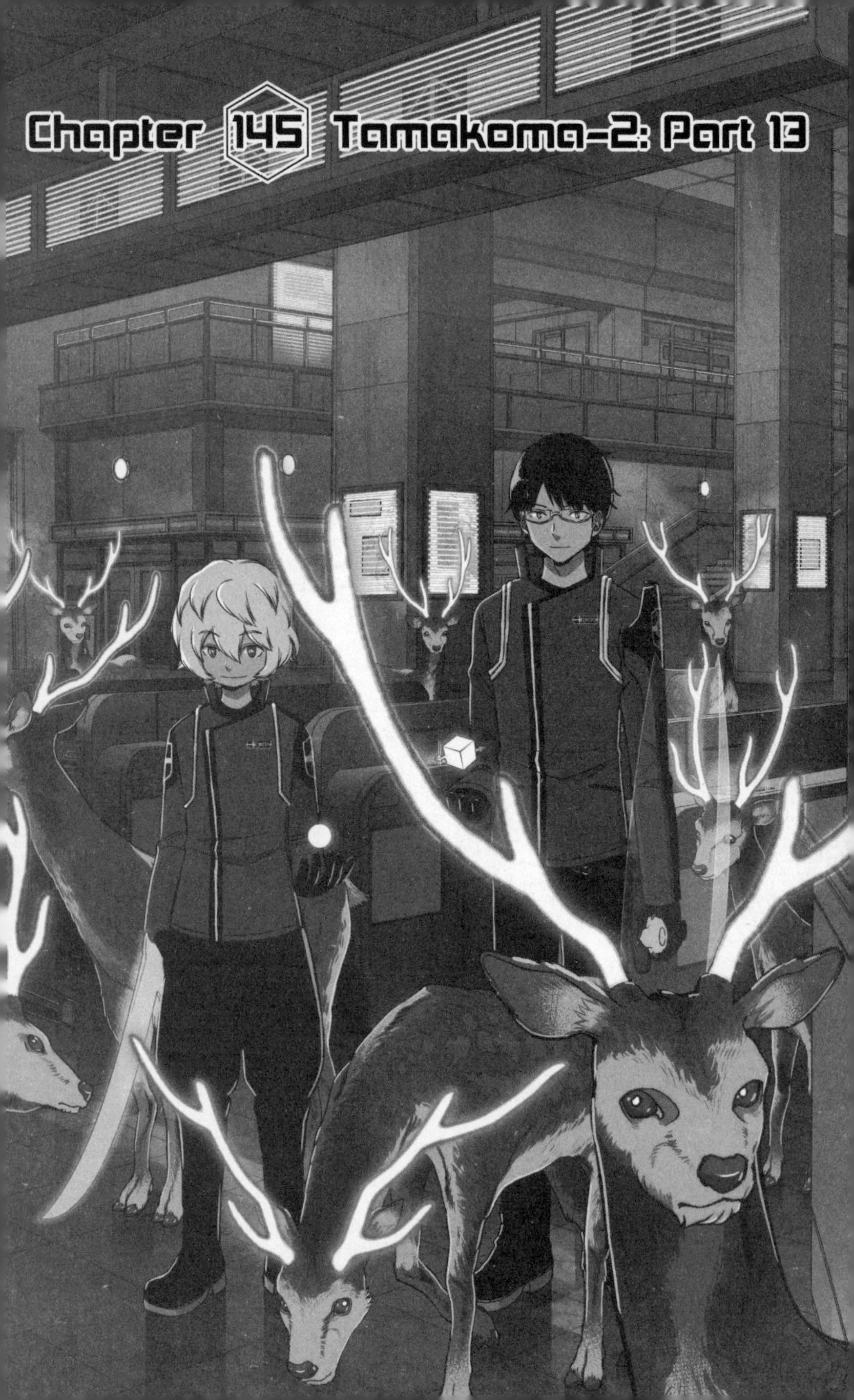
Chapter 145 Tamakoma-2: Part 13

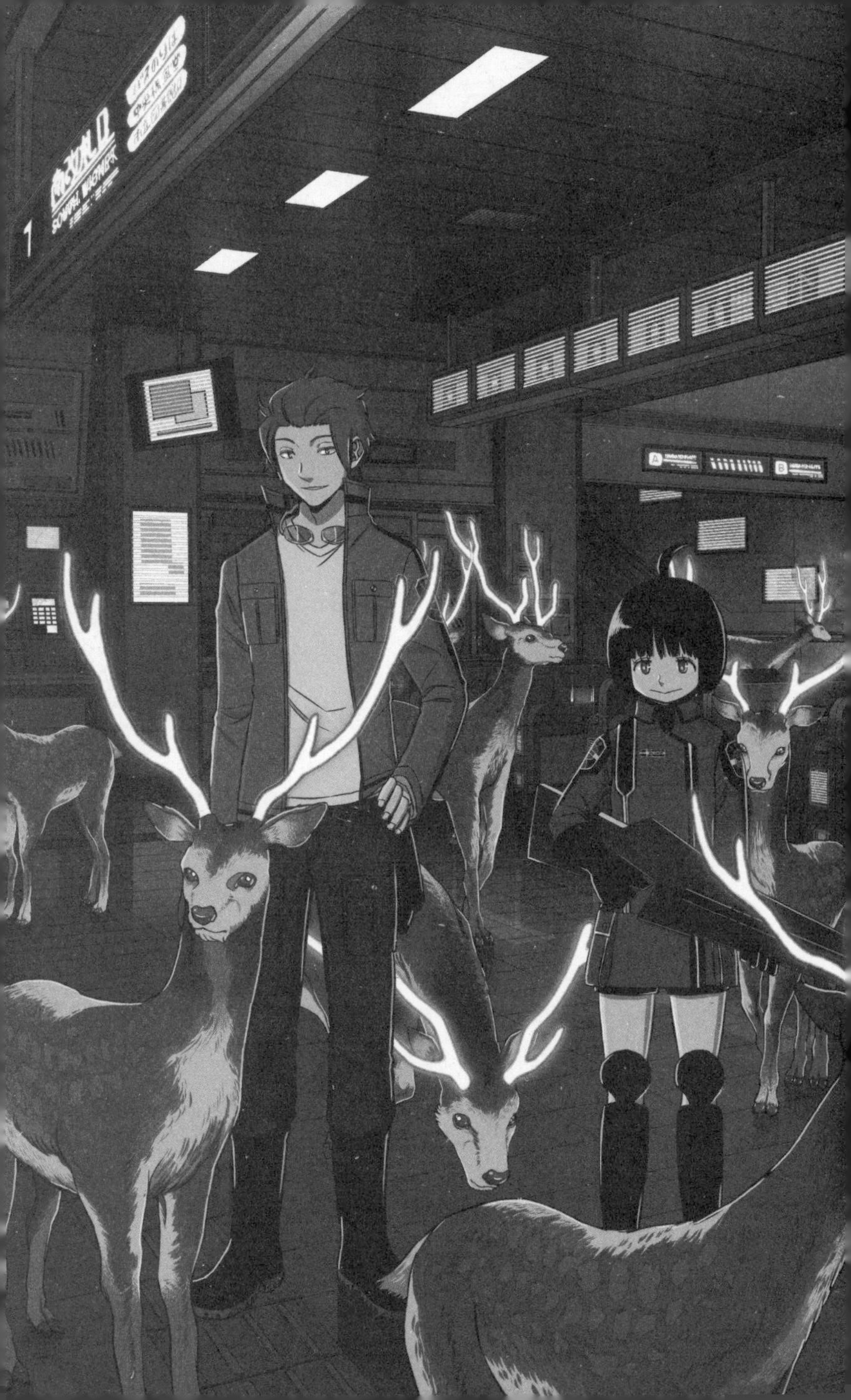

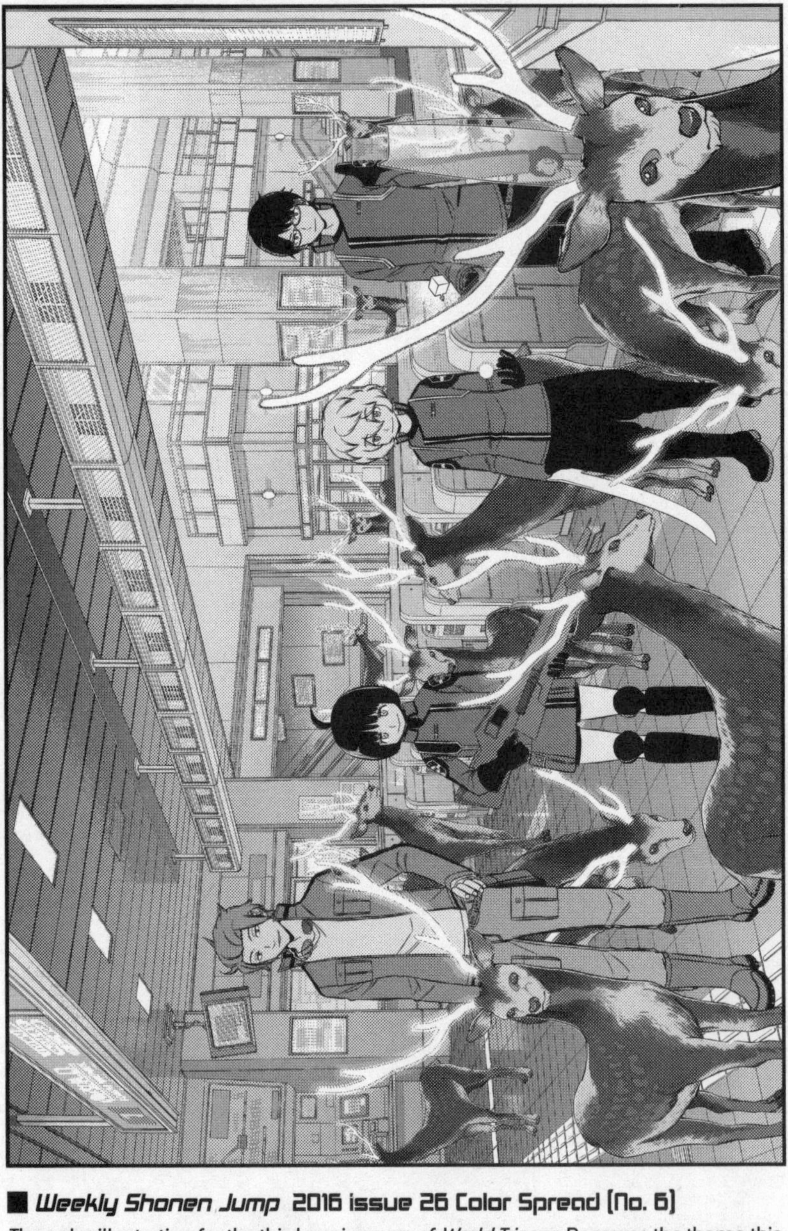

■ *Weekly Shonen Jump* 2016 issue 26 Color Spread [No. 6]

The color illustration for the third anniversary of *World Trigger*. Deer was the theme this year. Thanks to my fans and readers for helping me get this far. Now it's time to get ready for the fourth anniversary!

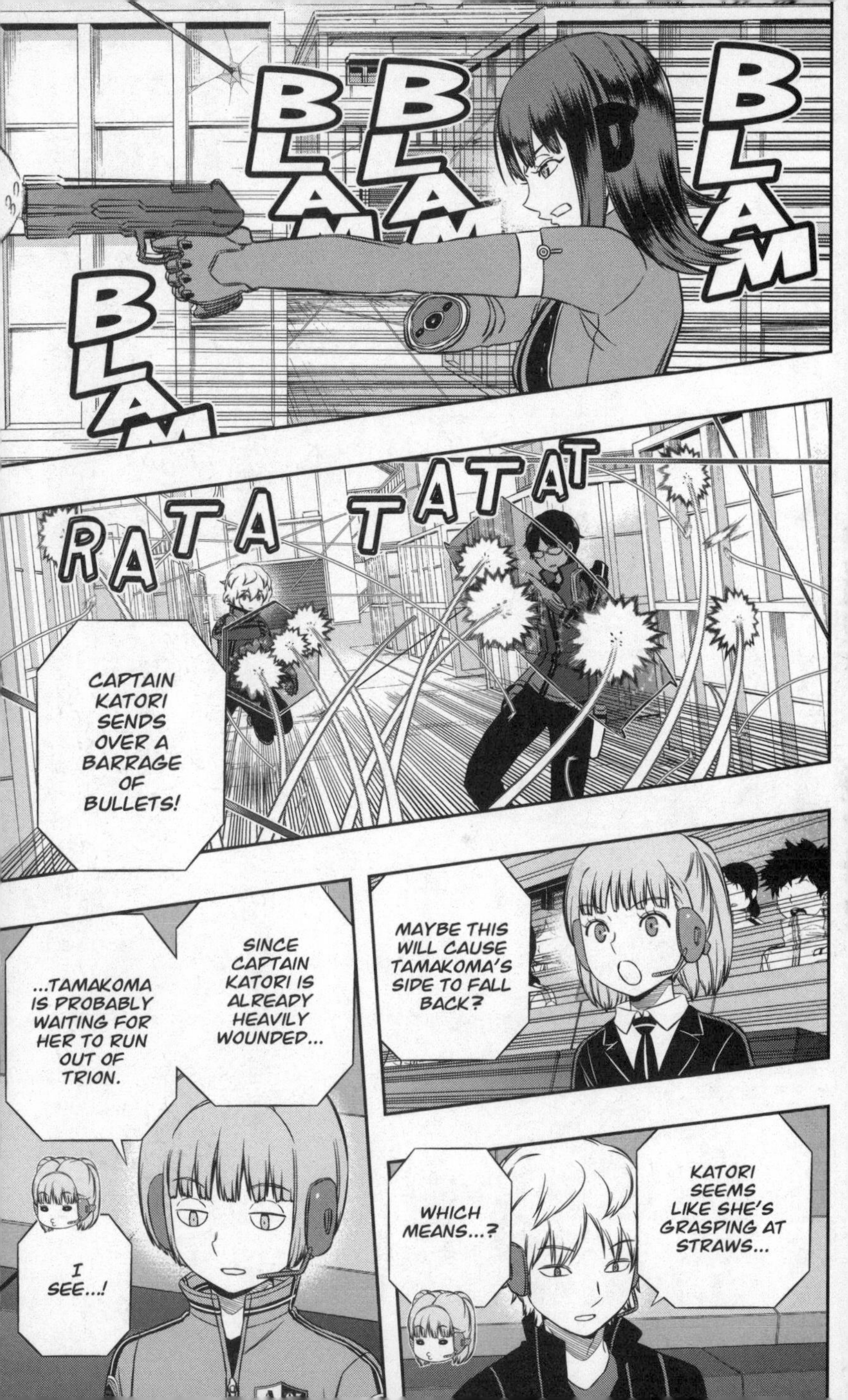
BLAM
BLAM
BLAM
BLAM
RATATATAT
CAPTAIN KATORI SENDS OVER A BARRAGE OF BULLETS!
MAYBE THIS WILL CAUSE TAMAKOMA'S SIDE TO FALL BACK?
KATORI SEEMS LIKE SHE'S GRASPING AT STRAWS...
WHICH MEANS...?
SINCE CAPTAIN KATORI IS ALREADY HEAVILY WOUNDED...
...TAMAKOMA IS PROBABLY WAITING FOR HER TO RUN OUT OF TRION.
I SEE...!

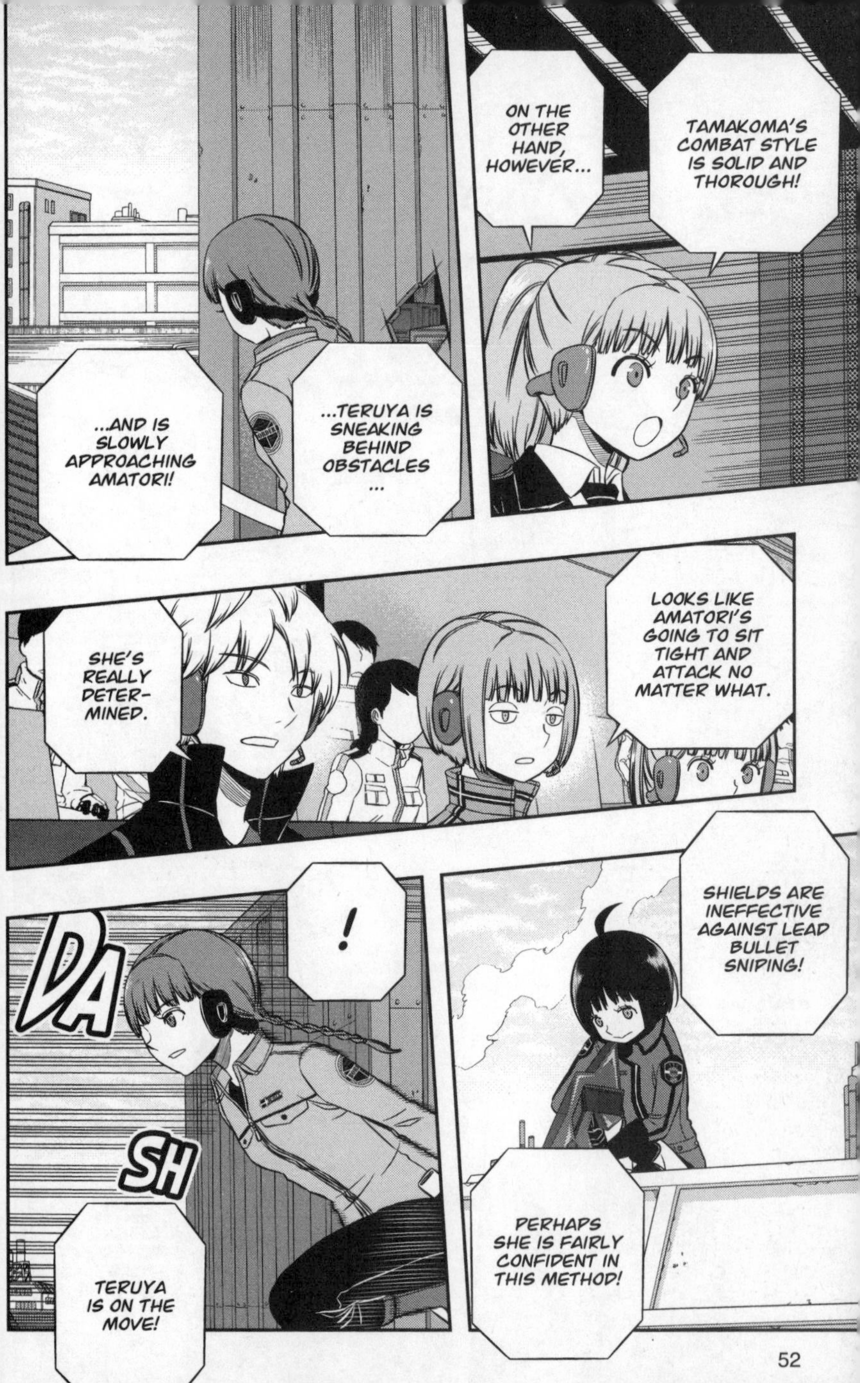
TAMAKOMA'S COMBAT STYLE IS SOLID AND THOROUGH!
ON THE OTHER HAND, HOWEVER...
...TERUYA IS SNEAKING BEHIND OBSTACLES ...
...AND IS SLOWLY APPROACHING AMATORI!
LOOKS LIKE AMATORI'S GOING TO SIT TIGHT AND ATTACK NO MATTER WHAT.
SHE'S REALLY DETER-MINED.
SHIELDS ARE INEFFECTIVE AGAINST LEAD BULLET SNIPING!
PERHAPS SHE IS FAIRLY CONFIDENT IN THIS METHOD!
!
DASH
TERUYA IS ON THE MOVE!

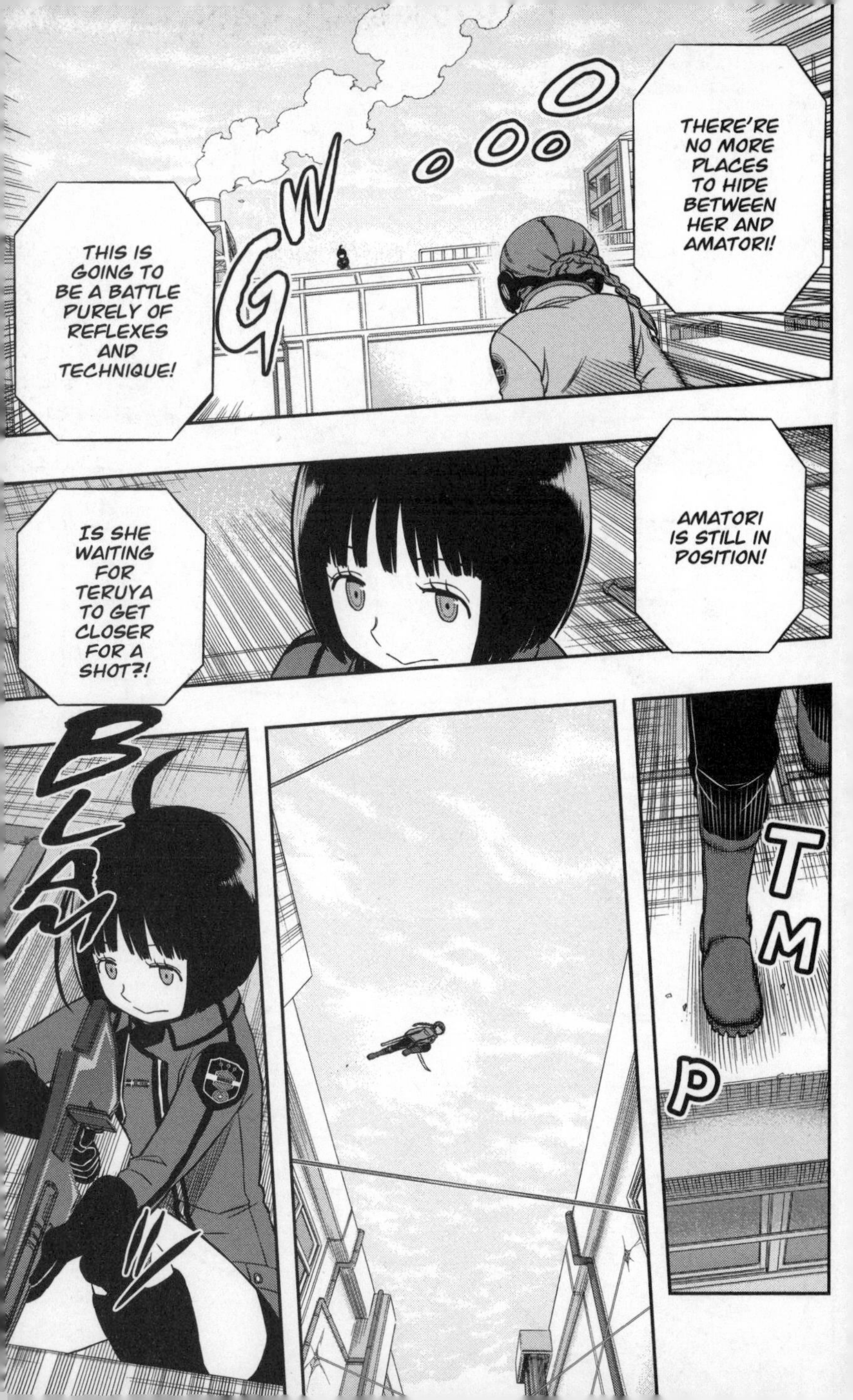
THERE'RE NO MORE PLACES TO HIDE BETWEEN HER AND AMATORI!
GWoOoO
THIS IS GOING TO BE A BATTLE PURELY OF REFLEXES AND TECHNIQUE!
AMATORI IS STILL IN POSITION!
IS SHE WAITING FOR TERUYA TO GET CLOSER FOR A SHOT?!
TMP
BLAM

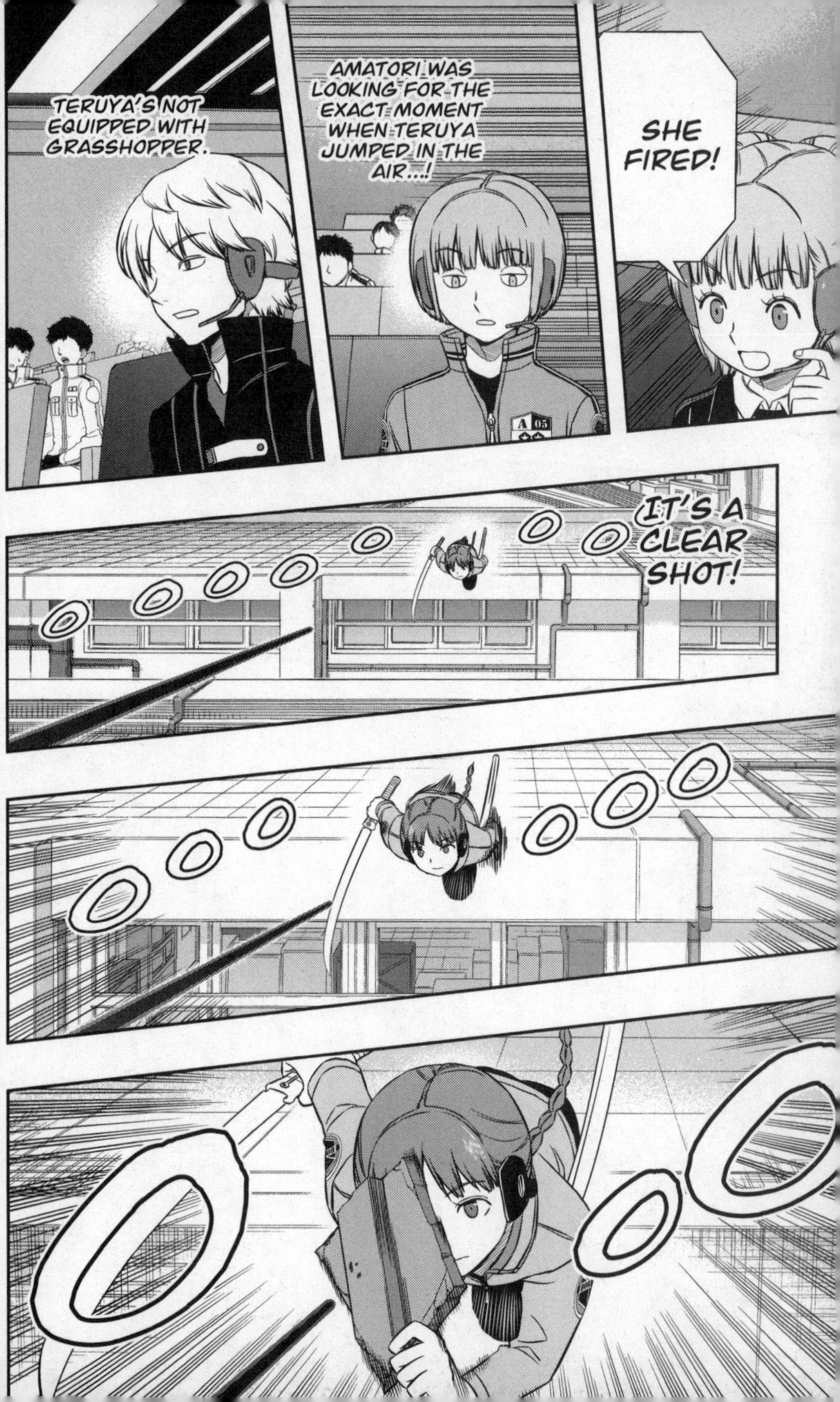
SHE FIRED!
AMATORI WAS LOOKING FOR THE EXACT MOMENT WHEN TERUYA JUMPED IN THE AIR...!
TERUYA'S NOT EQUIPPED WITH GRASSHOPPER.
IT'S A CLEAR SHOT!

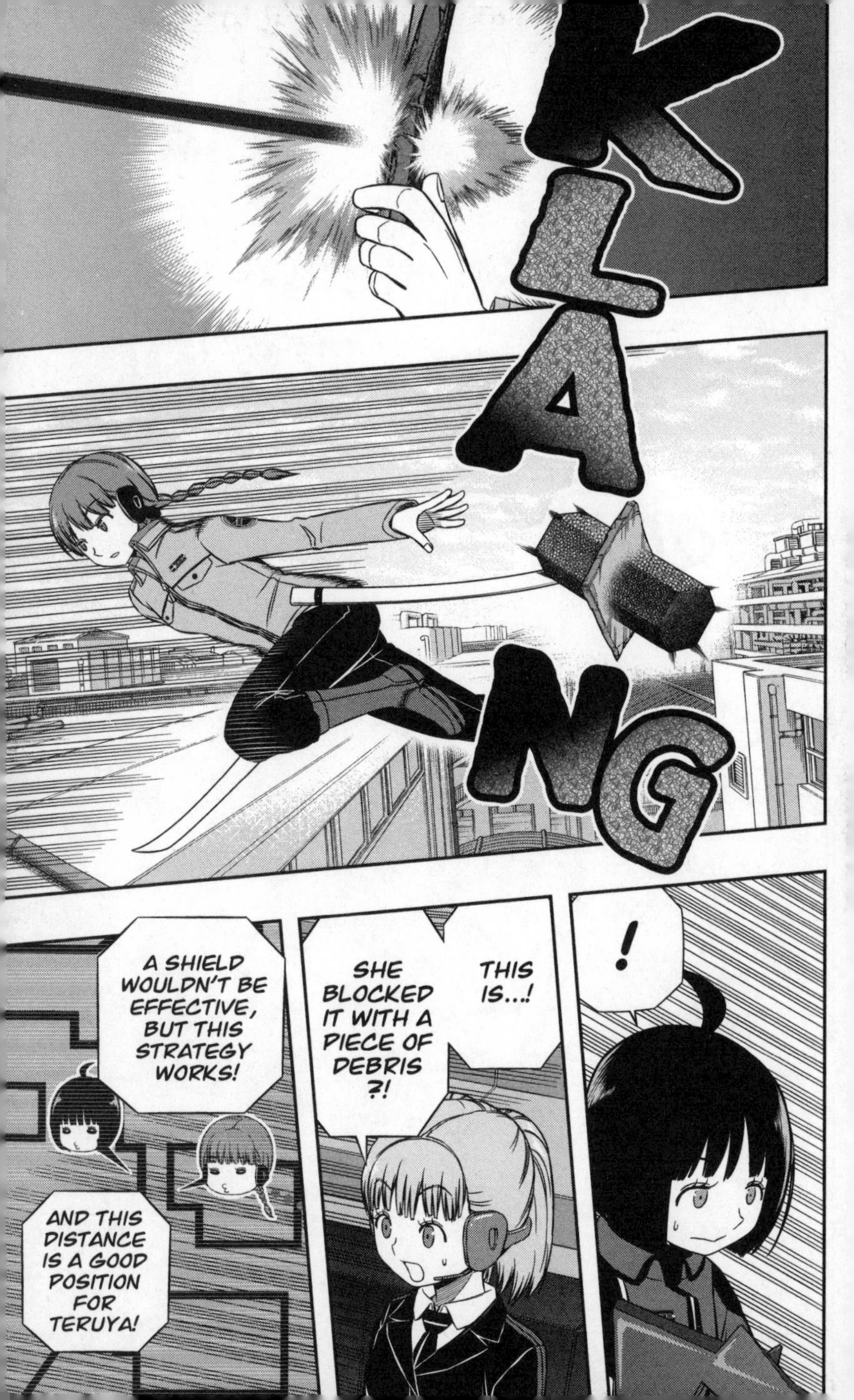
KLANG
!
THIS IS...!
SHE BLOCKED IT WITH A PIECE OF DEBRIS ?!
A SHIELD WOULDN'T BE EFFECTIVE, BUT THIS STRATEGY WORKS!
AND THIS DISTANCE IS A GOOD POSITION FOR TERUYA!

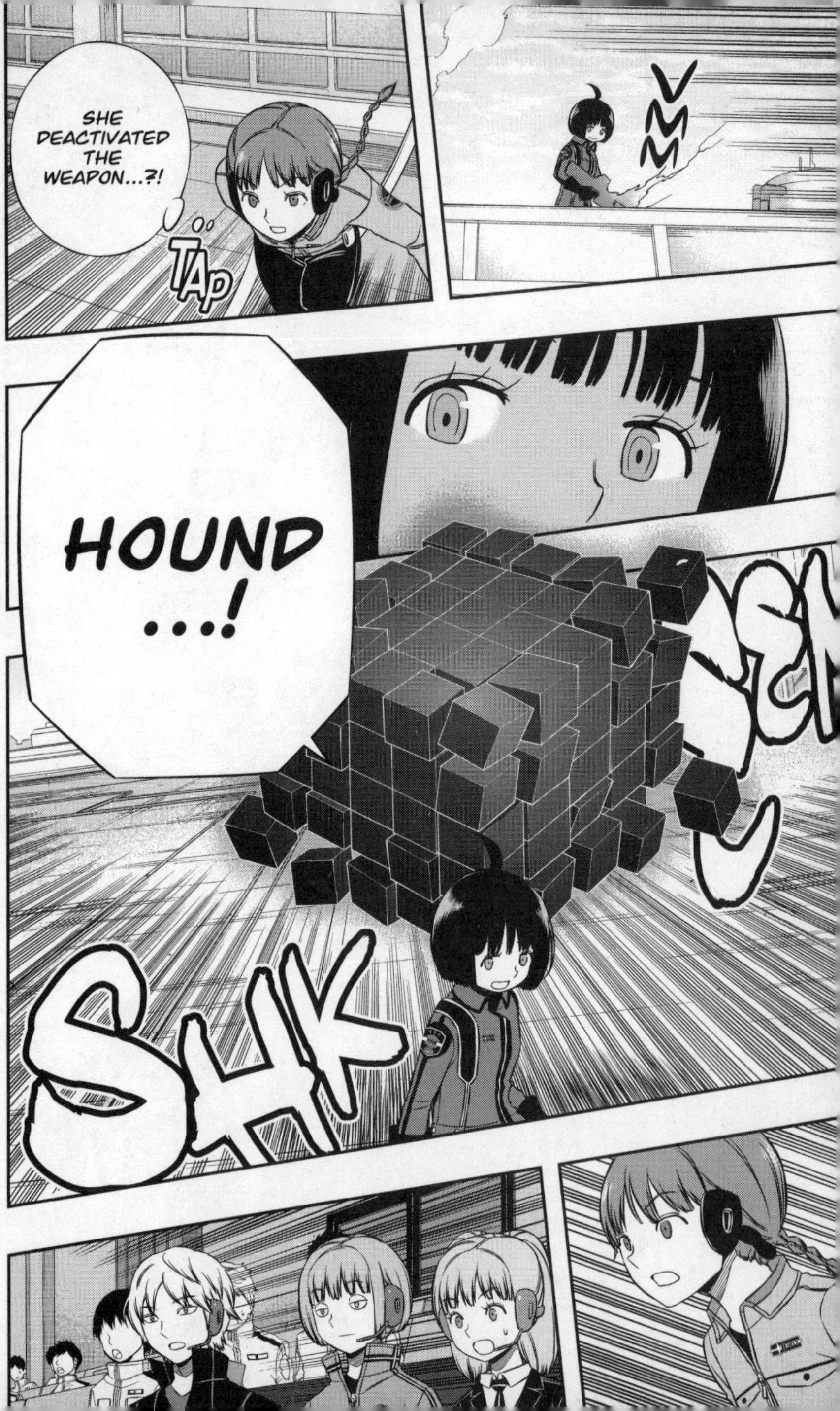
VMM
SHE DEACTIVATED THE WEAPON...?!
TAp
HOUND...!
SHK

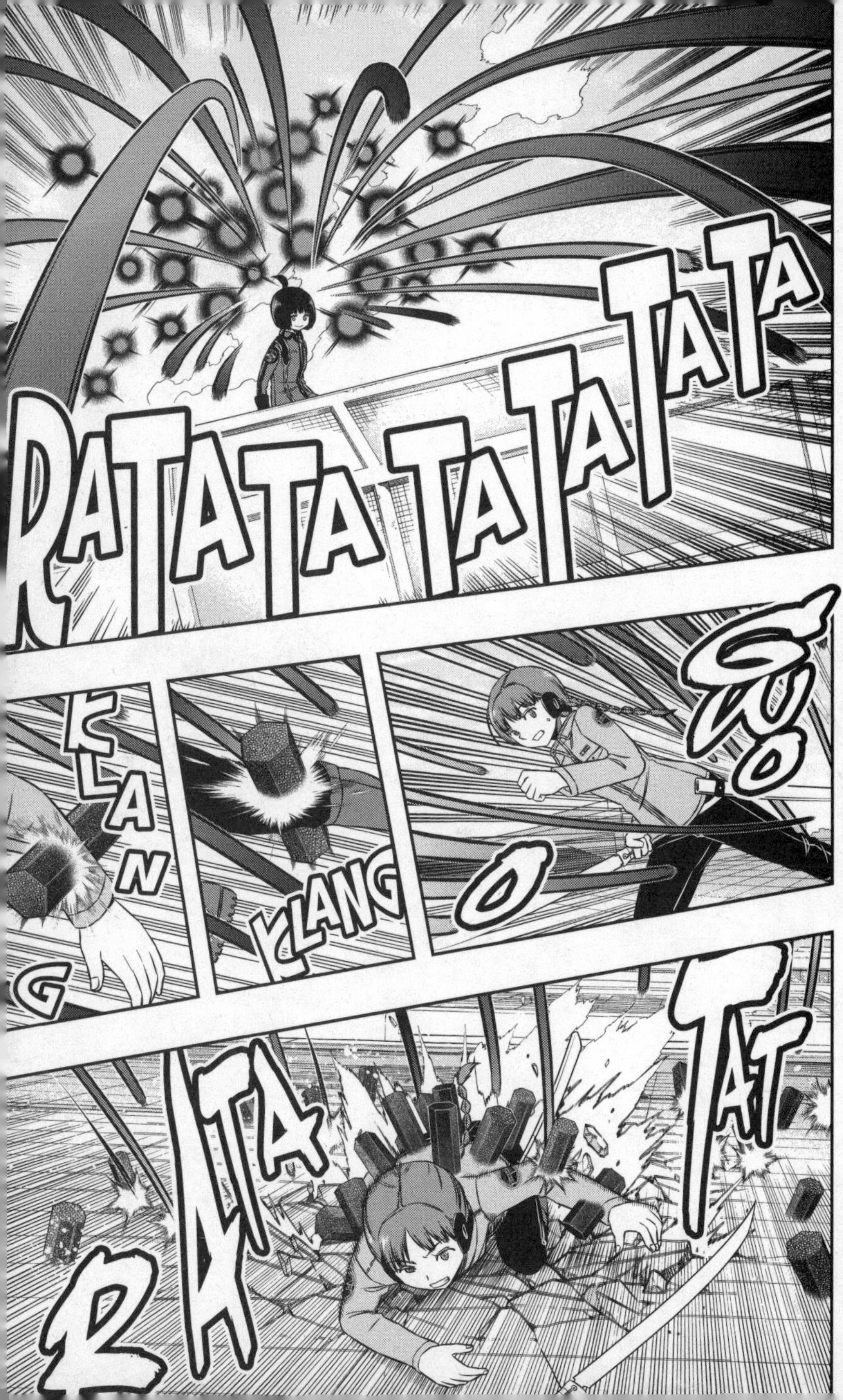
RATATATATATA
GUOO
KLANG
KLANG
RATATAT

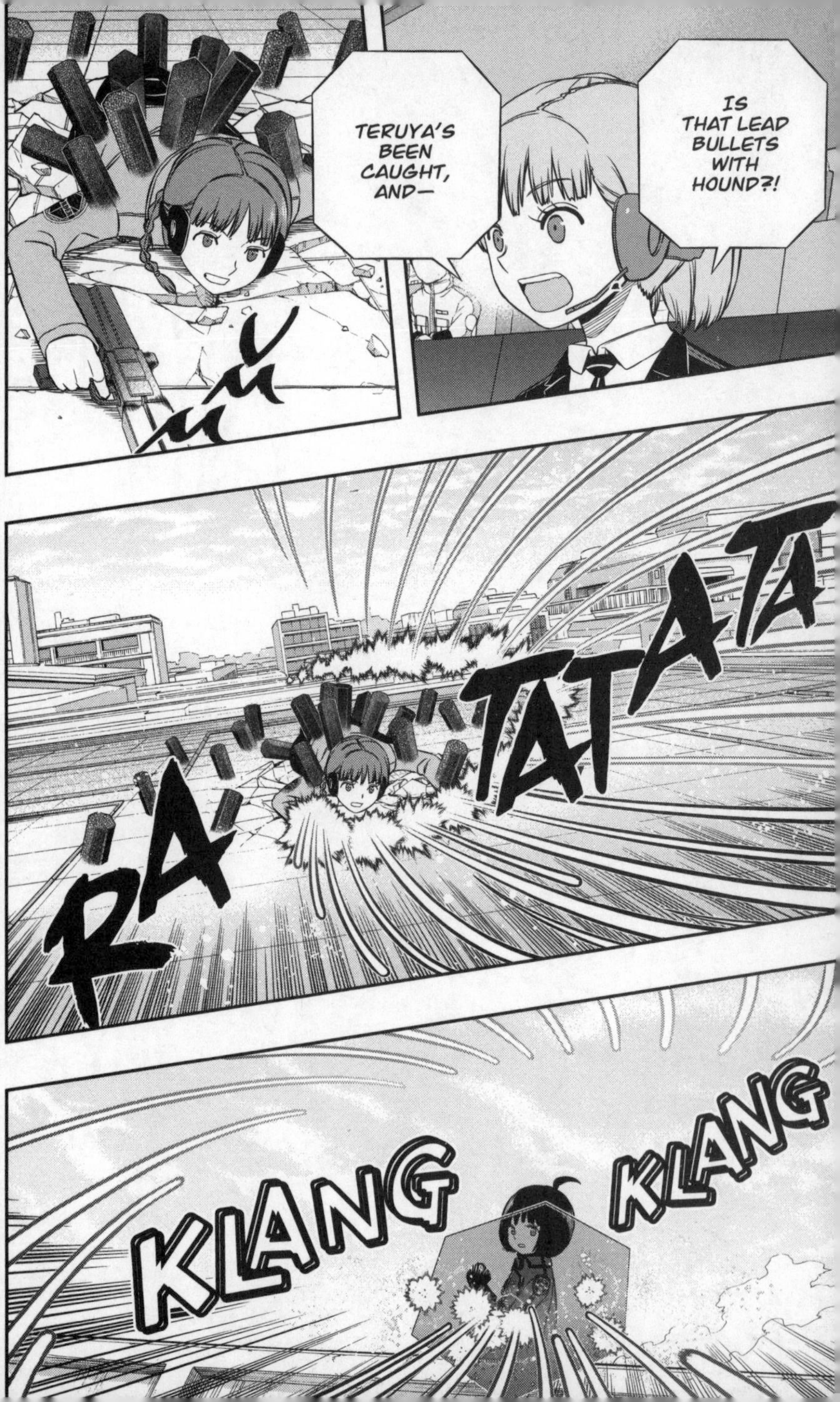
IS THAT LEAD BULLETS WITH HOUND?!
TERUYA'S BEEN CAUGHT, AND—
RATATATA
KLANG
KLANG

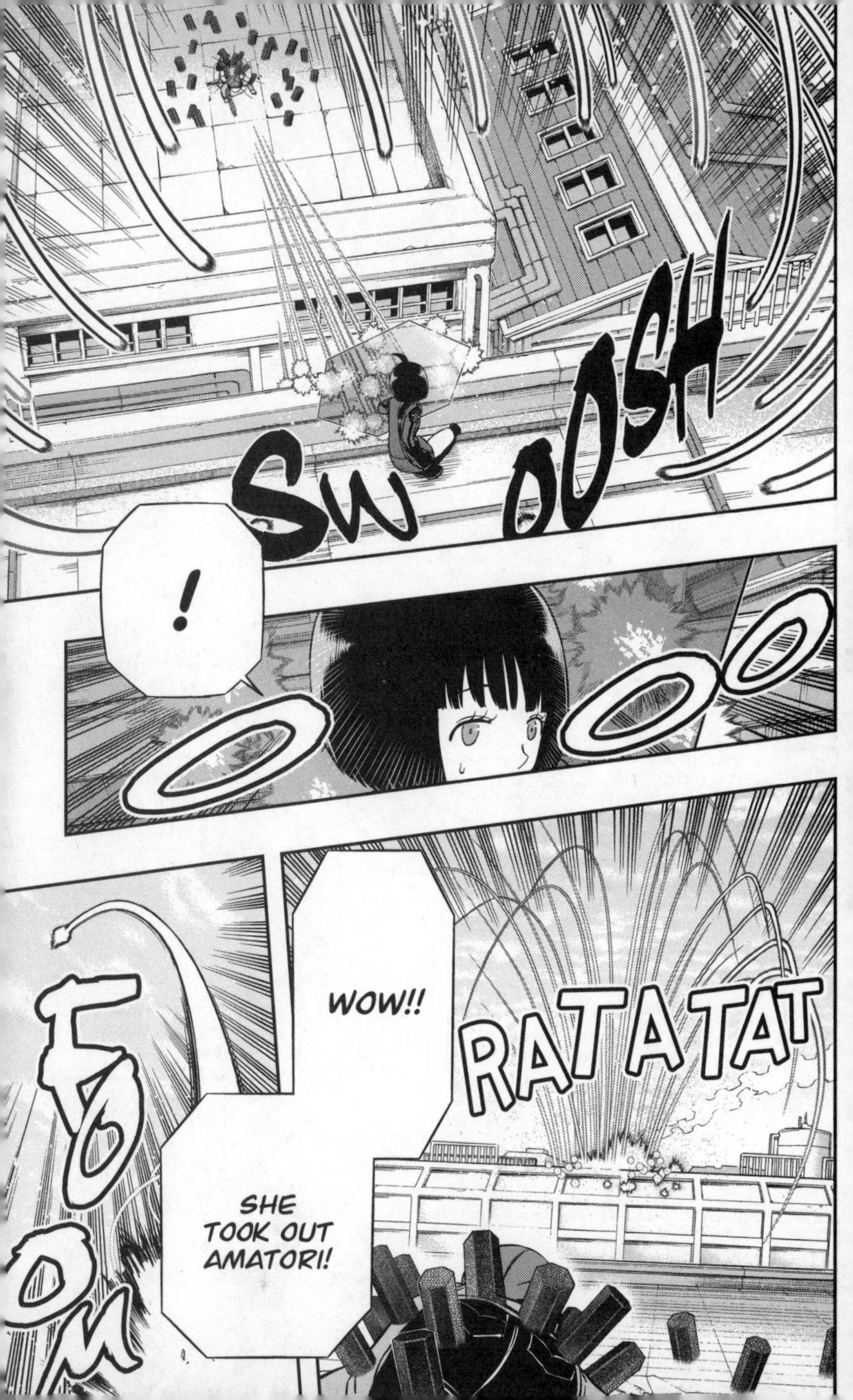
SWOOSH
!
OOO
RATATAT
WOW!!
SHE TOOK OUT AMATORI!
FOOM

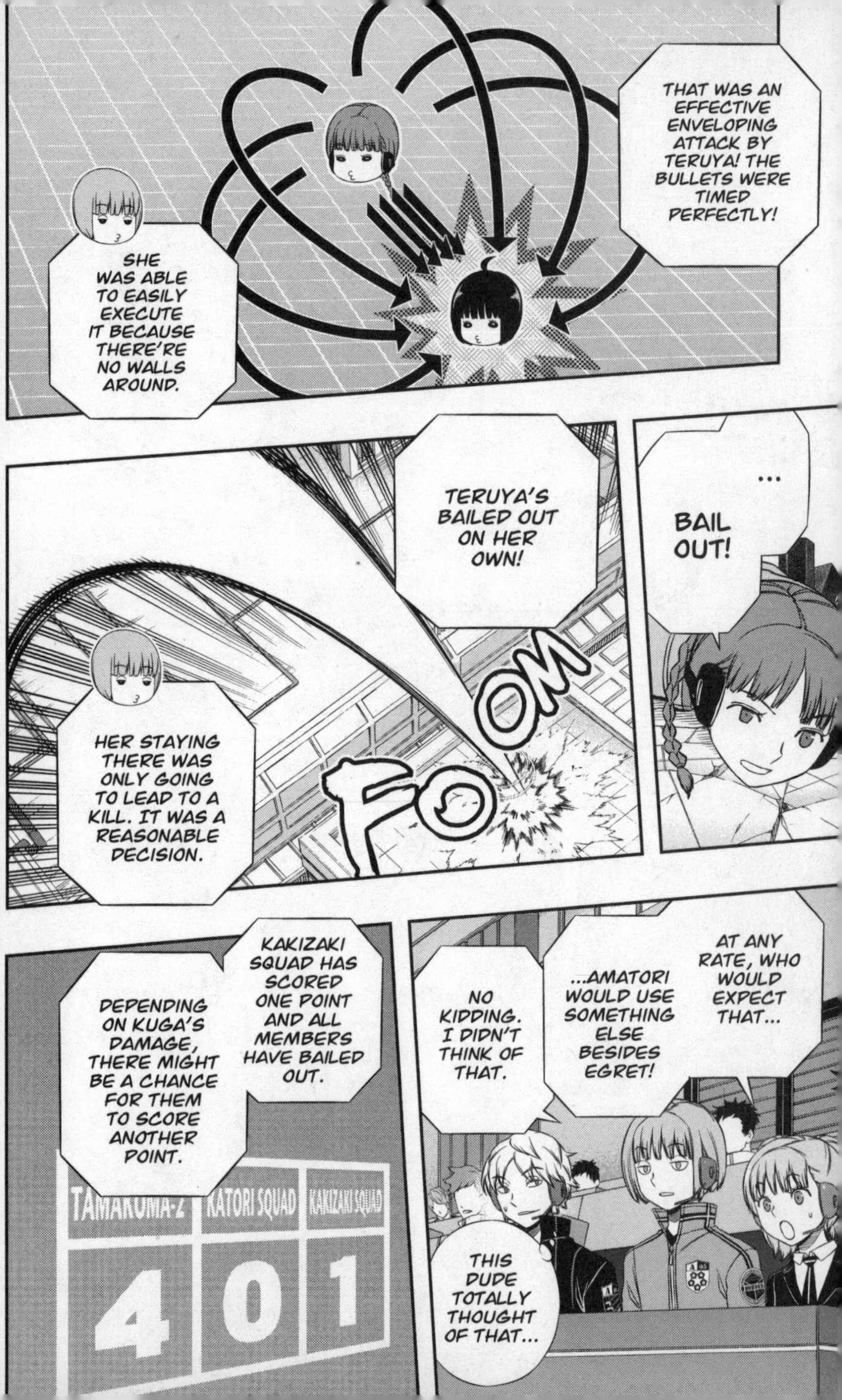
THAT WAS AN EFFECTIVE ENVELOPING ATTACK BY TERUYA! THE BULLETS WERE TIMED PERFECTLY!
SHE WAS ABLE TO EASILY EXECUTE IT BECAUSE THERE'RE NO WALLS AROUND.
...
BAIL OUT!
TERUYA'S BAILED OUT ON HER OWN!
FOOM
HER STAYING THERE WAS ONLY GOING TO LEAD TO A KILL. IT WAS A REASONABLE DECISION.
AT ANY RATE, WHO WOULD EXPECT THAT...
...AMATORI WOULD USE SOMETHING ELSE BESIDES EGRET!
NO KIDDING. I DIDN'T THINK OF THAT.
THIS DUDE TOTALLY THOUGHT OF THAT...
KAKIZAKI SQUAD HAS SCORED ONE POINT AND ALL MEMBERS HAVE BAILED OUT.
DEPENDING ON KUGA'S DAMAGE, THERE MIGHT BE A CHANCE FOR THEM TO SCORE ANOTHER POINT.
TAMAKOMA-2
KATORI SQUAD
KAKIZAKI SQUAD
4
0
1

NICE WORK, CHIKA.

NO, YOU DID WELL.

I GOT TAKEN OUT.

I'M SORRY...

WE HAVE ONLY ONE JOB LEFT HERE.

WITH MY SURVIVAL BONUS, WE COULD TIE WITH TAMAKOMA.

IF I TAKE DOWN THE OTHER TWO GUYS...

TAMAKOMA-2	KATORI SQUAD	KARIZAKI SQUAD
4	4	1

2+2
(SCORE + SURVIVAL BONUS)

THEIR SNIPER WAS TAKEN OUT BY TERUYA.

IT LOOKS LIKE TERUYA BAILED OUT ON HER OWN.

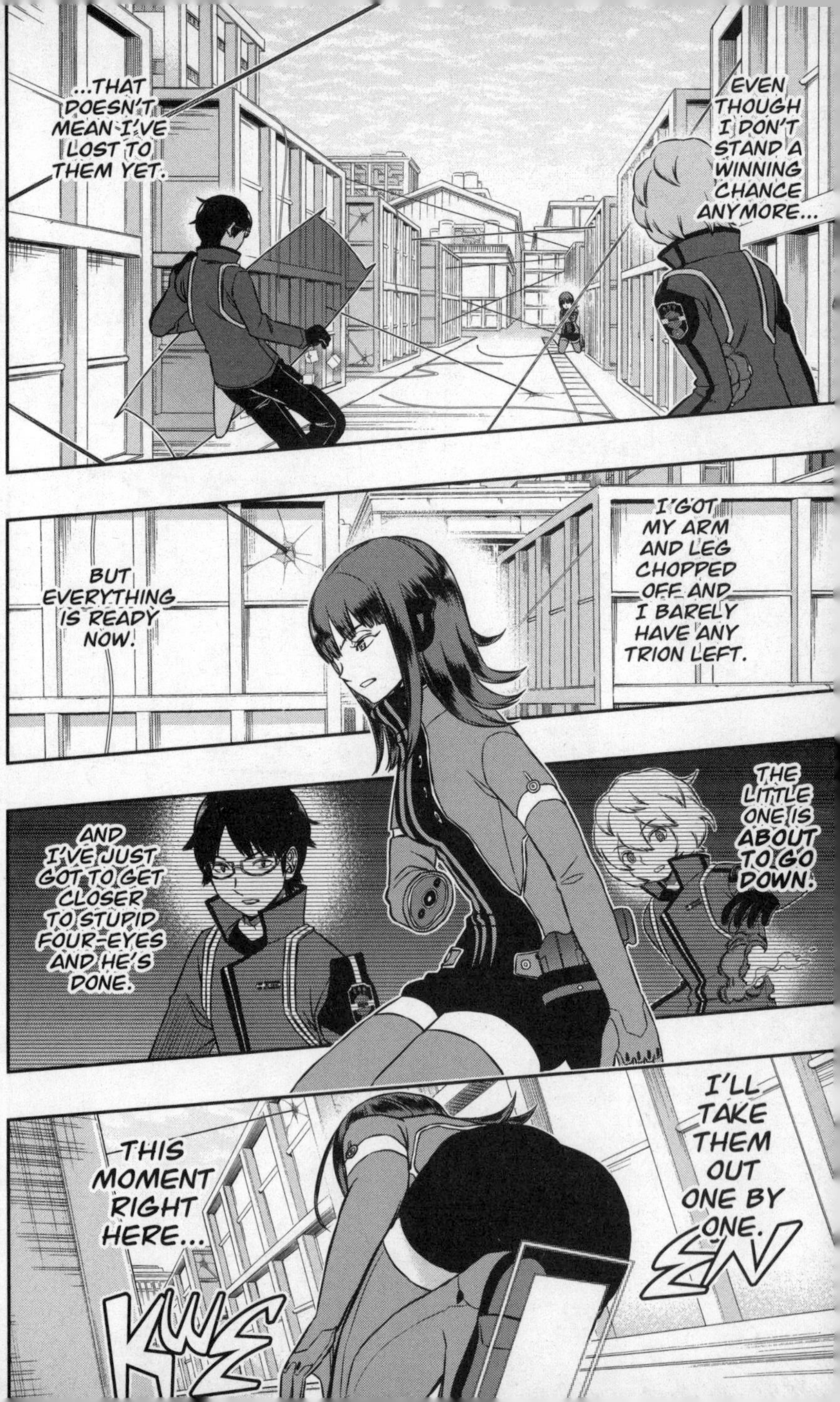
EVEN THOUGH I DON'T STAND A WINNING CHANCE ANYMORE...
...THAT DOESN'T MEAN I'VE LOST TO THEM YET.
I GOT MY ARM AND LEG CHOPPED OFF AND I BARELY HAVE ANY TRION LEFT.
BUT EVERYTHING IS READY NOW.
THE LITTLE ONE IS ABOUT TO GO DOWN.
AND I'VE JUST GOT TO GET CLOSER TO STUPID FOUR-EYES AND HE'S DONE.
I'LL TAKE THEM OUT ONE BY ONE.
EN
THIS MOMENT RIGHT HERE...
KWE

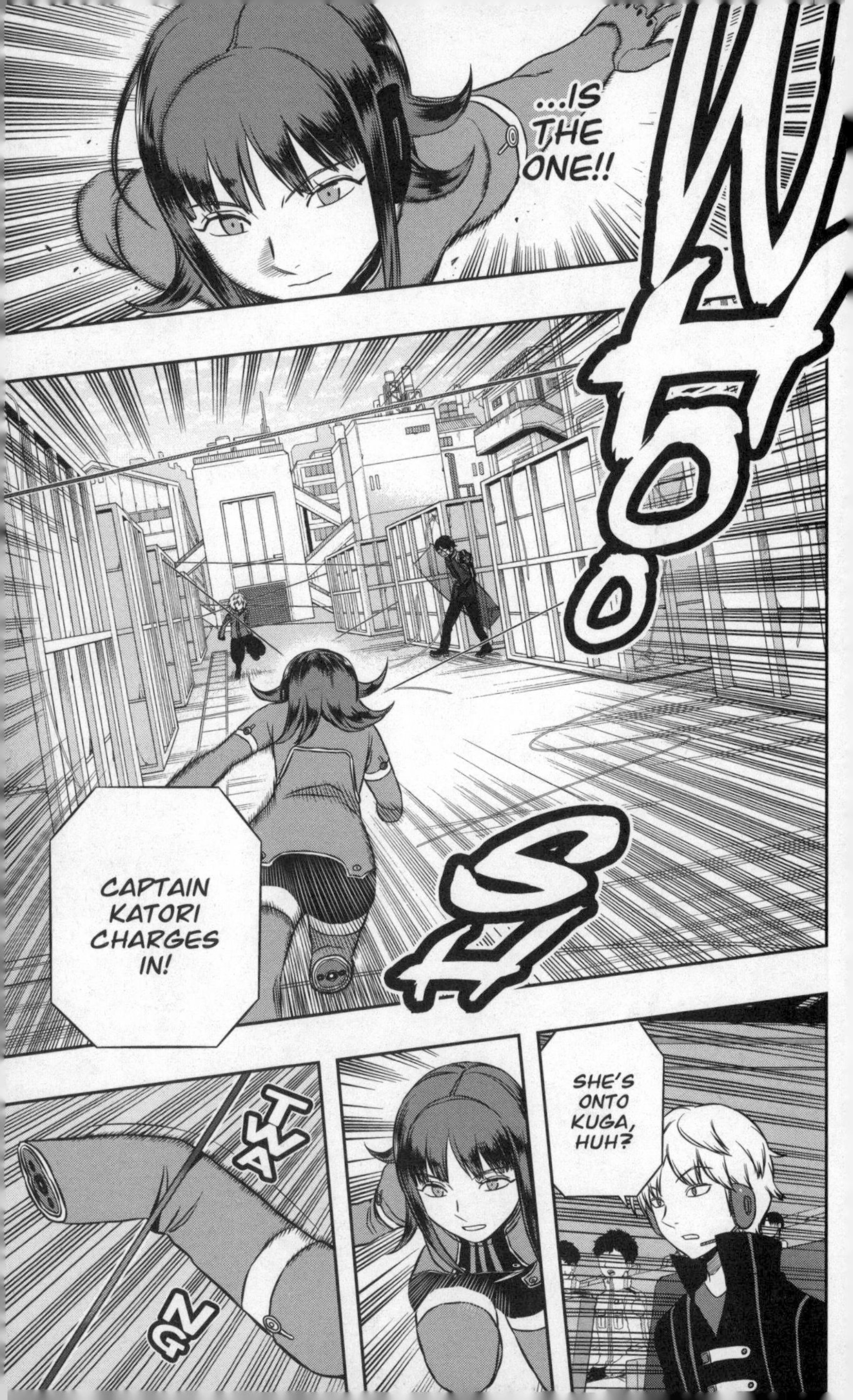
...IS THE ONE!!
WHOOSH
CAPTAIN KATORI CHARGES IN!
SHE'S ONTO KUGA, HUH?
TWA
ZG

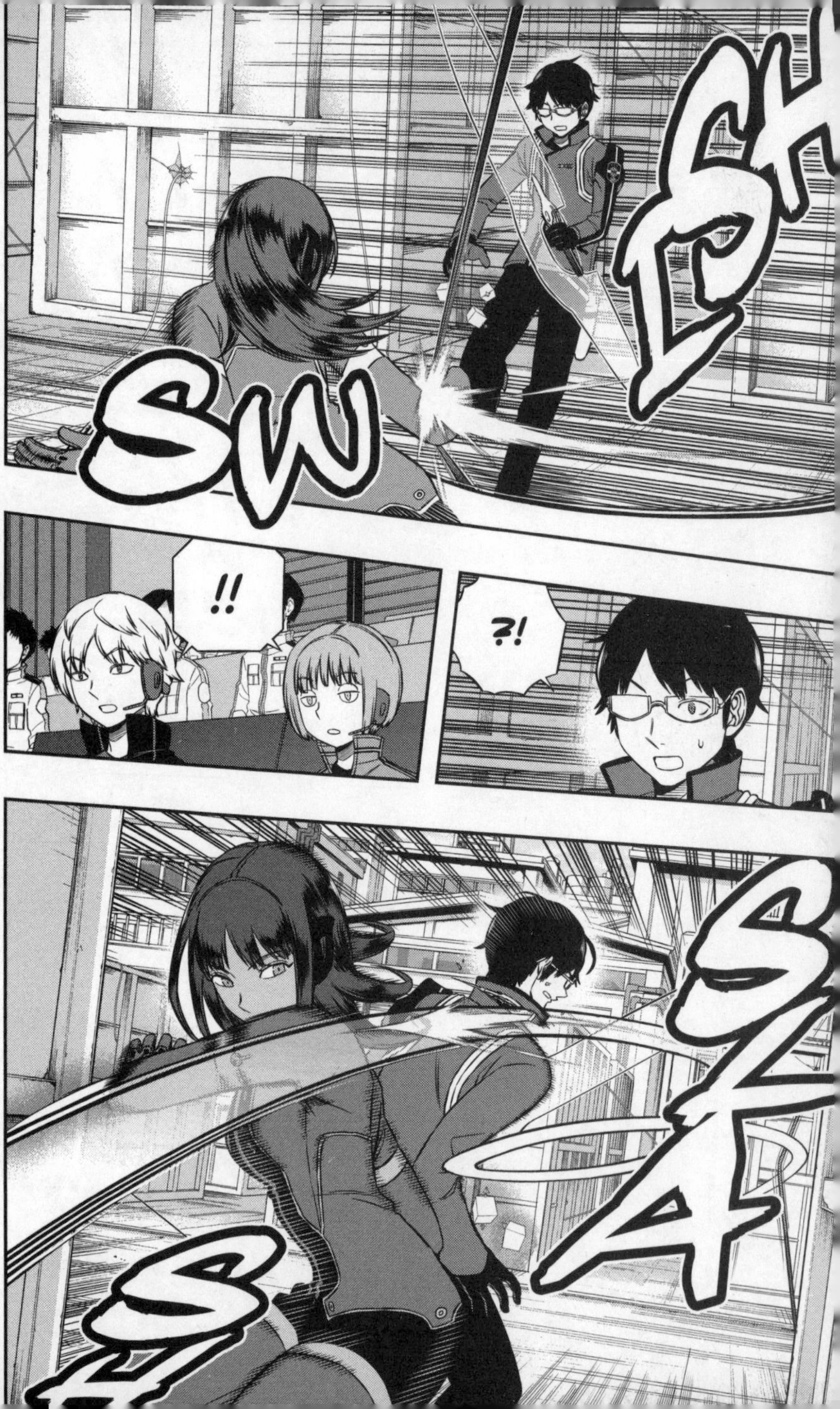
SW
?!
!!

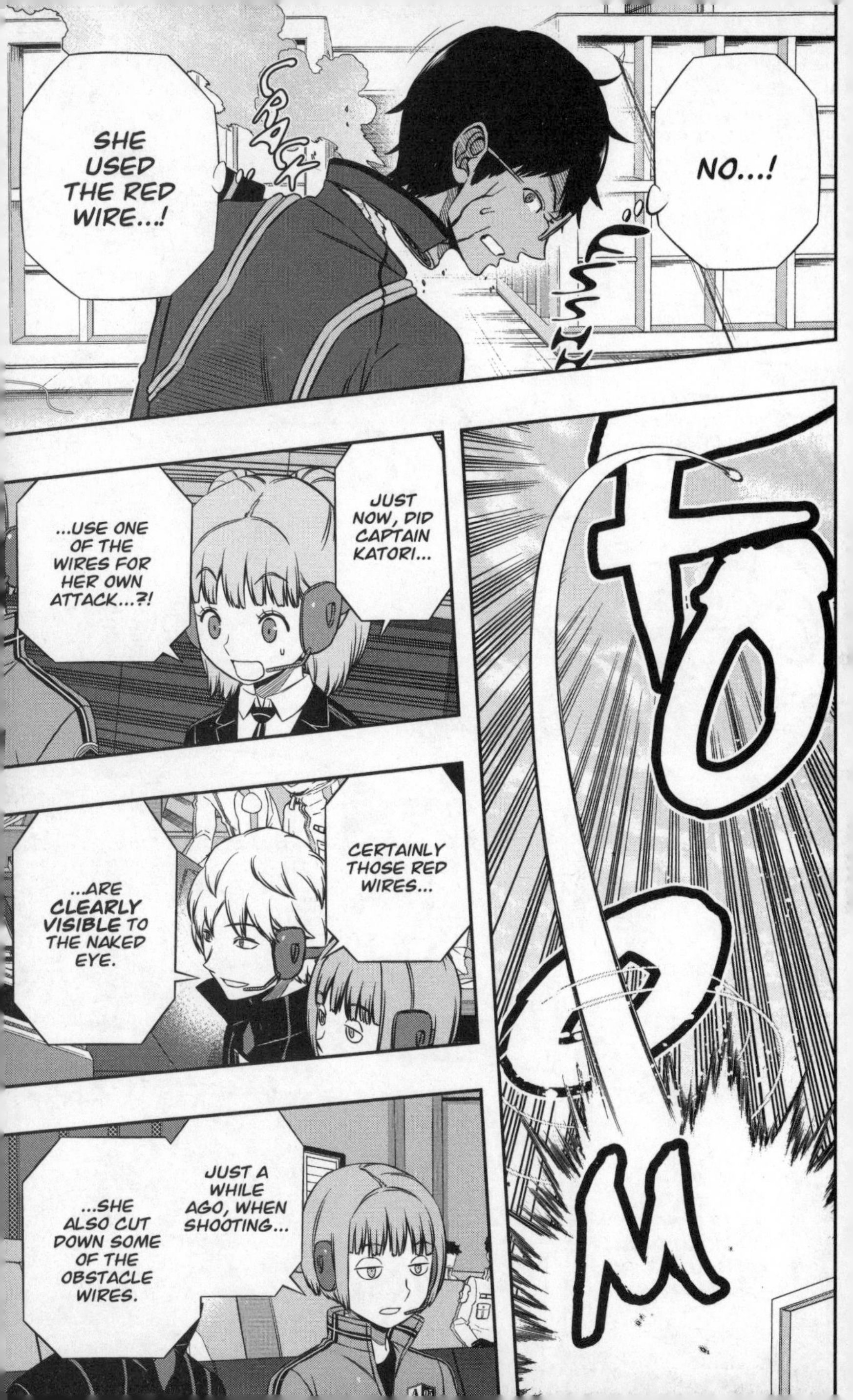
NO...!
CRACK
SHE USED THE RED WIRE...!
JUST NOW, DID CAPTAIN KATORI...
...USE ONE OF THE WIRES FOR HER OWN ATTACK...?!
CERTAINLY THOSE RED WIRES...
...ARE CLEARLY VISIBLE TO THE NAKED EYE.
JUST A WHILE AGO, WHEN SHOOTING...
...SHE ALSO CUT DOWN SOME OF THE OBSTACLE WIRES.

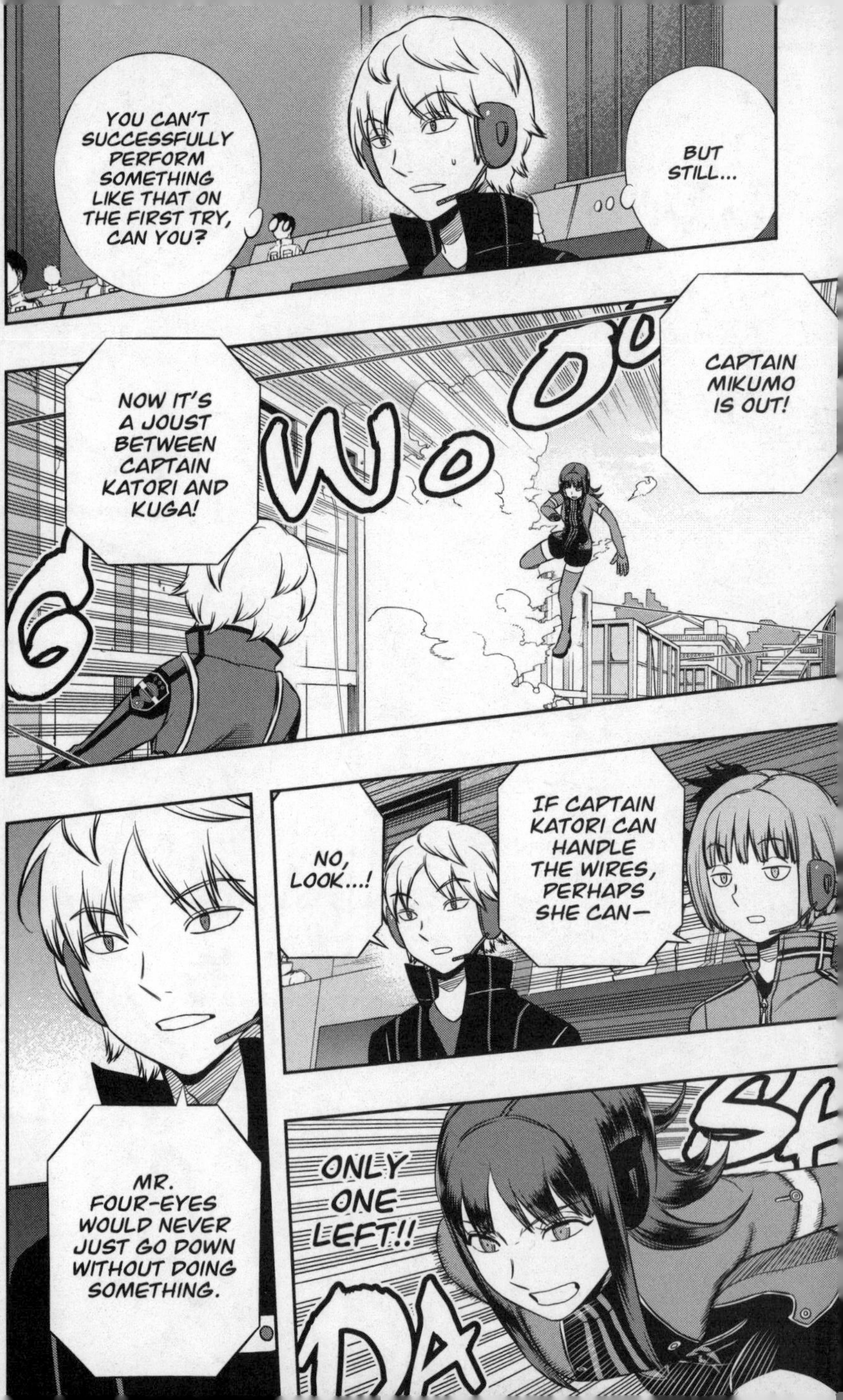
YOU CAN'T SUCCESSFULLY PERFORM SOMETHING LIKE THAT ON THE FIRST TRY, CAN YOU?
BUT STILL...
CAPTAIN MIKUMO IS OUT!
GWOOO
NOW IT'S A JOUST BETWEEN CAPTAIN KATORI AND KUGA!
IF CAPTAIN KATORI CAN HANDLE THE WIRES, PERHAPS SHE CAN—
NO, LOOK...!
SH
ONLY ONE LEFT!!
DA
MR. FOUR-EYES WOULD NEVER JUST GO DOWN WITHOUT DOING SOMETHING.

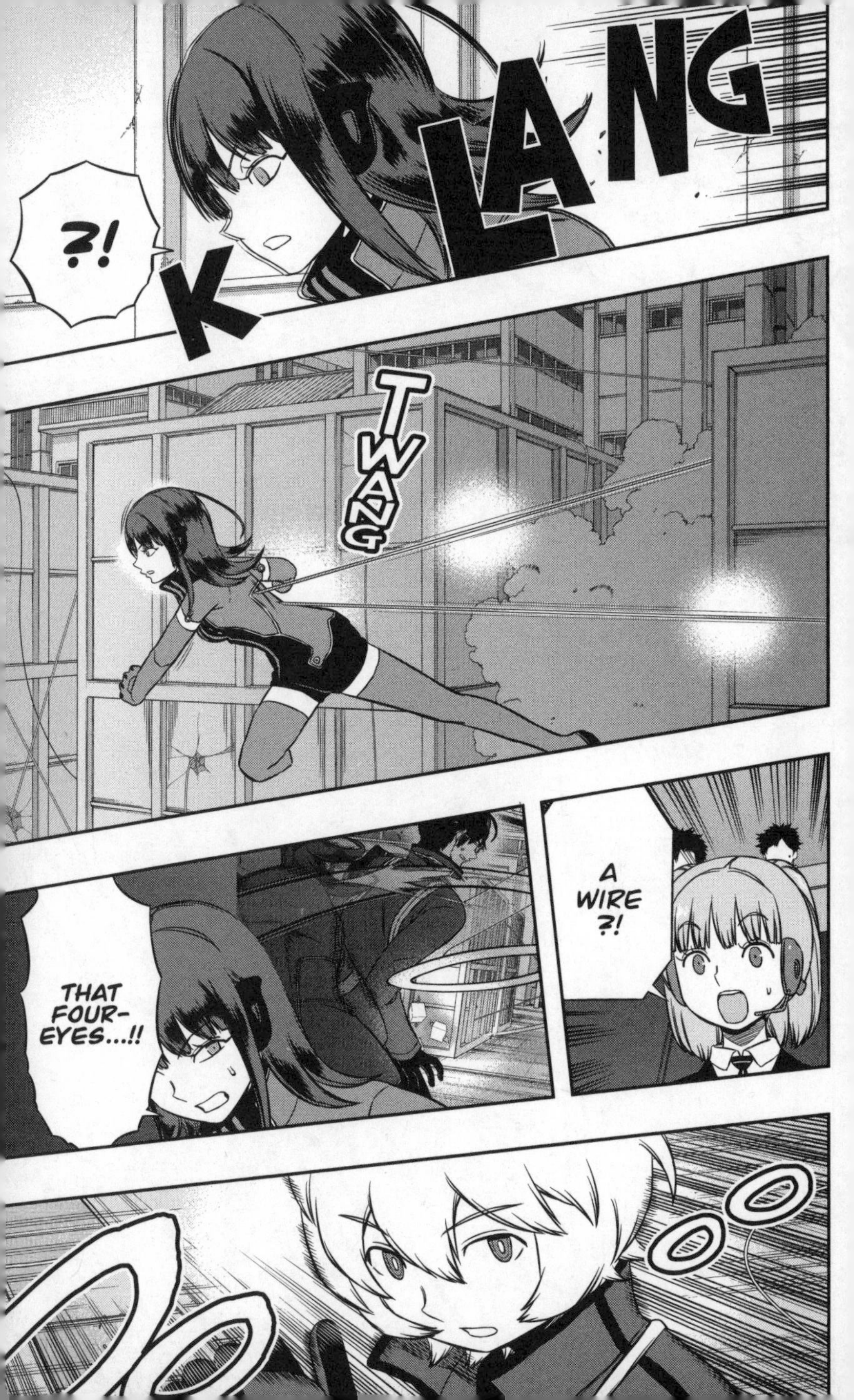
KLANG
?!
TWANG
A WIRE ?!
THAT FOUR-EYES...!!

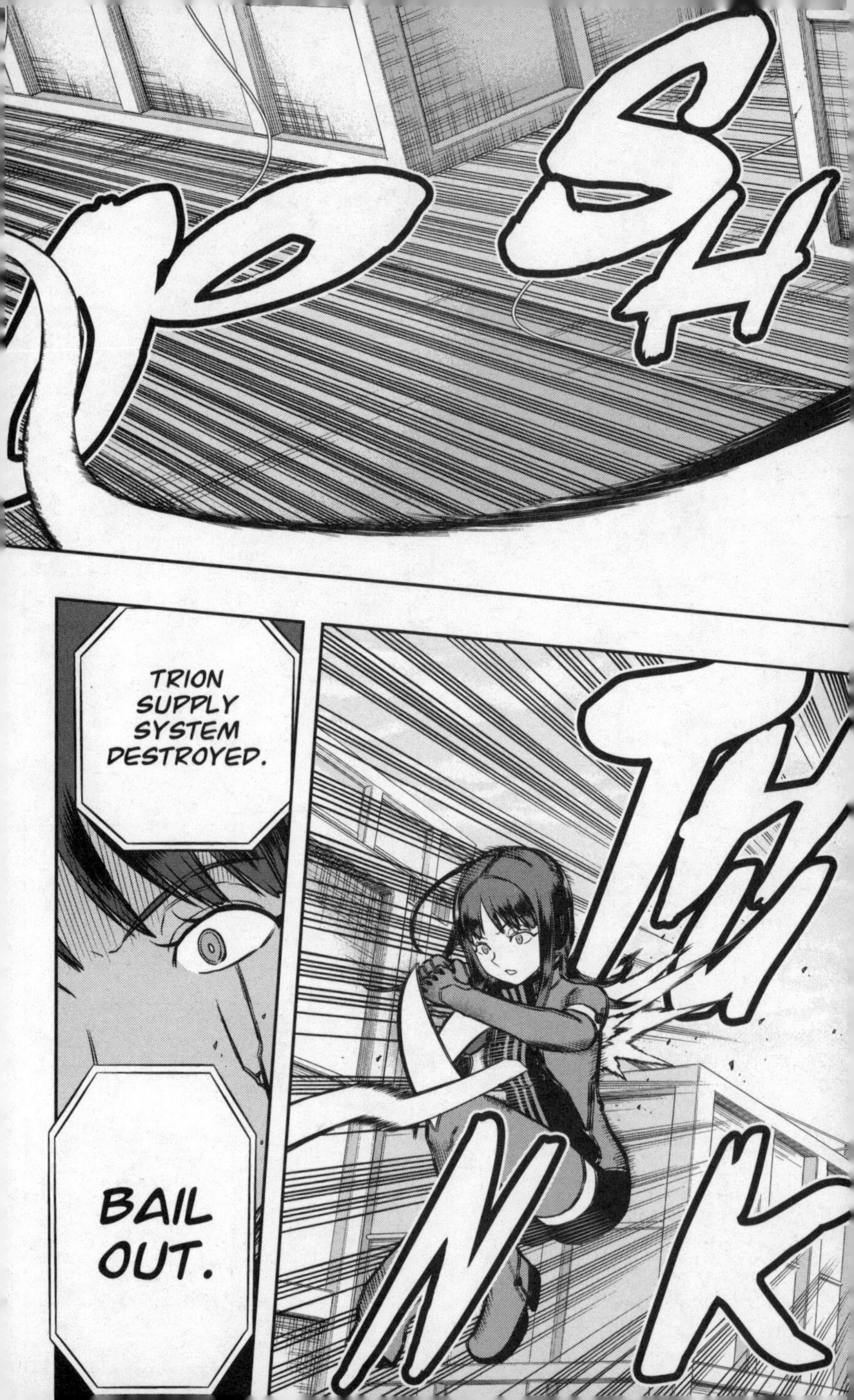
SHH
THNK
TRION SUPPLY SYSTEM DESTROYED.
BAIL OUT.

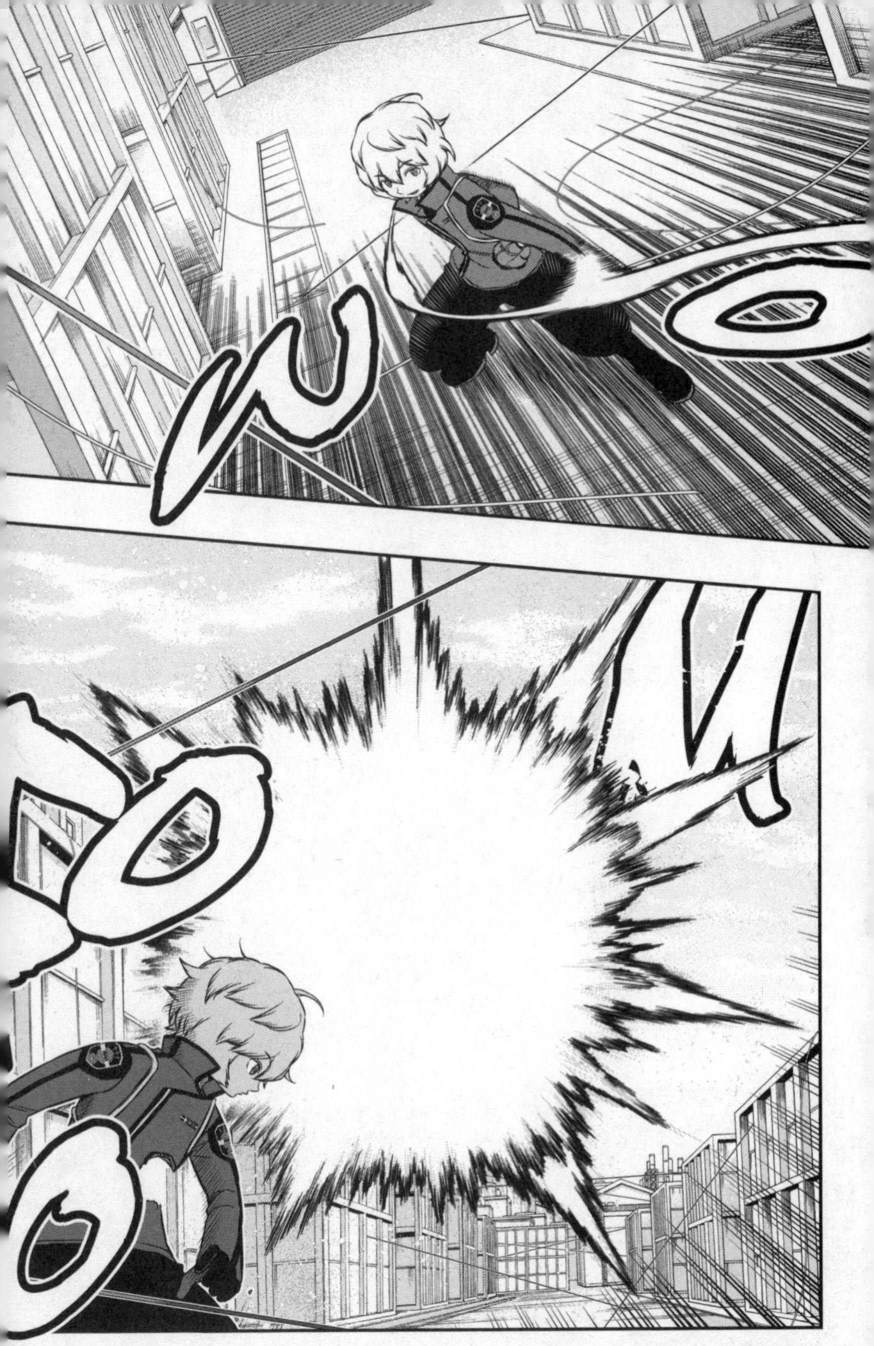

Burger Queen
Mikado City Flagship Store

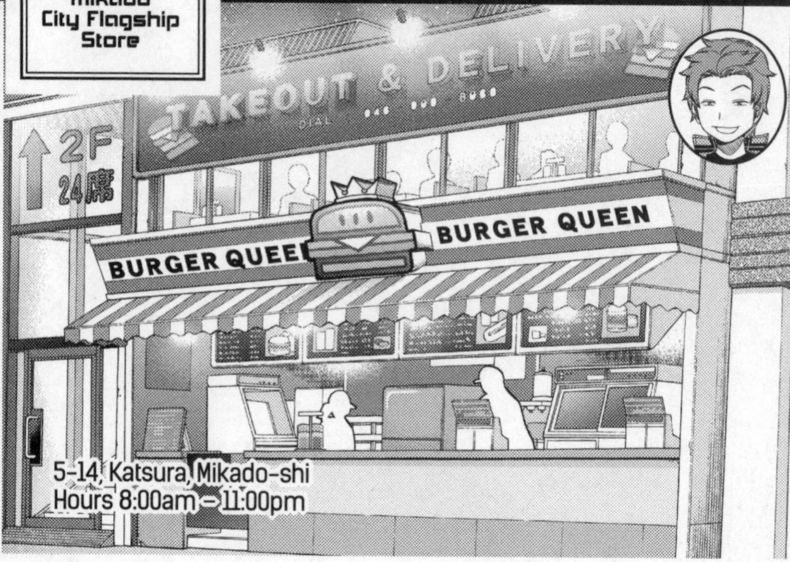
TAKEOUT & DELIVERY
2F
24席
BURGER QUEEN
BURGER QUEE

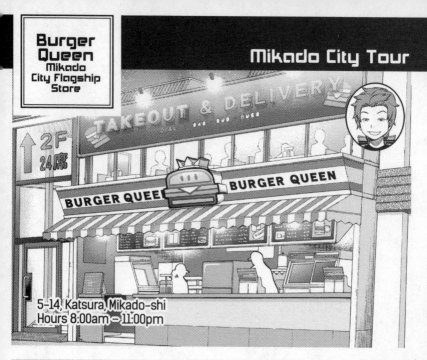

5-14, Katsura, Mikado-shi
Hours 8:00am – 11:00pm

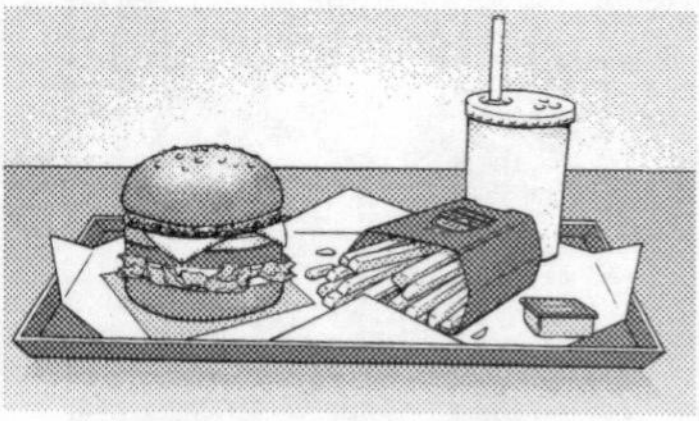

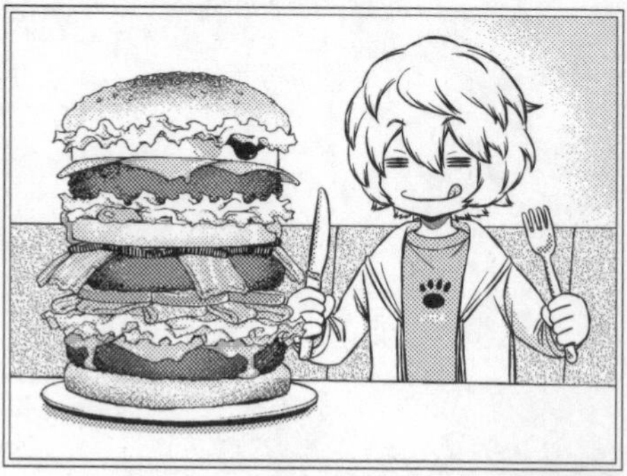

↑ A standard "Queen Burger set" is 640 yen.

→ The famous "Crazy Burger." It feeds at least ten people!

A major hamburger chain. The hamburger that Osamu gave to Yuma in chapter 2 is probably from this place. One of Yuma's favorites.

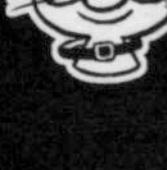

A major burger chain that has four stores in Mikado City alone. This place is regularly visted by Border Agents too. Satori from Arashiyama Squad's autograph is apparently on the wall in this particular storefront.

You can ask for delivery service for orders over 2,000 yen.

Snack queen

THE BATTLE IS OVER!

CAPTAIN KATORI HAS BAILED OUT!

FOOM

Chapter 146
Tamakoma-2: Part 14

TAMA-KOMA-2 WINS!

FINAL SCORE: 7-1-1!

	Points	Survival Bonus	Total
Tamakoma-2:	5	2	7
Katori Squad	1	0	1
Kakizaki Squad	1	0	1

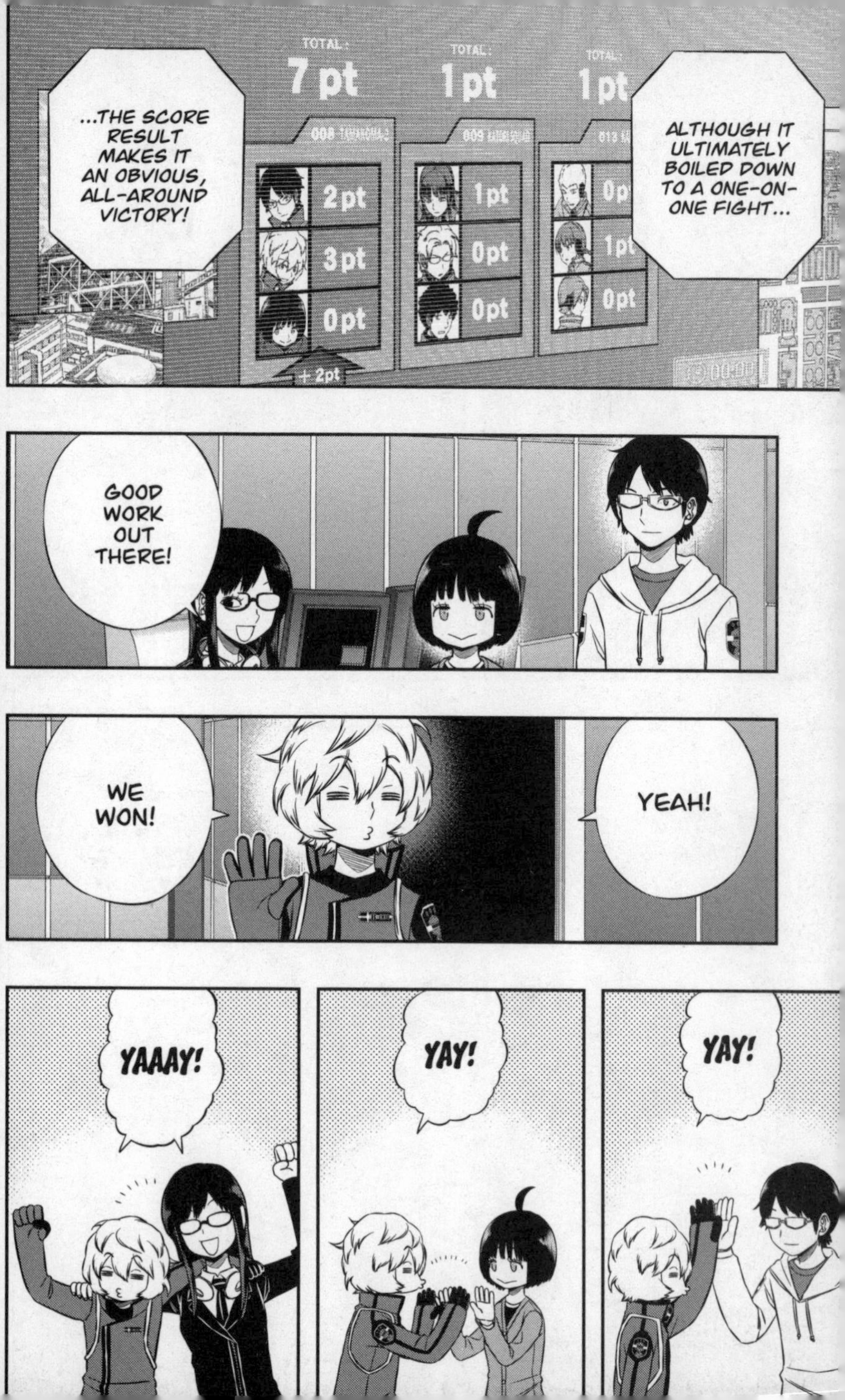
ALTHOUGH IT ULTIMATELY BOILED DOWN TO A ONE-ON-ONE FIGHT...
...THE SCORE RESULT MAKES IT AN OBVIOUS, ALL-AROUND VICTORY!
TOTAL: 7 pt
TOTAL: 1 pt
TOTAL: 1 pt
2pt
3pt
0pt
+2pt
1pt
0pt
0pt
1pt
0pt
YEAH!
WE WON!
GOOD WORK OUT THERE!
YAY!
YAY!
YAAAY!

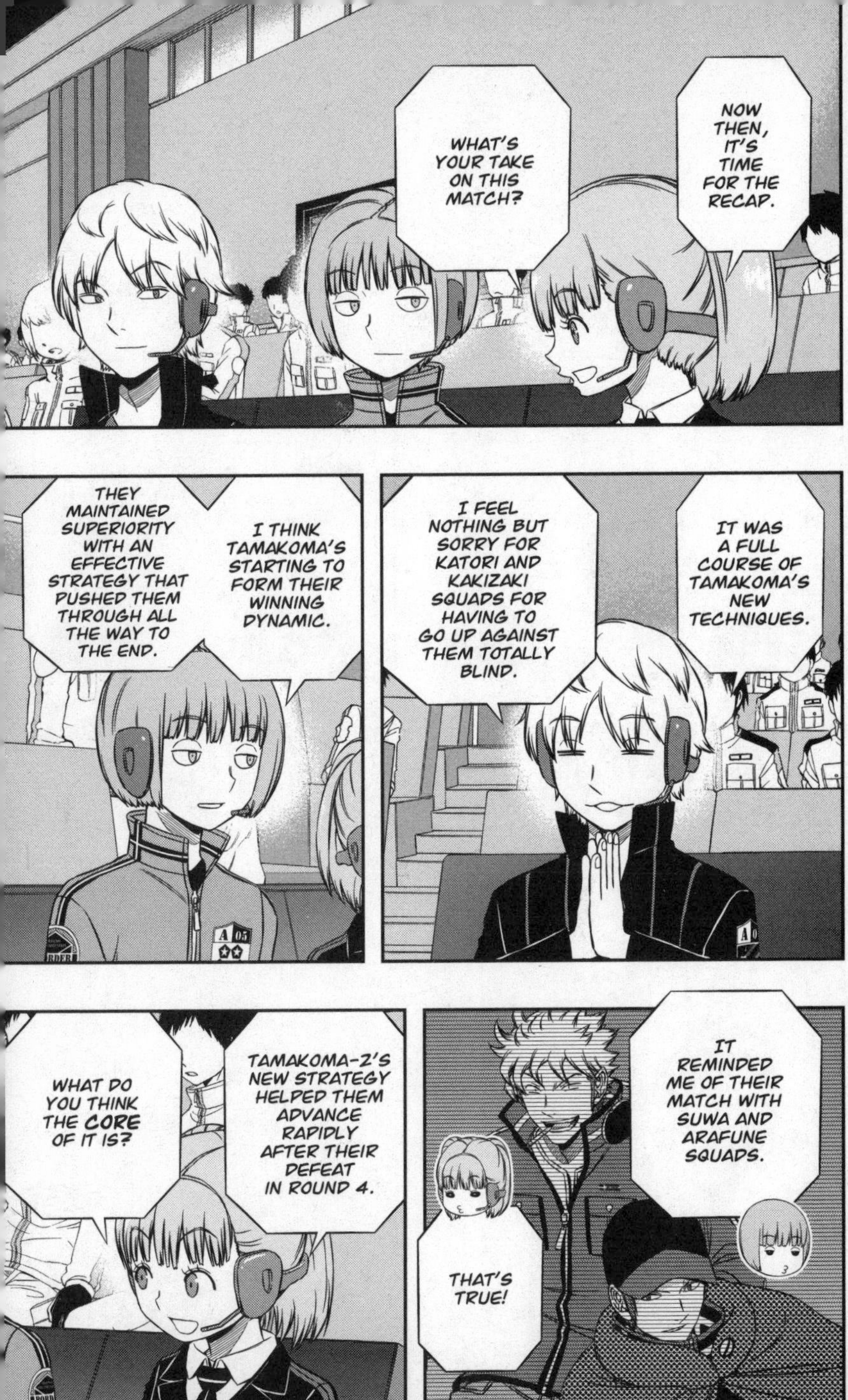
NOW THEN, IT'S TIME FOR THE RECAP.
WHAT'S YOUR TAKE ON THIS MATCH?
IT WAS A FULL COURSE OF TAMAKOMA'S NEW TECHNIQUES.
I FEEL NOTHING BUT SORRY FOR KATORI AND KAKIZAKI SQUADS FOR HAVING TO GO UP AGAINST THEM TOTALLY BLIND.
I THINK TAMAKOMA'S STARTING TO FORM THEIR WINNING DYNAMIC.
THEY MAINTAINED SUPERIORITY WITH AN EFFECTIVE STRATEGY THAT PUSHED THEM THROUGH ALL THE WAY TO THE END.
IT REMINDED ME OF THEIR MATCH WITH SUWA AND ARAFUNE SQUADS.
THAT'S TRUE!
TAMAKOMA-2'S NEW STRATEGY HELPED THEM ADVANCE RAPIDLY AFTER THEIR DEFEAT IN ROUND 4.
WHAT DO YOU THINK THE **CORE** OF IT IS?

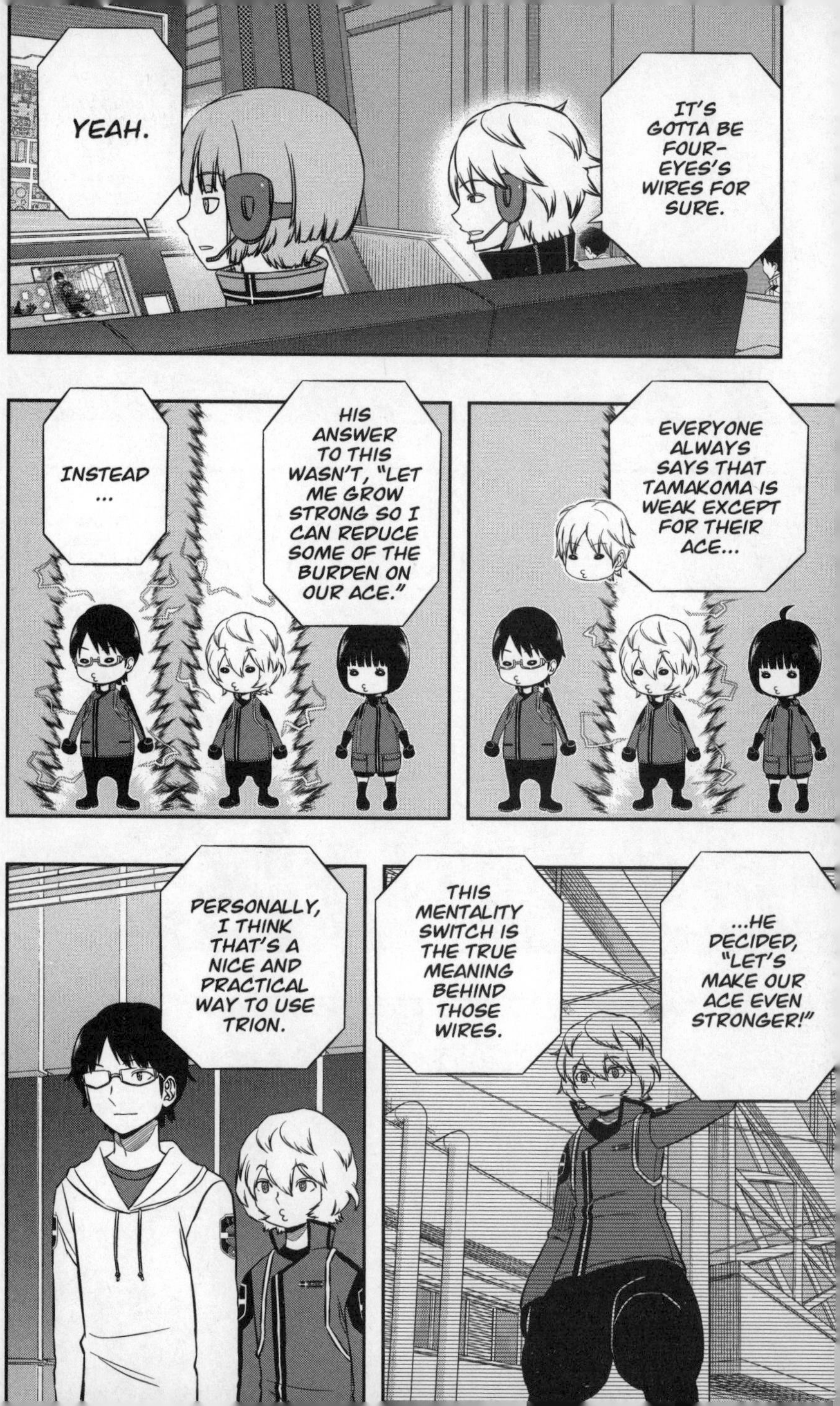
IT'S GOTTA BE FOUR-EYES'S WIRES FOR SURE.
YEAH.
EVERYONE ALWAYS SAYS THAT TAMAKOMA IS WEAK EXCEPT FOR THEIR ACE...
HIS ANSWER TO THIS WASN'T, "LET ME GROW STRONG SO I CAN REDUCE SOME OF THE BURDEN ON OUR ACE."
INSTEAD...
...HE DECIDED, "LET'S MAKE OUR ACE EVEN STRONGER!"
THIS MENTALITY SWITCH IS THE TRUE MEANING BEHIND THOSE WIRES.
PERSONALLY, I THINK THAT'S A NICE AND PRACTICAL WAY TO USE TRION.

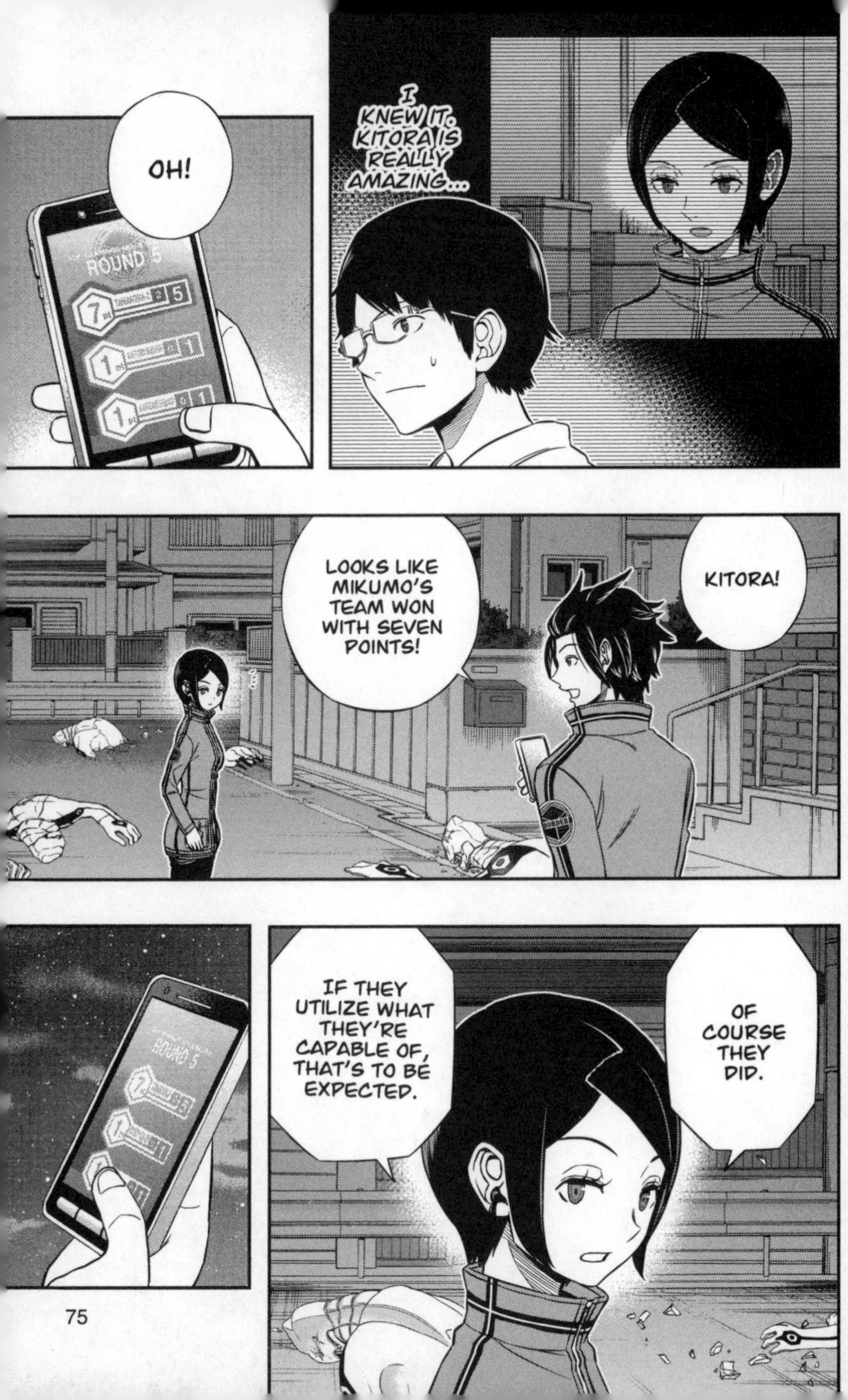
I KNEW IT. KITORA IS REALLY AMAZING...
OH!
ROUND 5
KITORA!
LOOKS LIKE MIKUMO'S TEAM WON WITH SEVEN POINTS!
OF COURSE THEY DID.
IF THEY UTILIZE WHAT THEY'RE CAPABLE OF, THAT'S TO BE EXPECTED.

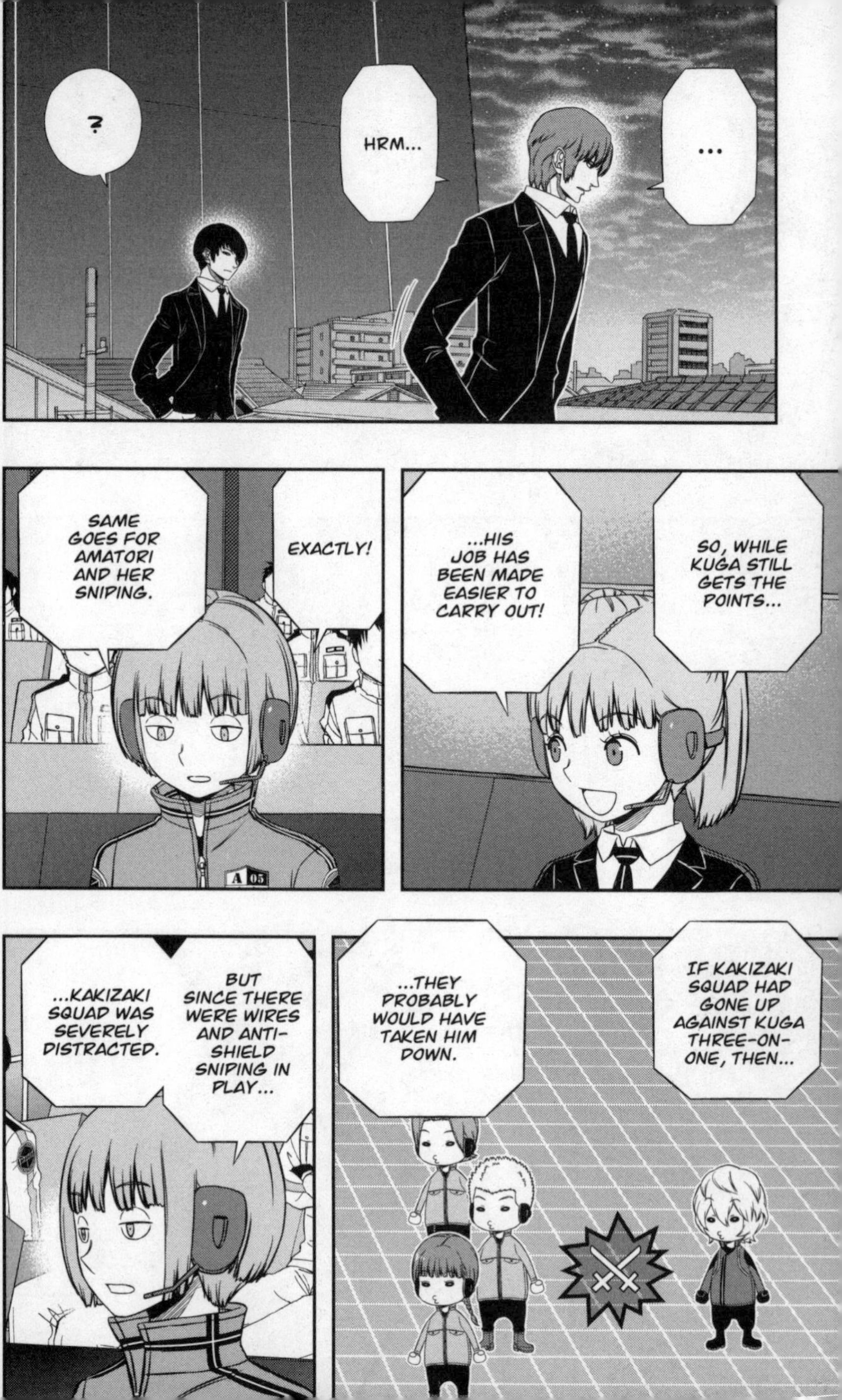
...
HRM...
?
SO, WHILE KUGA STILL GETS THE POINTS...
...HIS JOB HAS BEEN MADE EASIER TO CARRY OUT!
EXACTLY!
SAME GOES FOR AMATORI AND HER SNIPING.
IF KAKIZAKI SQUAD HAD GONE UP AGAINST KUGA THREE-ON-ONE, THEN...
...THEY PROBABLY WOULD HAVE TAKEN HIM DOWN.
BUT SINCE THERE WERE WIRES AND ANTI-SHIELD SNIPING IN PLAY...
...KAKIZAKI SQUAD WAS SEVERELY DISTRACTED.

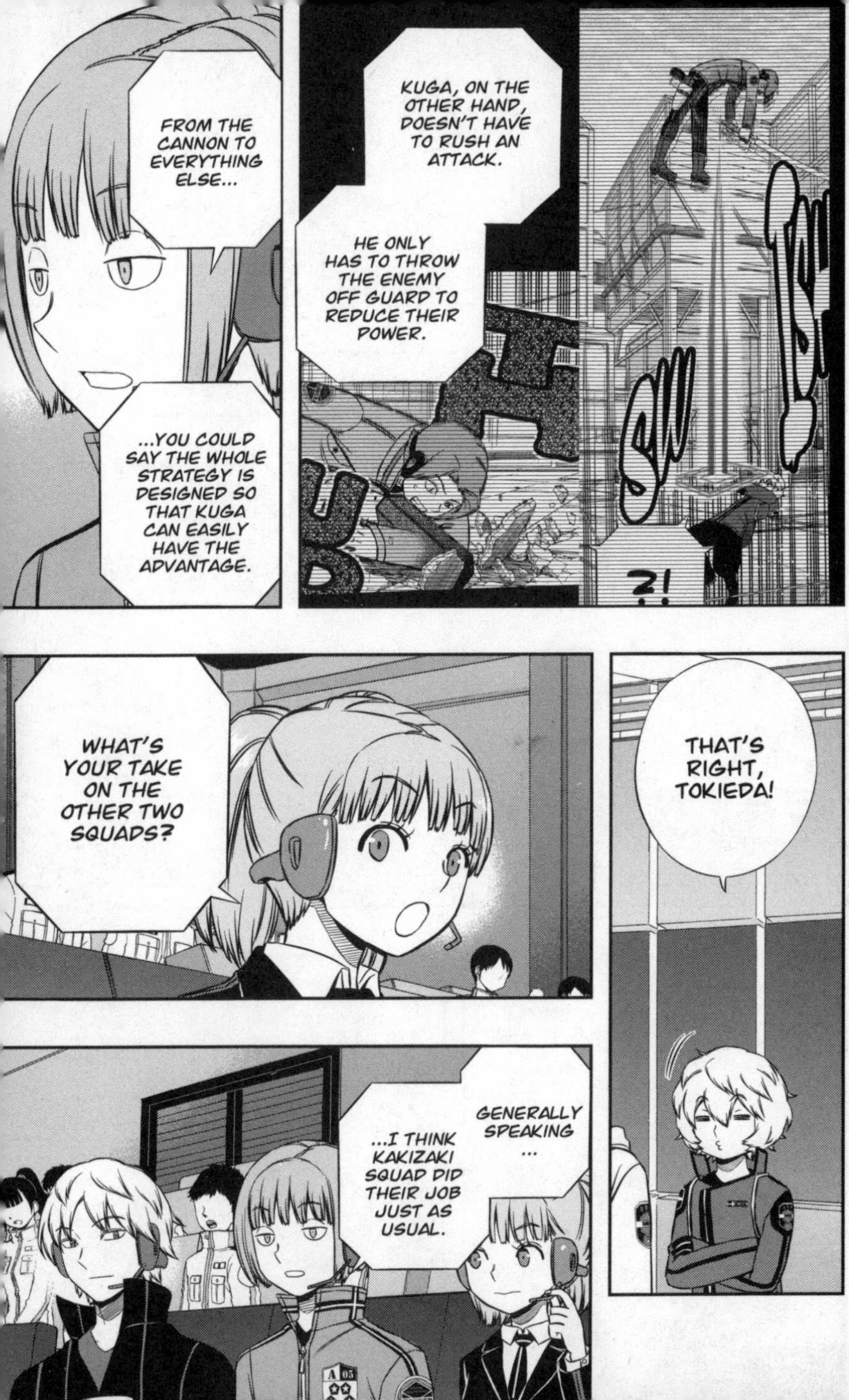
?!
KUGA, ON THE OTHER HAND, DOESN'T HAVE TO RUSH AN ATTACK.
HE ONLY HAS TO THROW THE ENEMY OFF GUARD TO REDUCE THEIR POWER.
FROM THE CANNON TO EVERYTHING ELSE...
...YOU COULD SAY THE WHOLE STRATEGY IS DESIGNED SO THAT KUGA CAN EASILY HAVE THE ADVANTAGE.
THAT'S RIGHT, TOKIEDA!
WHAT'S YOUR TAKE ON THE OTHER TWO SQUADS?
GENERALLY SPEAKING...
...I THINK KAKIZAKI SQUAD DID THEIR JOB JUST AS USUAL.

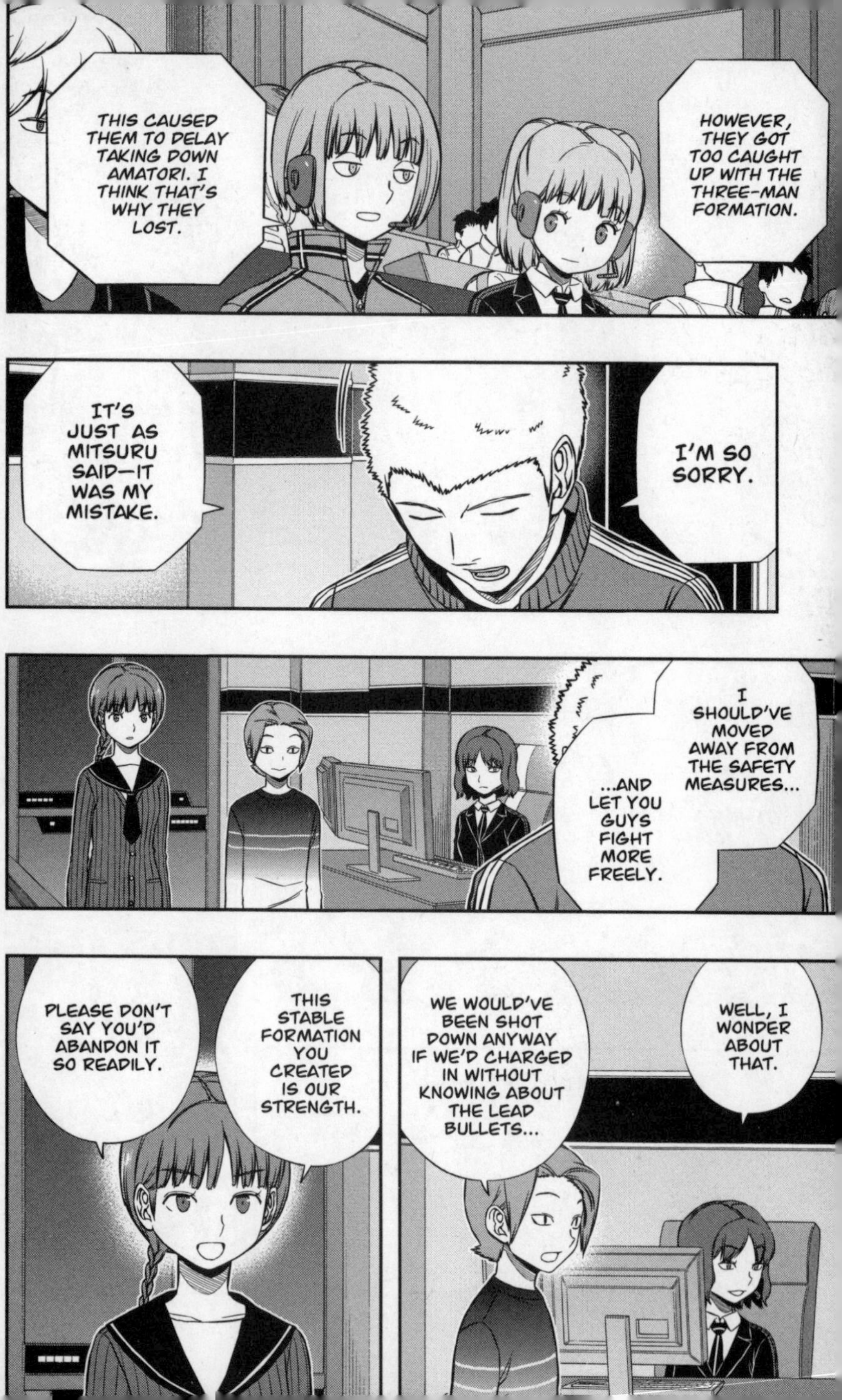
HOWEVER, THEY GOT TOO CAUGHT UP WITH THE THREE-MAN FORMATION.
THIS CAUSED THEM TO DELAY TAKING DOWN AMATORI. I THINK THAT'S WHY THEY LOST.
I'M SO SORRY.
IT'S JUST AS MITSURU SAID—IT WAS MY MISTAKE.
I SHOULD'VE MOVED AWAY FROM THE SAFETY MEASURES...
...AND LET YOU GUYS FIGHT MORE FREELY.
WELL, I WONDER ABOUT THAT.
WE WOULD'VE BEEN SHOT DOWN ANYWAY IF WE'D CHARGED IN WITHOUT KNOWING ABOUT THE LEAD BULLETS...
THIS STABLE FORMATION YOU CREATED IS OUR STRENGTH.
PLEASE DON'T SAY YOU'D ABANDON IT SO READILY.

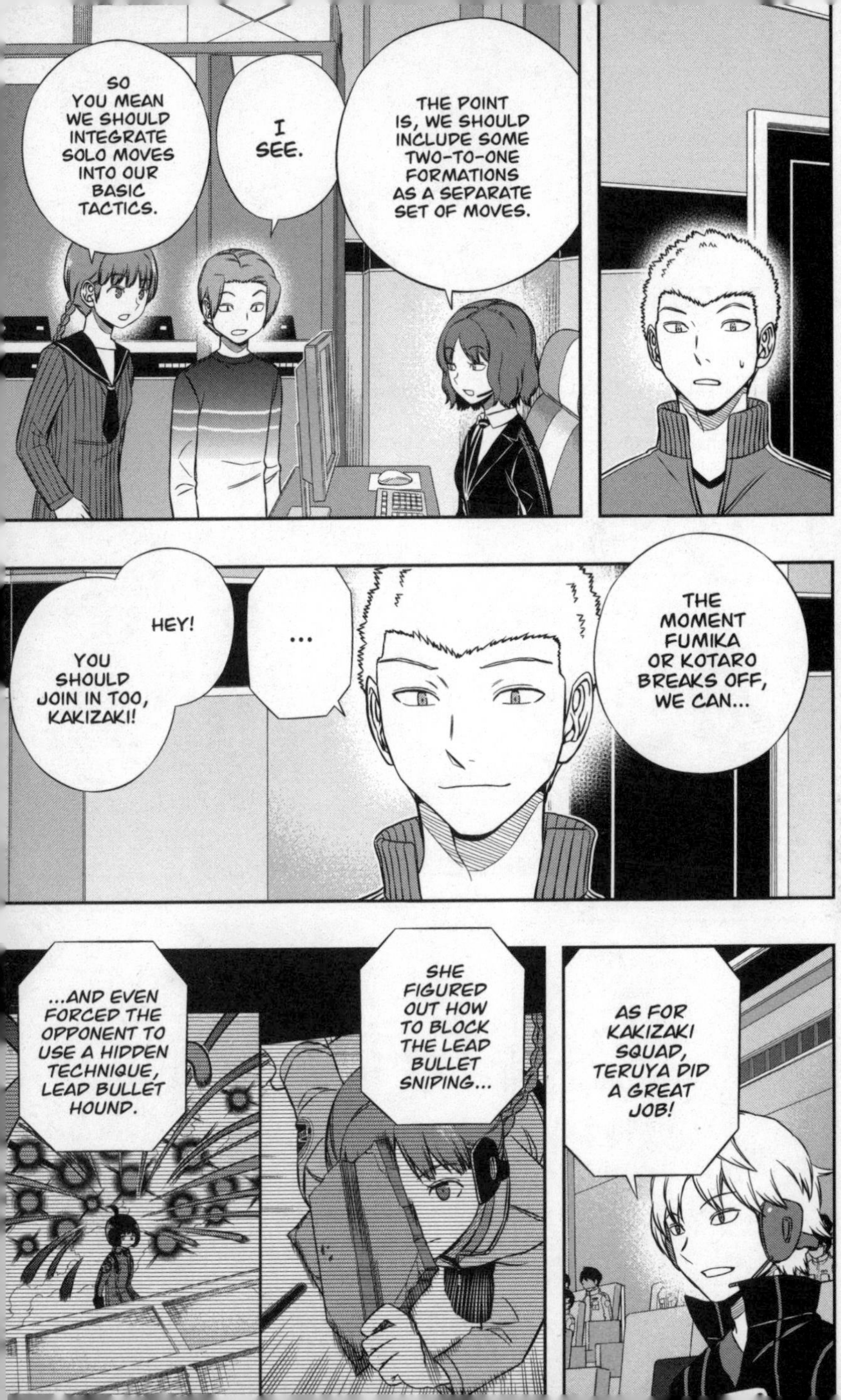
THE POINT IS, WE SHOULD INCLUDE SOME TWO-TO-ONE FORMATIONS AS A SEPARATE SET OF MOVES.
I SEE.
SO YOU MEAN WE SHOULD INTEGRATE SOLO MOVES INTO OUR BASIC TACTICS.
THE MOMENT FUMIKA OR KOTARO BREAKS OFF, WE CAN...
...
HEY! YOU SHOULD JOIN IN TOO, KAKIZAKI!
AS FOR KAKIZAKI SQUAD, TERUYA DID A GREAT JOB!
SHE FIGURED OUT HOW TO BLOCK THE LEAD BULLET SNIPING...
...AND EVEN FORCED THE OPPONENT TO USE A HIDDEN TECHNIQUE, LEAD BULLET HOUND.

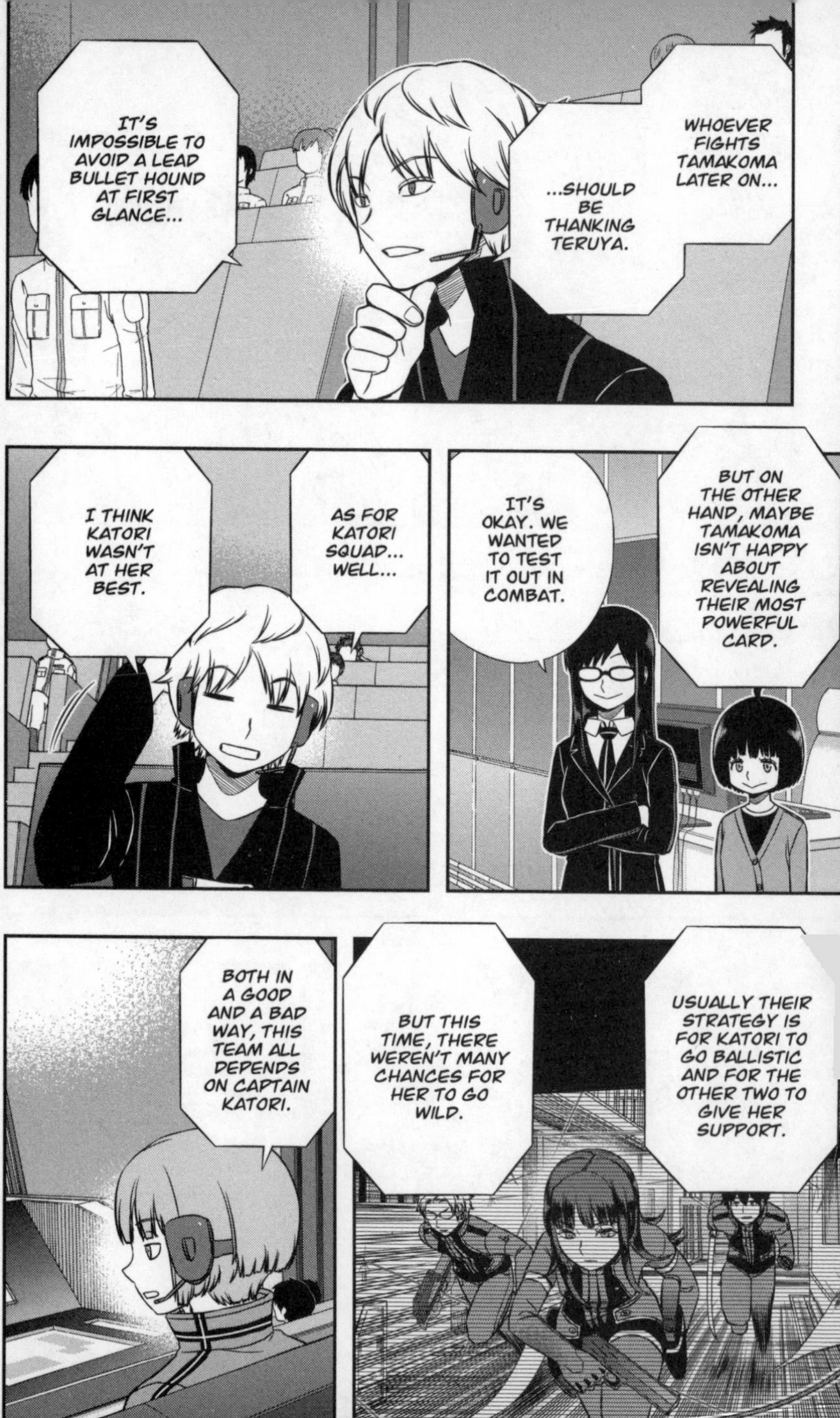
WHOEVER FIGHTS TAMAKOMA LATER ON...
...SHOULD BE THANKING TERUYA.
IT'S IMPOSSIBLE TO AVOID A LEAD BULLET HOUND AT FIRST GLANCE...
BUT ON THE OTHER HAND, MAYBE TAMAKOMA ISN'T HAPPY ABOUT REVEALING THEIR MOST POWERFUL CARD.
IT'S OKAY. WE WANTED TO TEST IT OUT IN COMBAT.
AS FOR KATORI SQUAD... WELL...
I THINK KATORI WASN'T AT HER BEST.
USUALLY THEIR STRATEGY IS FOR KATORI TO GO BALLISTIC AND FOR THE OTHER TWO TO GIVE HER SUPPORT.
BUT THIS TIME, THERE WEREN'T MANY CHANCES FOR HER TO GO WILD.
BOTH IN A GOOD AND A BAD WAY, THIS TEAM ALL DEPENDS ON CAPTAIN KATORI.

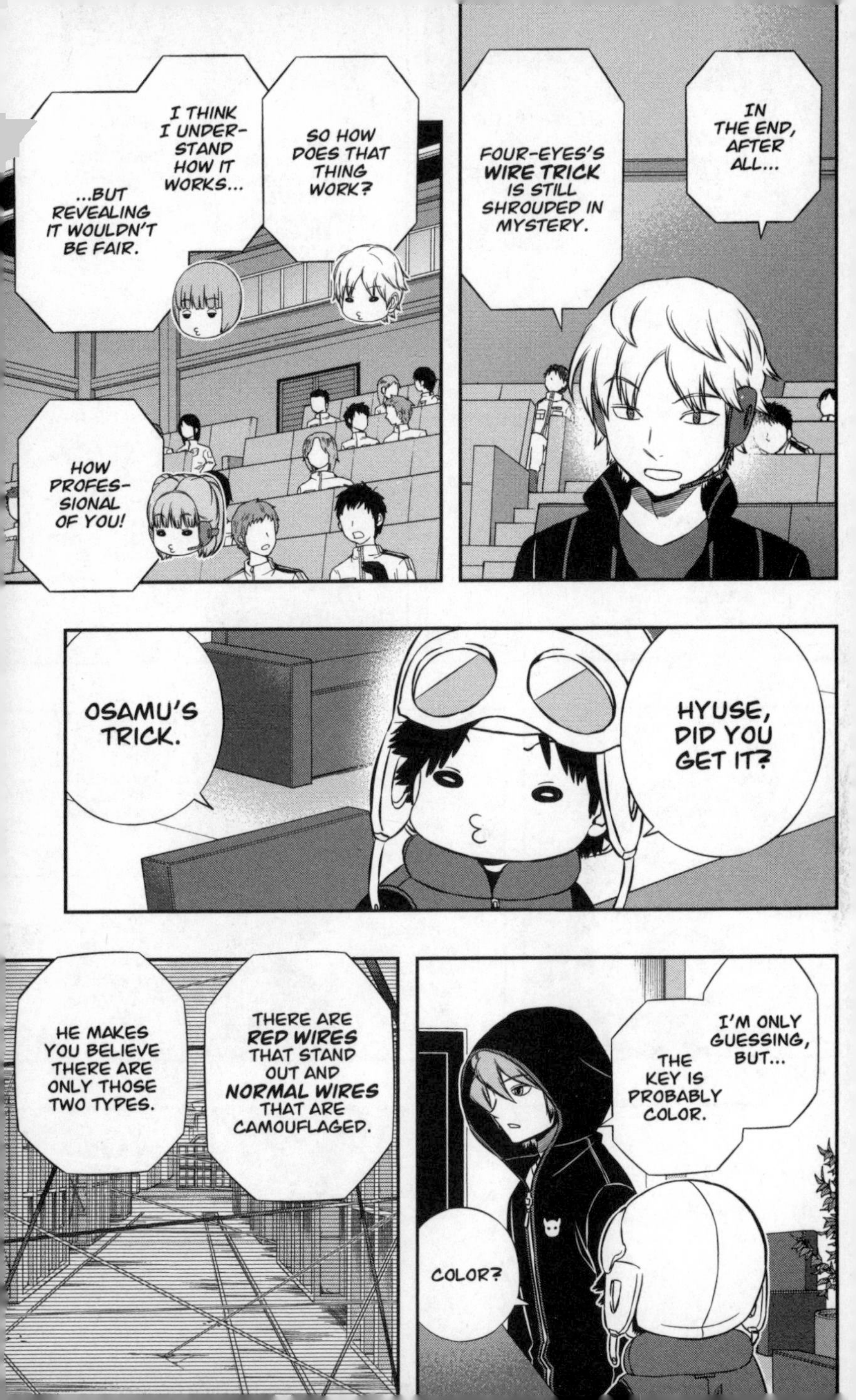
IN THE END, AFTER ALL...
FOUR-EYES'S WIRE TRICK IS STILL SHROUDED IN MYSTERY.
SO HOW DOES THAT THING WORK?
I THINK I UNDER-STAND HOW IT WORKS...
...BUT REVEALING IT WOULDN'T BE FAIR.
HOW PROFES-SIONAL OF YOU!
HYUSE, DID YOU GET IT?
OSAMU'S TRICK.
I'M ONLY GUESSING, BUT...
THE KEY IS PROBABLY COLOR.
COLOR?
THERE ARE RED WIRES THAT STAND OUT AND NORMAL WIRES THAT ARE CAMOUFLAGED.
HE MAKES YOU BELIEVE THERE ARE ONLY THOSE TWO TYPES.

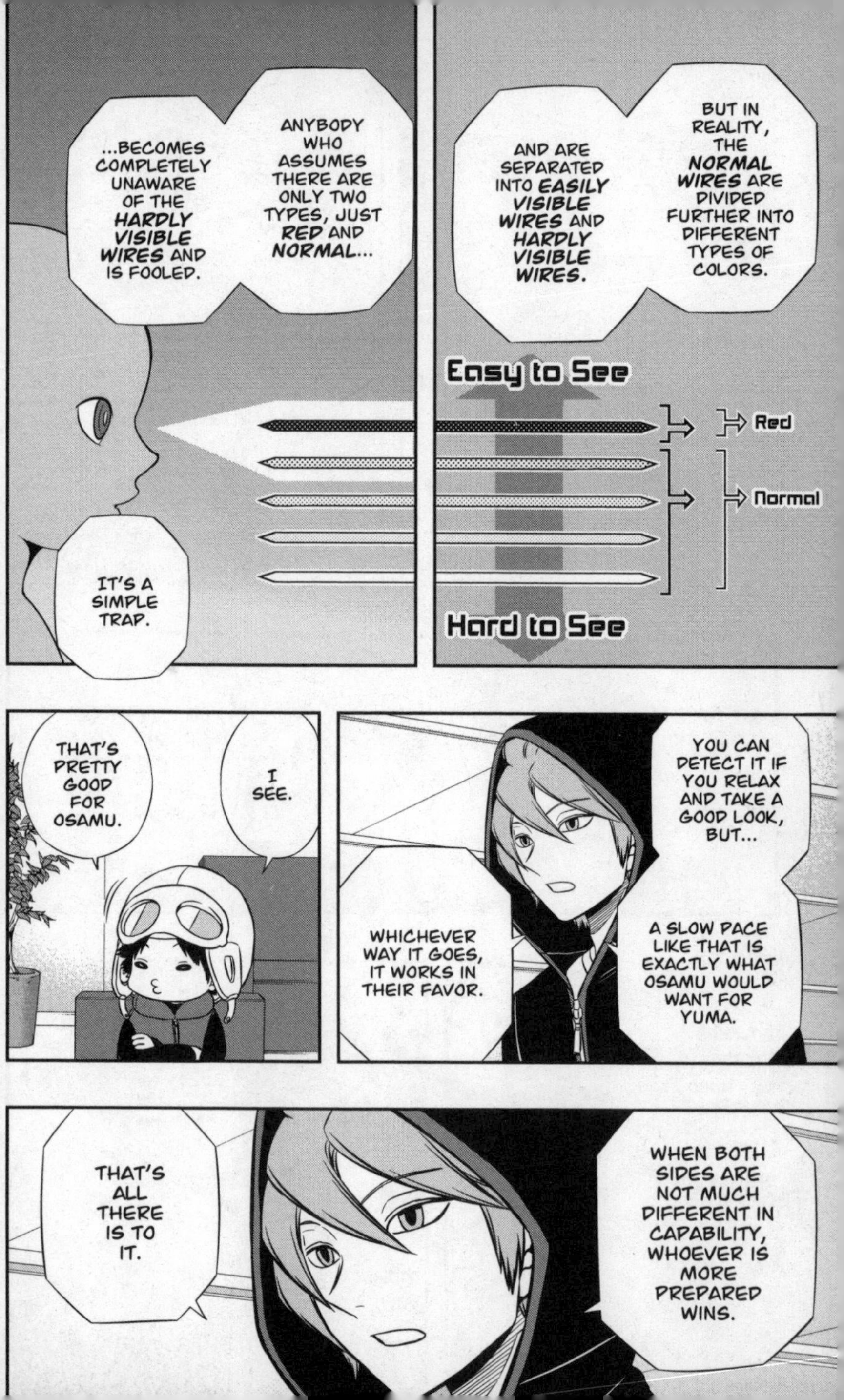
BUT IN REALITY, THE NORMAL WIRES ARE DIVIDED FURTHER INTO DIFFERENT TYPES OF COLORS.
AND ARE SEPARATED INTO EASILY VISIBLE WIRES AND HARDLY VISIBLE WIRES.
Easy to See
Red
Normal
Hard to See
ANYBODY WHO ASSUMES THERE ARE ONLY TWO TYPES, JUST RED AND NORMAL...
...BECOMES COMPLETELY UNAWARE OF THE HARDLY VISIBLE WIRES AND IS FOOLED.
IT'S A SIMPLE TRAP.
YOU CAN DETECT IT IF YOU RELAX AND TAKE A GOOD LOOK, BUT...
A SLOW PACE LIKE THAT IS EXACTLY WHAT OSAMU WOULD WANT FOR YUMA.
WHICHEVER WAY IT GOES, IT WORKS IN THEIR FAVOR.
I SEE.
THAT'S PRETTY GOOD FOR OSAMU.
WHEN BOTH SIDES ARE NOT MUCH DIFFERENT IN CAPABILITY, WHOEVER IS MORE PREPARED WINS.
THAT'S ALL THERE IS TO IT.

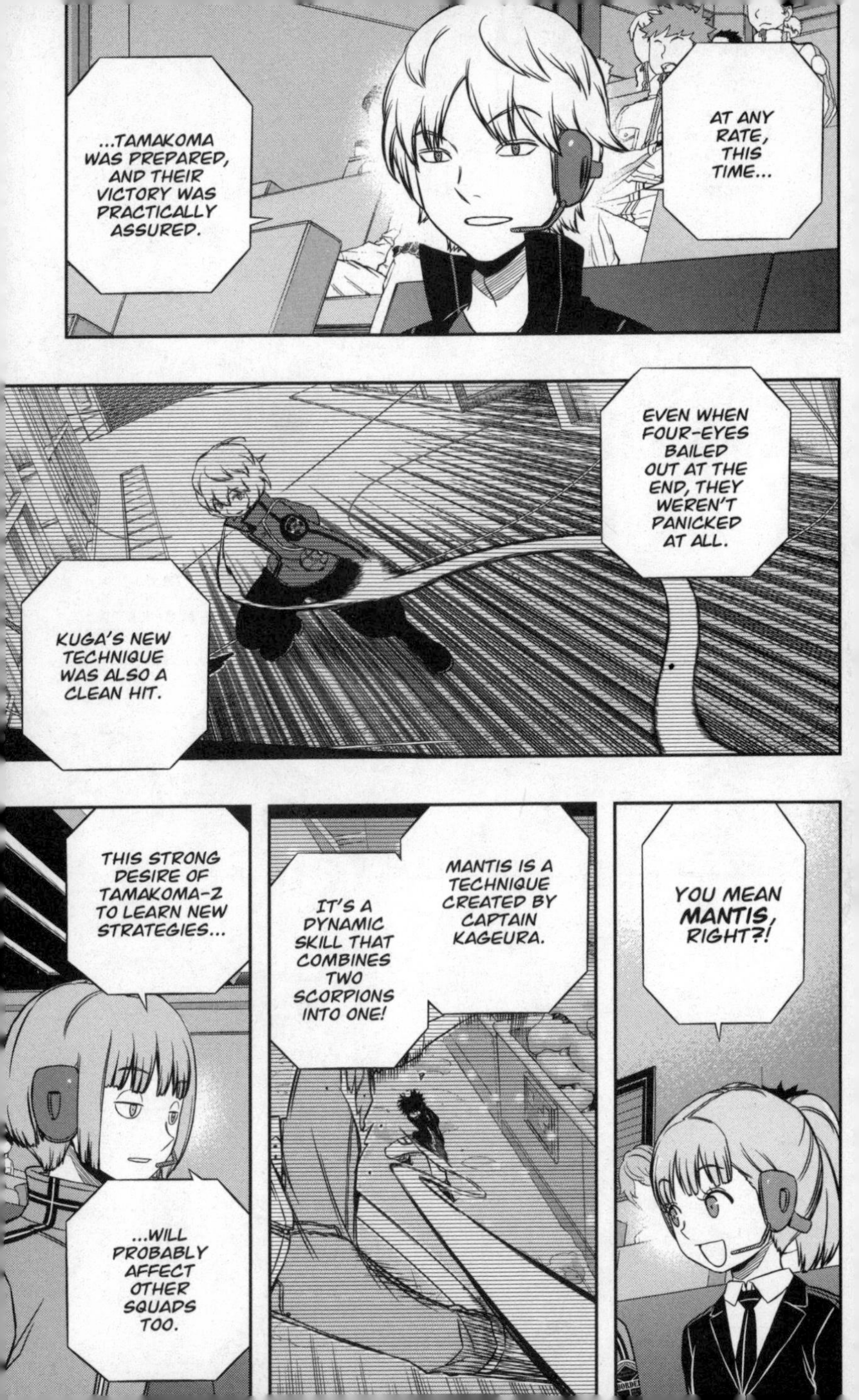
AT ANY RATE, THIS TIME...
...TAMAKOMA WAS PREPARED, AND THEIR VICTORY WAS PRACTICALLY ASSURED.
EVEN WHEN FOUR-EYES BAILED OUT AT THE END, THEY WEREN'T PANICKED AT ALL.
KUGA'S NEW TECHNIQUE WAS ALSO A CLEAN HIT.
YOU MEAN MANTIS, RIGHT?!
MANTIS IS A TECHNIQUE CREATED BY CAPTAIN KAGEURA.
IT'S A DYNAMIC SKILL THAT COMBINES TWO SCORPIONS INTO ONE!
THIS STRONG DESIRE OF TAMAKOMA-2 TO LEARN NEW STRATEGIES...
...WILL PROBABLY AFFECT OTHER SQUADS TOO.

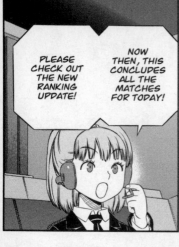

DO YOU EXPECT THIS WIRE STRATEGY TO SPREAD TO THE OTHER SQUADS...?
WELL, THIS STRATEGY IS BASED SOLELY ON KUGA'S PHYSICAL ABILITY AND THEIR CANNON.
SO I GUESS NOT MANY GROUPS COULD IMITATE IT JUST AS WE SAW IT TODAY.
NOW THEN, THIS CONCLUDES ALL THE MATCHES FOR TODAY!
PLEASE CHECK OUT THE NEW RANKING UPDATE!
TAMAKOMA-2, WITH THE HIGHEST SCORE, JUMPED UP TO NO. 4!
003 IKOMA SQUAD
004 TAMAKOMA-2
005 OJI SQUAD
006 AZUMA SQUAD
007 SUZUNARI-1
008 YUBA SQUAD
009 KATORI SQUAD
010 SUWA SQUAD
BOTH KATORI AND KAKIZAKI SQUADS STAYED WHERE THEY WERE!
NINOMIYA SQUAD
KAGEURA SQUAD
IKOMA SQUAD
TAMAKOMA-2
005 OJI SQUAD
I BELIEVE TAMAKOMA-2 WILL REMAIN AT THE CENTER OF THE STORM.
AS OF NOW...
...WE ARE FINISHED WITH THE ROUND 5 NIGHT DIVISION MATCHES!
THANK YOU ALL FOR PARTICIPATING!

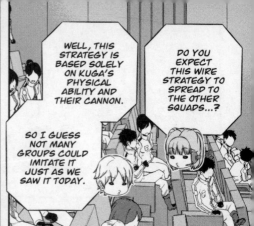

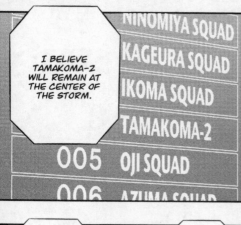

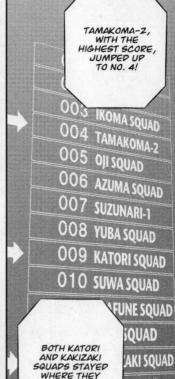

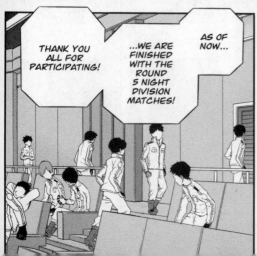

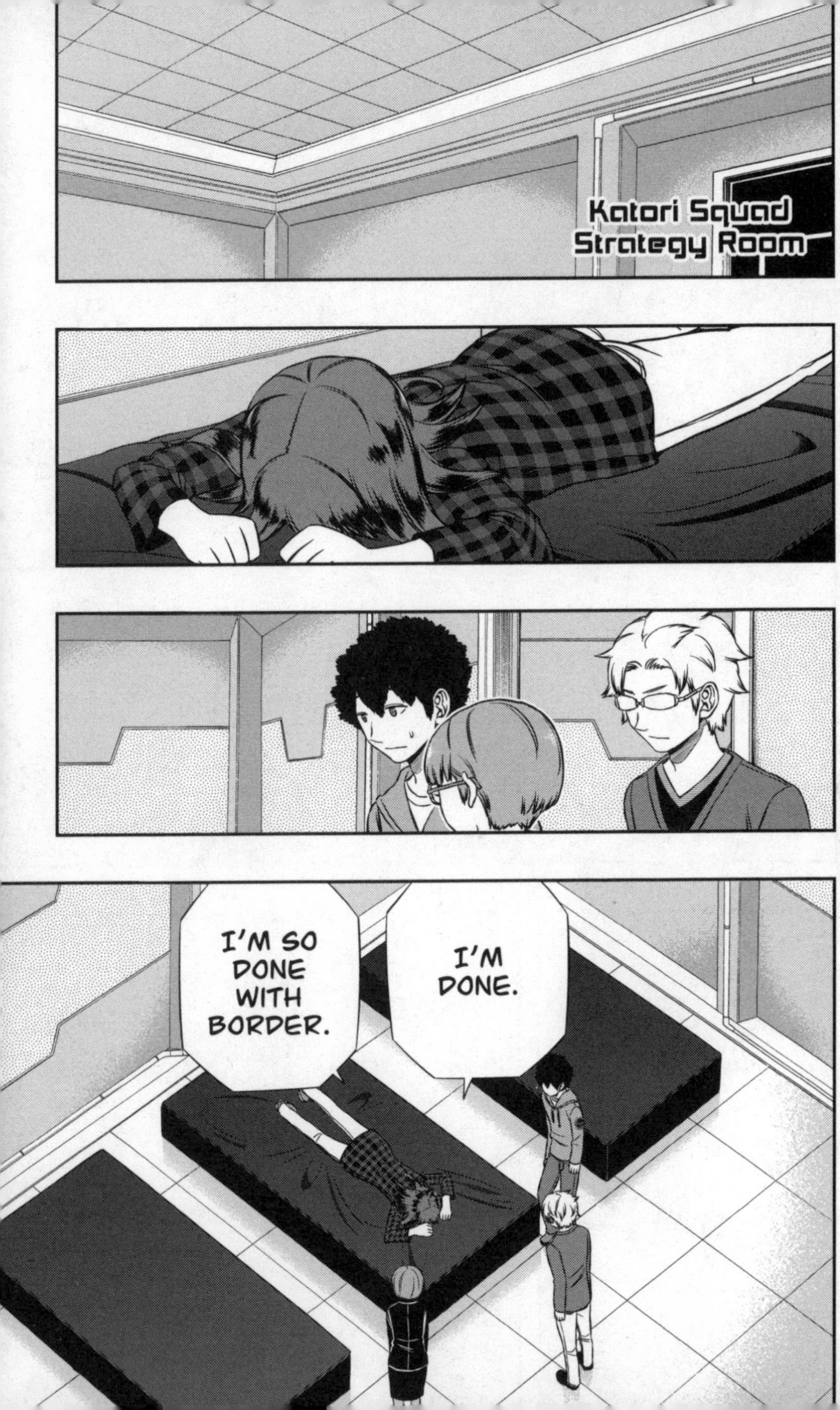
Katori Squad Strategy Room
I'M DONE.
I'M SO DONE WITH BORDER.

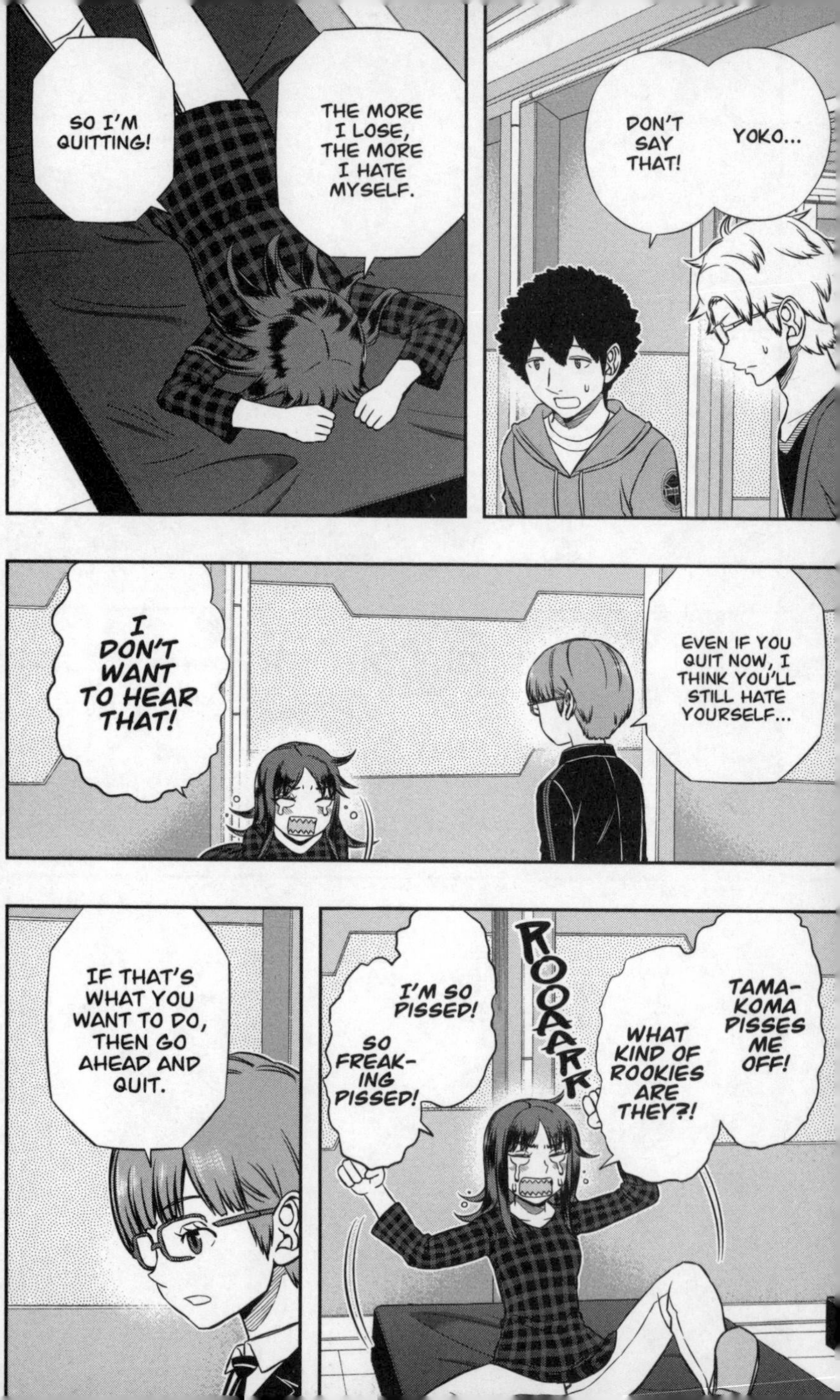
YOKO...
DON'T SAY THAT!
THE MORE I LOSE, THE MORE I HATE MYSELF.
SO I'M QUITTING!
EVEN IF YOU QUIT NOW, I THINK YOU'LL STILL HATE YOURSELF...
I DON'T WANT TO HEAR THAT!
TAMA-KOMA PISSES ME OFF!
WHAT KIND OF ROOKIES ARE THEY?!
ROOOAARR
I'M SO PISSED!
SO FREAK-ING PISSED!
IF THAT'S WHAT YOU WANT TO DO, THEN GO AHEAD AND QUIT.

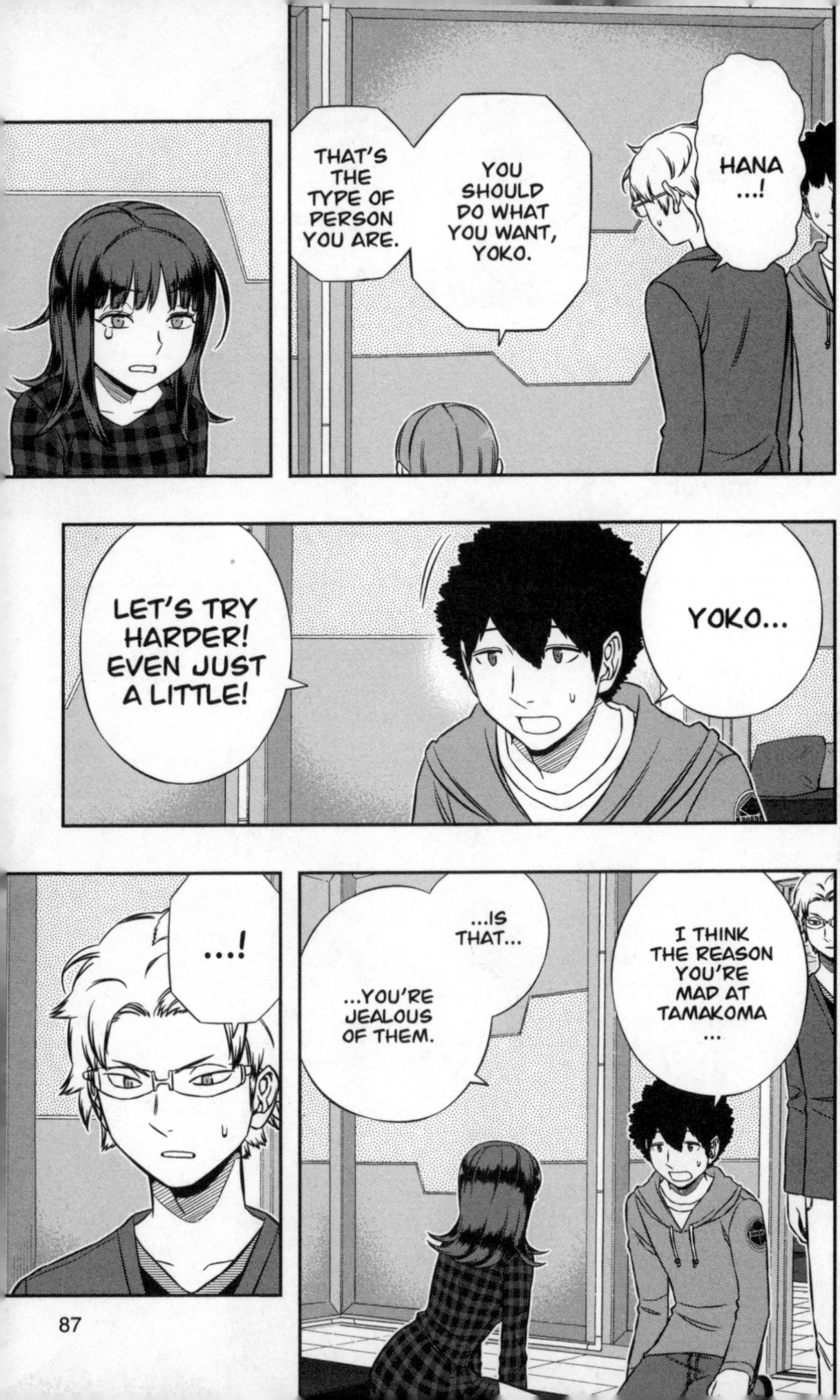
HANA ...!
YOU SHOULD DO WHAT YOU WANT, YOKO.
THAT'S THE TYPE OF PERSON YOU ARE.
YOKO...
LET'S TRY HARDER! EVEN JUST A LITTLE!
I THINK THE REASON YOU'RE MAD AT TAMAKOMA ...
...IS THAT...
...YOU'RE JEALOUS OF THEM.
...!

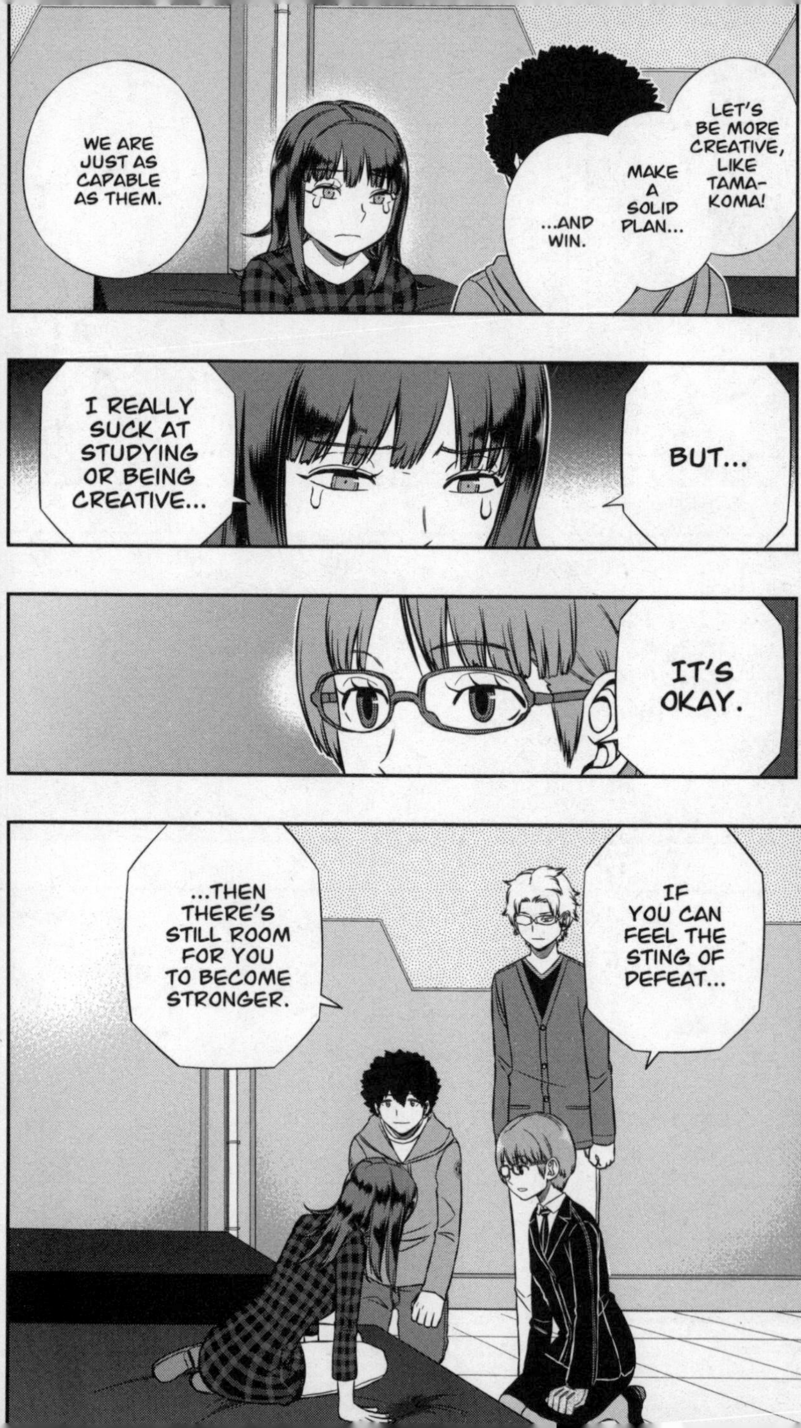
LET'S BE MORE CREATIVE, LIKE TAMA-KOMA!
MAKE A SOLID PLAN...
...AND WIN.
WE ARE JUST AS CAPABLE AS THEM.
BUT...
I REALLY SUCK AT STUDYING OR BEING CREATIVE...
IT'S OKAY.
IF YOU CAN FEEL THE STING OF DEFEAT...
...THEN THERE'S STILL ROOM FOR YOU TO BECOME STRONGER.

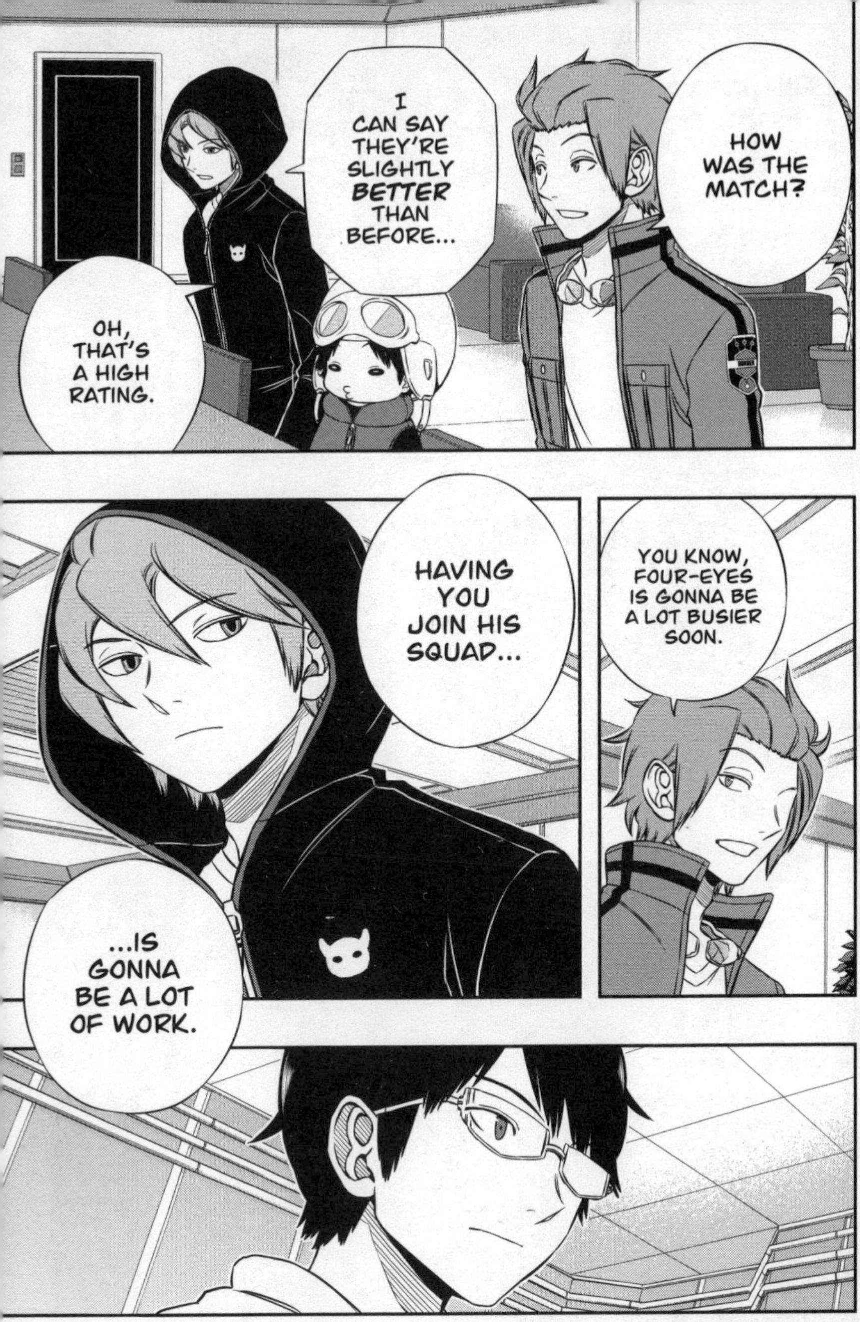
HOW WAS THE MATCH?
I CAN SAY THEY'RE SLIGHTLY BETTER THAN BEFORE...
OH, THAT'S A HIGH RATING.
YOU KNOW, FOUR-EYES IS GONNA BE A LOT BUSIER SOON.
HAVING YOU JOIN HIS SQUAD...
...IS GONNA BE A LOT OF WORK.

Aji-jiman Ramen
Mikado Store

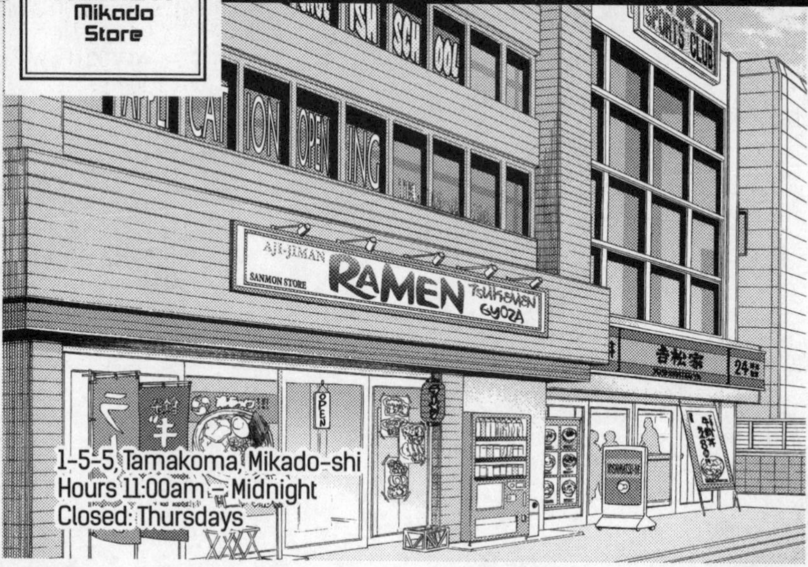
AJI-JIMAN
SANMON STORE
RAMEN
TSUKEMEN
GYOZA
SPORTS CLUB
OPEN

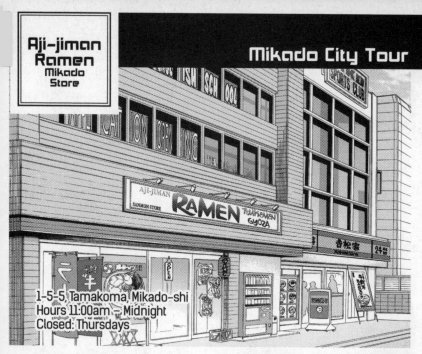

1-5-5, Tamakoma, Mikado-shi
Hours 11:00am – Midnight
Closed: Thursdays

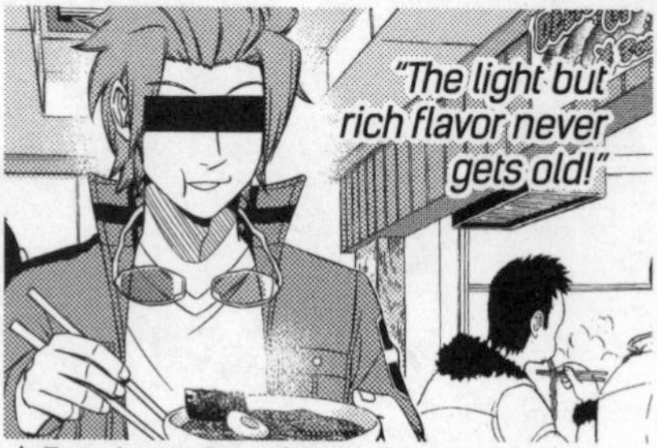
"The light but rich flavor never gets old!"

↑ Tamakoma Branch members are regular customers.

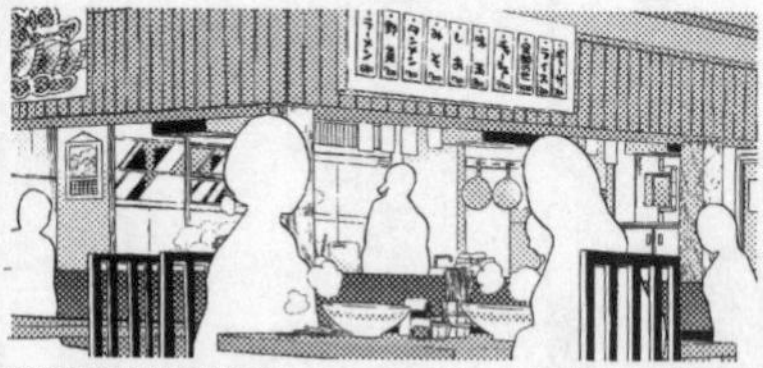

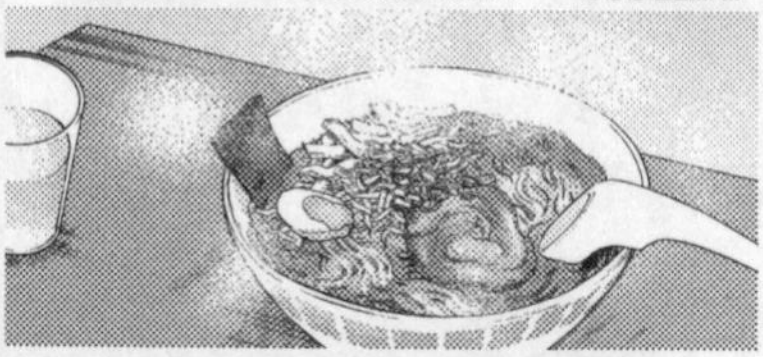

← Thick noodle with tonkotsu-soy sauce for 680 yen

A ramen place that Jin and Reiji use for their secret talks. They take Chika with them sometimes too. Director Rindo and Yotaro probably come here too. It's a nice place to return to often.

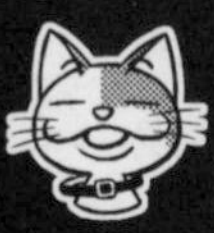

A ramen chain near the Tamakoma Branch.

A husband-and-wife pair with over a decade of ramen experience run this shop. The menu is pretty standard, but regulars flood the shop on a daily basis.

Home-cooked flavor

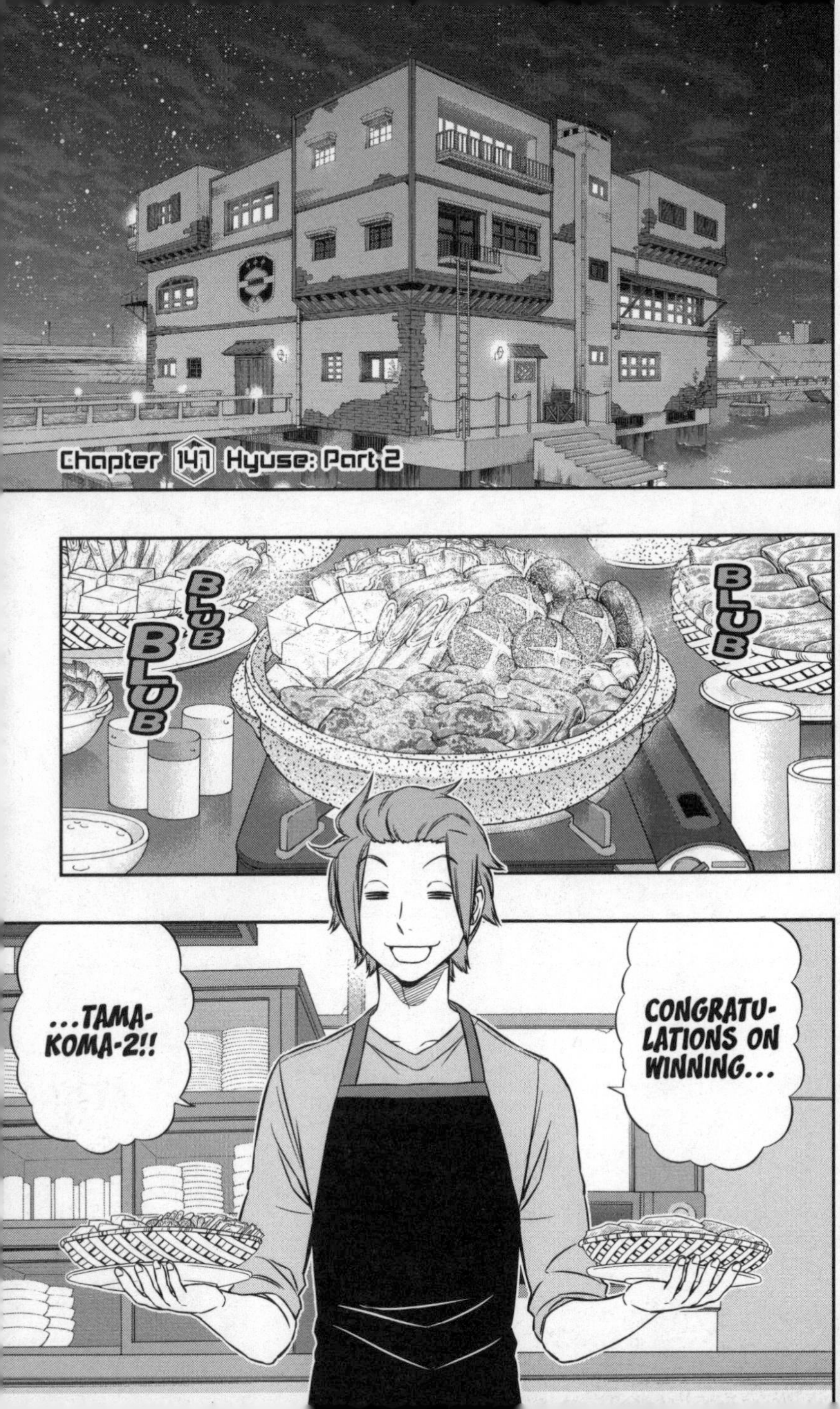
Chapter 147 Hyuse: Part 2
BLUB
BLUB
BLUB
CONGRATU-LATIONS ON WINNING...
...TAMA-KOMA-2!!

Chapter 147 Hyuse: Part 2

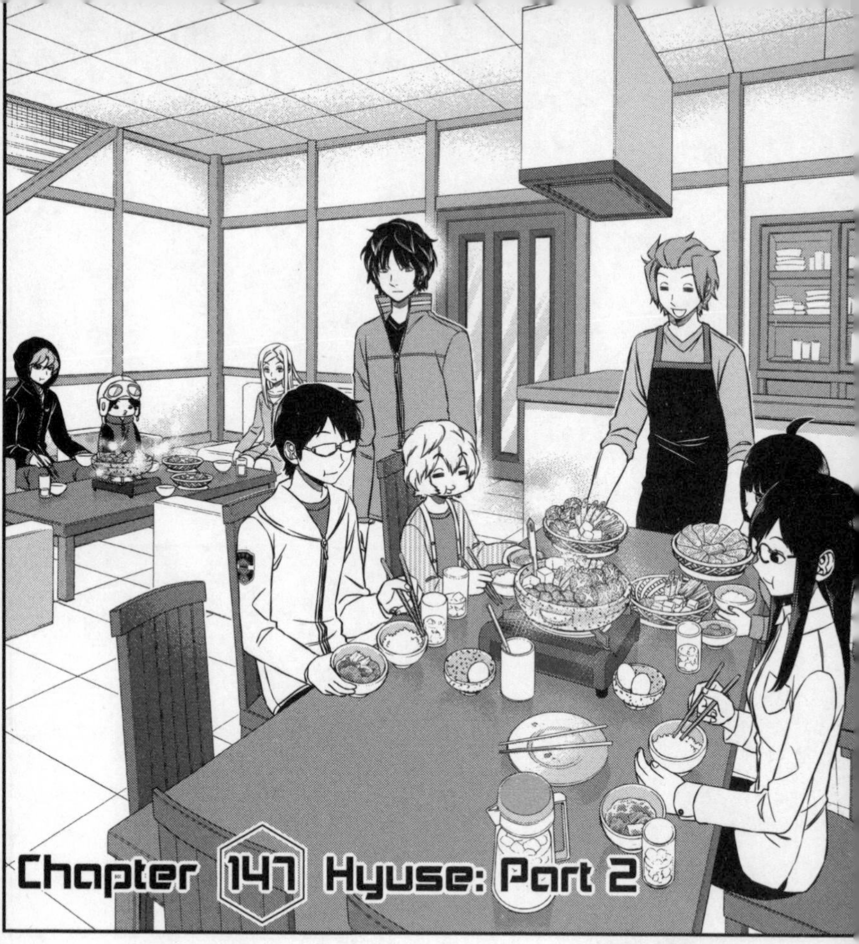

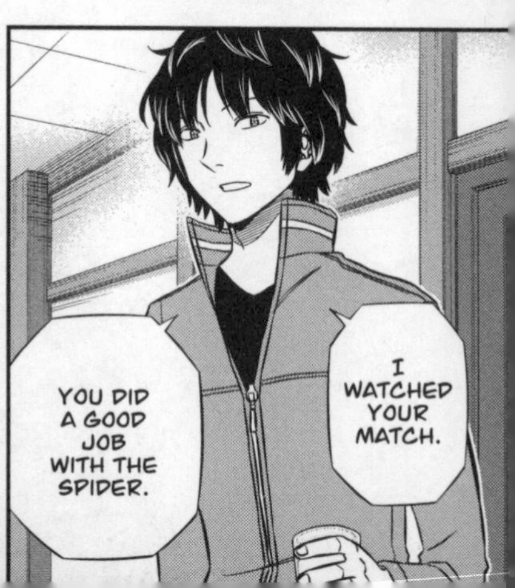
I WATCHED YOUR MATCH.
YOU DID A GOOD JOB WITH THE SPIDER.

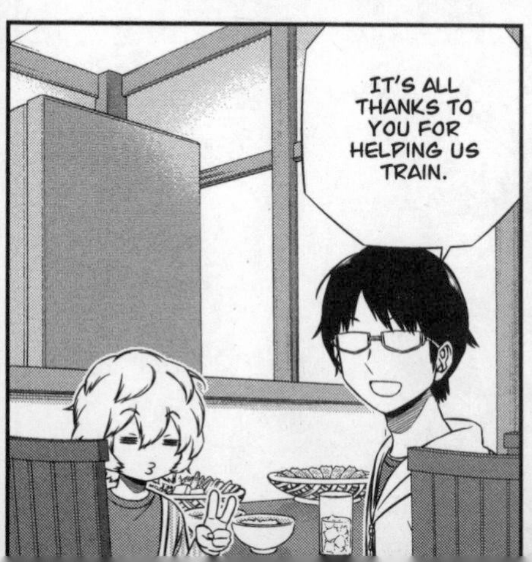
IT'S ALL THANKS TO YOU FOR HELPING US TRAIN.

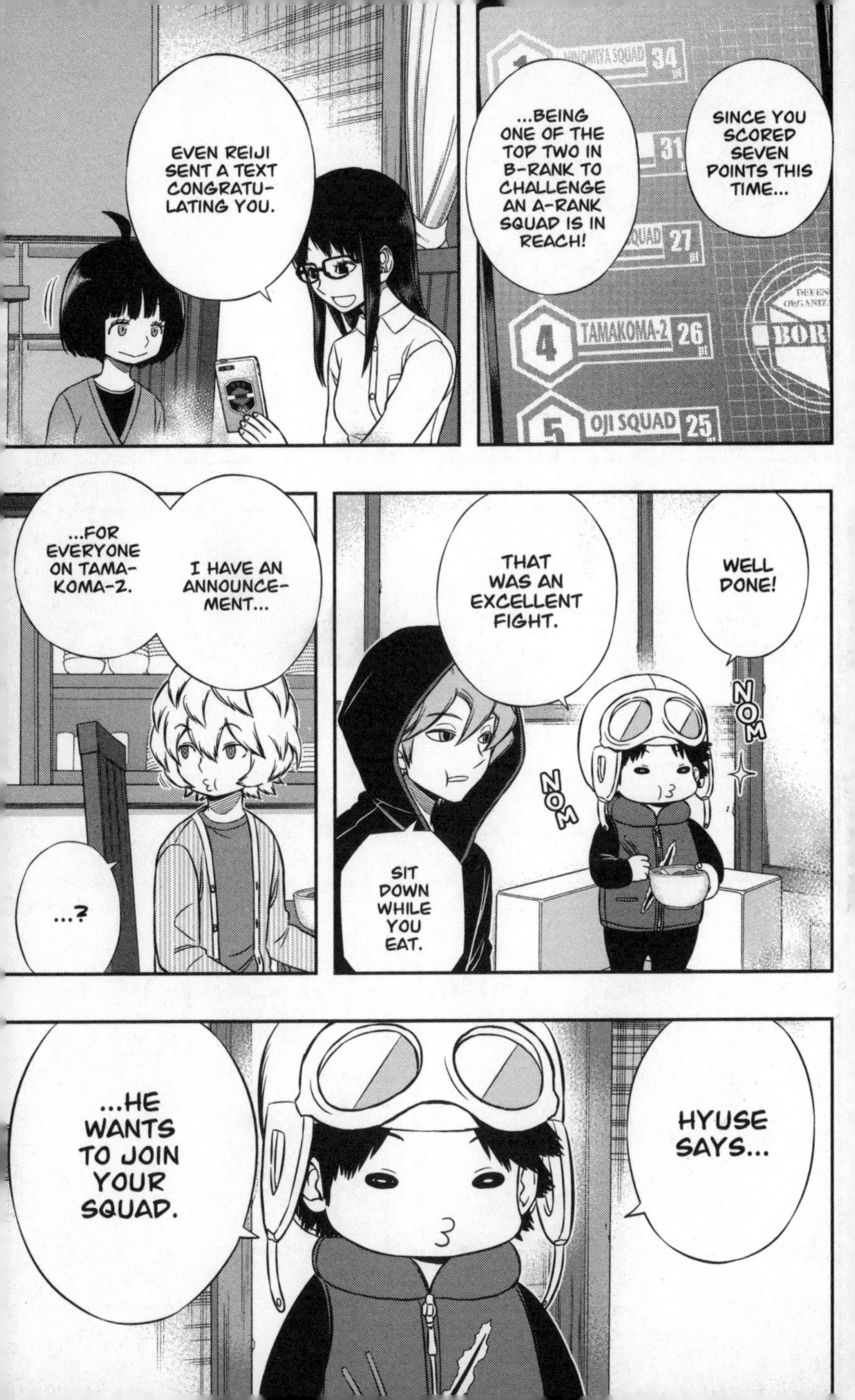
SINCE YOU SCORED SEVEN POINTS THIS TIME...
...BEING ONE OF THE TOP TWO IN B-RANK TO CHALLENGE AN A-RANK SQUAD IS IN REACH!
4 TAMAKOMA-2 26
5 OJI SQUAD 25
EVEN REIJI SENT A TEXT CONGRATU-LATING YOU.
WELL DONE!
NOM
THAT WAS AN EXCELLENT FIGHT.
NOM
SIT DOWN WHILE YOU EAT.
I HAVE AN ANNOUNCE-MENT...
...FOR EVERYONE ON TAMA-KOMA-2.
...?
HYUSE SAYS...
...HE WANTS TO JOIN YOUR SQUAD.

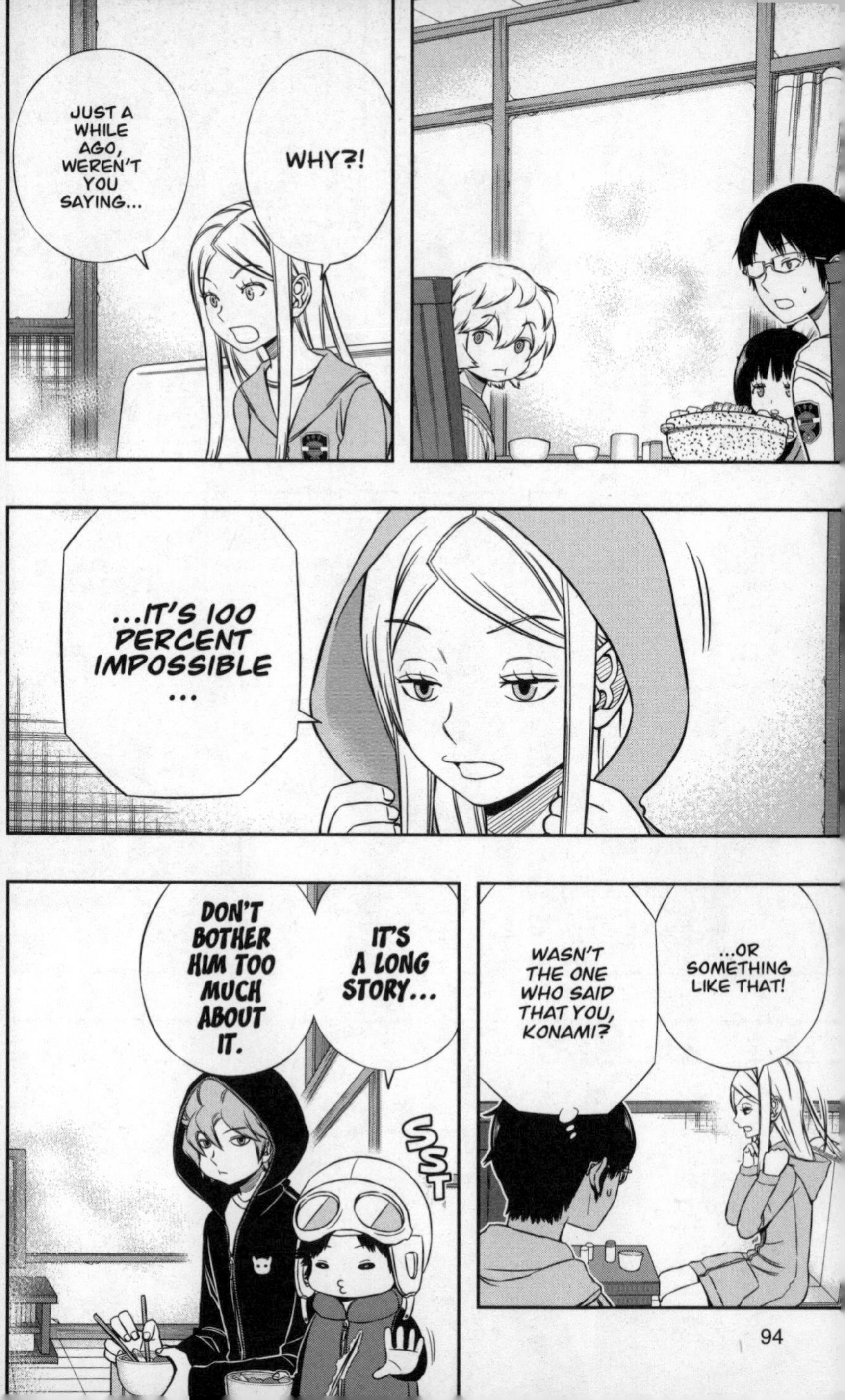
WHY?!
JUST A WHILE AGO, WEREN'T YOU SAYING...
...IT'S 100 PERCENT IMPOSSIBLE ...
...OR SOMETHING LIKE THAT!
WASN'T THE ONE WHO SAID THAT YOU, KONAMI?
IT'S A LONG STORY...
DON'T BOTHER HIM TOO MUCH ABOUT IT.
SST

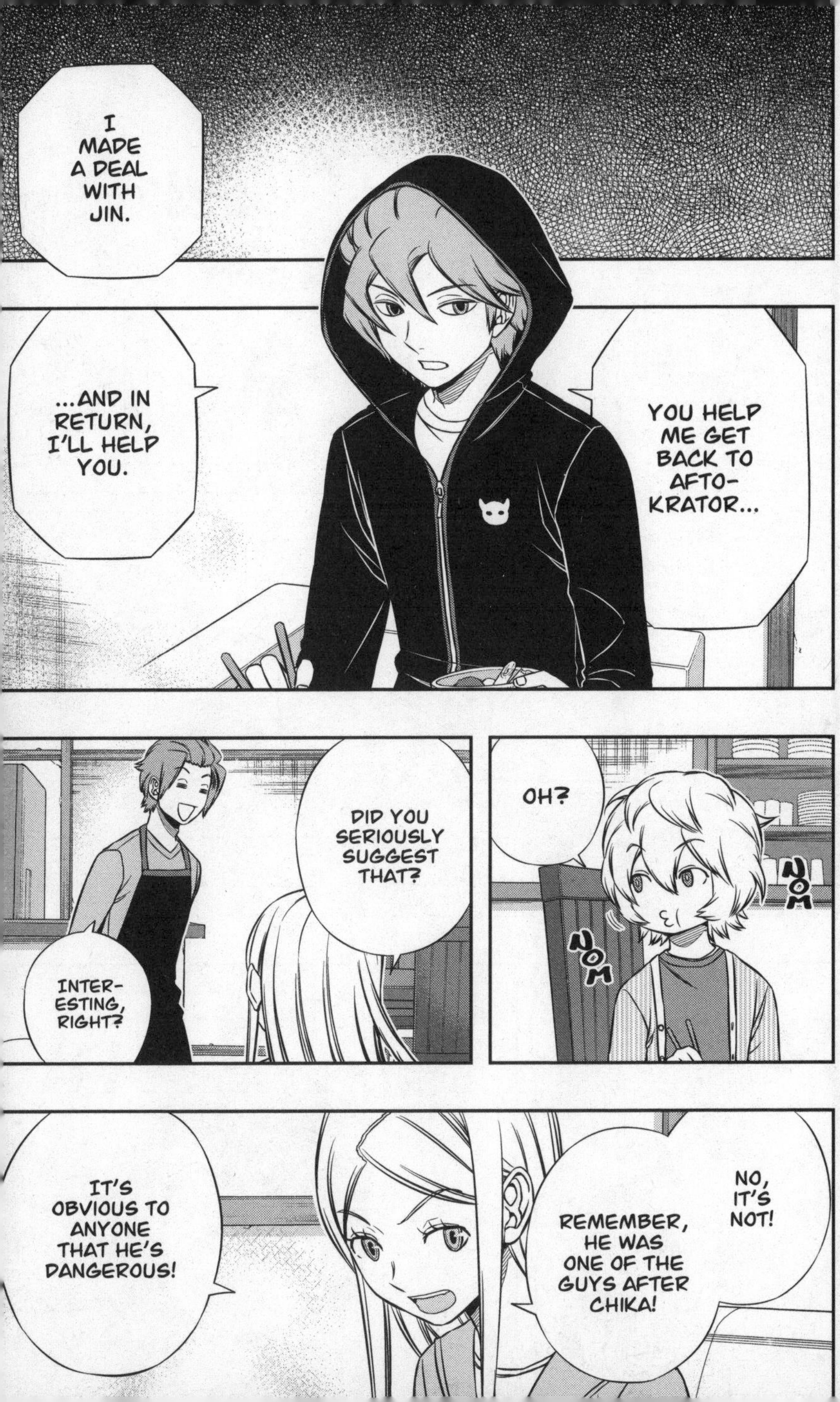
I MADE A DEAL WITH JIN.
YOU HELP ME GET BACK TO AFTO-KRATOR...
...AND IN RETURN, I'LL HELP YOU.
OH?
NOM
NOM
DID YOU SERIOUSLY SUGGEST THAT?
INTER-ESTING, RIGHT?
NO, IT'S NOT!
REMEMBER, HE WAS ONE OF THE GUYS AFTER CHIKA!
IT'S OBVIOUS TO ANYONE THAT HE'S DANGEROUS!

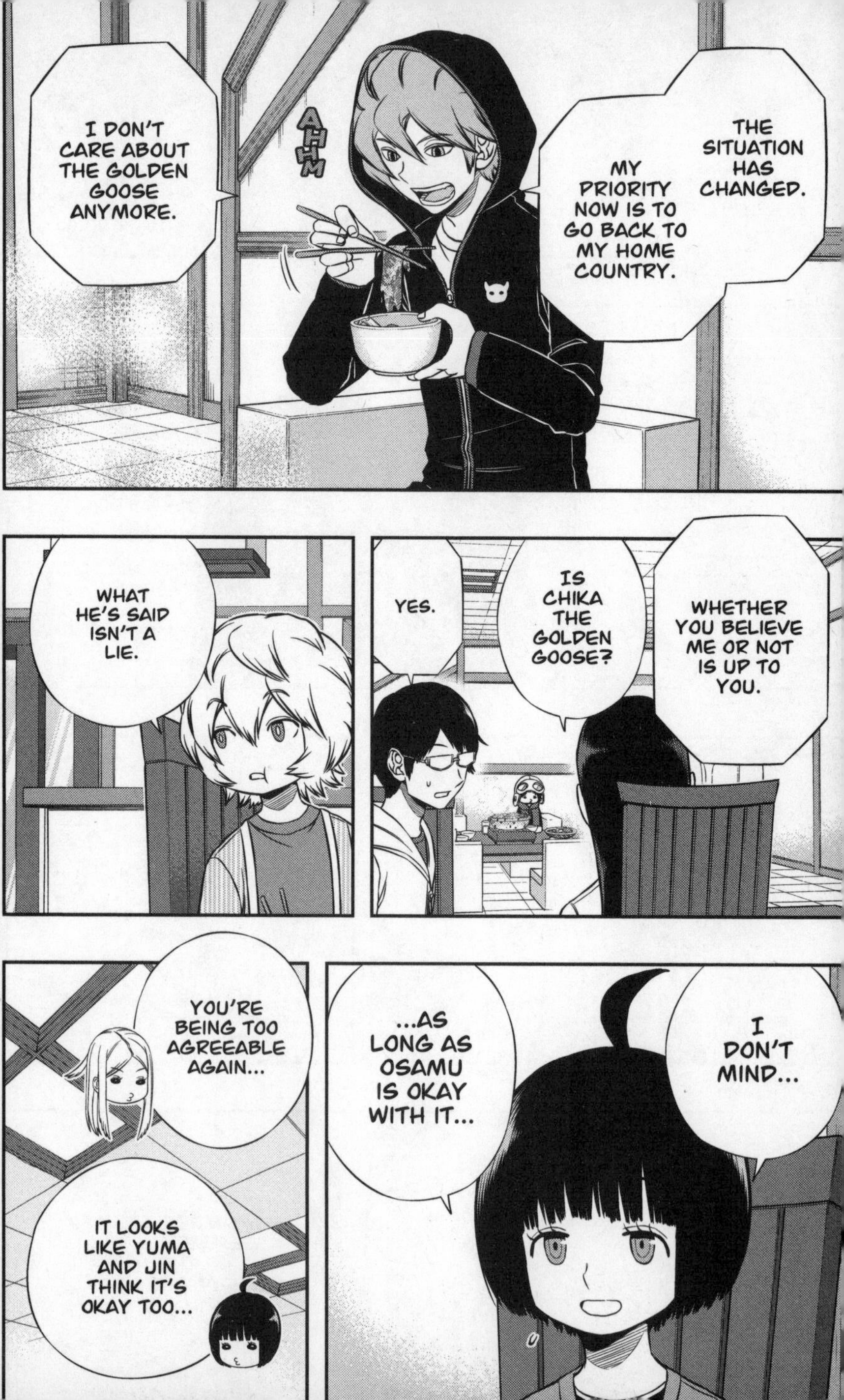
THE SITUATION HAS CHANGED.
MY PRIORITY NOW IS TO GO BACK TO MY HOME COUNTRY.
AHHM
I DON'T CARE ABOUT THE GOLDEN GOOSE ANYMORE.
WHETHER YOU BELIEVE ME OR NOT IS UP TO YOU.
IS CHIKA THE GOLDEN GOOSE?
YES.
WHAT HE'S SAID ISN'T A LIE.
I DON'T MIND...
...AS LONG AS OSAMU IS OKAY WITH IT...
YOU'RE BEING TOO AGREEABLE AGAIN...
IT LOOKS LIKE YUMA AND JIN THINK IT'S OKAY TOO...

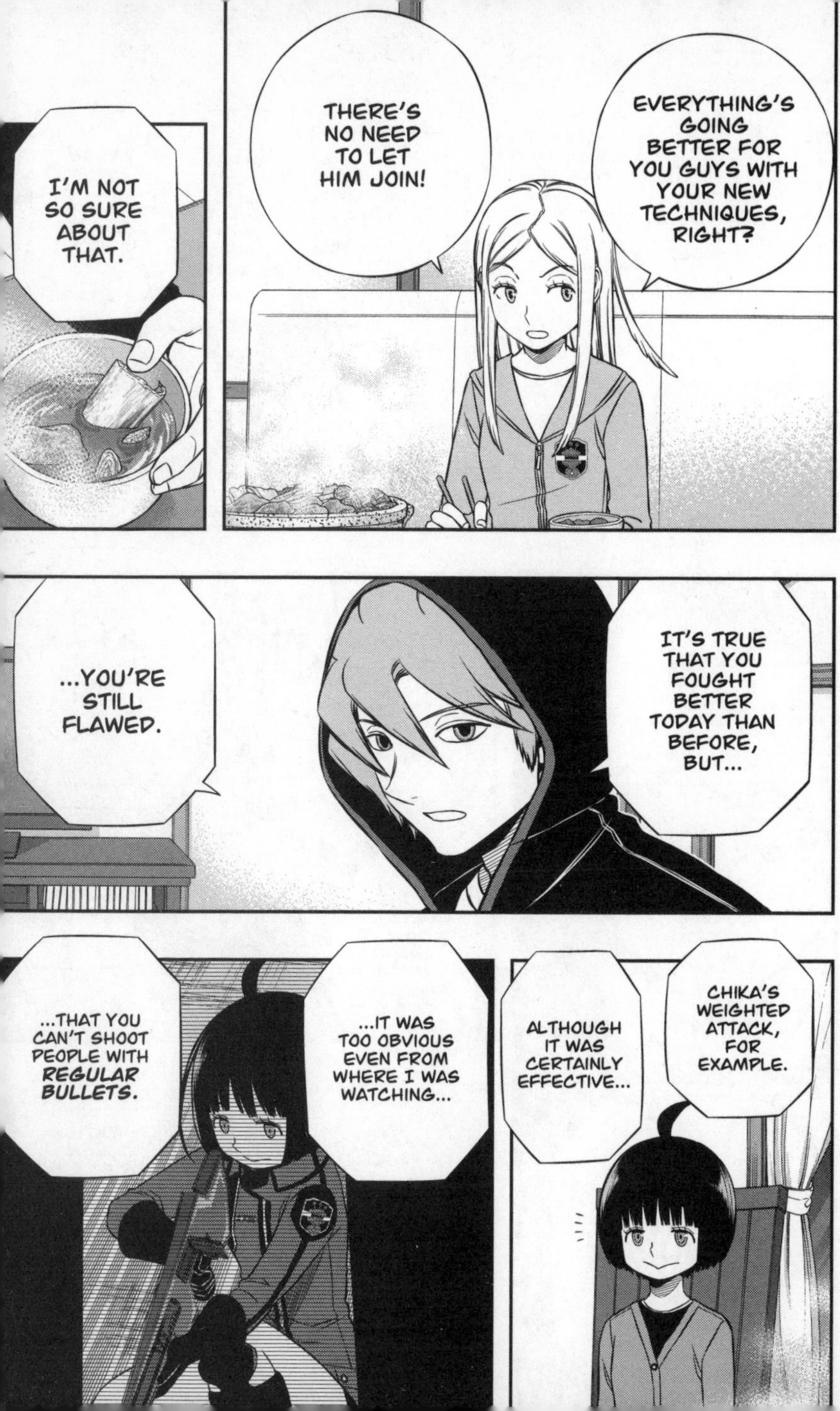

EVERYTHING'S GOING BETTER FOR YOU GUYS WITH YOUR NEW TECHNIQUES, RIGHT?
THERE'S NO NEED TO LET HIM JOIN!
I'M NOT SO SURE ABOUT THAT.
IT'S TRUE THAT YOU FOUGHT BETTER TODAY THAN BEFORE, BUT...
...YOU'RE STILL FLAWED.
CHIKA'S WEIGHTED ATTACK, FOR EXAMPLE.
ALTHOUGH IT WAS CERTAINLY EFFECTIVE...
...IT WAS TOO OBVIOUS EVEN FROM WHERE I WAS WATCHING...
...THAT YOU CAN'T SHOOT PEOPLE WITH **REGULAR BULLETS**.

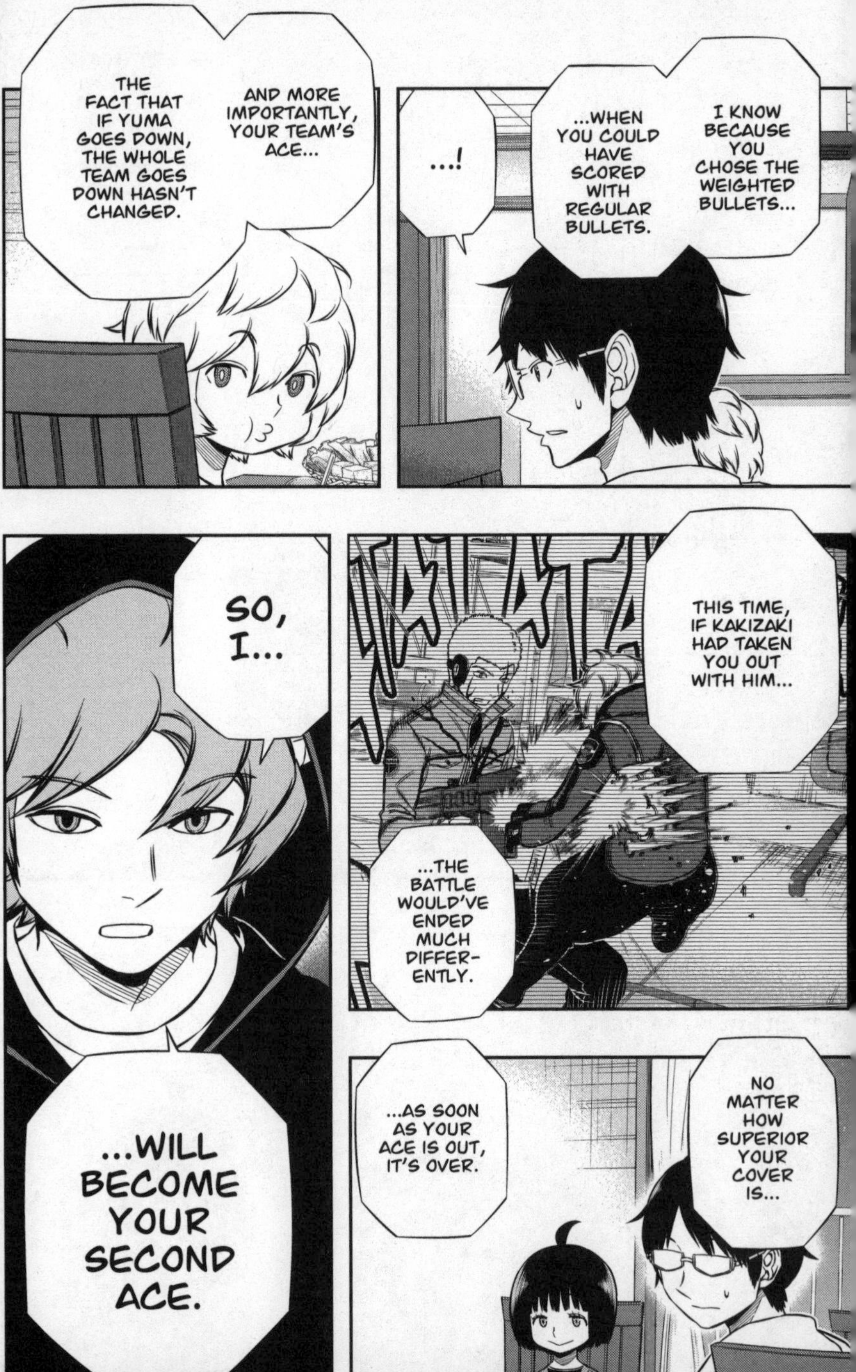
I KNOW BECAUSE YOU CHOSE THE WEIGHTED BULLETS...
...WHEN YOU COULD HAVE SCORED WITH REGULAR BULLETS.
...!
AND MORE IMPORTANTLY, YOUR TEAM'S ACE...
THE FACT THAT IF YUMA GOES DOWN, THE WHOLE TEAM GOES DOWN HASN'T CHANGED.
THIS TIME, IF KAKIZAKI HAD TAKEN YOU OUT WITH HIM...
...THE BATTLE WOULD'VE ENDED MUCH DIFFER-ENTLY.
NO MATTER HOW SUPERIOR YOUR COVER IS...
...AS SOON AS YOUR ACE IS OUT, IT'S OVER.
SO, I...
...WILL BECOME YOUR SECOND ACE.

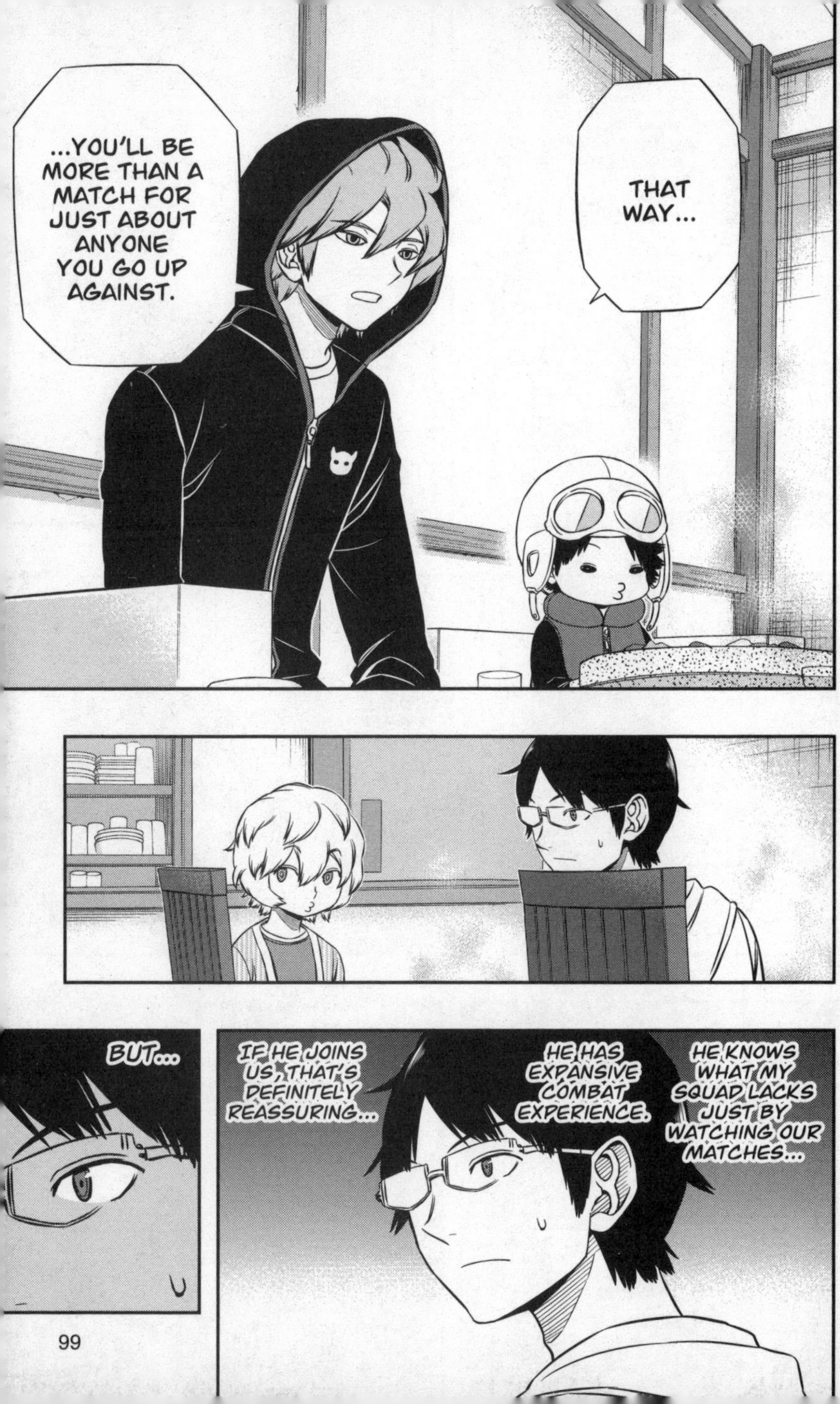
THAT WAY...
...YOU'LL BE MORE THAN A MATCH FOR JUST ABOUT ANYONE YOU GO UP AGAINST.
HE KNOWS WHAT MY SQUAD LACKS JUST BY WATCHING OUR MATCHES...
HE HAS EXPANSIVE COMBAT EXPERIENCE.
IF HE JOINS US, THAT'S DEFINITELY REASSURING...
BUT...

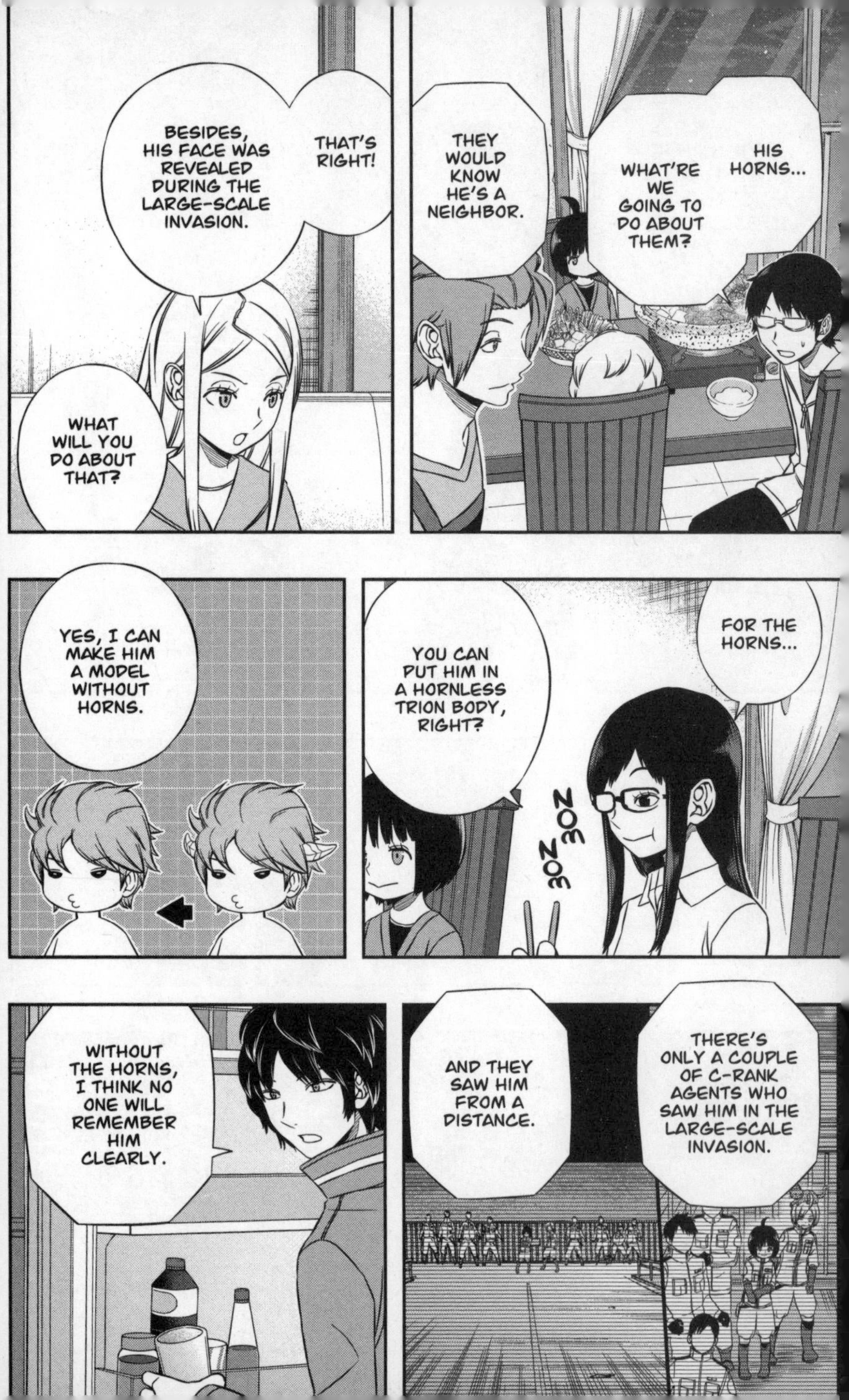
HIS HORNS...
WHAT'RE WE GOING TO DO ABOUT THEM?
THEY WOULD KNOW HE'S A NEIGHBOR.
THAT'S RIGHT!
BESIDES, HIS FACE WAS REVEALED DURING THE LARGE-SCALE INVASION.
WHAT WILL YOU DO ABOUT THAT?
FOR THE HORNS...
YOU CAN PUT HIM IN A HORNLESS TRION BODY, RIGHT?
NOM NOM
YES, I CAN MAKE HIM A MODEL WITHOUT HORNS.
THERE'S ONLY A COUPLE OF C-RANK AGENTS WHO SAW HIM IN THE LARGE-SCALE INVASION.
AND THEY SAW HIM FROM A DISTANCE.
WITHOUT THE HORNS, I THINK NO ONE WILL REMEMBER HIM CLEARLY.

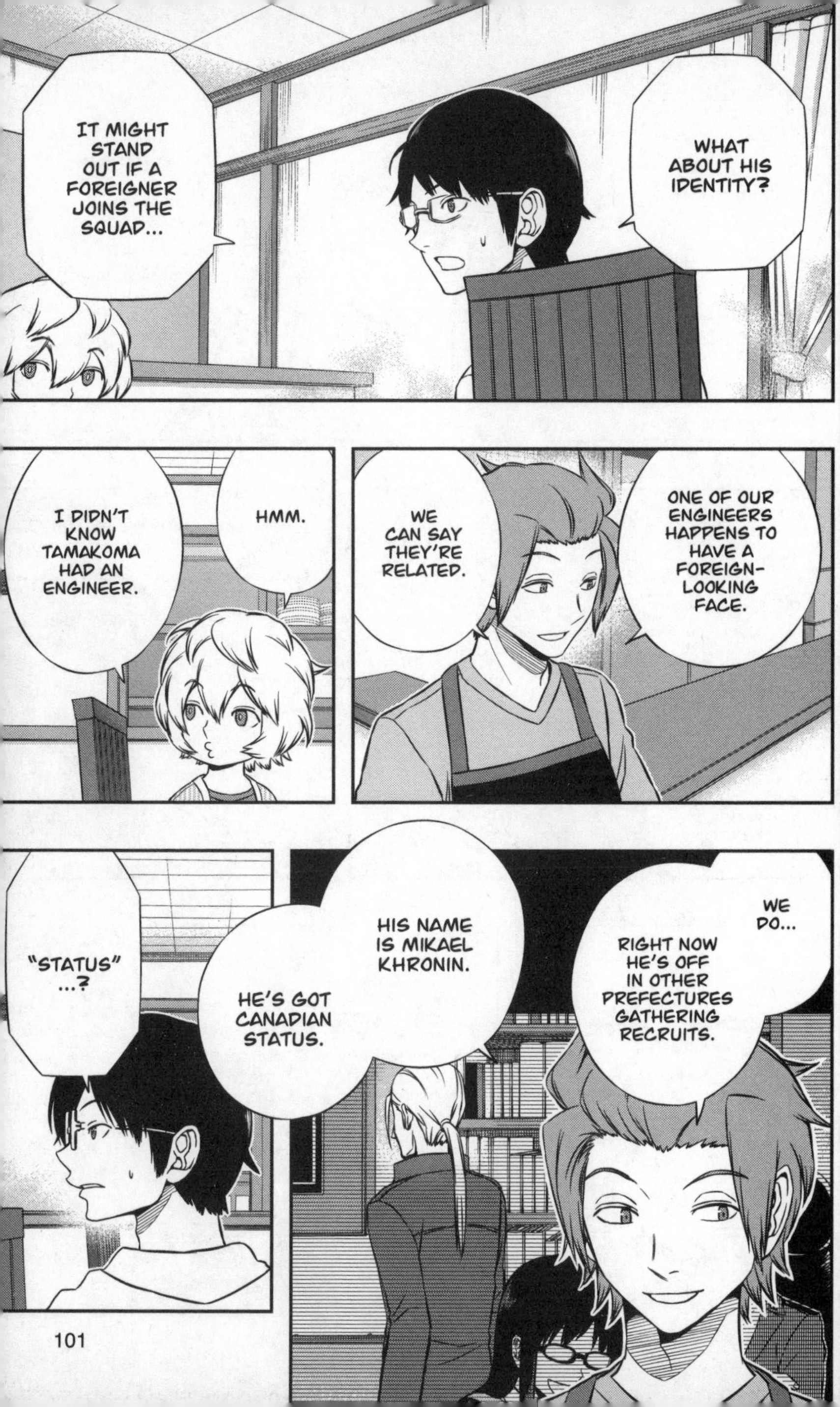
WHAT ABOUT HIS IDENTITY?
IT MIGHT STAND OUT IF A FOREIGNER JOINS THE SQUAD...
ONE OF OUR ENGINEERS HAPPENS TO HAVE A FOREIGN-LOOKING FACE.
WE CAN SAY THEY'RE RELATED.
HMM.
I DIDN'T KNOW TAMAKOMA HAD AN ENGINEER.
WE DO...
RIGHT NOW HE'S OFF IN OTHER PREFECTURES GATHERING RECRUITS.
HIS NAME IS MIKAEL KHRONIN.
HE'S GOT CANADIAN STATUS.
"STATUS" ...?

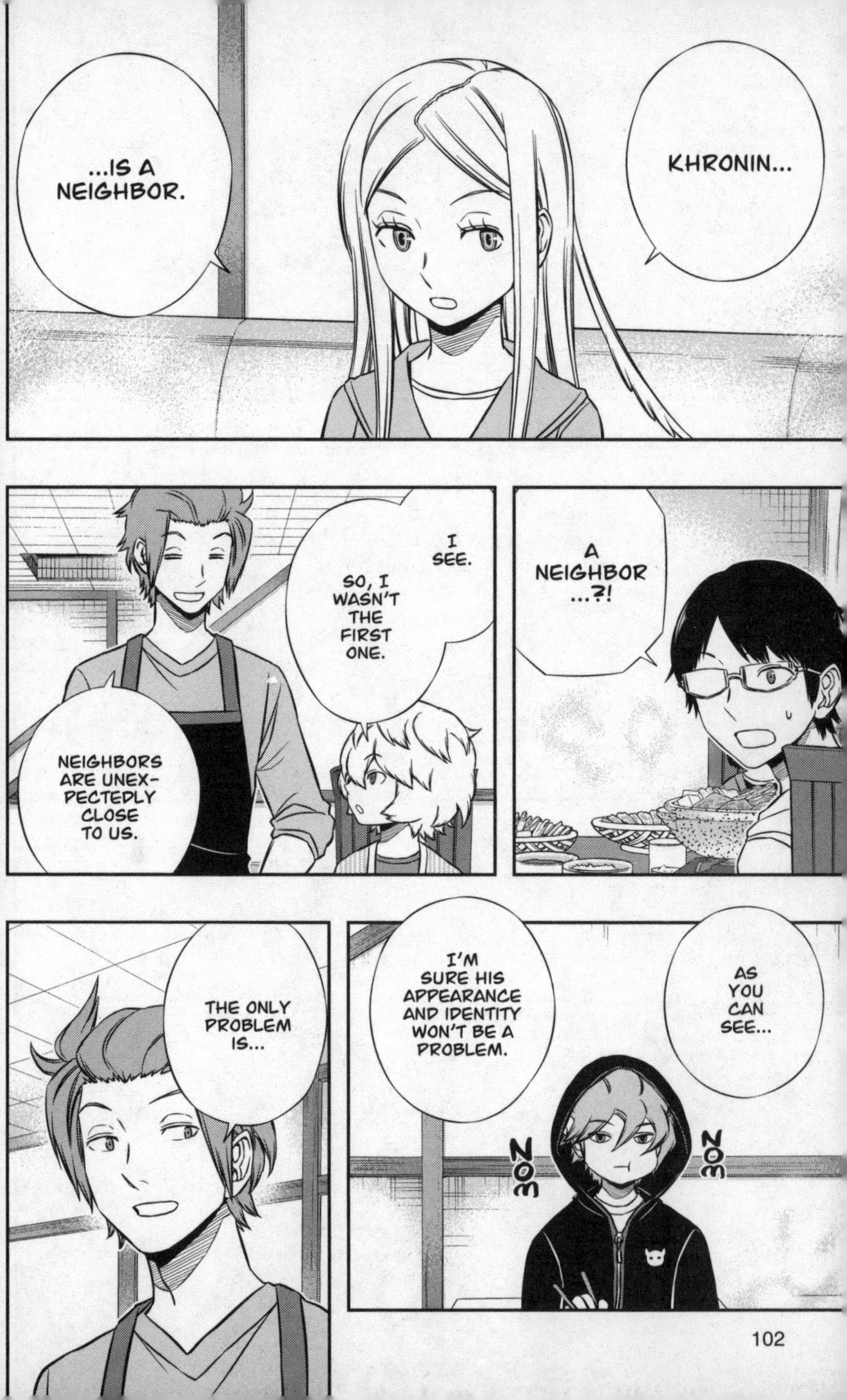
KHRONIN...
...IS A NEIGHBOR.
A NEIGHBOR ...?!
I SEE.
SO, I WASN'T THE FIRST ONE.
NEIGHBORS ARE UNEXPECTEDLY CLOSE TO US.
AS YOU CAN SEE...
I'M SURE HIS APPEARANCE AND IDENTITY WON'T BE A PROBLEM.
NOM
NOM
THE ONLY PROBLEM IS...

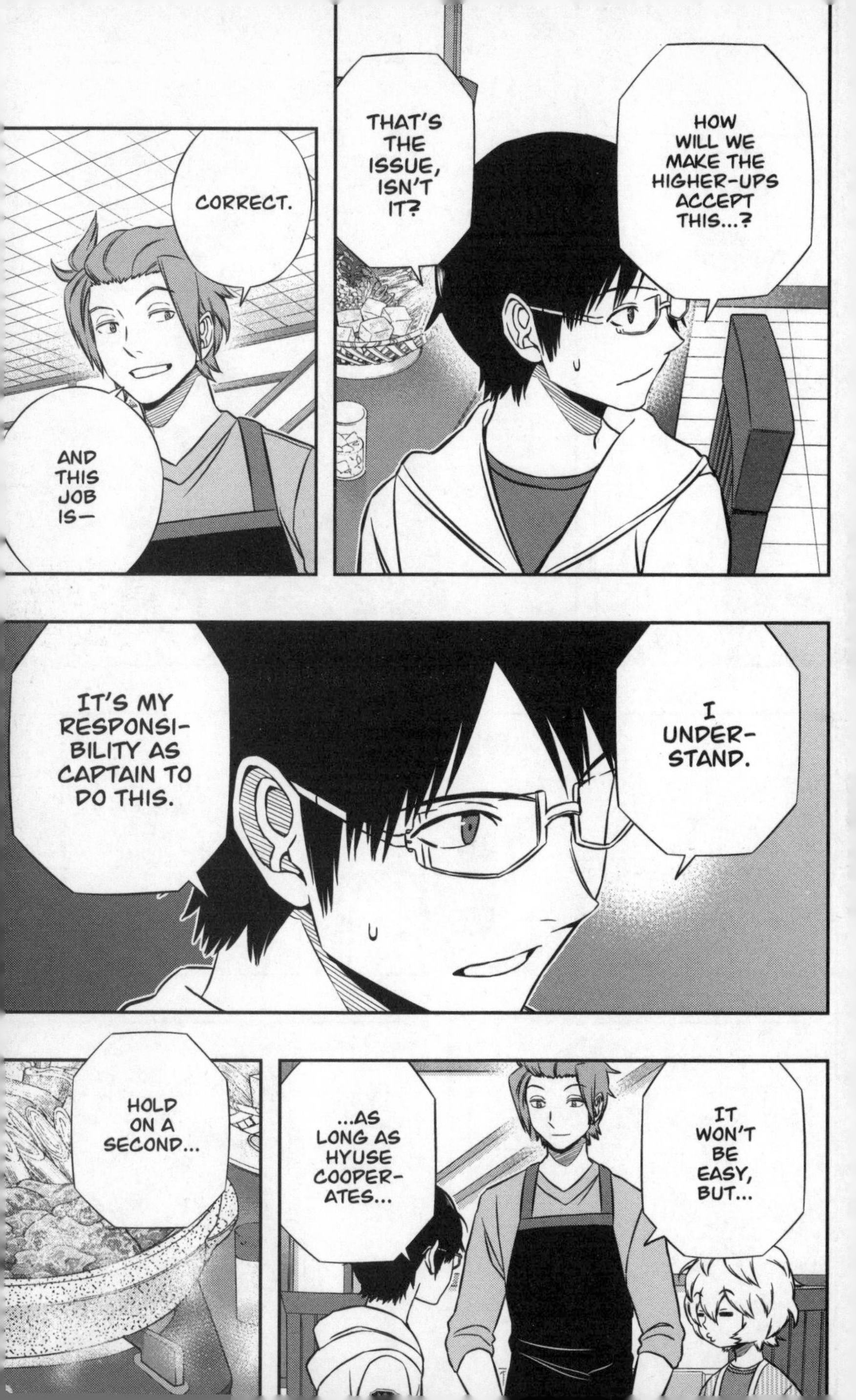
HOW WILL WE MAKE THE HIGHER-UPS ACCEPT THIS...?
THAT'S THE ISSUE, ISN'T IT?
CORRECT.
AND THIS JOB IS—
I UNDERSTAND.
IT'S MY RESPONSIBILITY AS CAPTAIN TO DO THIS.
IT WON'T BE EASY, BUT...
...AS LONG AS HYUSE COOPERATES...
HOLD ON A SECOND...

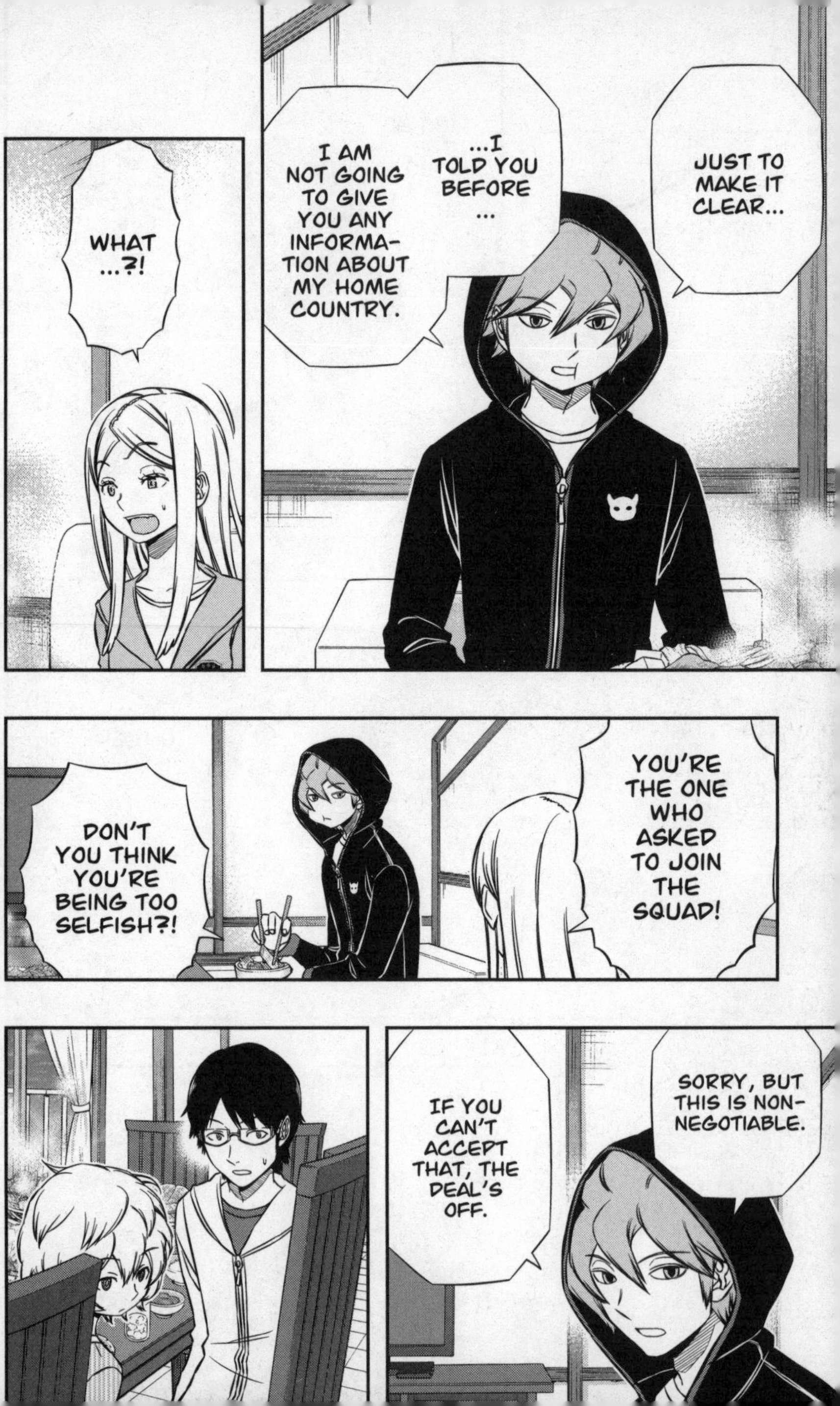
JUST TO MAKE IT CLEAR...
...I TOLD YOU BEFORE ...
I AM NOT GOING TO GIVE YOU ANY INFORMATION ABOUT MY HOME COUNTRY.
WHAT ...?!
YOU'RE THE ONE WHO ASKED TO JOIN THE SQUAD!
DON'T YOU THINK YOU'RE BEING TOO SELFISH?!
SORRY, BUT THIS IS NON-NEGOTIABLE.
IF YOU CAN'T ACCEPT THAT, THE DEAL'S OFF.

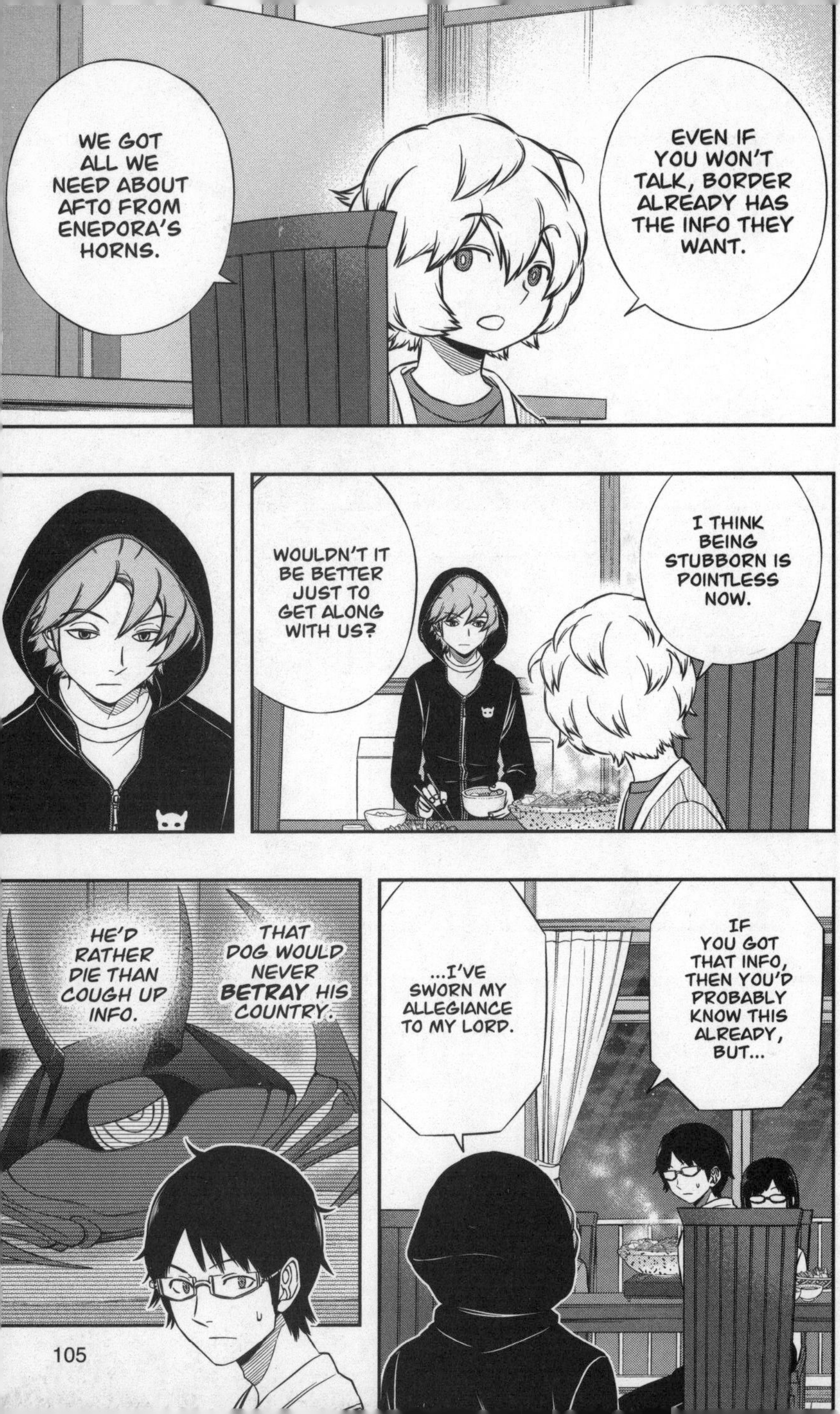
EVEN IF YOU WON'T TALK, BORDER ALREADY HAS THE INFO THEY WANT.
WE GOT ALL WE NEED ABOUT AFTO FROM ENEDORA'S HORNS.
I THINK BEING STUBBORN IS POINTLESS NOW.
WOULDN'T IT BE BETTER JUST TO GET ALONG WITH US?
IF YOU GOT THAT INFO, THEN YOU'D PROBABLY KNOW THIS ALREADY, BUT...
...I'VE SWORN MY ALLEGIANCE TO MY LORD.
THAT DOG WOULD NEVER **BETRAY** HIS COUNTRY.
HE'D RATHER DIE THAN COUGH UP INFO.

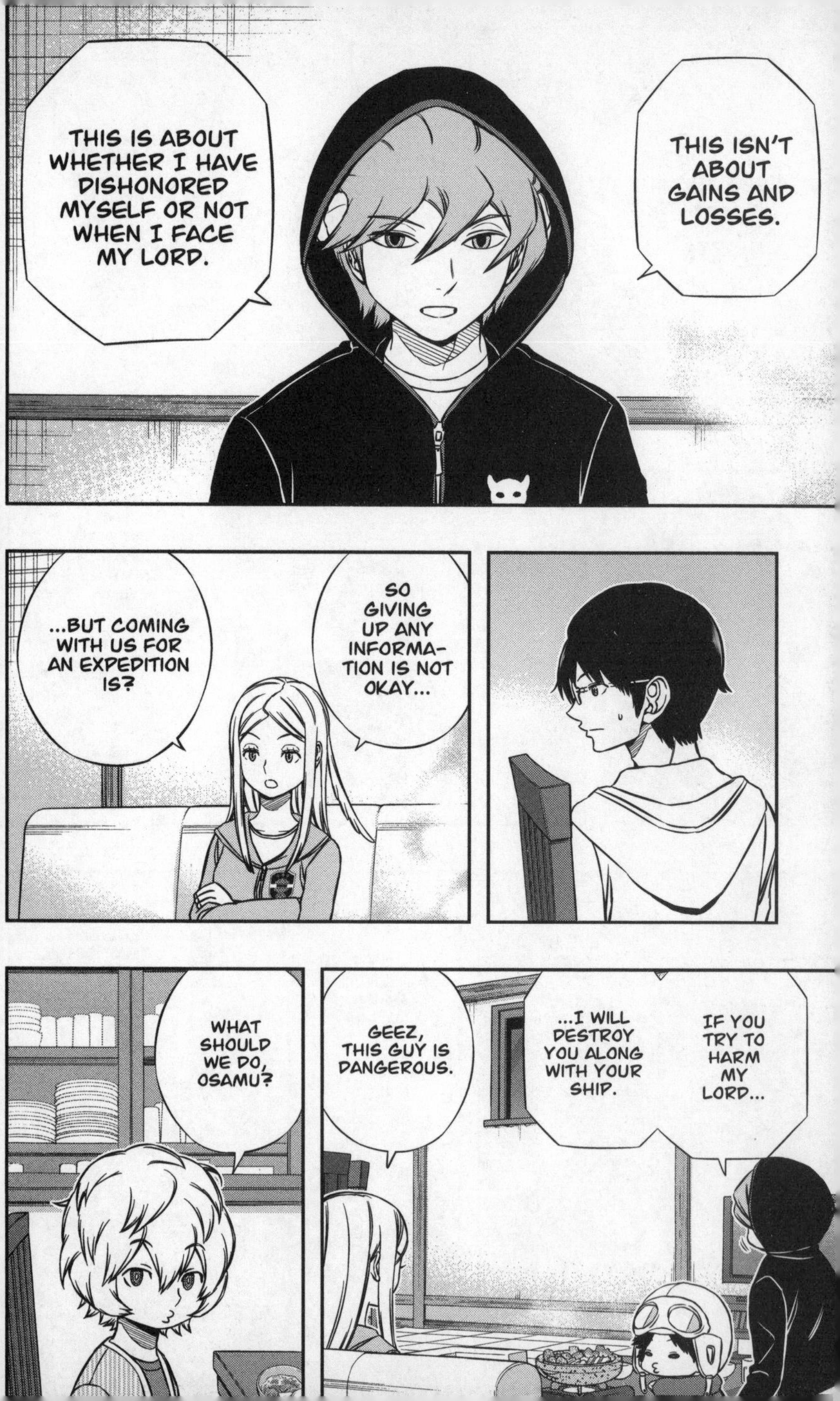
THIS ISN'T ABOUT GAINS AND LOSSES.
THIS IS ABOUT WHETHER I HAVE DISHONORED MYSELF OR NOT WHEN I FACE MY LORD.
SO GIVING UP ANY INFORMATION IS NOT OKAY...
...BUT COMING WITH US FOR AN EXPEDITION IS?
IF YOU TRY TO HARM MY LORD...
...I WILL DESTROY YOU ALONG WITH YOUR SHIP.
GEEZ, THIS GUY IS DANGEROUS.
WHAT SHOULD WE DO, OSAMU?

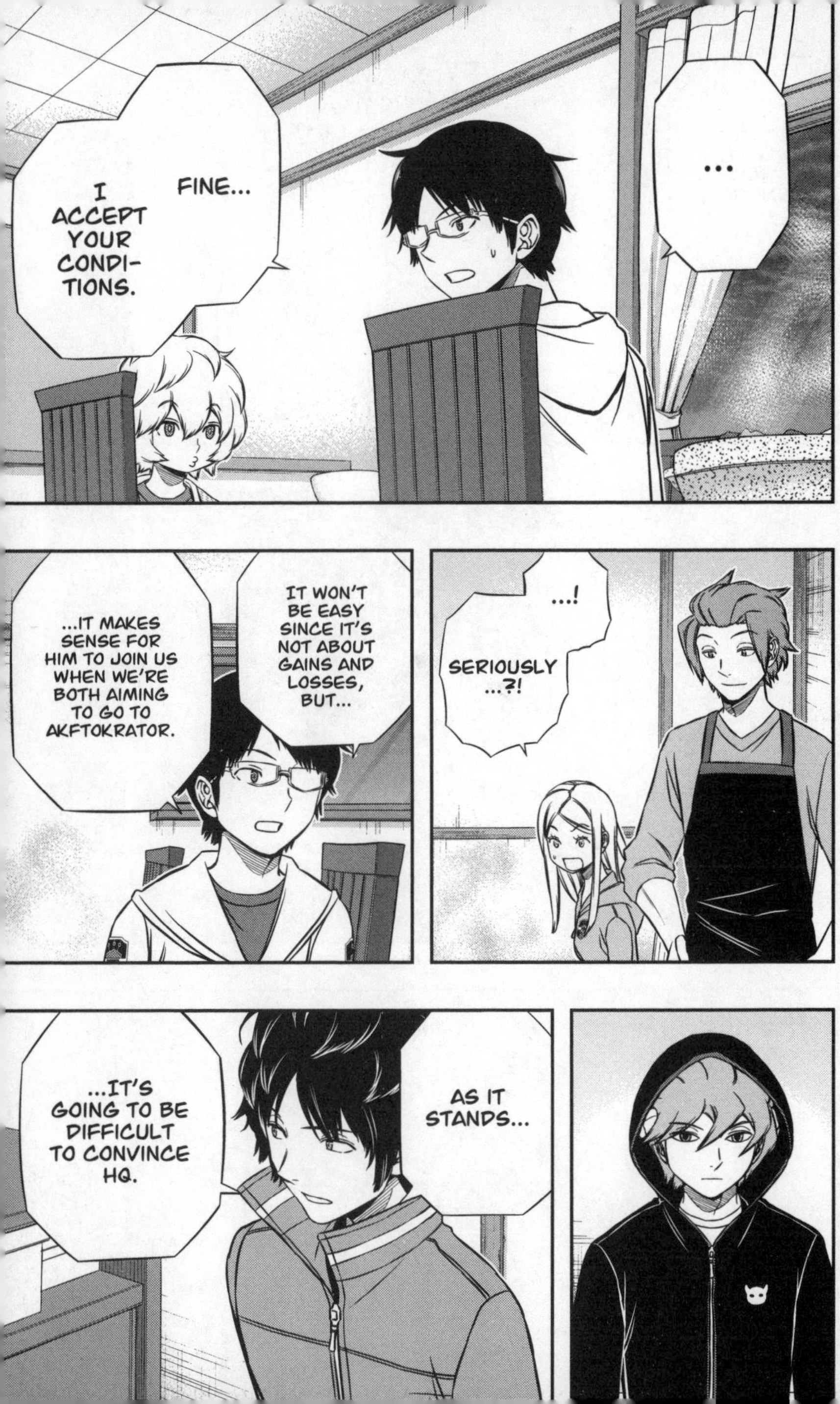
...
FINE...
I ACCEPT YOUR CONDITIONS.
...!
SERIOUSLY ...?!
IT WON'T BE EASY SINCE IT'S NOT ABOUT GAINS AND LOSSES, BUT...
...IT MAKES SENSE FOR HIM TO JOIN US WHEN WE'RE BOTH AIMING TO GO TO AKFTOKRATOR.
AS IT STANDS...
...IT'S GOING TO BE DIFFICULT TO CONVINCE HQ.

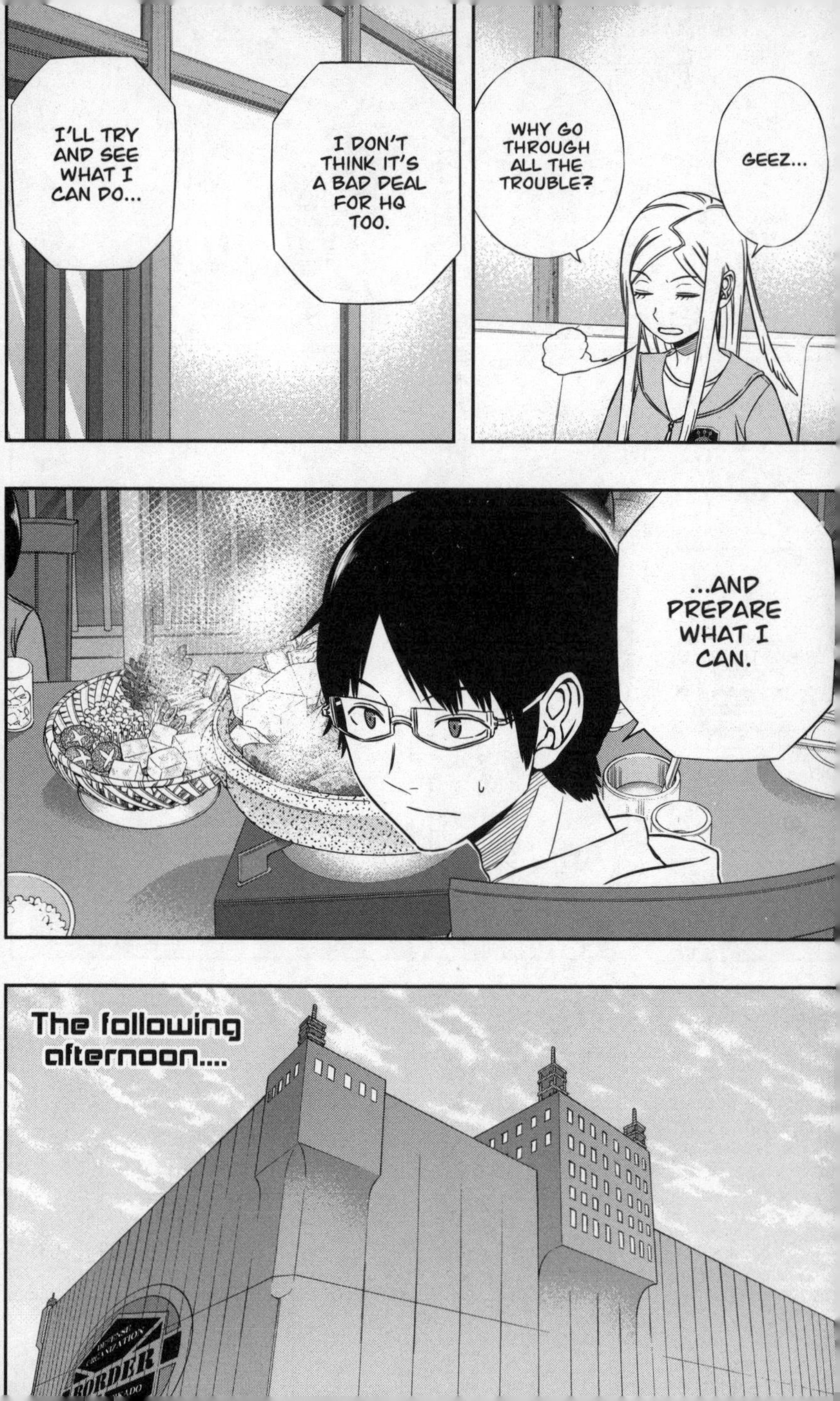
GEEZ...
WHY GO THROUGH ALL THE TROUBLE?
I DON'T THINK IT'S A BAD DEAL FOR HQ TOO.
I'LL TRY AND SEE WHAT I CAN DO...
...AND PREPARE WHAT I CAN.
The following afternoon....
BORDER

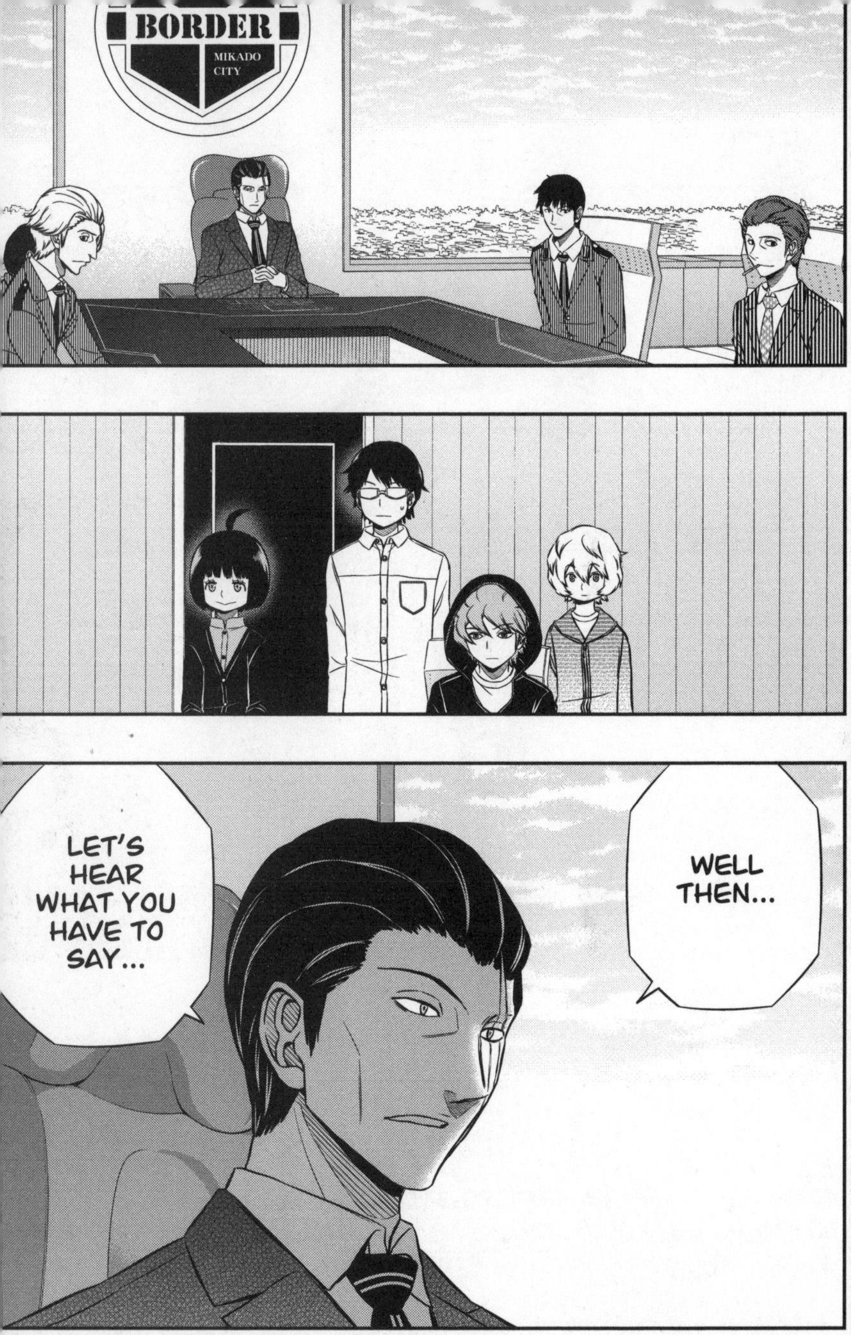
BORDER
MIKADO CITY
WELL THEN...
LET'S HEAR WHAT YOU HAVE TO SAY...

■ *Weekly Shonen Jump* 2016 36-37 Combined Issue

A drawing for *Weekly Shonen Jump*'s Combined Issue cover. The theme is "Yuma trying to come up with a betting plan." It's hard to tell, but he's wearing a tailcoat.

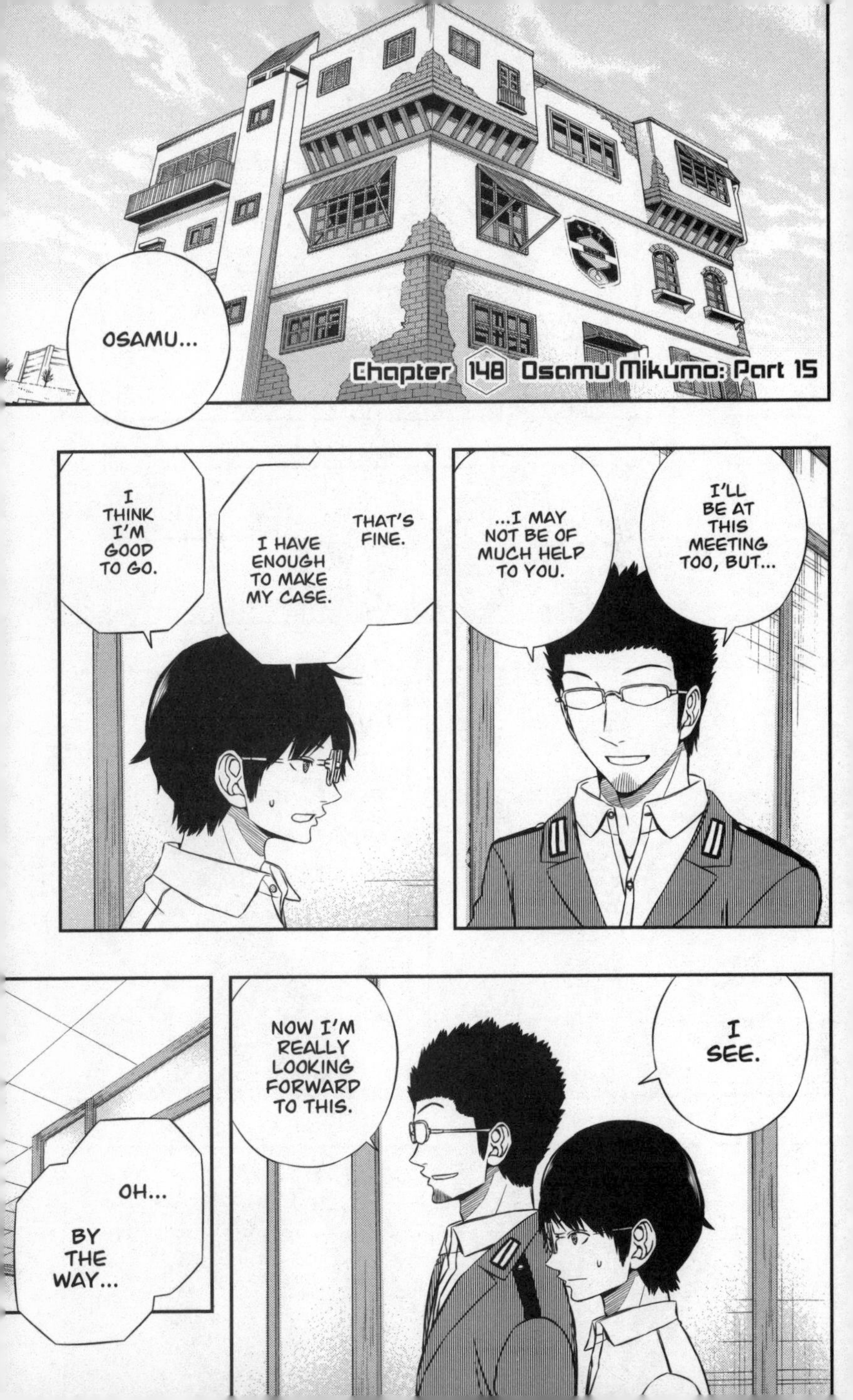
Chapter 148 Osamu Mikumo: Part 15
OSAMU...
I'LL BE AT THIS MEETING TOO, BUT...
...I MAY NOT BE OF MUCH HELP TO YOU.
THAT'S FINE.
I HAVE ENOUGH TO MAKE MY CASE.
I THINK I'M GOOD TO GO.
I SEE.
NOW I'M REALLY LOOKING FORWARD TO THIS.
OH...
BY THE WAY...

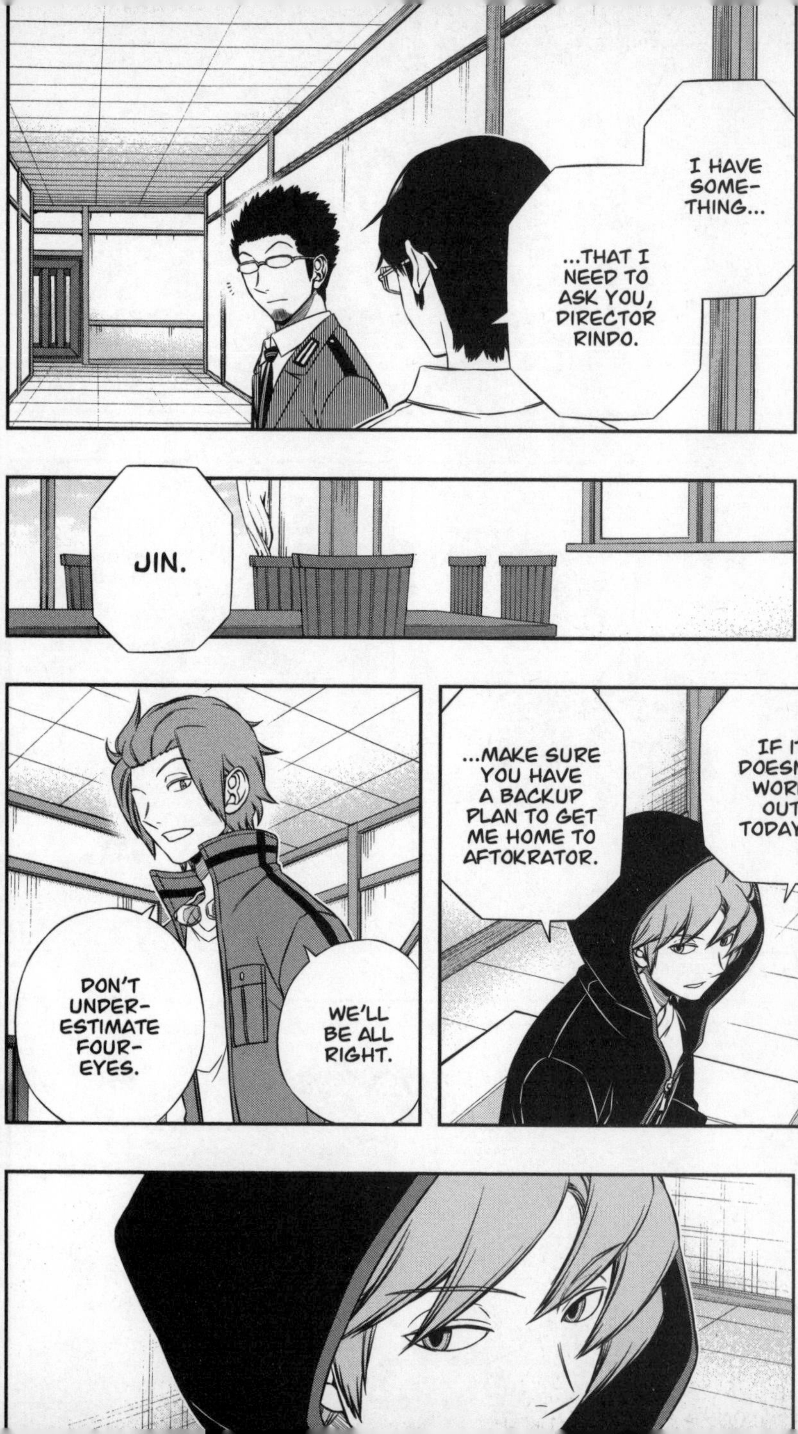
I HAVE SOMETHING...
...THAT I NEED TO ASK YOU, DIRECTOR RINDO.
JIN.
IF IT DOESN'T WORK OUT TODAY...
...MAKE SURE YOU HAVE A BACKUP PLAN TO GET ME HOME TO AFTOKRATOR.
WE'LL BE ALL RIGHT.
DON'T UNDER-ESTIMATE FOUR-EYES.

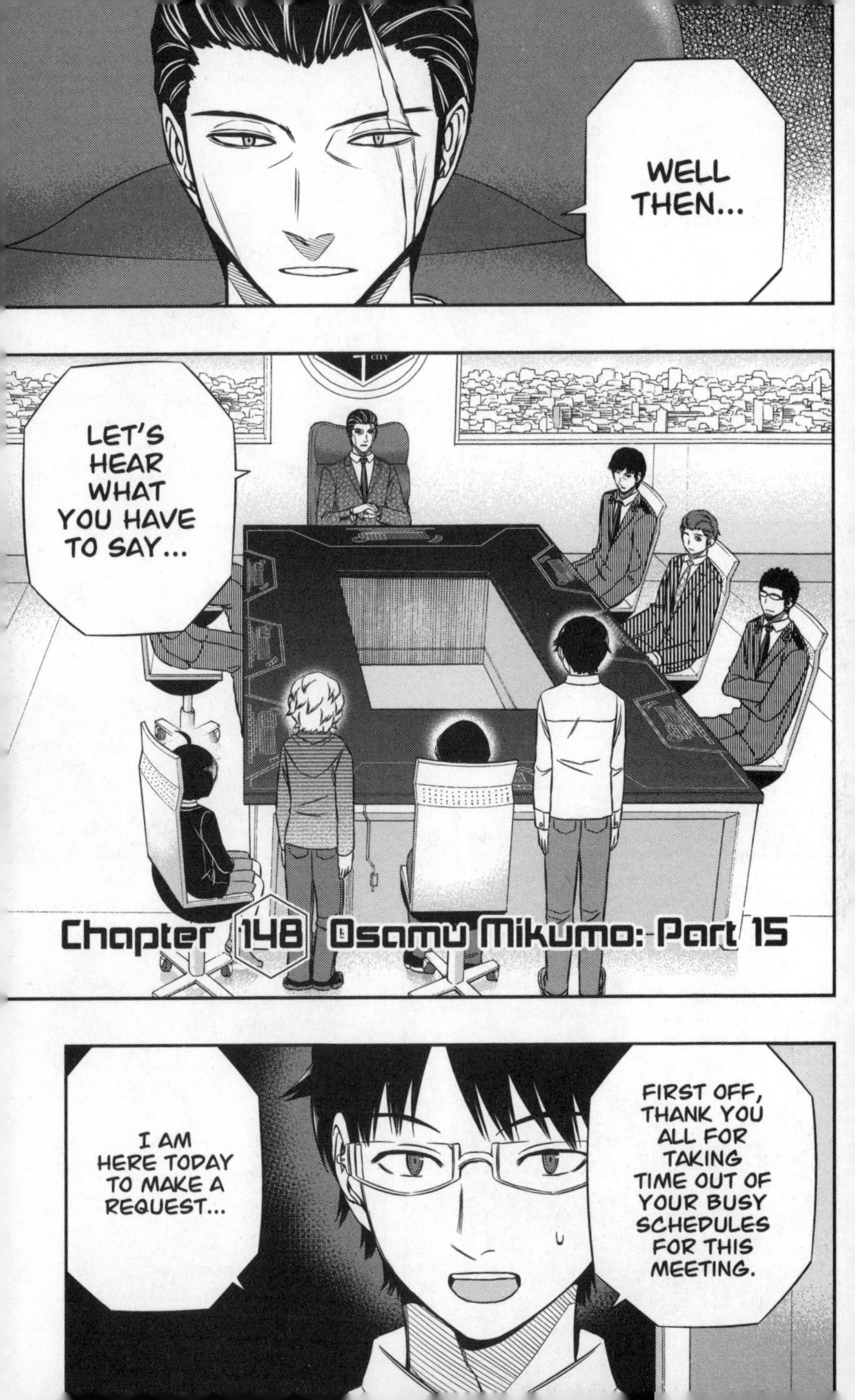
WELL THEN...
LET'S HEAR WHAT YOU HAVE TO SAY...
Chapter 148 Osamu Mikumo: Part 15
FIRST OFF, THANK YOU ALL FOR TAKING TIME OUT OF YOUR BUSY SCHEDULES FOR THIS MEETING.
I AM HERE TODAY TO MAKE A REQUEST...

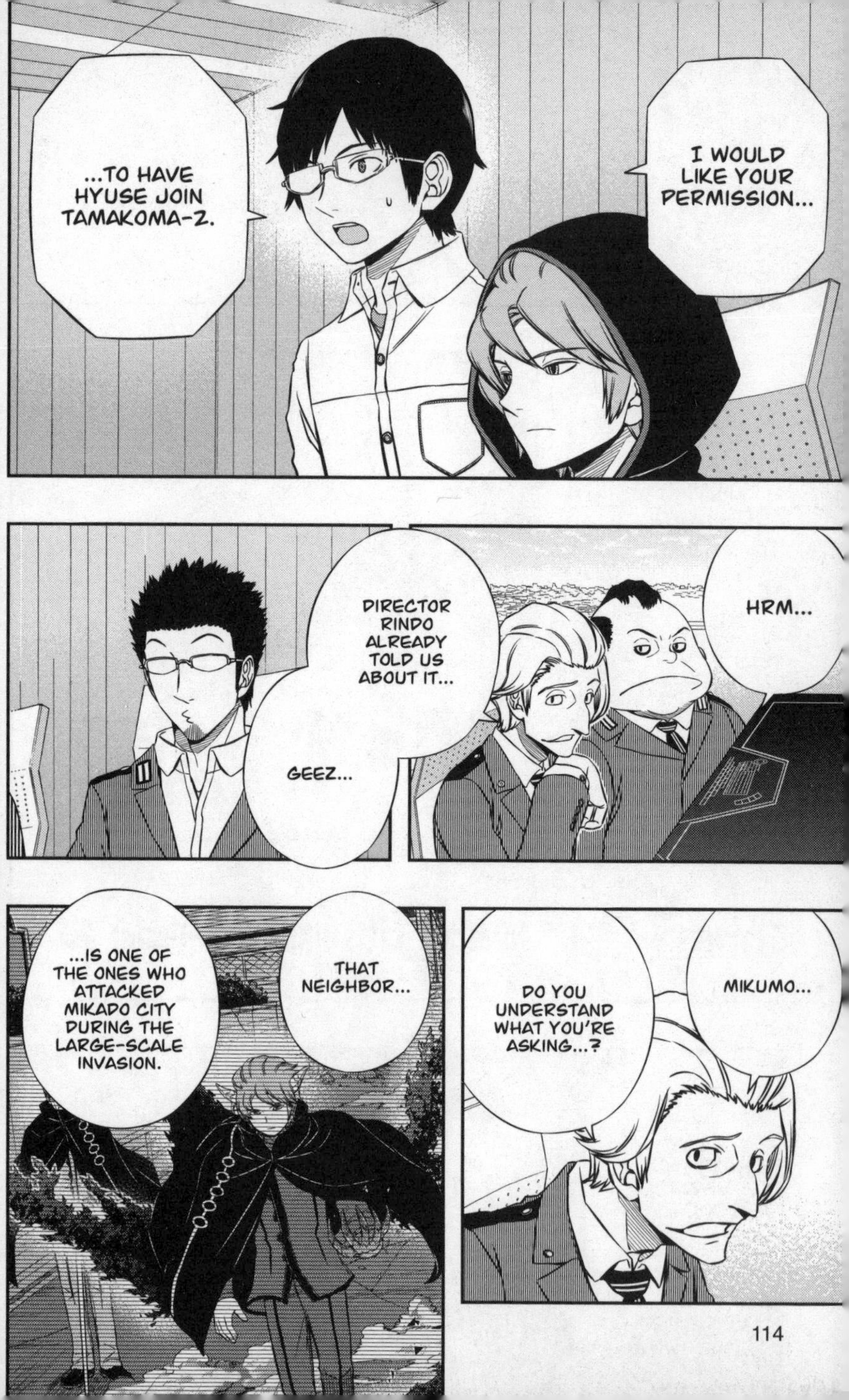
I WOULD LIKE YOUR PERMISSION...
...TO HAVE HYUSE JOIN TAMAKOMA-2.
HRM...
DIRECTOR RINDO ALREADY TOLD US ABOUT IT...
GEEZ...
MIKUMO...
DO YOU UNDERSTAND WHAT YOU'RE ASKING...?
THAT NEIGHBOR...
...IS ONE OF THE ONES WHO ATTACKED MIKADO CITY DURING THE LARGE-SCALE INVASION.

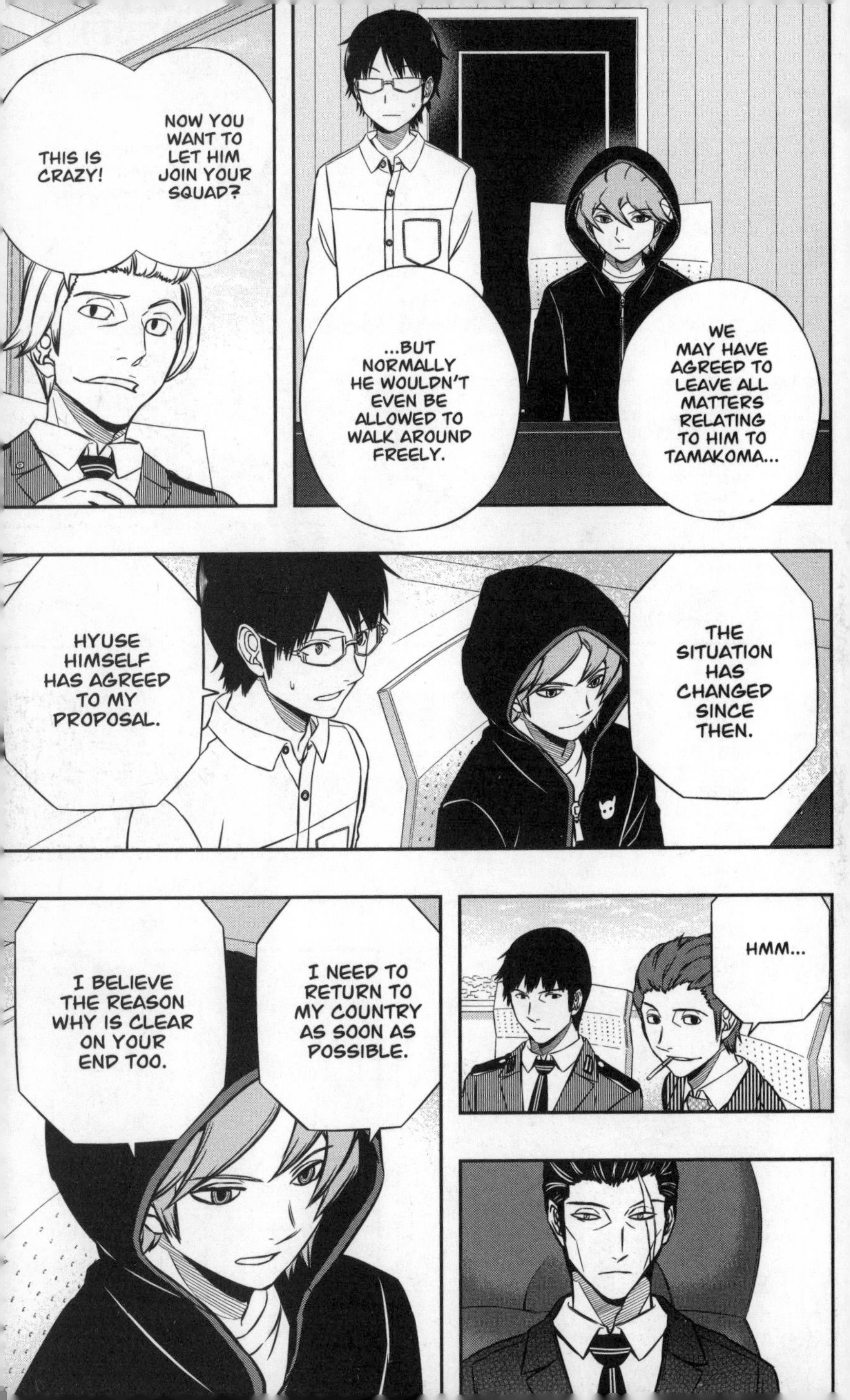
WE MAY HAVE AGREED TO LEAVE ALL MATTERS RELATING TO HIM TO TAMAKOMA...
...BUT NORMALLY HE WOULDN'T EVEN BE ALLOWED TO WALK AROUND FREELY.
NOW YOU WANT TO LET HIM JOIN YOUR SQUAD?
THIS IS CRAZY!
THE SITUATION HAS CHANGED SINCE THEN.
HYUSE HIMSELF HAS AGREED TO MY PROPOSAL.
HMM...
I NEED TO RETURN TO MY COUNTRY AS SOON AS POSSIBLE.
I BELIEVE THE REASON WHY IS CLEAR ON YOUR END TOO.

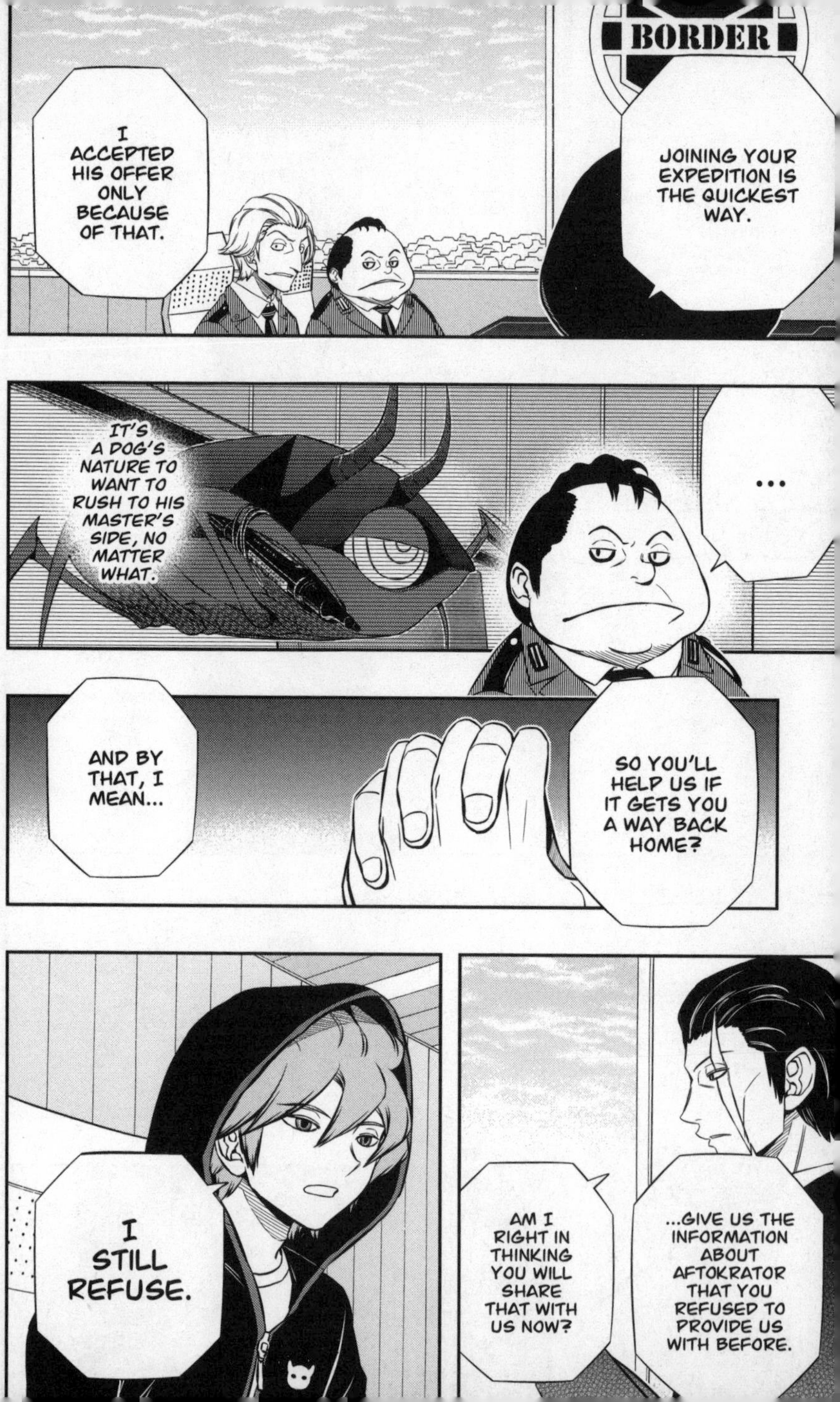
BORDER
JOINING YOUR EXPEDITION IS THE QUICKEST WAY.
I ACCEPTED HIS OFFER ONLY BECAUSE OF THAT.
...
IT'S A DOG'S NATURE TO WANT TO RUSH TO HIS MASTER'S SIDE, NO MATTER WHAT.
SO YOU'LL HELP US IF IT GETS YOU A WAY BACK HOME?
AND BY THAT, I MEAN...
...GIVE US THE INFORMATION ABOUT AFTOKRATOR THAT YOU REFUSED TO PROVIDE US WITH BEFORE.
AM I RIGHT IN THINKING YOU WILL SHARE THAT WITH US NOW?
I STILL REFUSE.

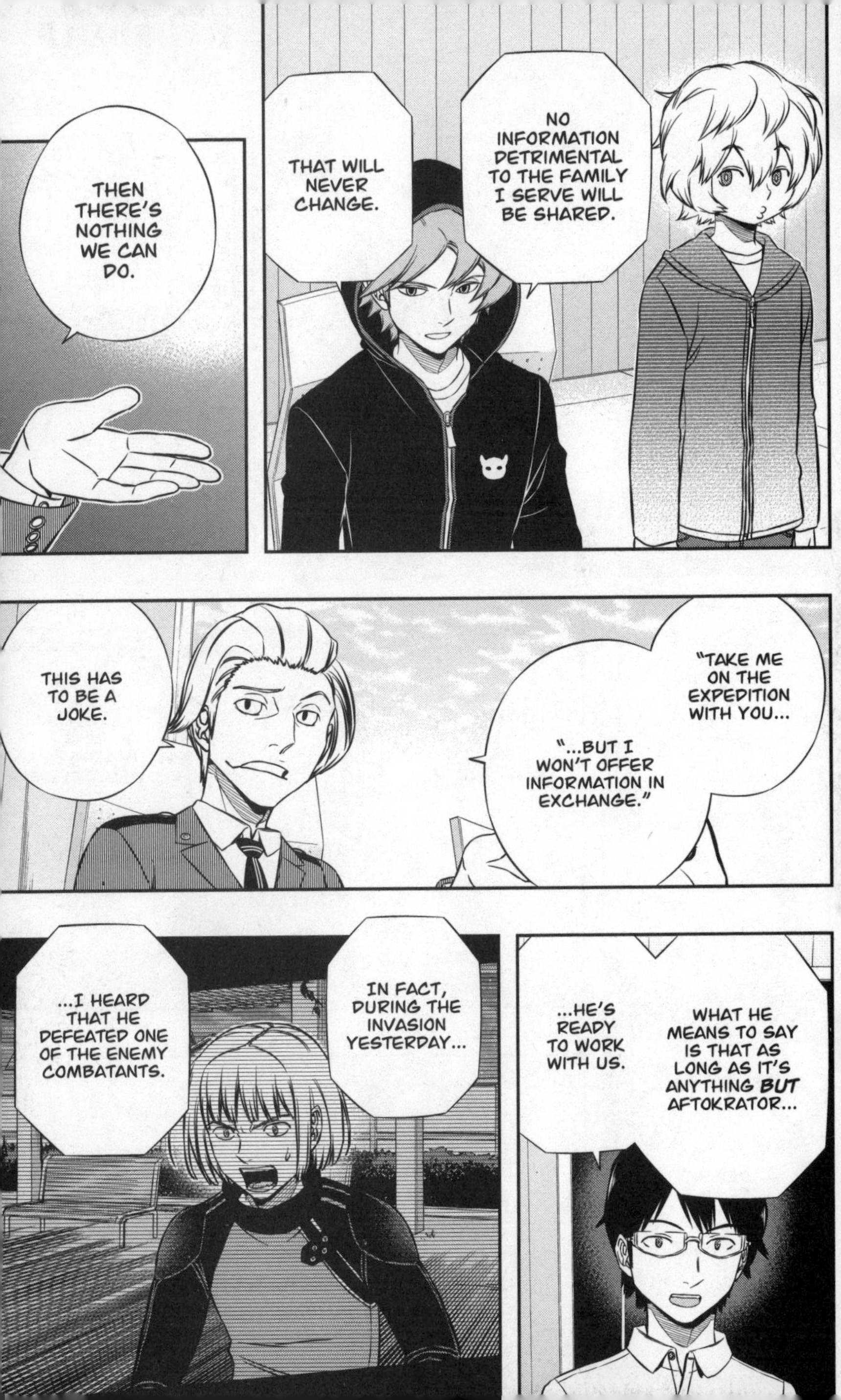
NO INFORMATION DETRIMENTAL TO THE FAMILY I SERVE WILL BE SHARED.
THAT WILL NEVER CHANGE.
THEN THERE'S NOTHING WE CAN DO.
"TAKE ME ON THE EXPEDITION WITH YOU...
"...BUT I WON'T OFFER INFORMATION IN EXCHANGE."
THIS HAS TO BE A JOKE.
WHAT HE MEANS TO SAY IS THAT AS LONG AS IT'S ANYTHING *BUT* AFTOKRATOR...
...HE'S READY TO WORK WITH US.
IN FACT, DURING THE INVASION YESTERDAY...
...I HEARD THAT HE DEFEATED ONE OF THE ENEMY COMBATANTS.

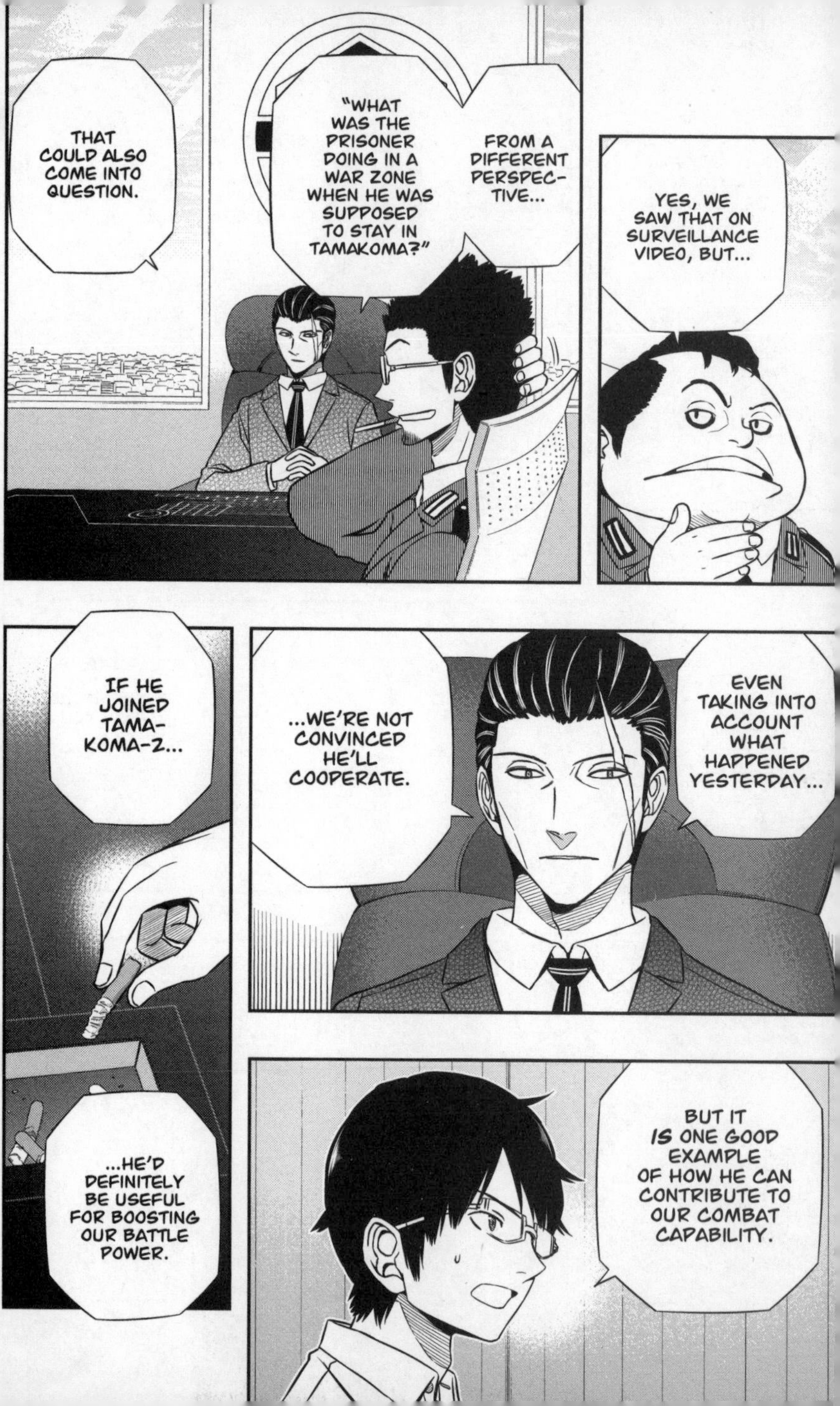
YES, WE SAW THAT ON SURVEILLANCE VIDEO, BUT...
FROM A DIFFERENT PERSPEC-TIVE...
"WHAT WAS THE PRISONER DOING IN A WAR ZONE WHEN HE WAS SUPPOSED TO STAY IN TAMAKOMA?"
THAT COULD ALSO COME INTO QUESTION.
EVEN TAKING INTO ACCOUNT WHAT HAPPENED YESTERDAY...
...WE'RE NOT CONVINCED HE'LL COOPERATE.
BUT IT *IS* ONE GOOD EXAMPLE OF HOW HE CAN CONTRIBUTE TO OUR COMBAT CAPABILITY.
IF HE JOINED TAMA-KOMA-2...
...HE'D DEFINITELY BE USEFUL FOR BOOSTING OUR BATTLE POWER.

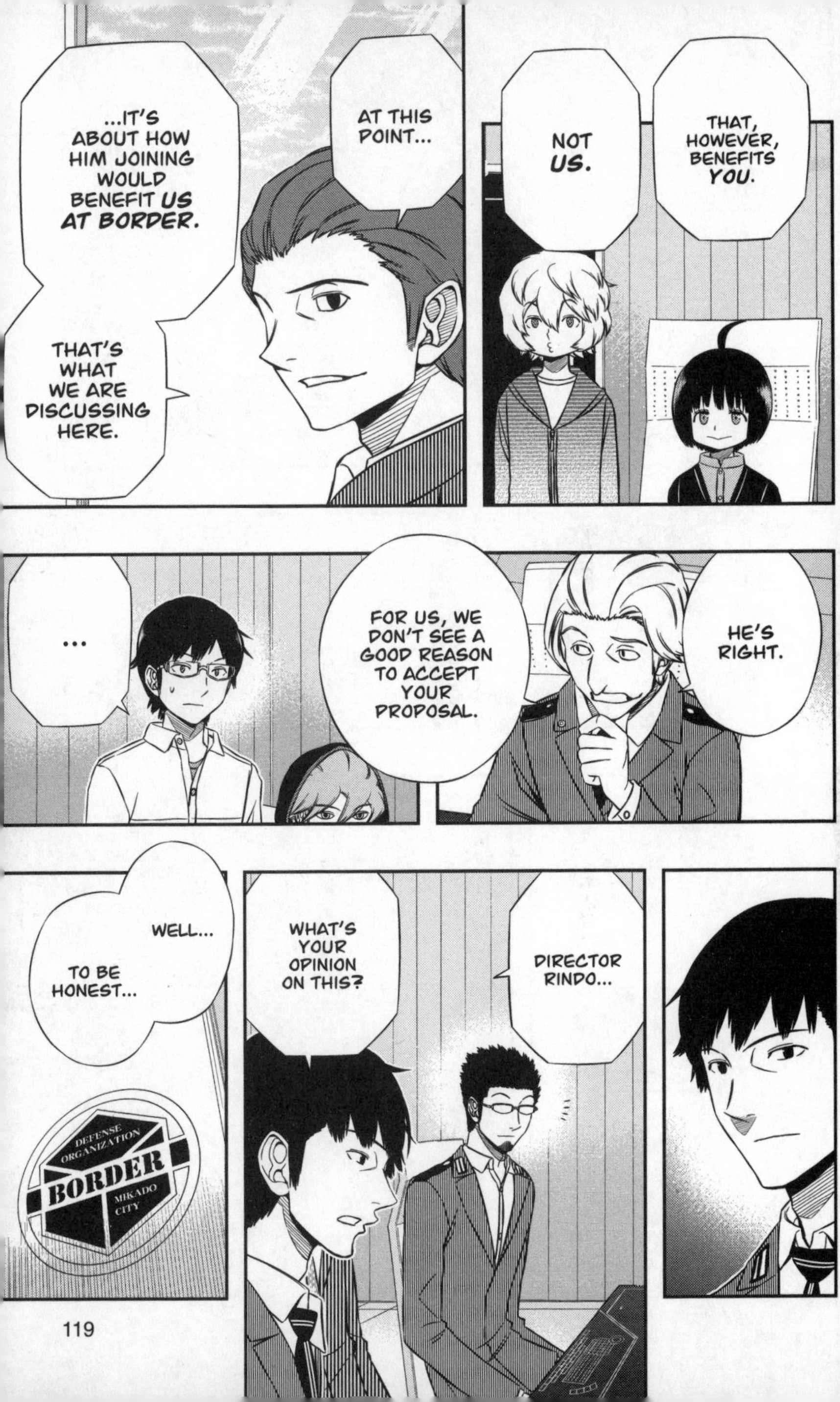
THAT, HOWEVER, BENEFITS YOU.
NOT US.
AT THIS POINT...
...IT'S ABOUT HOW HIM JOINING WOULD BENEFIT US AT BORDER.
THAT'S WHAT WE ARE DISCUSSING HERE.
HE'S RIGHT.
FOR US, WE DON'T SEE A GOOD REASON TO ACCEPT YOUR PROPOSAL.
...
DIRECTOR RINDO...
WHAT'S YOUR OPINION ON THIS?
WELL...
TO BE HONEST...
DEFENSE ORGANIZATION
BORDER
MIKADO CITY

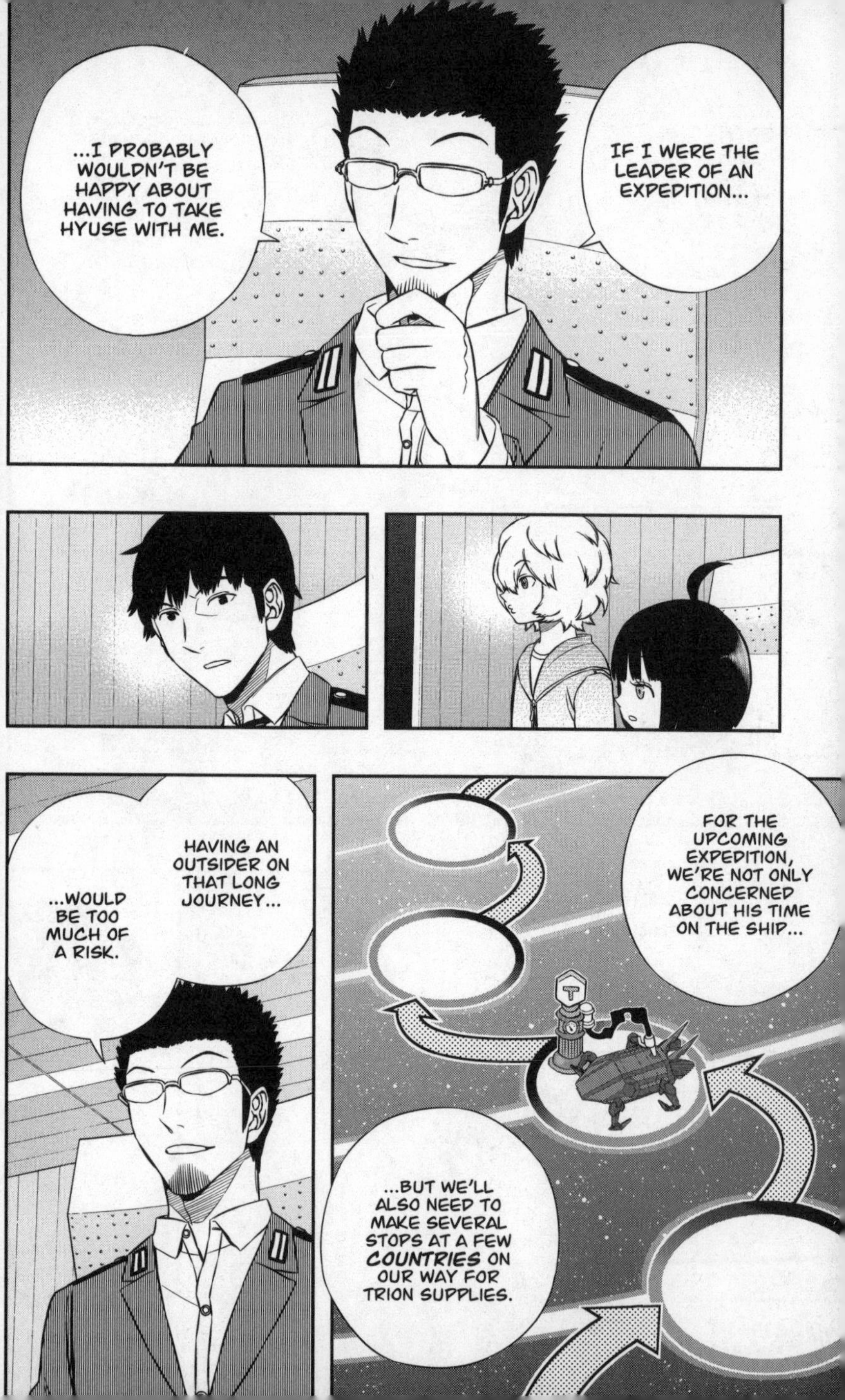
IF I WERE THE LEADER OF AN EXPEDITION...
...I PROBABLY WOULDN'T BE HAPPY ABOUT HAVING TO TAKE HYUSE WITH ME.
FOR THE UPCOMING EXPEDITION, WE'RE NOT ONLY CONCERNED ABOUT HIS TIME ON THE SHIP...
...BUT WE'LL ALSO NEED TO MAKE SEVERAL STOPS AT A FEW **COUNTRIES** ON OUR WAY FOR TRION SUPPLIES.
HAVING AN OUTSIDER ON THAT LONG JOURNEY...
...WOULD BE TOO MUCH OF A RISK.

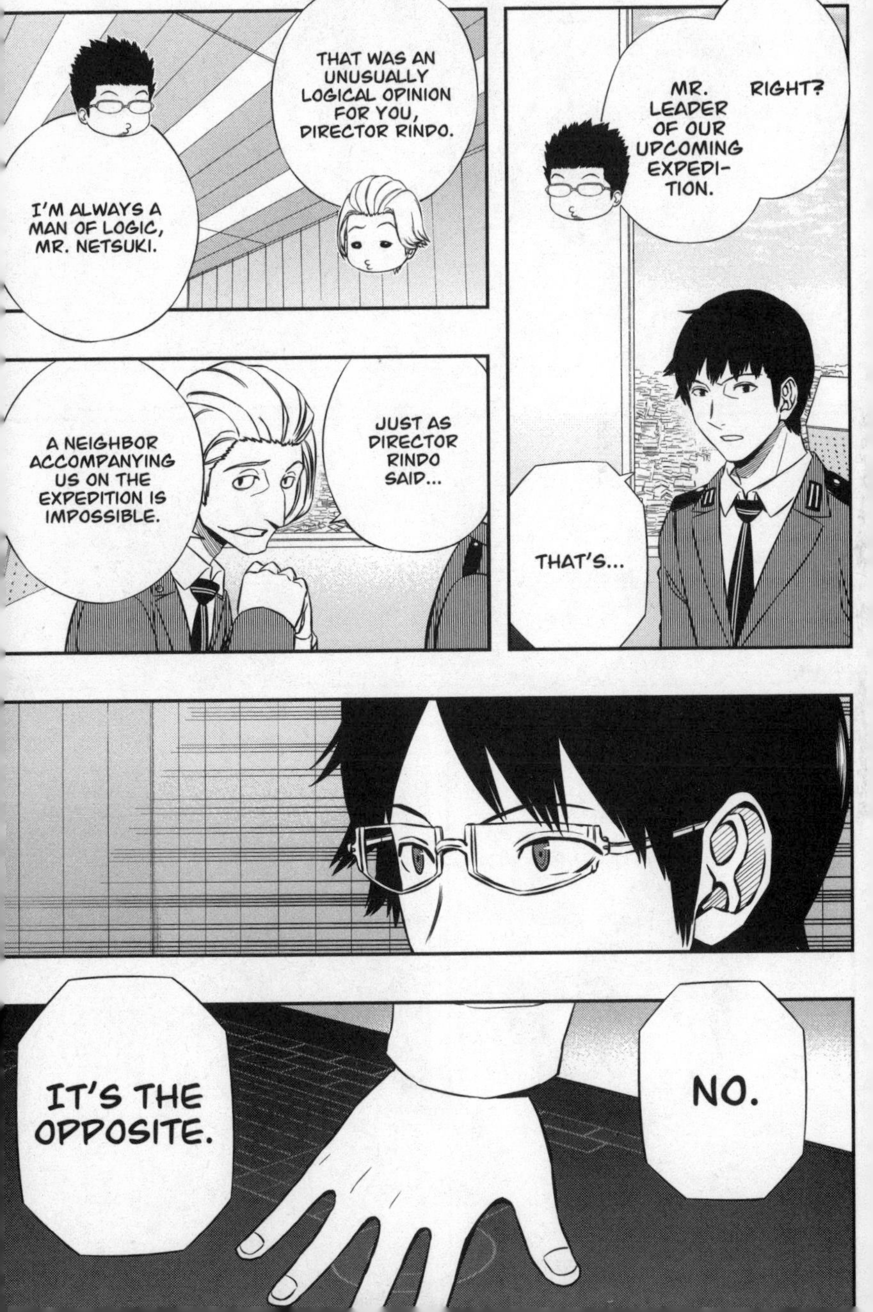
RIGHT? MR. LEADER OF OUR UPCOMING EXPEDITION.
THAT'S...
THAT WAS AN UNUSUALLY LOGICAL OPINION FOR YOU, DIRECTOR RINDO.
I'M ALWAYS A MAN OF LOGIC, MR. NETSUKI.
JUST AS DIRECTOR RINDO SAID...
A NEIGHBOR ACCOMPANYING US ON THE EXPEDITION IS IMPOSSIBLE.
NO.
IT'S THE OPPOSITE.

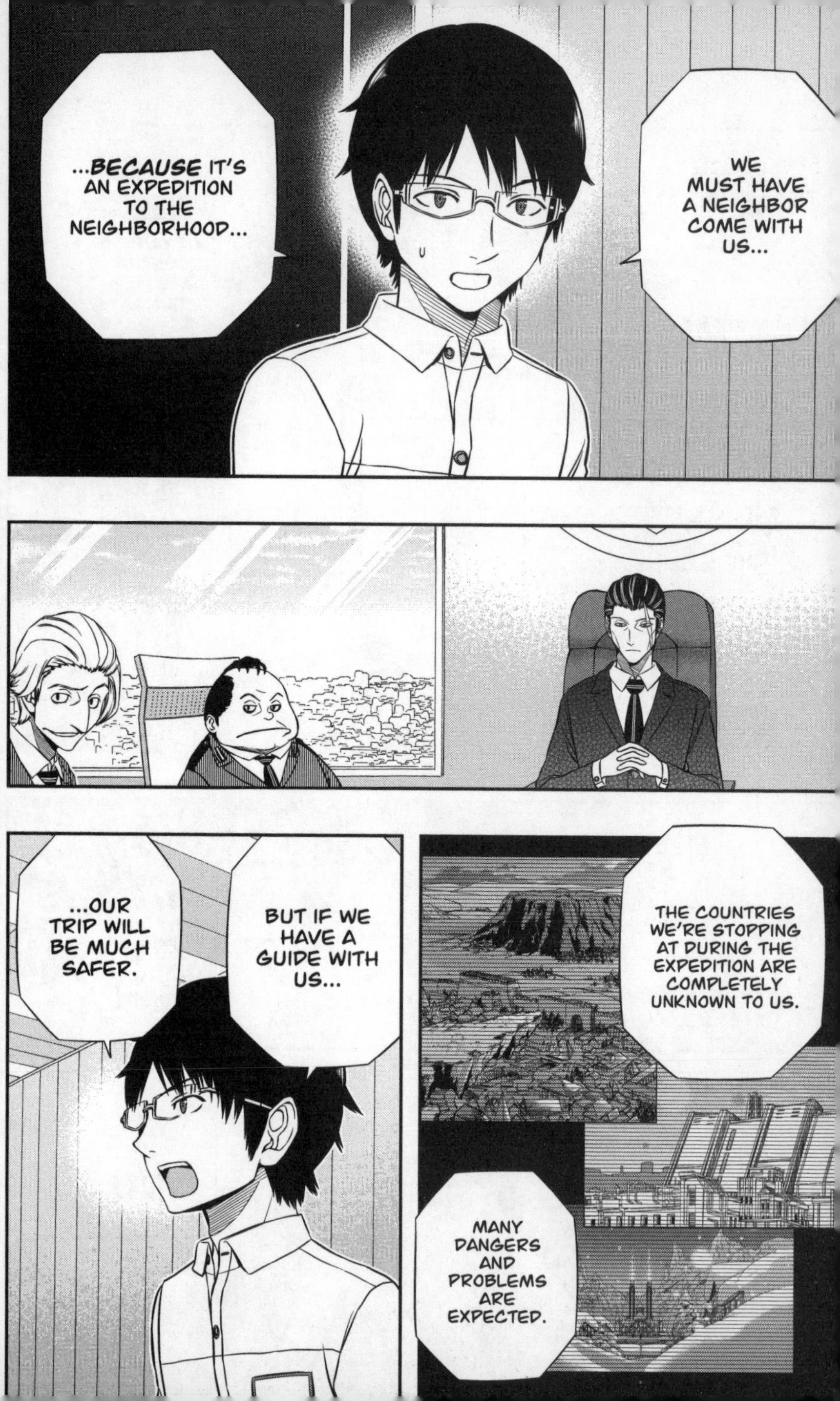
WE MUST HAVE A NEIGHBOR COME WITH US...
...BECAUSE IT'S AN EXPEDITION TO THE NEIGHBORHOOD...
THE COUNTRIES WE'RE STOPPING AT DURING THE EXPEDITION ARE COMPLETELY UNKNOWN TO US.
MANY DANGERS AND PROBLEMS ARE EXPECTED.
BUT IF WE HAVE A GUIDE WITH US...
...OUR TRIP WILL BE MUCH SAFER.

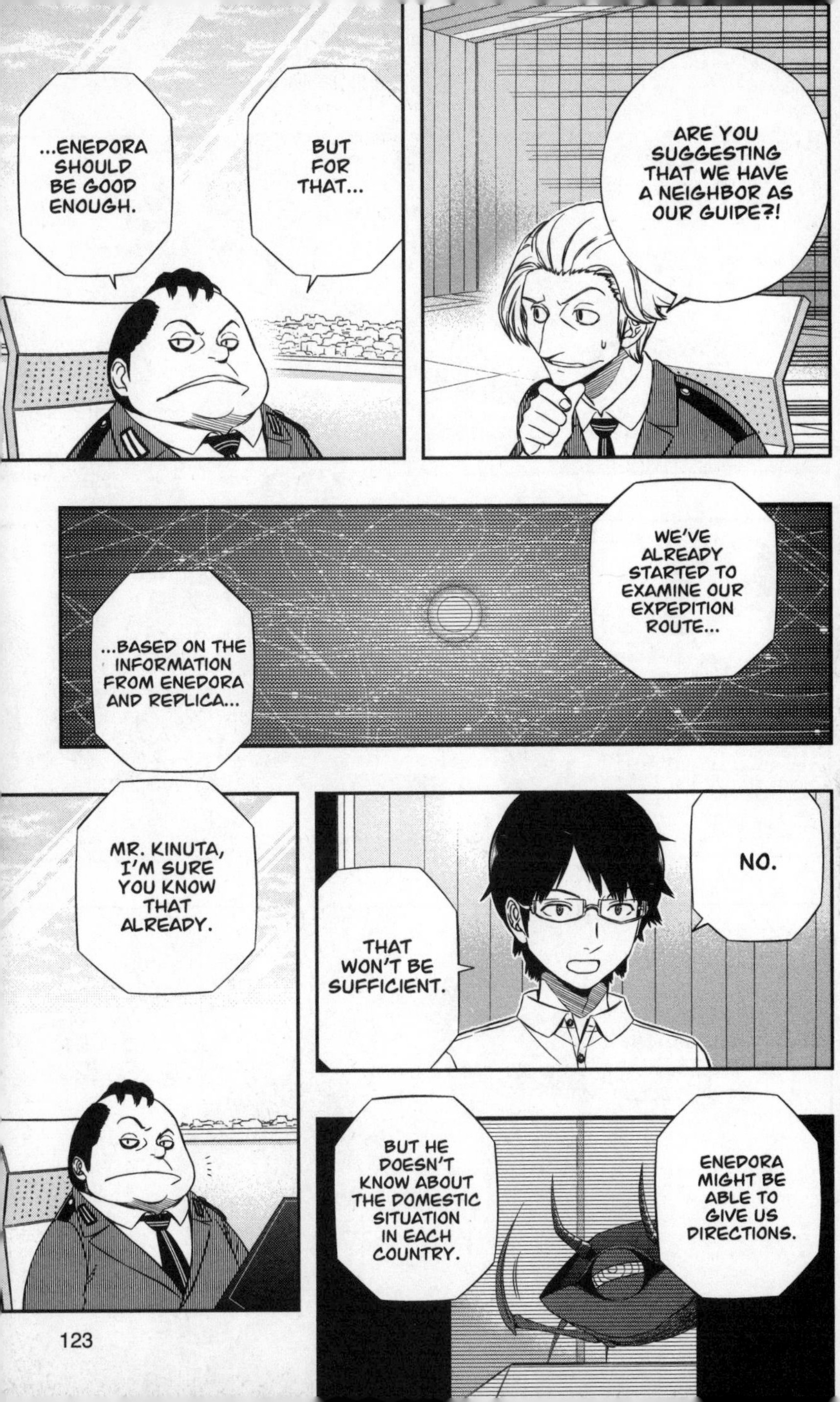

ARE YOU SUGGESTING THAT WE HAVE A NEIGHBOR AS OUR GUIDE?!
BUT FOR THAT...
...ENEDORA SHOULD BE GOOD ENOUGH.
WE'VE ALREADY STARTED TO EXAMINE OUR EXPEDITION ROUTE...
...BASED ON THE INFORMATION FROM ENEDORA AND REPLICA...
NO.
THAT WON'T BE SUFFICIENT.
ENEDORA MIGHT BE ABLE TO GIVE US DIRECTIONS.
BUT HE DOESN'T KNOW ABOUT THE DOMESTIC SITUATION IN EACH COUNTRY.
MR. KINUTA, I'M SURE YOU KNOW THAT ALREADY.

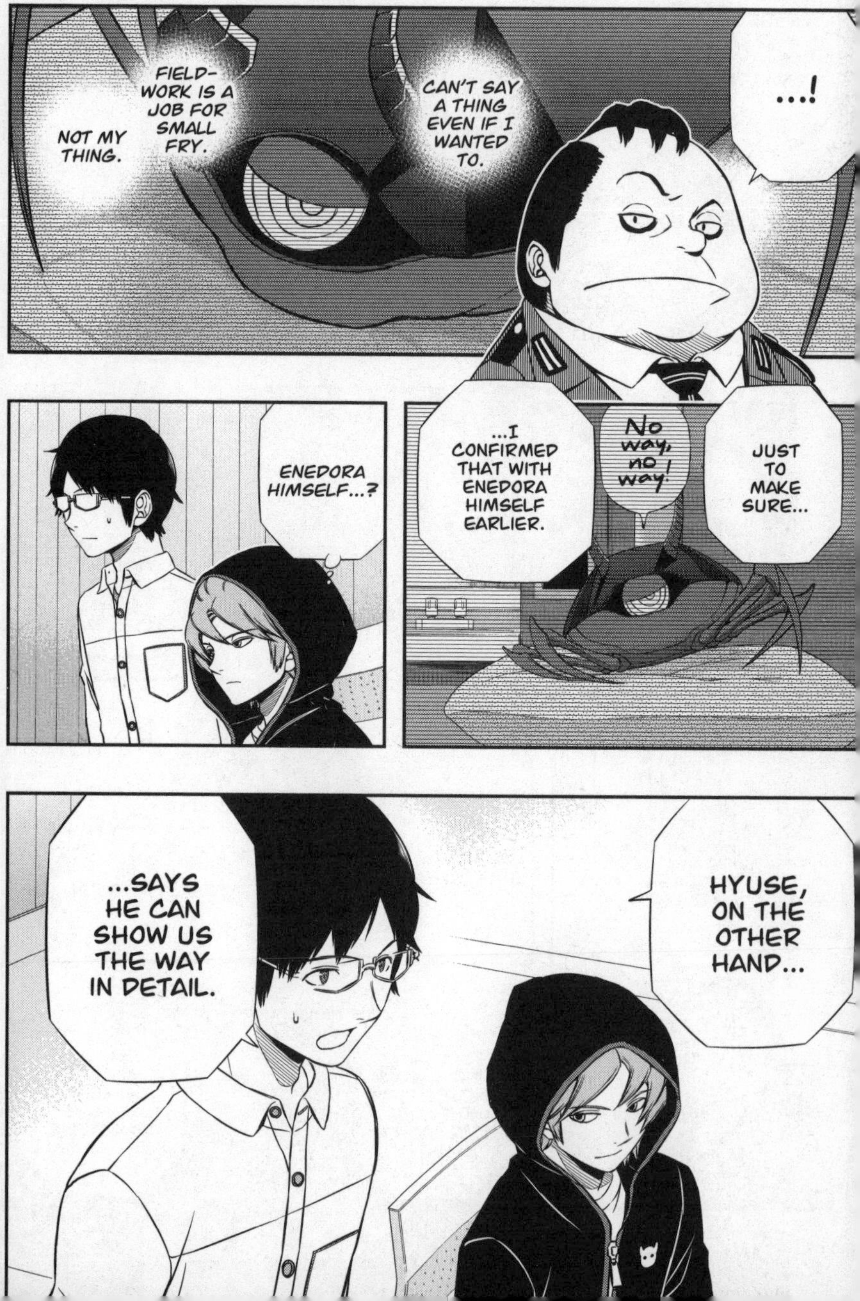
...!
CAN'T SAY A THING EVEN IF I WANTED TO.
FIELD-WORK IS A JOB FOR SMALL FRY.
NOT MY THING.
JUST TO MAKE SURE...
No way, no way!
...I CONFIRMED THAT WITH ENEDORA HIMSELF EARLIER.
ENEDORA HIMSELF...?
HYUSE, ON THE OTHER HAND...
...SAYS HE CAN SHOW US THE WAY IN DETAIL.

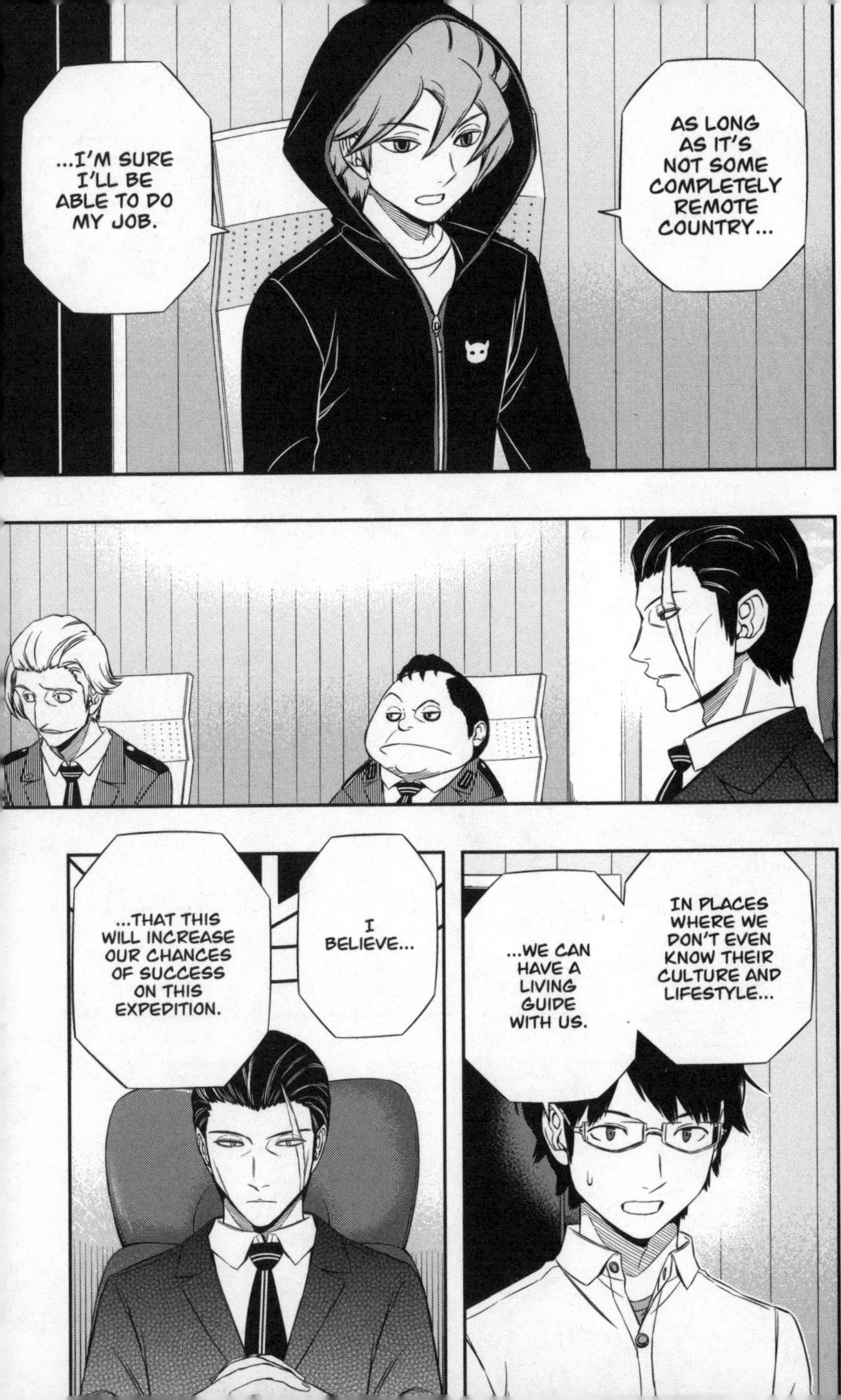
AS LONG AS IT'S NOT SOME COMPLETELY REMOTE COUNTRY...
...I'M SURE I'LL BE ABLE TO DO MY JOB.
IN PLACES WHERE WE DON'T EVEN KNOW THEIR CULTURE AND LIFESTYLE...
...WE CAN HAVE A LIVING GUIDE WITH US.
I BELIEVE...
...THAT THIS WILL INCREASE OUR CHANCES OF SUCCESS ON THIS EXPEDITION.

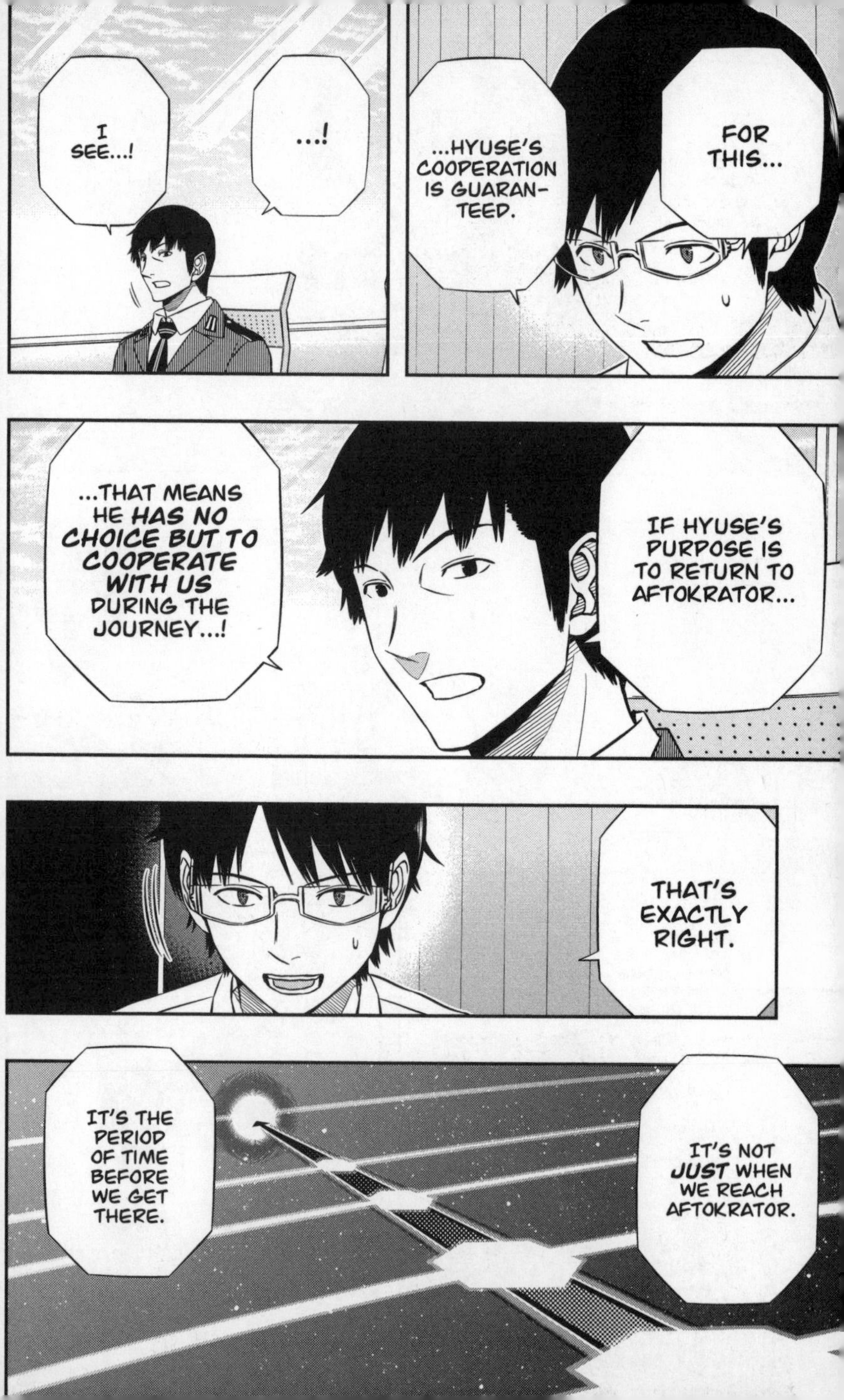
FOR THIS...
...HYUSE'S COOPERATION IS GUARAN-TEED.
...!
I SEE...!
IF HYUSE'S PURPOSE IS TO RETURN TO AFTOKRATOR...
...THAT MEANS HE HAS NO CHOICE BUT TO COOPERATE WITH US DURING THE JOURNEY...!
THAT'S EXACTLY RIGHT.
IT'S NOT JUST WHEN WE REACH AFTOKRATOR.
IT'S THE PERIOD OF TIME BEFORE WE GET THERE.

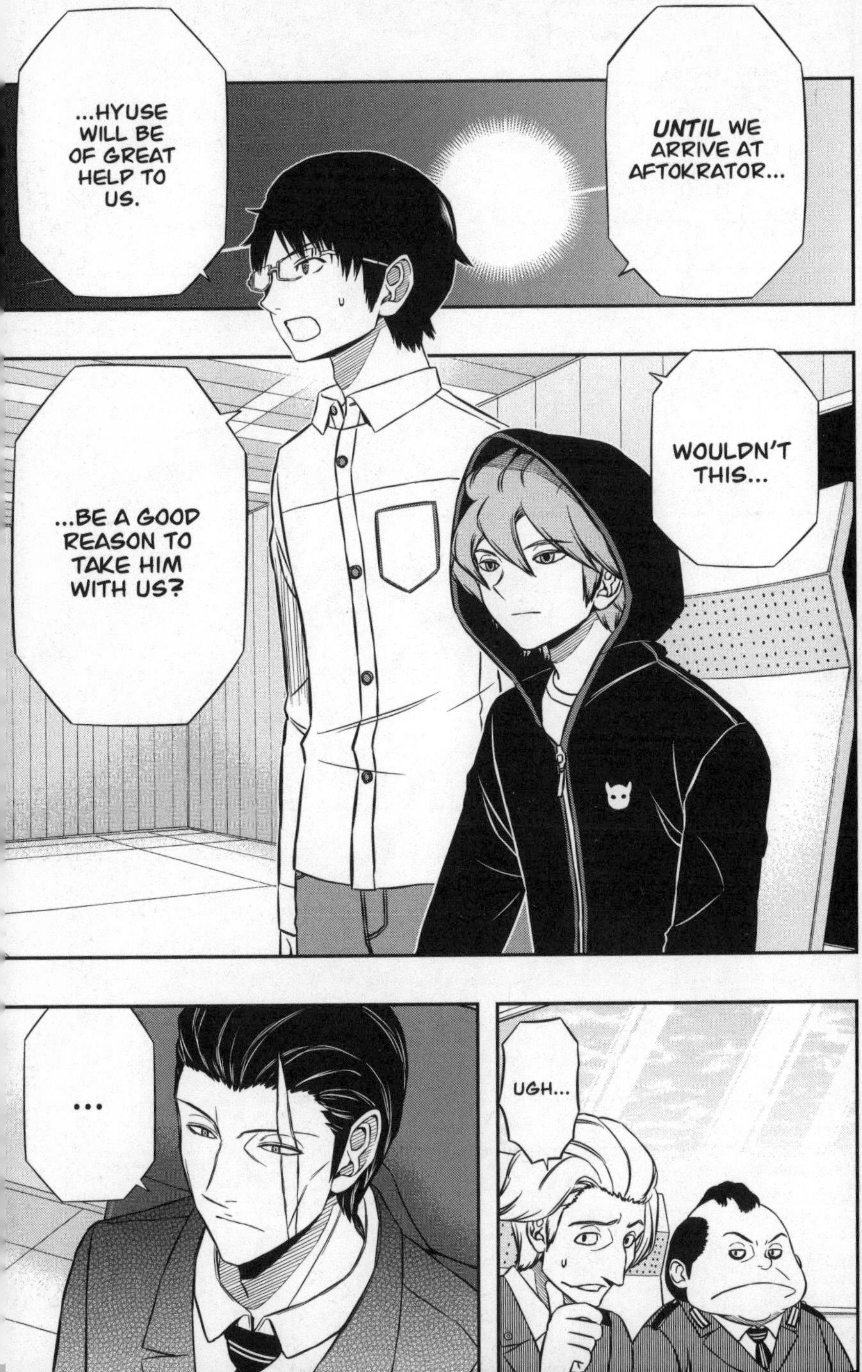
UNTIL WE ARRIVE AT AFTOKRATOR...
...HYUSE WILL BE OF GREAT HELP TO US.
WOULDN'T THIS...
...BE A GOOD REASON TO TAKE HIM WITH US?
UGH...
...

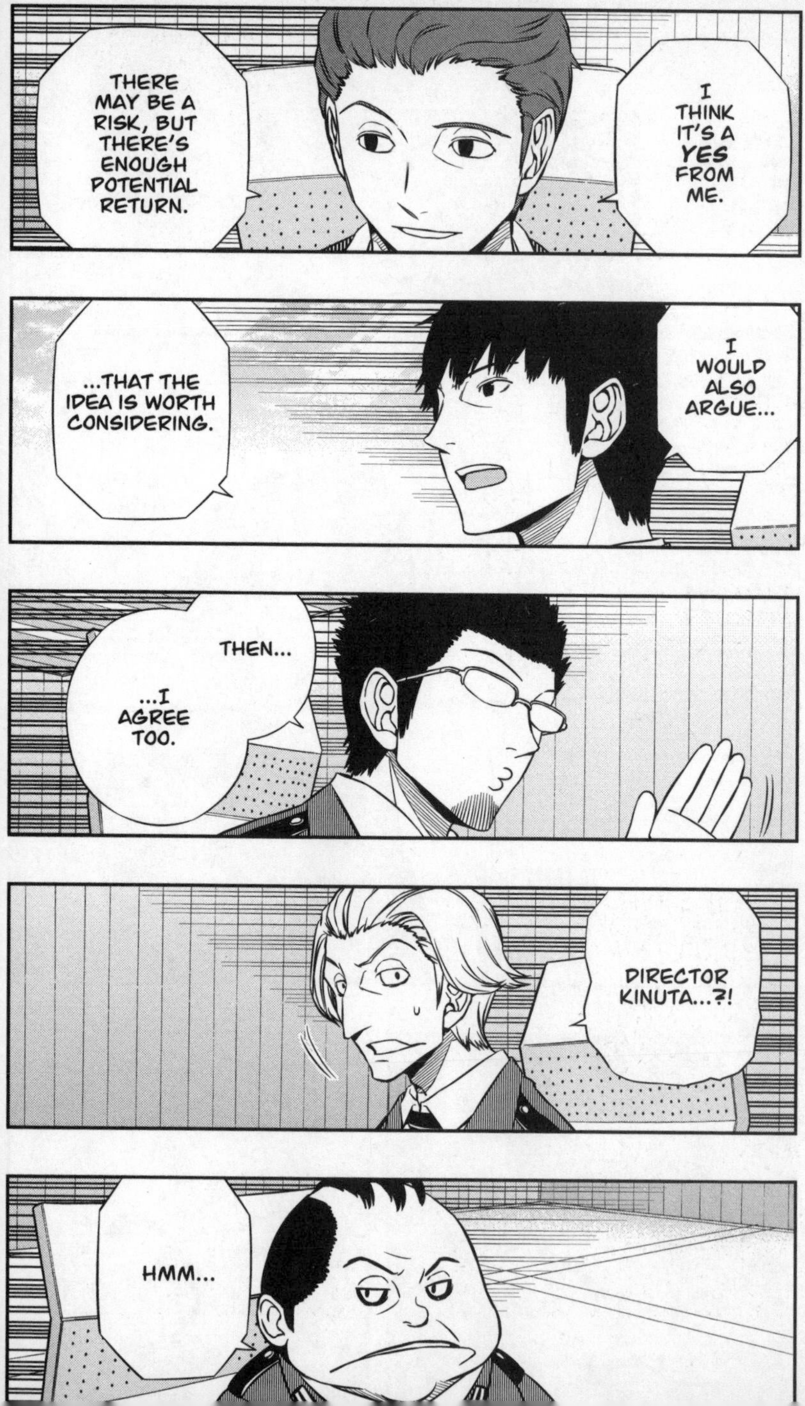
I THINK IT'S A YES FROM ME.
THERE MAY BE A RISK, BUT THERE'S ENOUGH POTENTIAL RETURN.
I WOULD ALSO ARGUE...
...THAT THE IDEA IS WORTH CONSIDERING.
THEN...
...I AGREE TOO.
DIRECTOR KINUTA...?!
HMM...

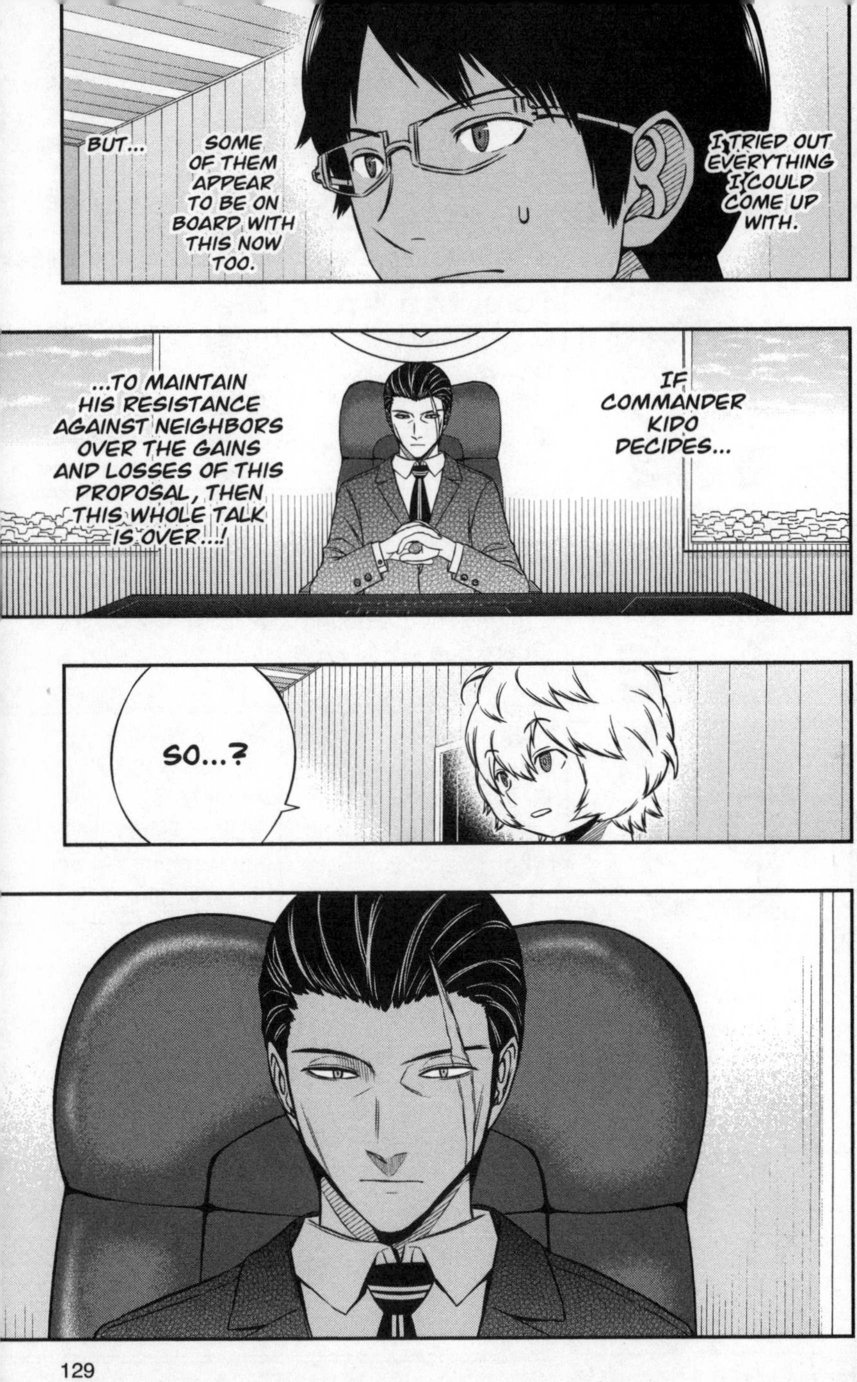
I TRIED OUT EVERYTHING I COULD COME UP WITH.
SOME OF THEM APPEAR TO BE ON BOARD WITH THIS NOW TOO.
BUT...
IF COMMANDER KIDO DECIDES...
...TO MAINTAIN HIS RESISTANCE AGAINST NEIGHBORS OVER THE GAINS AND LOSSES OF THIS PROPOSAL, THEN THIS WHOLE TALK IS OVER...!
SO...?

Ikoma Squad

Border HQ B-Rank #3

B-003

Tatsuhito Ikoma

Captain, Attacker
- 19 years old
  (College student)
- Born April 29

- Felis
  Blood type B
- Height: 5'8"
- Likes: Girls, new
menu in the dining hall,
soccer, eggplant curry

Satoshi Mizukami

Shooter
- 18 years old
  (High school student)
- Born Dec. 5

- Cetacea
  Blood type B
- Height: 5'10"
- Likes: Rakugo, shogi,
udon, spring rolls

Koji Oki

Sniper
- 17 years old
  (High school student)
- Born Sept. 30

- Luna Falcata
  Blood type AB
- Height: 5'9"
- Likes: Akashi-style
egg dumplings, oden,
cats, shopping

Kai Minamisawa

Attacker
- 16 years old
  (High school student)
- Born Nov. 7

- Chronos
  Blood type A
- Height: 5'7"
- Likes: Scallops,
cheeseburgers, fried
stuffed pepper

Maori Hosoi

Operator
- 17 years old
  (High school student)
- Born July 14

- Gladius
  Blood type O
- Height: 5'2"
- Likes: Inari sushi,
dandan noodles,
flowers, cute things

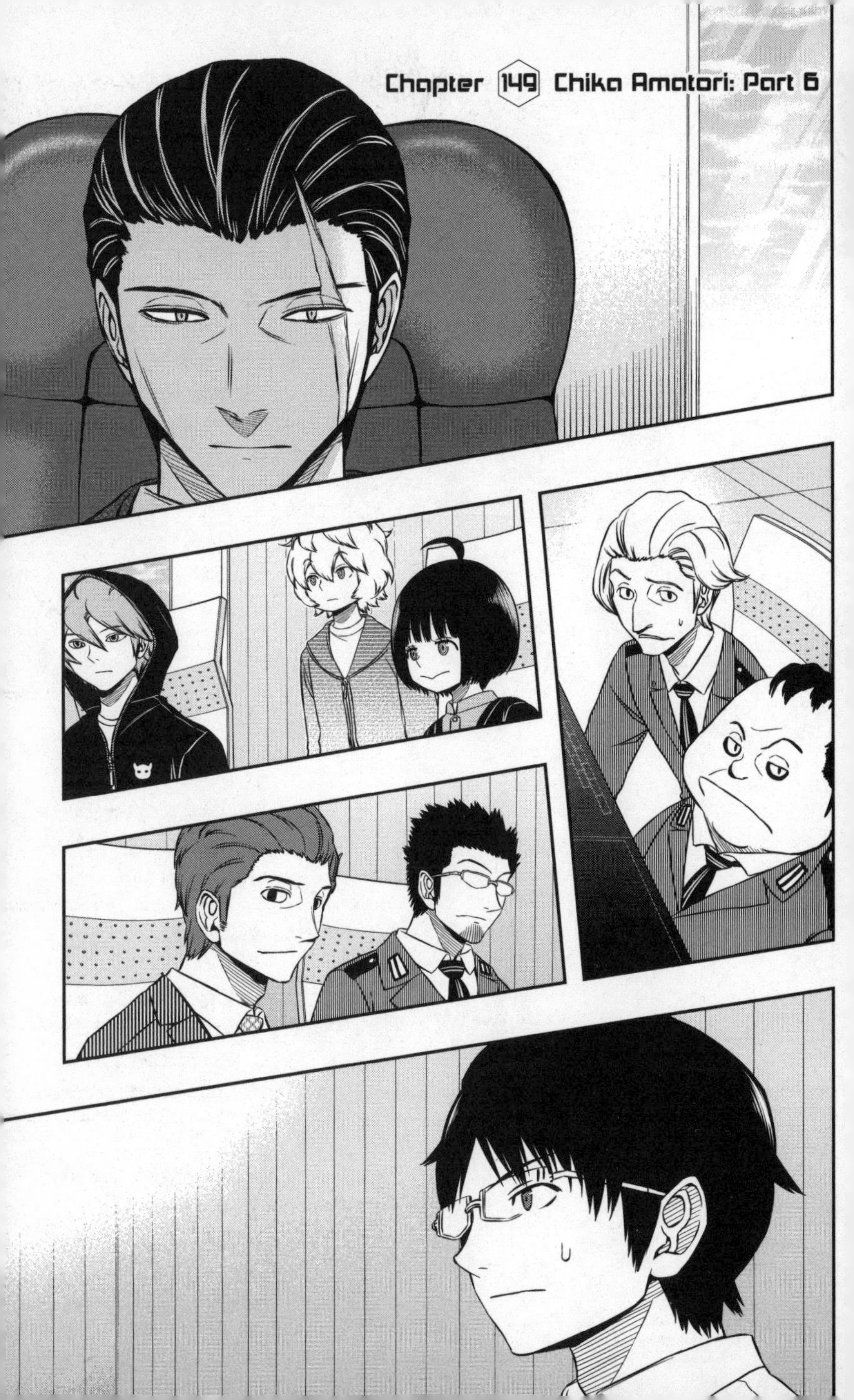
Chapter 149 Chika Amatori: Part 6

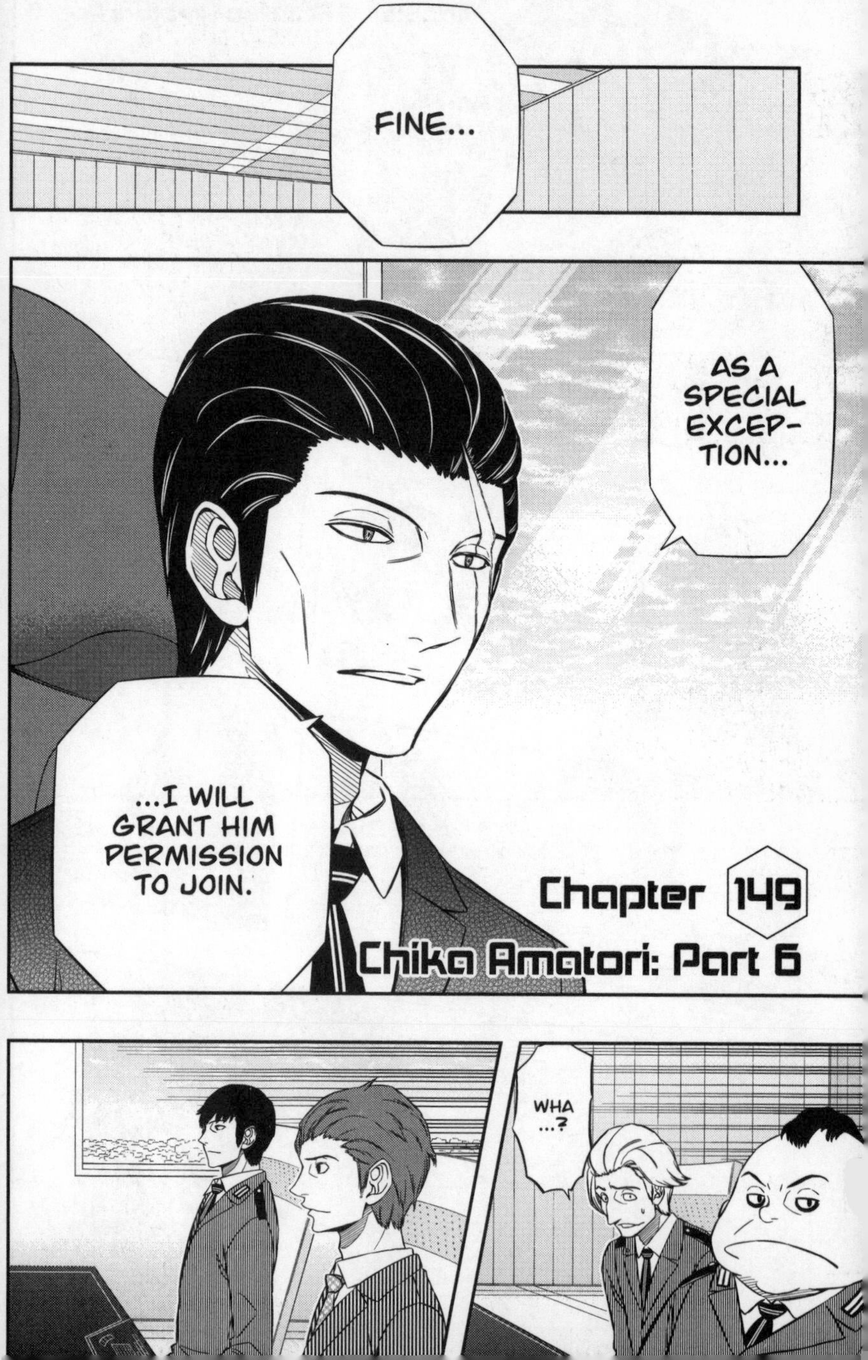
FINE...
AS A SPECIAL EXCEPTION...
...I WILL GRANT HIM PERMISSION TO JOIN.
Chapter 149
Chika Amatori: Part 6
WHA ...?

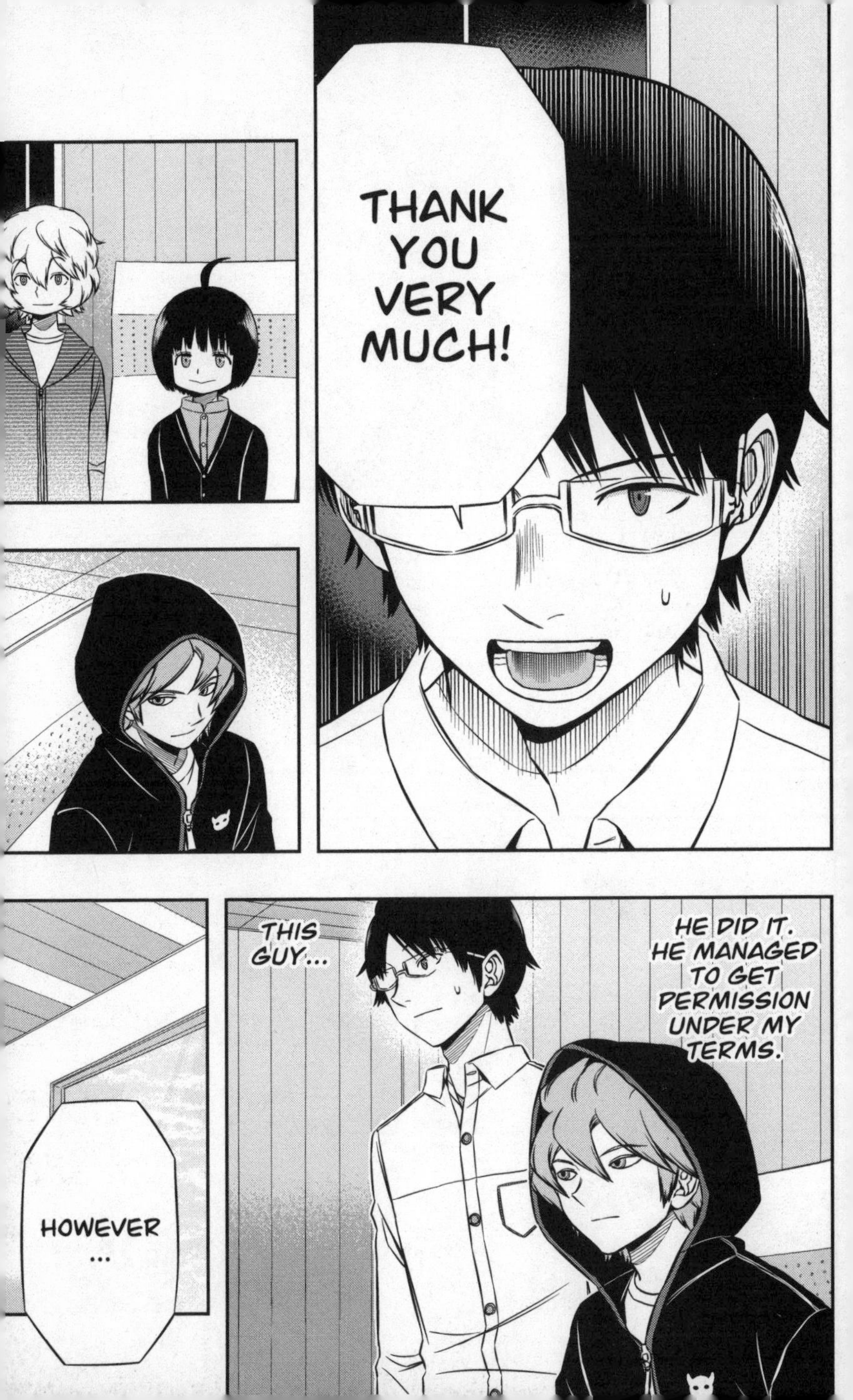
THANK YOU VERY MUCH!
HE DID IT. HE MANAGED TO GET PERMISSION UNDER MY TERMS.
THIS GUY...
HOWEVER ...

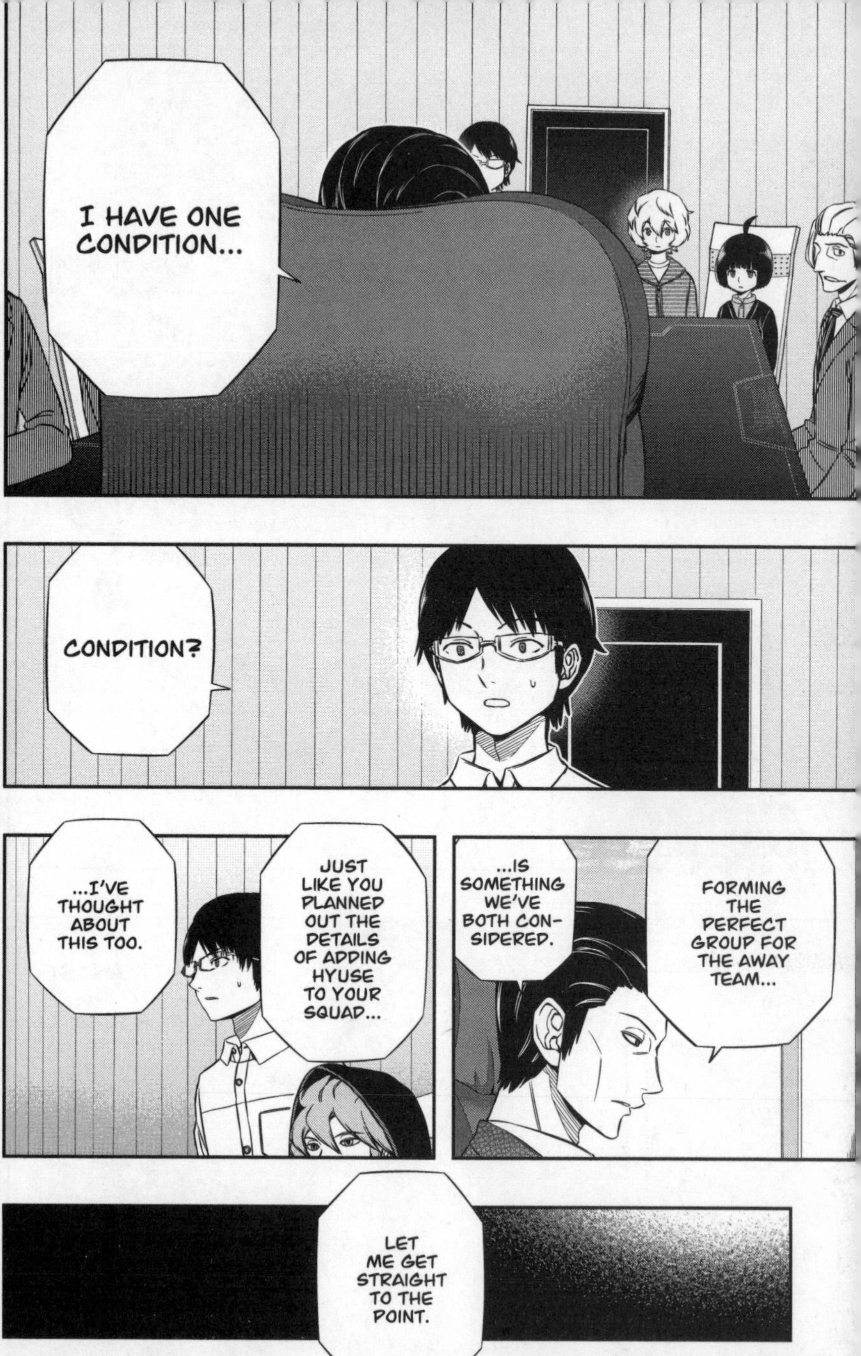
I HAVE ONE CONDITION...
CONDITION?
FORMING THE PERFECT GROUP FOR THE AWAY TEAM...
...IS SOMETHING WE'VE BOTH CON-SIDERED.
JUST LIKE YOU PLANNED OUT THE DETAILS OF ADDING HYUSE TO YOUR SQUAD...
...I'VE THOUGHT ABOUT THIS TOO.
LET ME GET STRAIGHT TO THE POINT.

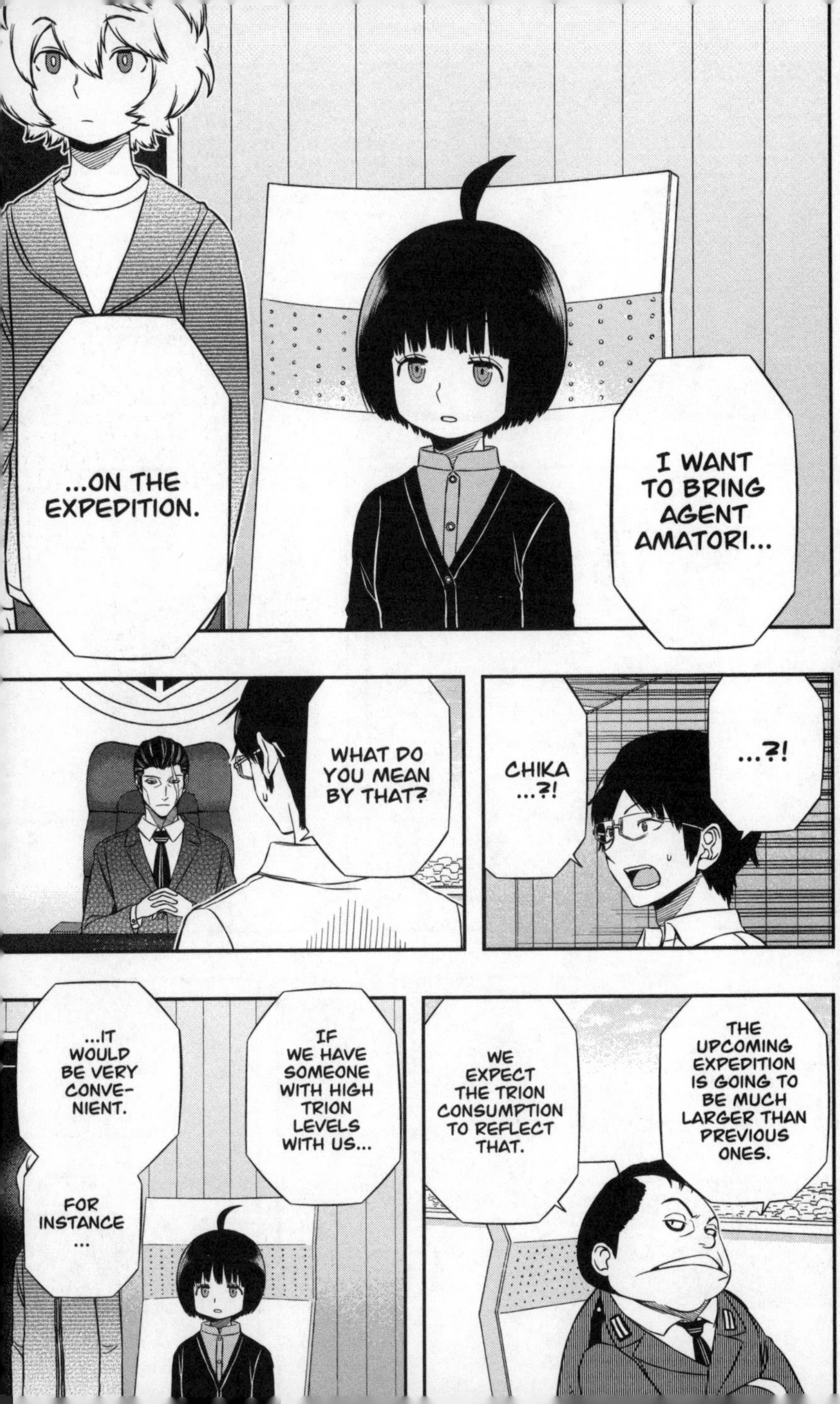
I WANT TO BRING AGENT AMATORI...
...ON THE EXPEDITION.
...?!
CHIKA ...?!
WHAT DO YOU MEAN BY THAT?
THE UPCOMING EXPEDITION IS GOING TO BE MUCH LARGER THAN PREVIOUS ONES.
WE EXPECT THE TRION CONSUMPTION TO REFLECT THAT.
IF WE HAVE SOMEONE WITH HIGH TRION LEVELS WITH US...
...IT WOULD BE VERY CONVE-NIENT.
FOR INSTANCE ...

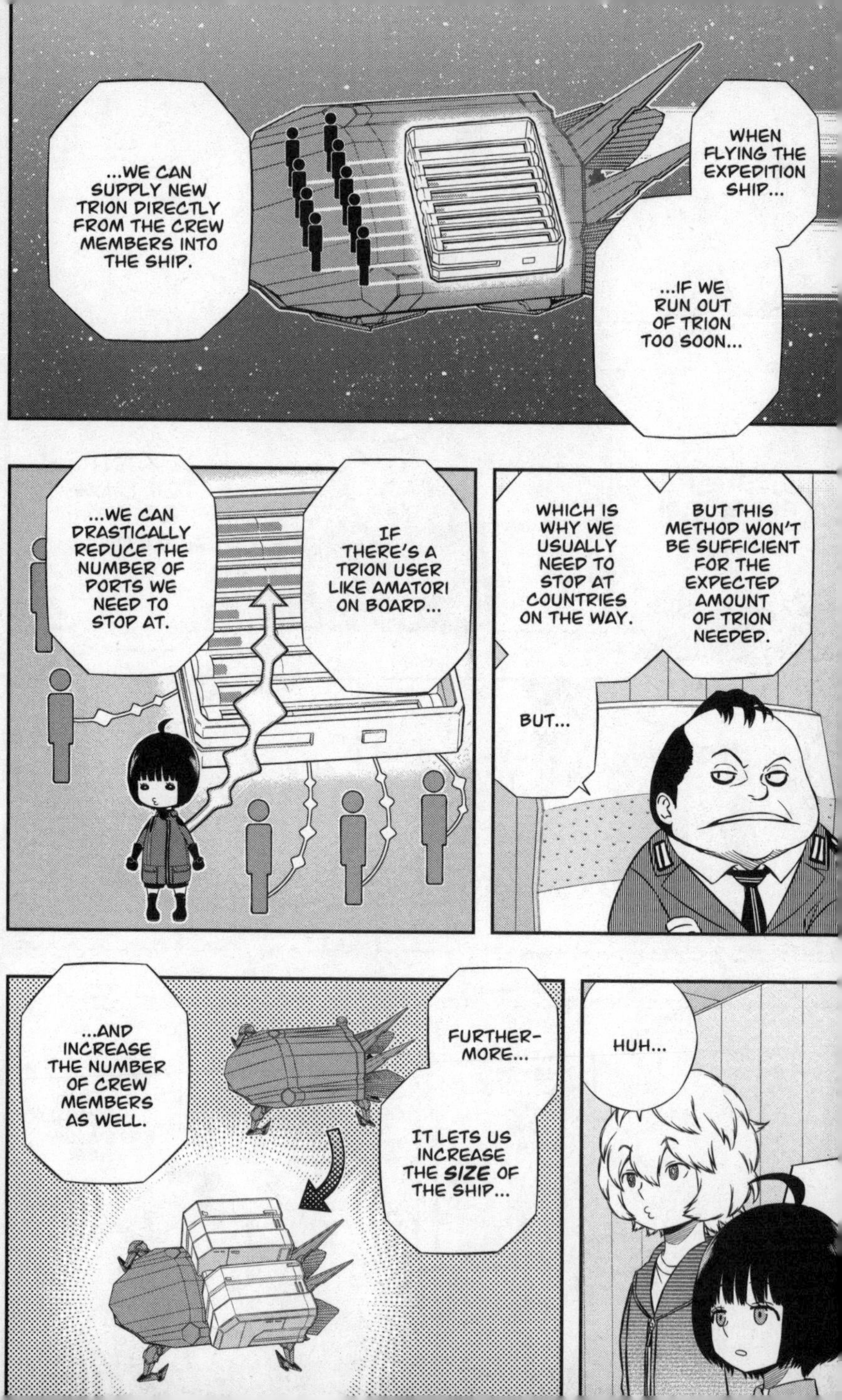
WHEN FLYING THE EXPEDITION SHIP...
...IF WE RUN OUT OF TRION TOO SOON...
...WE CAN SUPPLY NEW TRION DIRECTLY FROM THE CREW MEMBERS INTO THE SHIP.
BUT THIS METHOD WON'T BE SUFFICIENT FOR THE EXPECTED AMOUNT OF TRION NEEDED.
WHICH IS WHY WE USUALLY NEED TO STOP AT COUNTRIES ON THE WAY.
BUT...
IF THERE'S A TRION USER LIKE AMATORI ON BOARD...
...WE CAN DRASTICALLY REDUCE THE NUMBER OF PORTS WE NEED TO STOP AT.
HUH...
FURTHER-MORE...
IT LETS US INCREASE THE *SIZE* OF THE SHIP...
...AND INCREASE THE NUMBER OF CREW MEMBERS AS WELL.

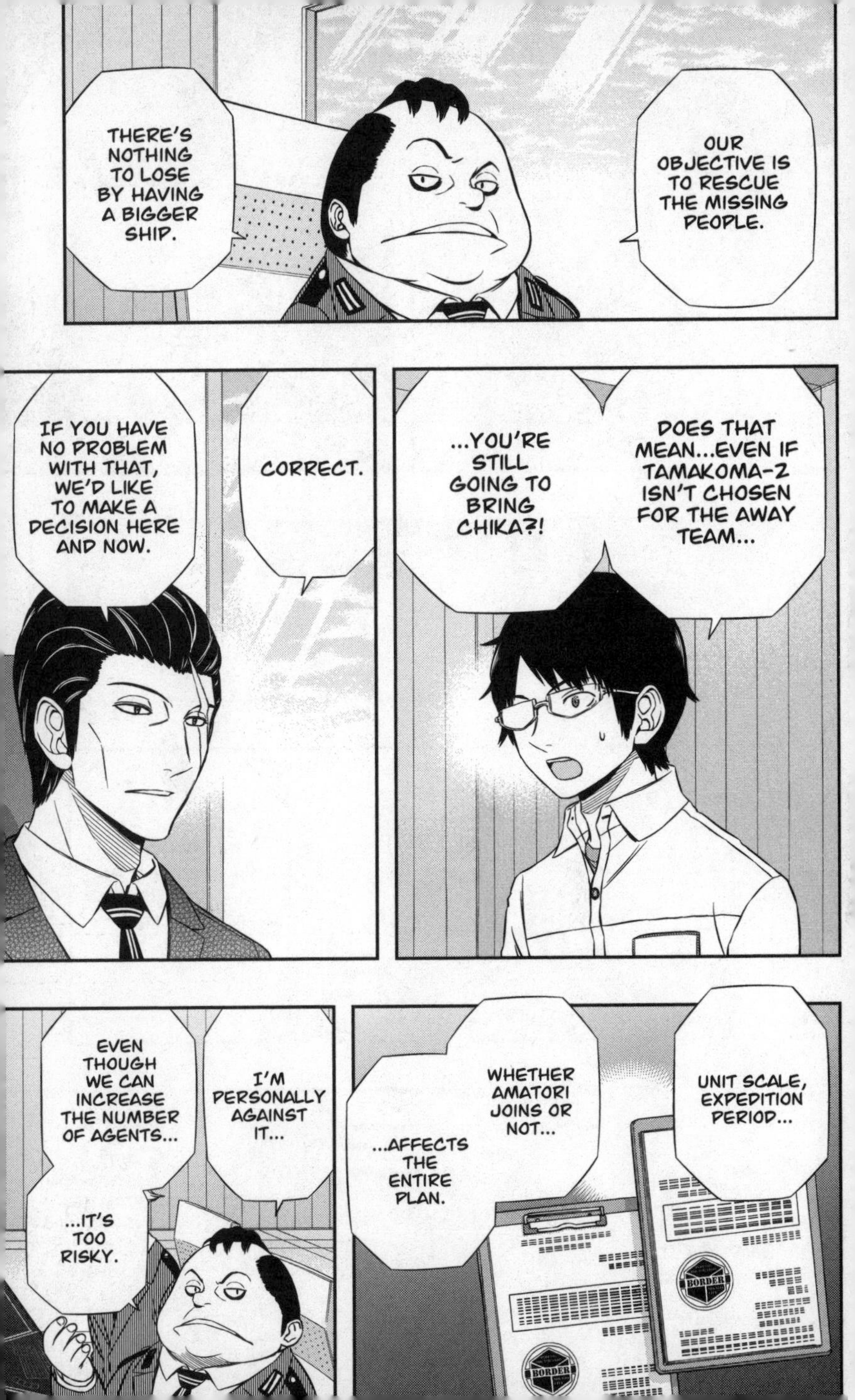
OUR OBJECTIVE IS TO RESCUE THE MISSING PEOPLE.
THERE'S NOTHING TO LOSE BY HAVING A BIGGER SHIP.
DOES THAT MEAN...EVEN IF TAMAKOMA-2 ISN'T CHOSEN FOR THE AWAY TEAM...
...YOU'RE STILL GOING TO BRING CHIKA?!
CORRECT.
IF YOU HAVE NO PROBLEM WITH THAT, WE'D LIKE TO MAKE A DECISION HERE AND NOW.
UNIT SCALE, EXPEDITION PERIOD...
WHETHER AMATORI JOINS OR NOT...
...AFFECTS THE ENTIRE PLAN.
I'M PERSONALLY AGAINST IT...
EVEN THOUGH WE CAN INCREASE THE NUMBER OF AGENTS...
...IT'S TOO RISKY.

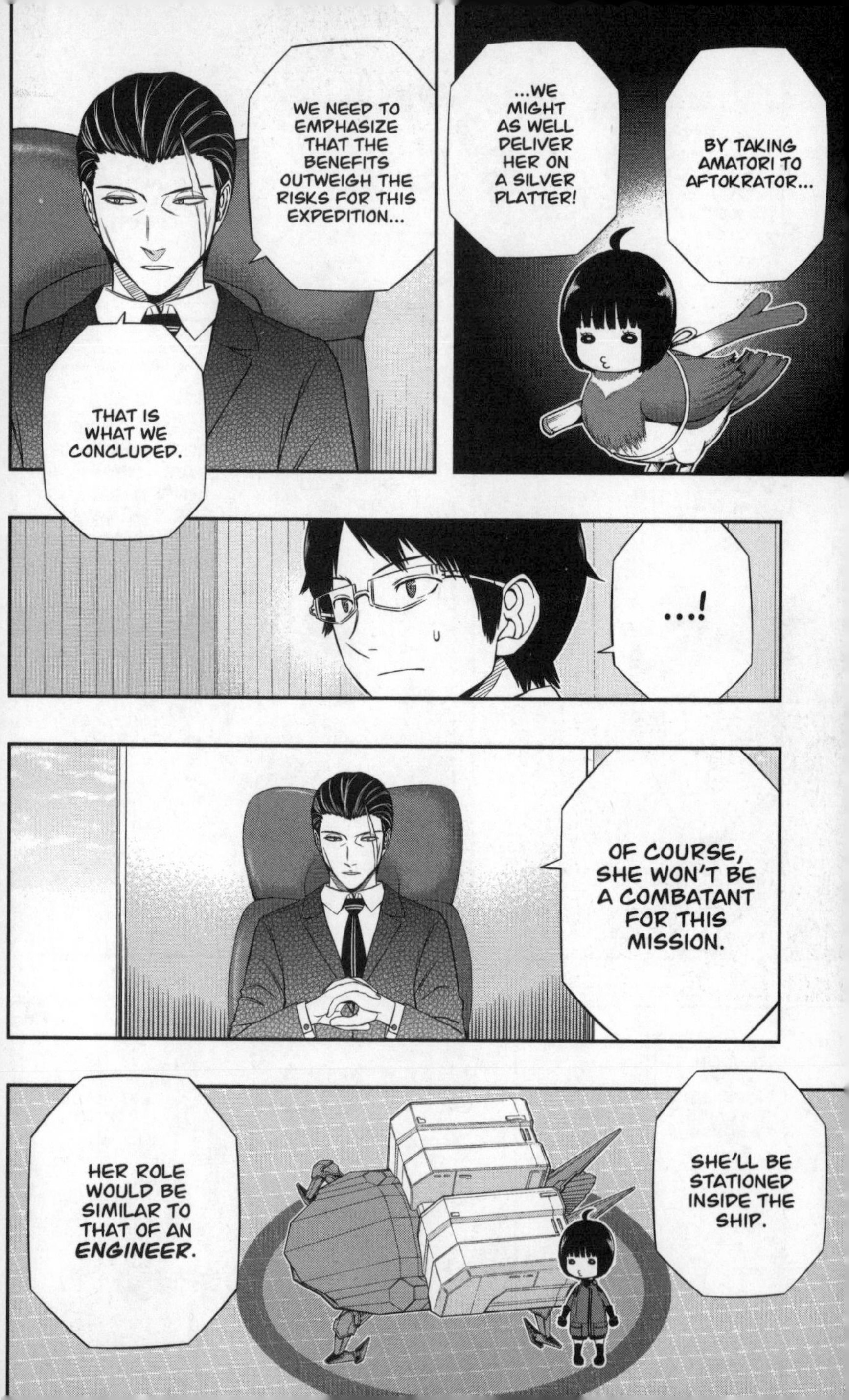
BY TAKING AMATORI TO AFTOKRATOR...
...WE MIGHT AS WELL DELIVER HER ON A SILVER PLATTER!
WE NEED TO EMPHASIZE THAT THE BENEFITS OUTWEIGH THE RISKS FOR THIS EXPEDITION...
THAT IS WHAT WE CONCLUDED.
...!
OF COURSE, SHE WON'T BE A COMBATANT FOR THIS MISSION.
SHE'LL BE STATIONED INSIDE THE SHIP.
HER ROLE WOULD BE SIMILAR TO THAT OF AN ENGINEER.

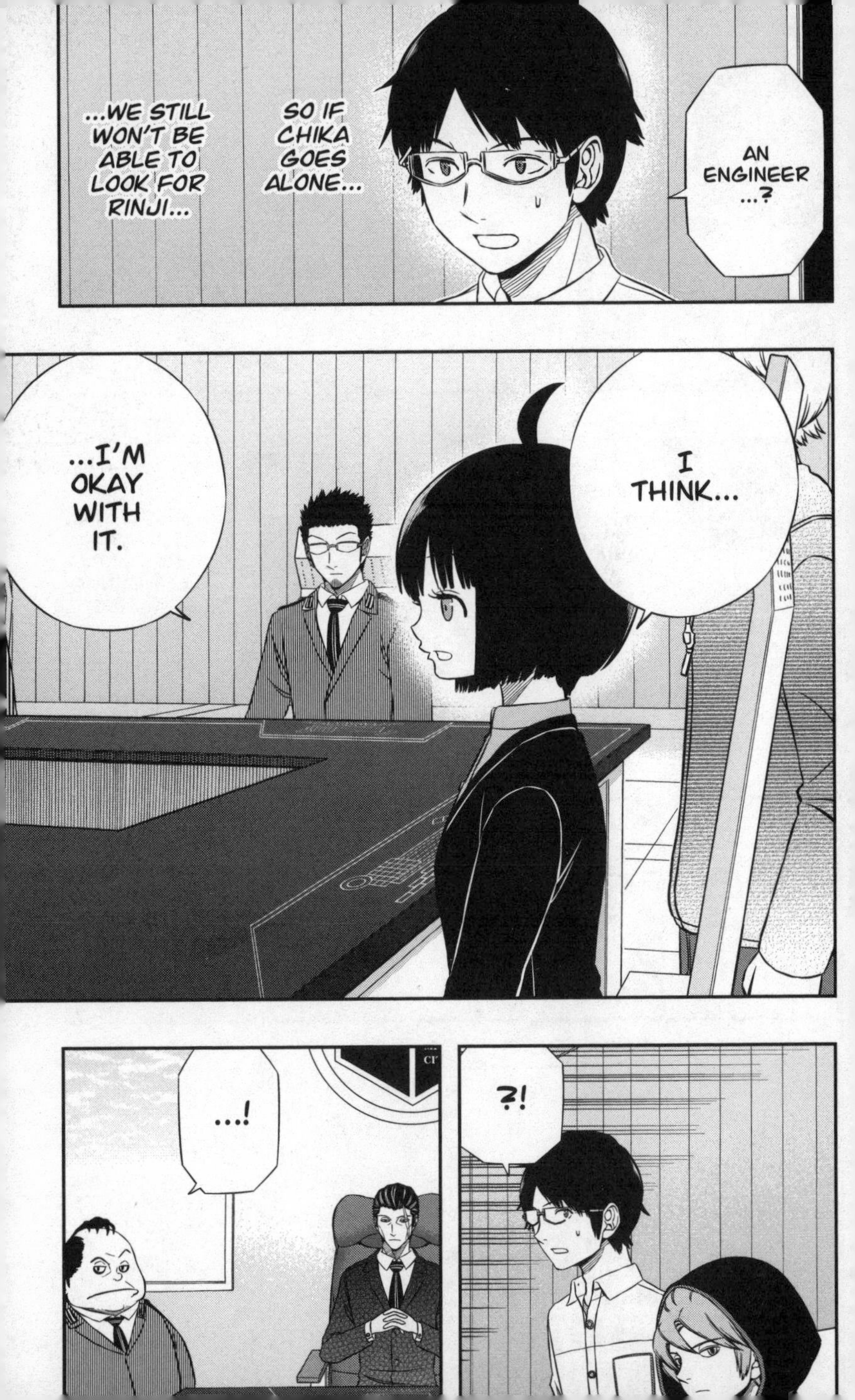
AN ENGINEER ...?
SO IF CHIKA GOES ALONE...
...WE STILL WON'T BE ABLE TO LOOK FOR RINJI...
I THINK...
...I'M OKAY WITH IT.
?!
...!

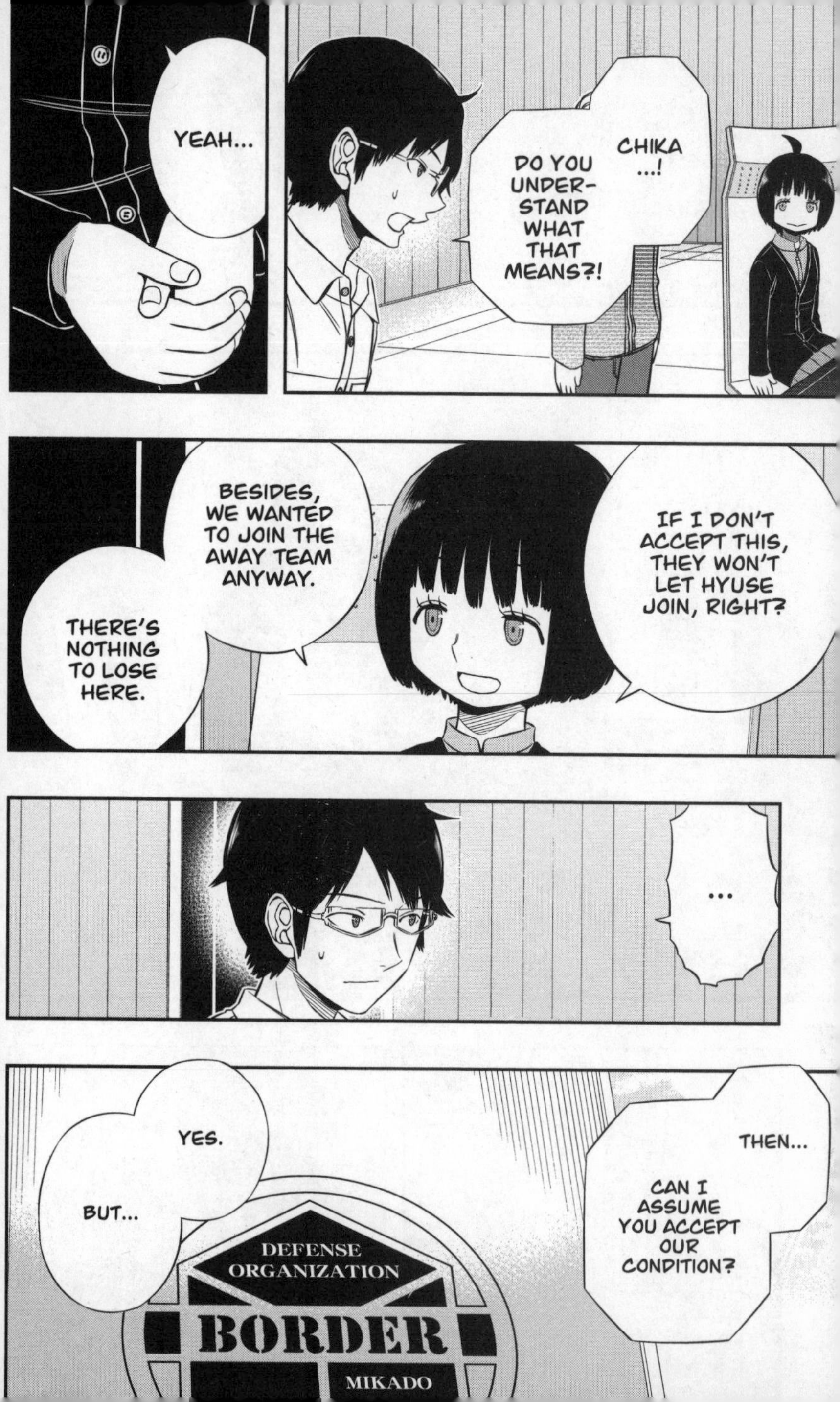
CHIKA ...!
DO YOU UNDER-STAND WHAT THAT MEANS?!
YEAH...
IF I DON'T ACCEPT THIS, THEY WON'T LET HYUSE JOIN, RIGHT?
BESIDES, WE WANTED TO JOIN THE AWAY TEAM ANYWAY.
THERE'S NOTHING TO LOSE HERE.
...
THEN...
CAN I ASSUME YOU ACCEPT OUR CONDITION?
YES.
BUT...
DEFENSE ORGANIZATION
BORDER
MIKADO

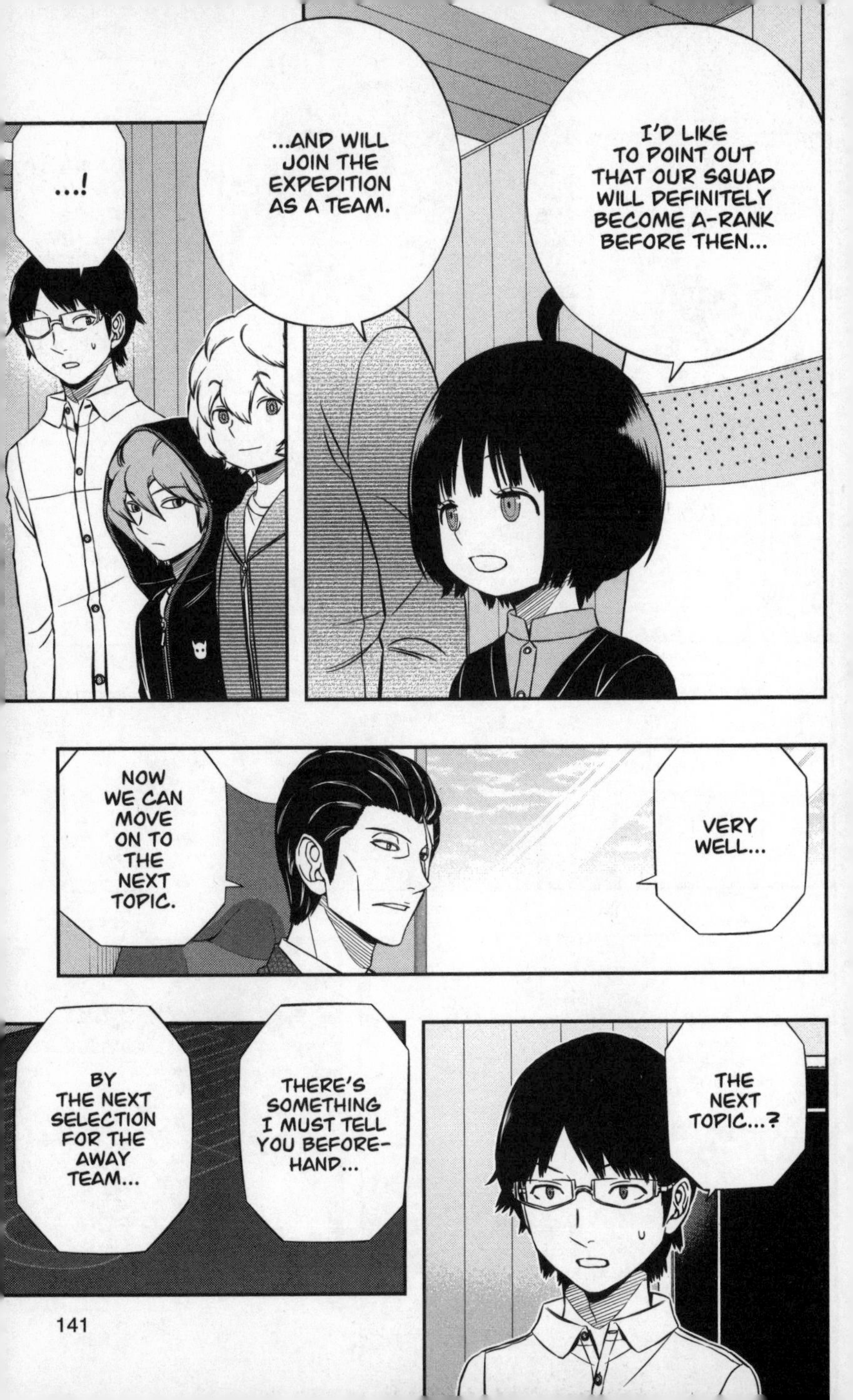
I'D LIKE TO POINT OUT THAT OUR SQUAD WILL DEFINITELY BECOME A-RANK BEFORE THEN...
...AND WILL JOIN THE EXPEDITION AS A TEAM.
...!
VERY WELL...
NOW WE CAN MOVE ON TO THE NEXT TOPIC.
THE NEXT TOPIC...?
THERE'S SOMETHING I MUST TELL YOU BEFORE-HAND...
BY THE NEXT SELECTION FOR THE AWAY TEAM...

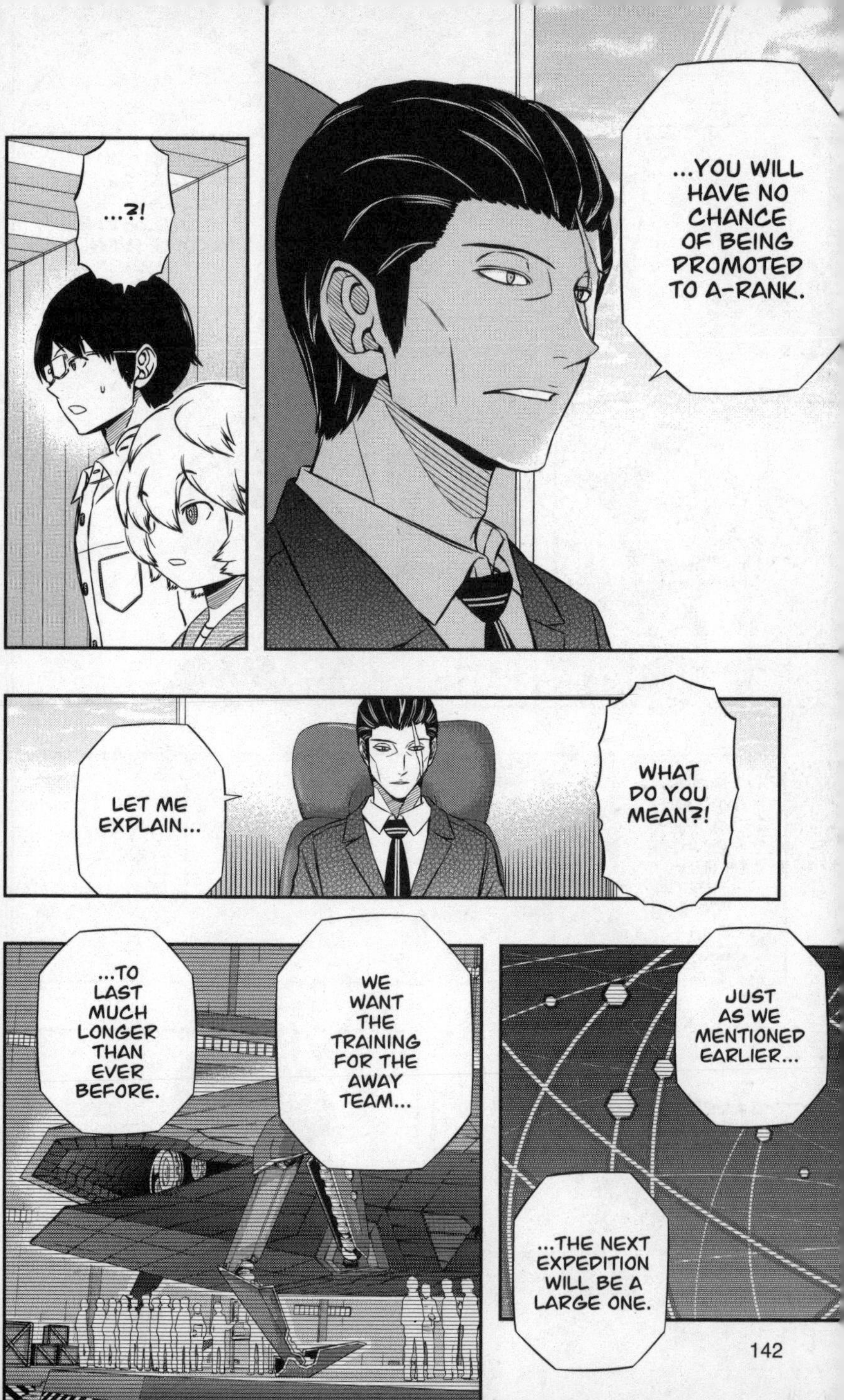
...YOU WILL HAVE NO CHANCE OF BEING PROMOTED TO A-RANK.
...?!
WHAT DO YOU MEAN?!
LET ME EXPLAIN...
JUST AS WE MENTIONED EARLIER...
...THE NEXT EXPEDITION WILL BE A LARGE ONE.
WE WANT THE TRAINING FOR THE AWAY TEAM...
...TO LAST MUCH LONGER THAN EVER BEFORE.

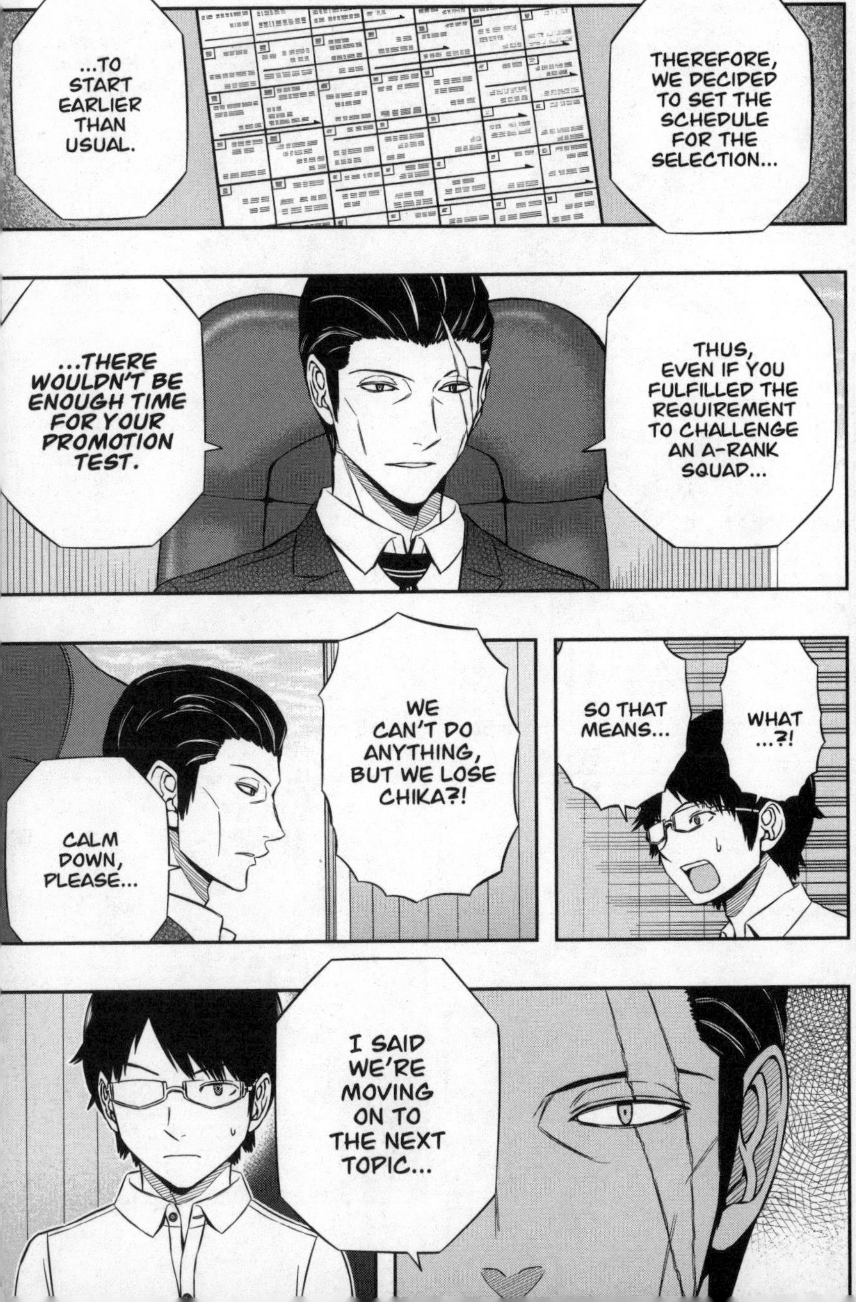
THEREFORE, WE DECIDED TO SET THE SCHEDULE FOR THE SELECTION...
...TO START EARLIER THAN USUAL.
THUS, EVEN IF YOU FULFILLED THE REQUIREMENT TO CHALLENGE AN A-RANK SQUAD...
...THERE WOULDN'T BE ENOUGH TIME FOR YOUR PROMOTION TEST.
WHAT ...?!
SO THAT MEANS...
WE CAN'T DO ANYTHING, BUT WE LOSE CHIKA?!
CALM DOWN, PLEASE...
I SAID WE'RE MOVING ON TO THE NEXT TOPIC...

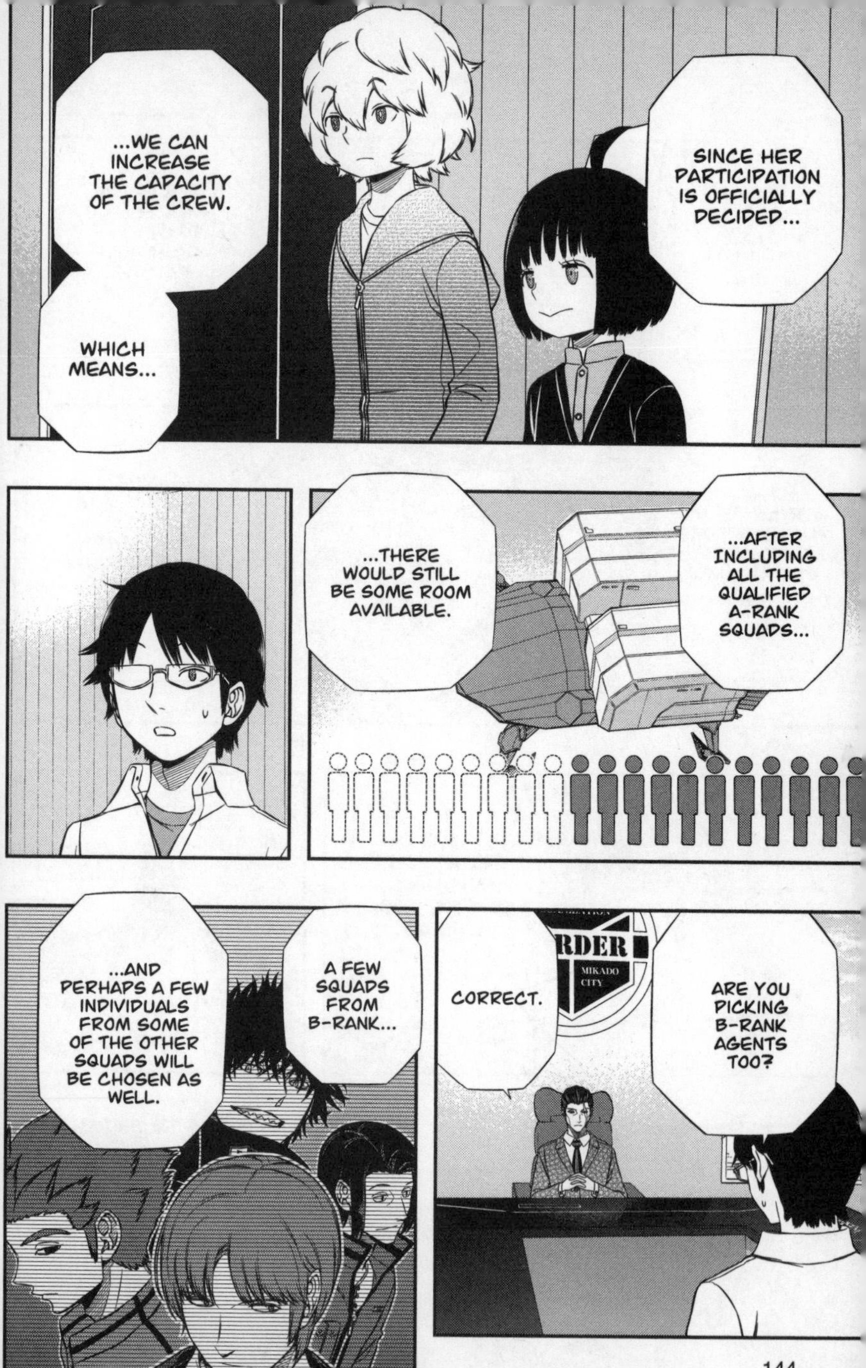
SINCE HER PARTICIPATION IS OFFICIALLY DECIDED...
...WE CAN INCREASE THE CAPACITY OF THE CREW.
WHICH MEANS...
...AFTER INCLUDING ALL THE QUALIFIED A-RANK SQUADS...
...THERE WOULD STILL BE SOME ROOM AVAILABLE.
ARE YOU PICKING B-RANK AGENTS TOO?
MIKADO CITY
CORRECT.
A FEW SQUADS FROM B-RANK...
...AND PERHAPS A FEW INDIVIDUALS FROM SOME OF THE OTHER SQUADS WILL BE CHOSEN AS WELL.

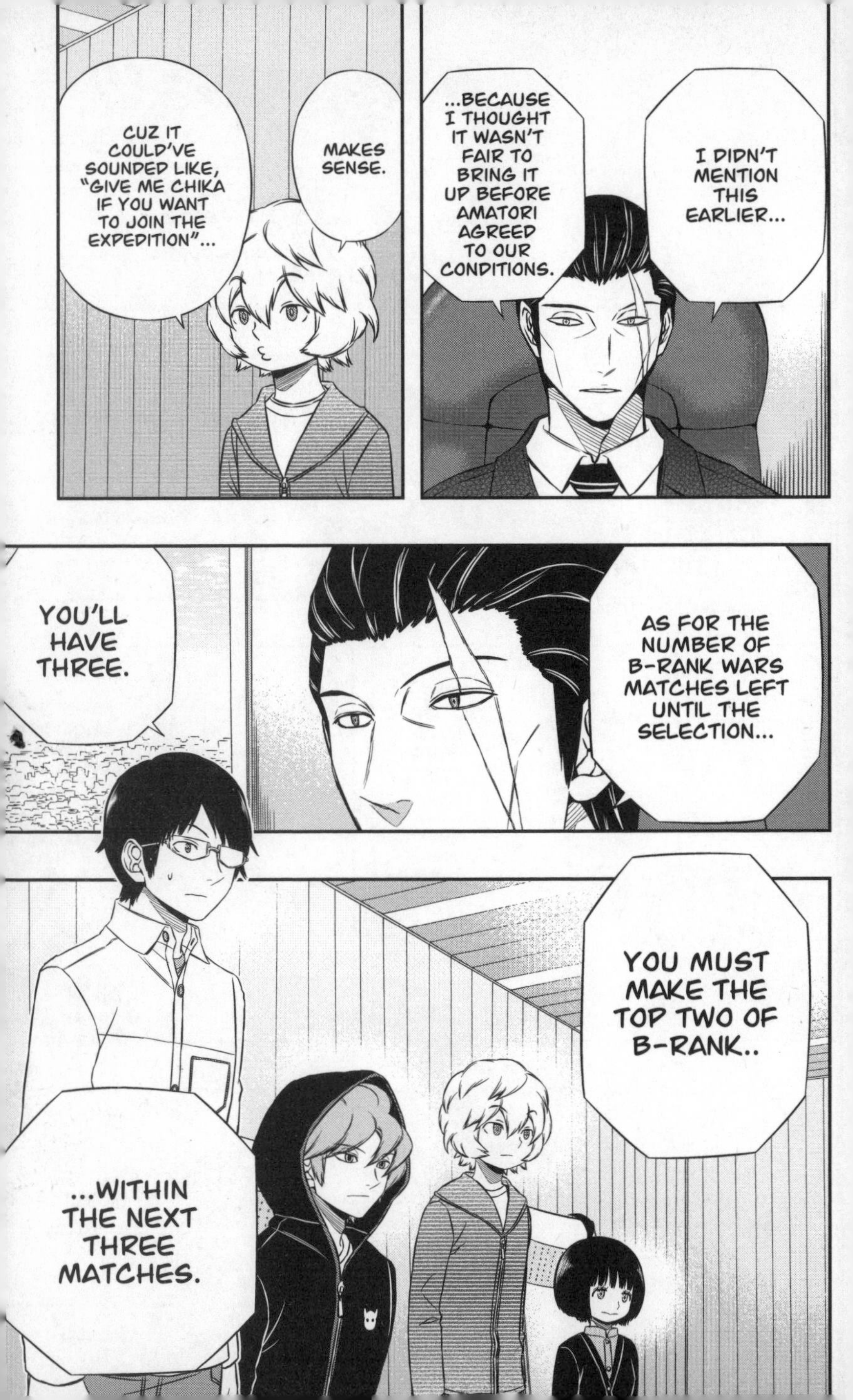
I DIDN'T MENTION THIS EARLIER...
...BECAUSE I THOUGHT IT WASN'T FAIR TO BRING IT UP BEFORE AMATORI AGREED TO OUR CONDITIONS.
MAKES SENSE.
CUZ IT COULD'VE SOUNDED LIKE, "GIVE ME CHIKA IF YOU WANT TO JOIN THE EXPEDITION"...
AS FOR THE NUMBER OF B-RANK WARS MATCHES LEFT UNTIL THE SELECTION...
YOU'LL HAVE THREE.
YOU MUST MAKE THE TOP TWO OF B-RANK..
...WITHIN THE NEXT THREE MATCHES.

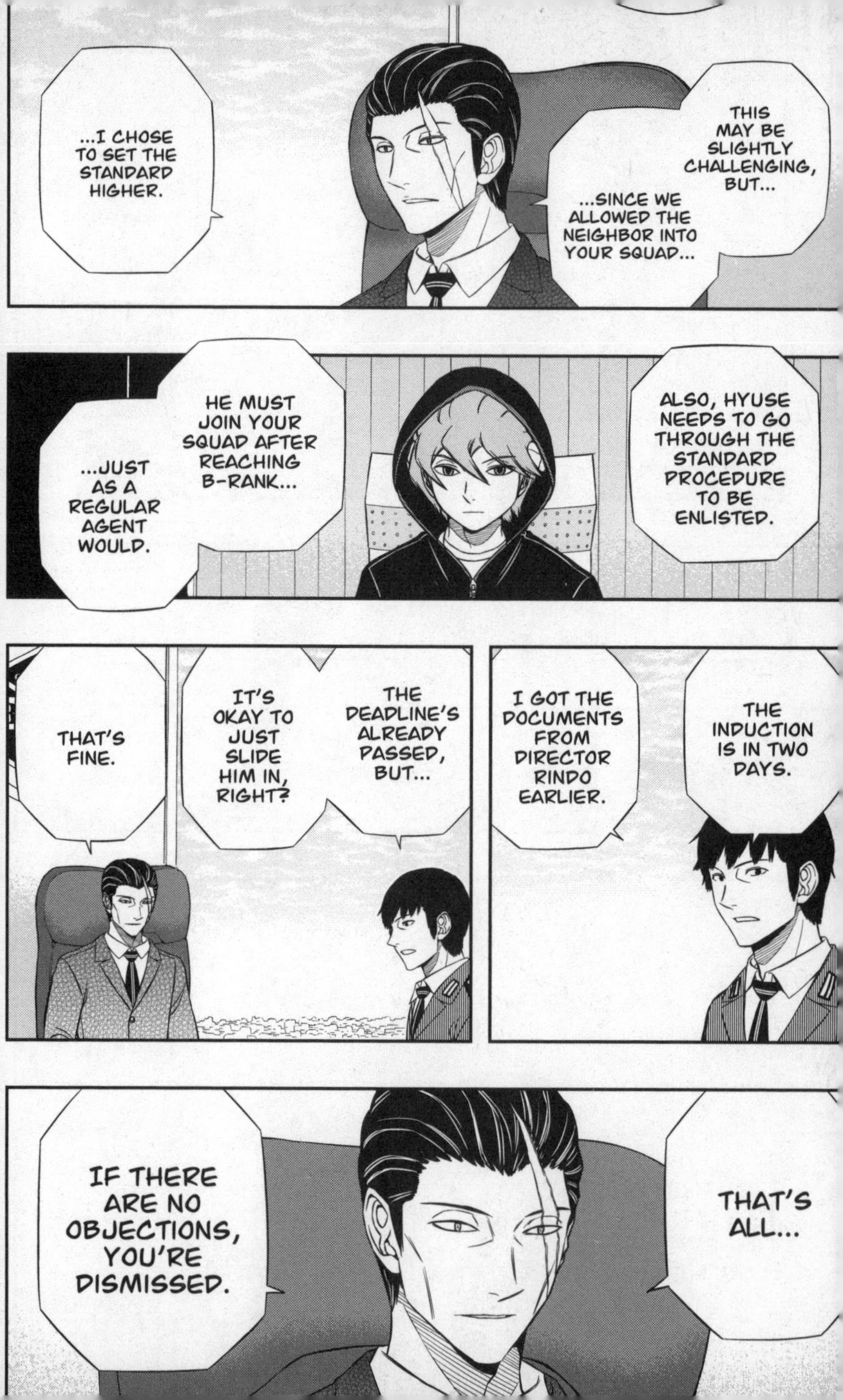
THIS MAY BE SLIGHTLY CHALLENGING, BUT...
...SINCE WE ALLOWED THE NEIGHBOR INTO YOUR SQUAD...
...I CHOSE TO SET THE STANDARD HIGHER.
ALSO, HYUSE NEEDS TO GO THROUGH THE STANDARD PROCEDURE TO BE ENLISTED.
HE MUST JOIN YOUR SQUAD AFTER REACHING B-RANK...
...JUST AS A REGULAR AGENT WOULD.
THE INDUCTION IS IN TWO DAYS.
I GOT THE DOCUMENTS FROM DIRECTOR RINDO EARLIER.
THE DEADLINE'S ALREADY PASSED, BUT...
IT'S OKAY TO JUST SLIDE HIM IN, RIGHT?
THAT'S FINE.
THAT'S ALL...
IF THERE ARE NO OBJECTIONS, YOU'RE DISMISSED.

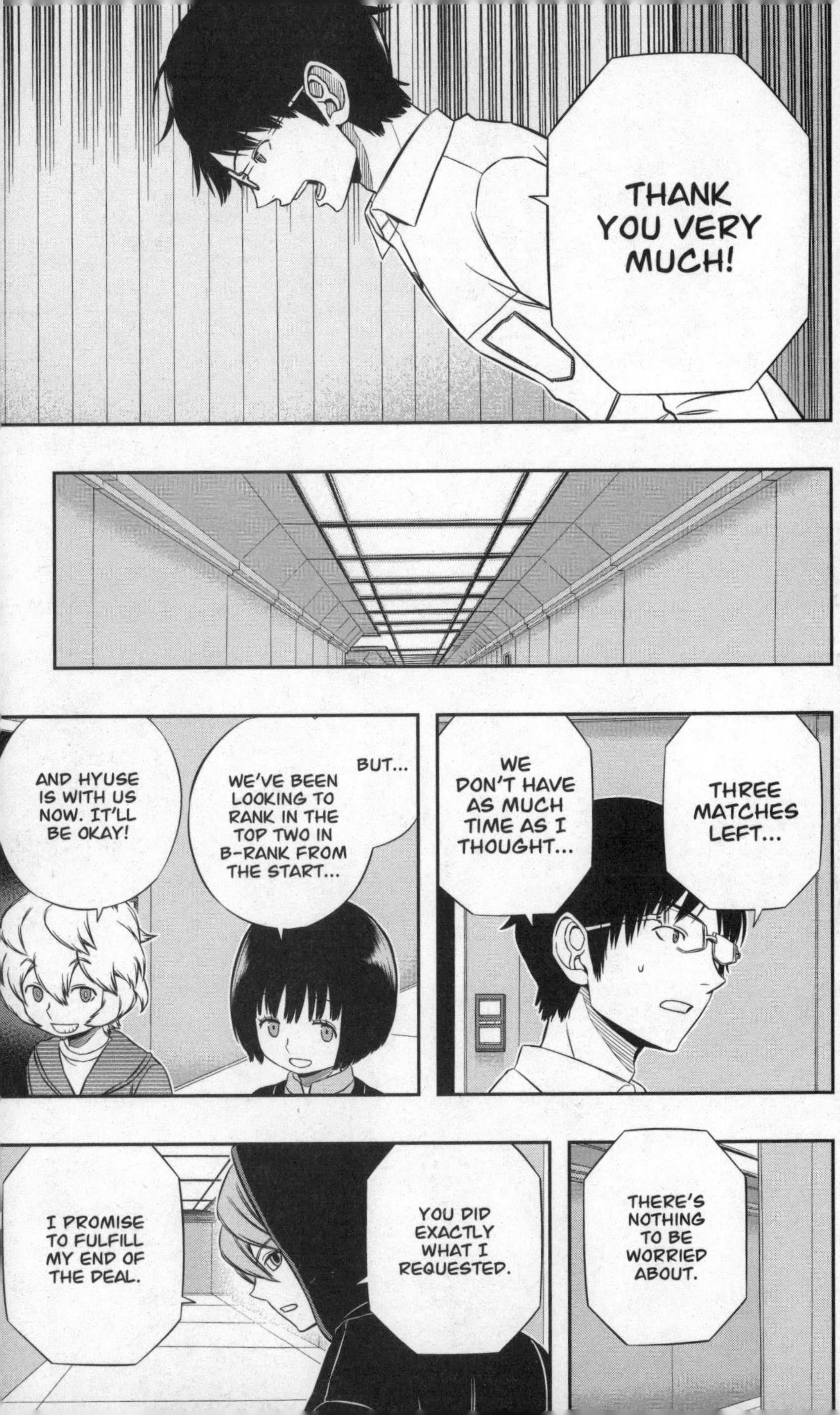
THANK YOU VERY MUCH!
THREE MATCHES LEFT...
WE DON'T HAVE AS MUCH TIME AS I THOUGHT...
BUT...
WE'VE BEEN LOOKING TO RANK IN THE TOP TWO IN B-RANK FROM THE START...
AND HYUSE IS WITH US NOW. IT'LL BE OKAY!
THERE'S NOTHING TO BE WORRIED ABOUT.
YOU DID EXACTLY WHAT I REQUESTED.
I PROMISE TO FULFILL MY END OF THE DEAL.

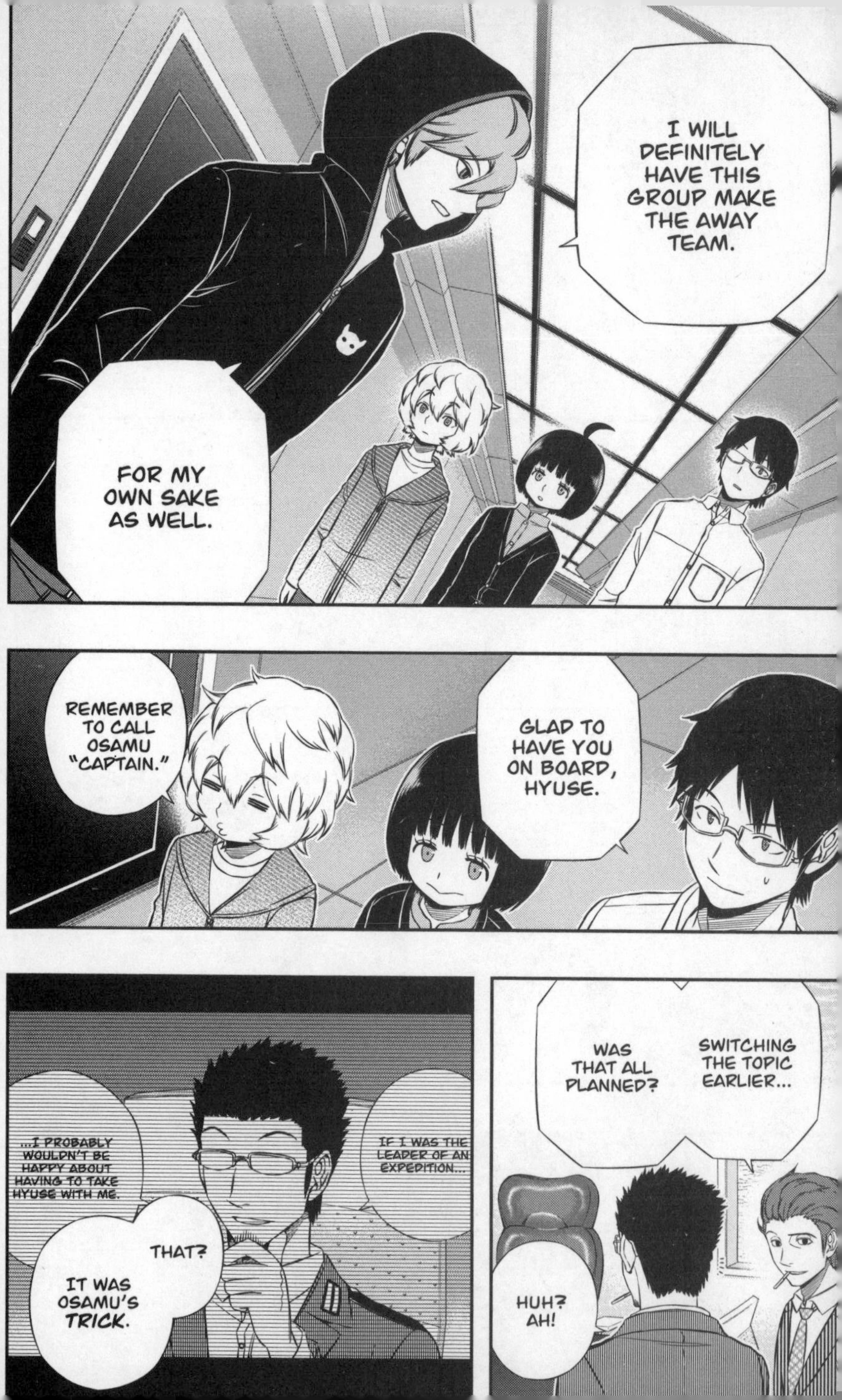
I WILL DEFINITELY HAVE THIS GROUP MAKE THE AWAY TEAM.
FOR MY OWN SAKE AS WELL.
GLAD TO HAVE YOU ON BOARD, HYUSE.
REMEMBER TO CALL OSAMU "CAPTAIN."
SWITCHING THE TOPIC EARLIER...
WAS THAT ALL PLANNED?
HUH? AH!
IF I WAS THE LEADER OF AN EXPEDITION...
...I PROBABLY WOULDN'T BE HAPPY ABOUT HAVING TO TAKE HYUSE WITH ME.
THAT?
IT WAS OSAMU'S TRICK.

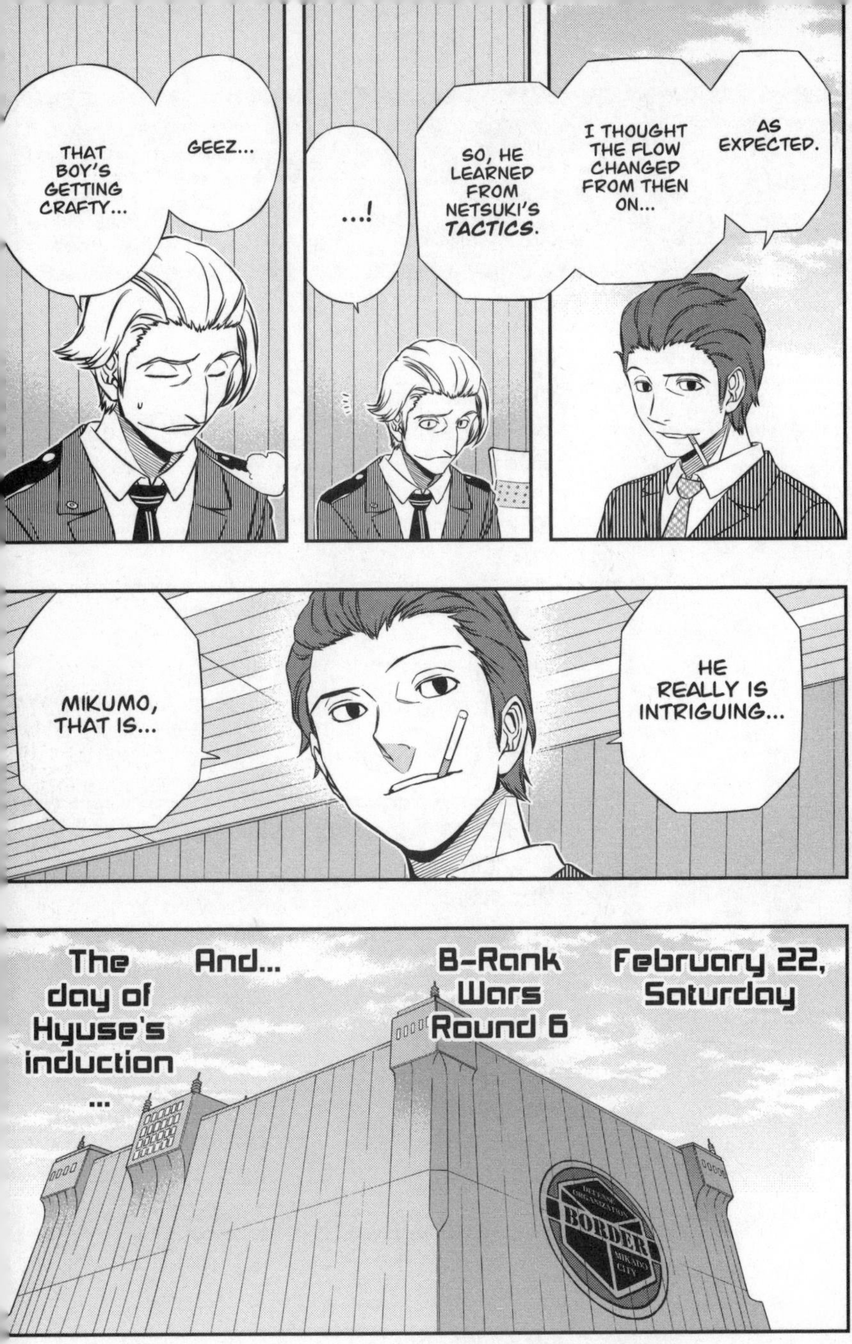
AS EXPECTED.
I THOUGHT THE FLOW CHANGED FROM THEN ON...
SO, HE LEARNED FROM NETSUKI'S TACTICS.
...!
GEEZ...
THAT BOY'S GETTING CRAFTY...
HE REALLY IS INTRIGUING...
MIKUMO, THAT IS...
February 22, Saturday
B-Rank Wars Round 6
And...
The day of Hyuse's induction ...
DEFENSE ORGANIZATION
BORDER
MIKADO CITY

Oji Squad
Border HQ B-Rank #5

Kazuaki Oji
Captain, Attacker
- 18 years old
  (High school student)
- Born Jan. 11

- Clavis
  Blood type B
- Height: 5'10"
- Likes: Omelets, croissants, horses, chess

Kazuki Kurauchi
Shooter
- 18 years old
  (High school student)
- Born Sept. 3

- Lupus
  Blood type A
- Height: 5'11"
- Likes: Sea bream with rice and tea, chicken and egg bowls, pickled thin-sliced turnips, aquariums

Yutaka Kashio
Attacker
- 15 years old
  (Middle school student)
- Born May 29

- Lepus
  Blood type A
- Height: 5'8"
- Likes: Lasagna, ramune soda, potato salad, studying

Haya Kittaka
Operator
- 19 years old
  (College student)
- Born Aug. 14

- Aptenodytes
  Blood type A
- Height: 5'5"
- Likes: Boiled spinach salad, kiwi, yogurt

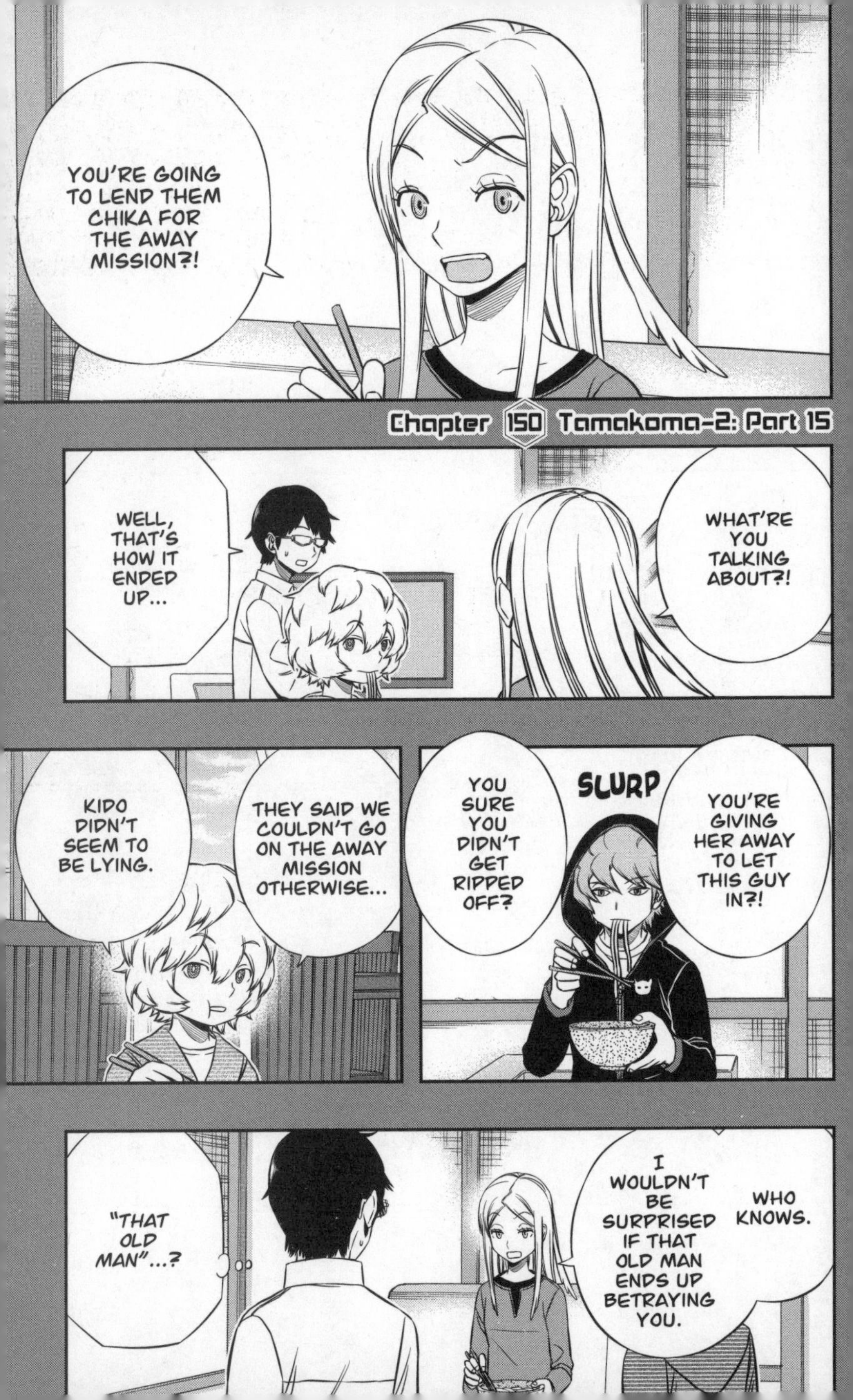
YOU'RE GOING TO LEND THEM CHIKA FOR THE AWAY MISSION?!
Chapter 150 Tamakoma-2: Part 15
WHAT'RE YOU TALKING ABOUT?!
WELL, THAT'S HOW IT ENDED UP...
YOU'RE GIVING HER AWAY TO LET THIS GUY IN?!
SLURP
YOU SURE YOU DIDN'T GET RIPPED OFF?
THEY SAID WE COULDN'T GO ON THE AWAY MISSION OTHERWISE...
KIDO DIDN'T SEEM TO BE LYING.
WHO KNOWS.
I WOULDN'T BE SURPRISED IF THAT OLD MAN ENDS UP BETRAYING YOU.
"THAT OLD MAN"...?

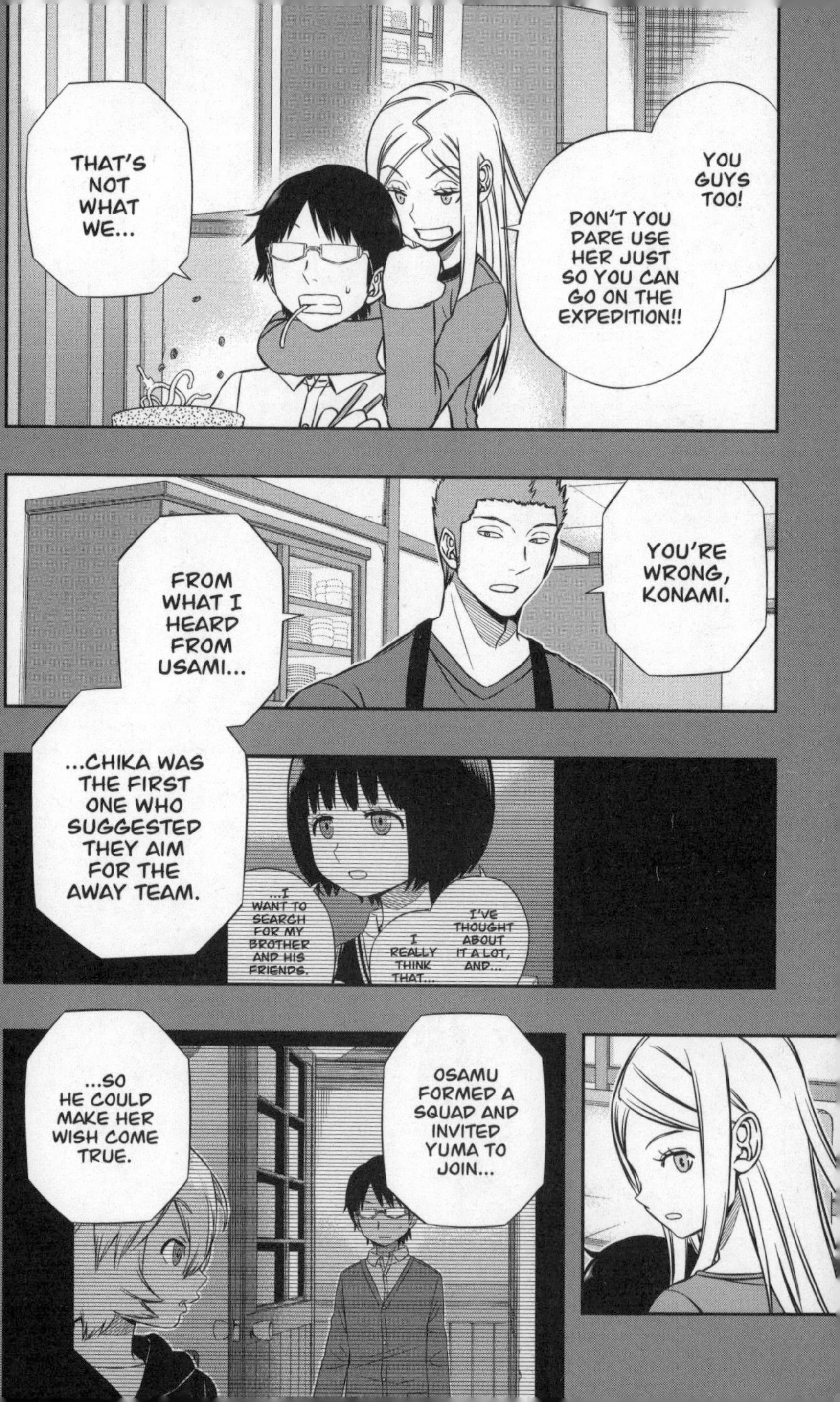
YOU GUYS TOO!
DON'T YOU DARE USE HER JUST SO YOU CAN GO ON THE EXPEDITION!!
THAT'S NOT WHAT WE...
YOU'RE WRONG, KONAMI.
FROM WHAT I HEARD FROM USAMI...
...CHIKA WAS THE FIRST ONE WHO SUGGESTED THEY AIM FOR THE AWAY TEAM.
I'VE THOUGHT ABOUT IT A LOT, AND...
I REALLY THINK THAT...
...I WANT TO SEARCH FOR MY BROTHER AND HIS FRIENDS.
OSAMU FORMED A SQUAD AND INVITED YUMA TO JOIN...
...SO HE COULD MAKE HER WISH COME TRUE.

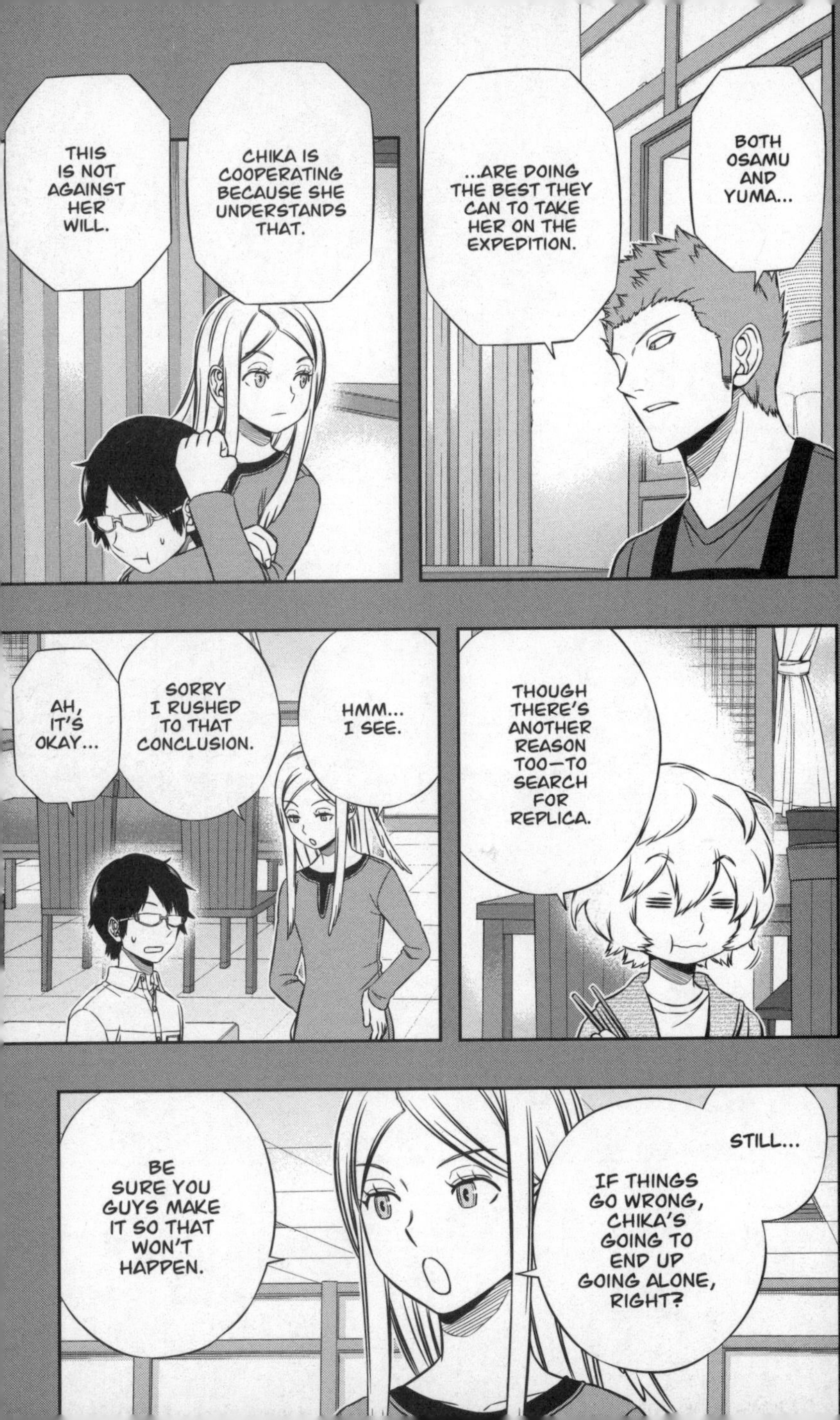
BOTH OSAMU AND YUMA...
...ARE DOING THE BEST THEY CAN TO TAKE HER ON THE EXPEDITION.
CHIKA IS COOPERATING BECAUSE SHE UNDERSTANDS THAT.
THIS IS NOT AGAINST HER WILL.
THOUGH THERE'S ANOTHER REASON TOO—TO SEARCH FOR REPLICA.
HMM... I SEE.
SORRY I RUSHED TO THAT CONCLUSION.
AH, IT'S OKAY...
STILL...
IF THINGS GO WRONG, CHIKA'S GOING TO END UP GOING ALONE, RIGHT?
BE SURE YOU GUYS MAKE IT SO THAT WON'T HAPPEN.

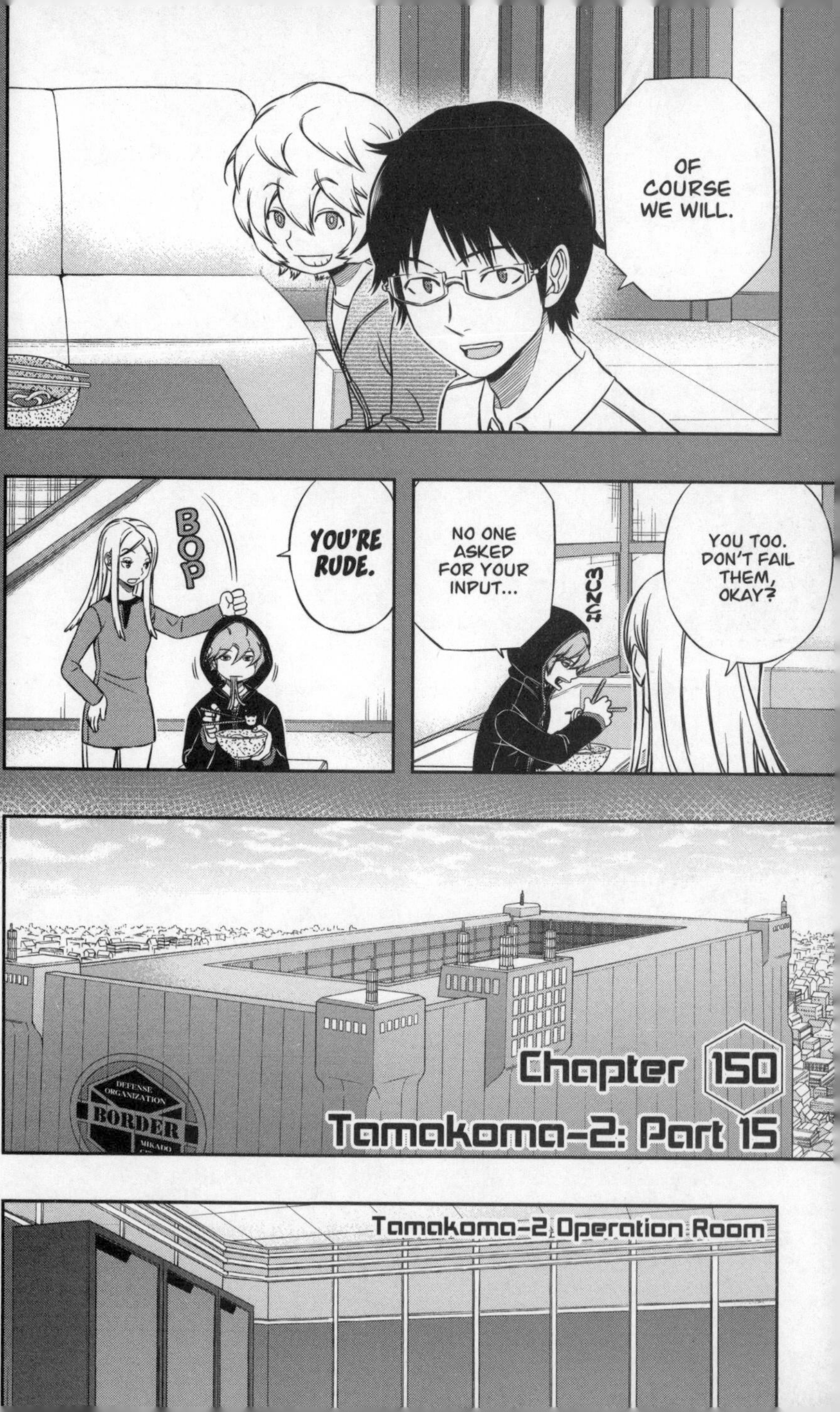
OF COURSE WE WILL.
YOU TOO. DON'T FAIL THEM, OKAY?
NO ONE ASKED FOR YOUR INPUT...
MUNCH
YOU'RE RUDE.
BOP
Chapter 150
Tamakoma-2: Part 15
DEFENSE ORGANIZATION
BORDER
MIKADO
Tamakoma-2 Operation Room

...UNTIL THE AWAY TEAM IS DECIDED.

WE HAVE THREE MATCHES...

SO THAT MEANS WE NEED SIX MORE POINTS TO AT LEAST REACH NO. 2.

HMPH...

...WE NEED EIGHT MORE POINTS THAN NINOMIYA SQUAD AND FIVE MORE THAN KAGEURA.

TO REACH THE TOP...

1	NINOMIYA SQUAD	34 pt
2	KAGEURA SQUAD	31 pt
3	IKOMA SQUAD	27 pt
4	TAMAKOMA-2	26 pt
5	OJI SQUAD	25 pt
	MA SQUAD	25 pt

WE NEED TO CATCH UP WITHIN OUR NEXT THREE MATCHES.

FOR NOW, WE HAVE TO SCORE AS MANY POINTS AS WE CAN...

BUT WE DON'T KNOW HOW MANY POINTS THEY'RE GOING TO GET EITHER.

RIGHT...

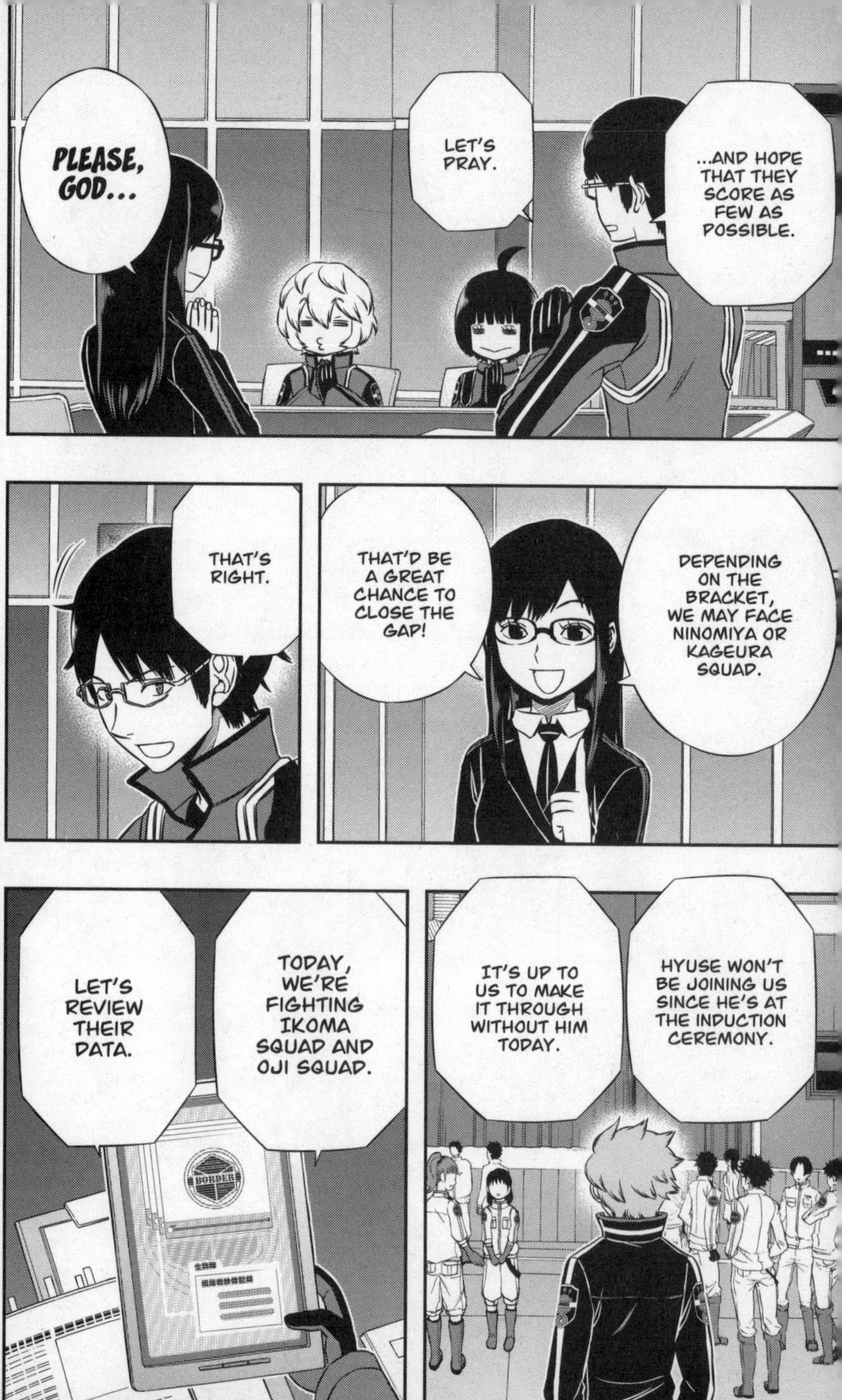
...AND HOPE THAT THEY SCORE AS FEW AS POSSIBLE.
LET'S PRAY.
PLEASE, GOD...
DEPENDING ON THE BRACKET, WE MAY FACE NINOMIYA OR KAGEURA SQUAD.
THAT'D BE A GREAT CHANCE TO CLOSE THE GAP!
THAT'S RIGHT.
HYUSE WON'T BE JOINING US SINCE HE'S AT THE INDUCTION CEREMONY.
IT'S UP TO US TO MAKE IT THROUGH WITHOUT HIM TODAY.
TODAY, WE'RE FIGHTING IKOMA SQUAD AND OJI SQUAD.
LET'S REVIEW THEIR DATA.
BORDER

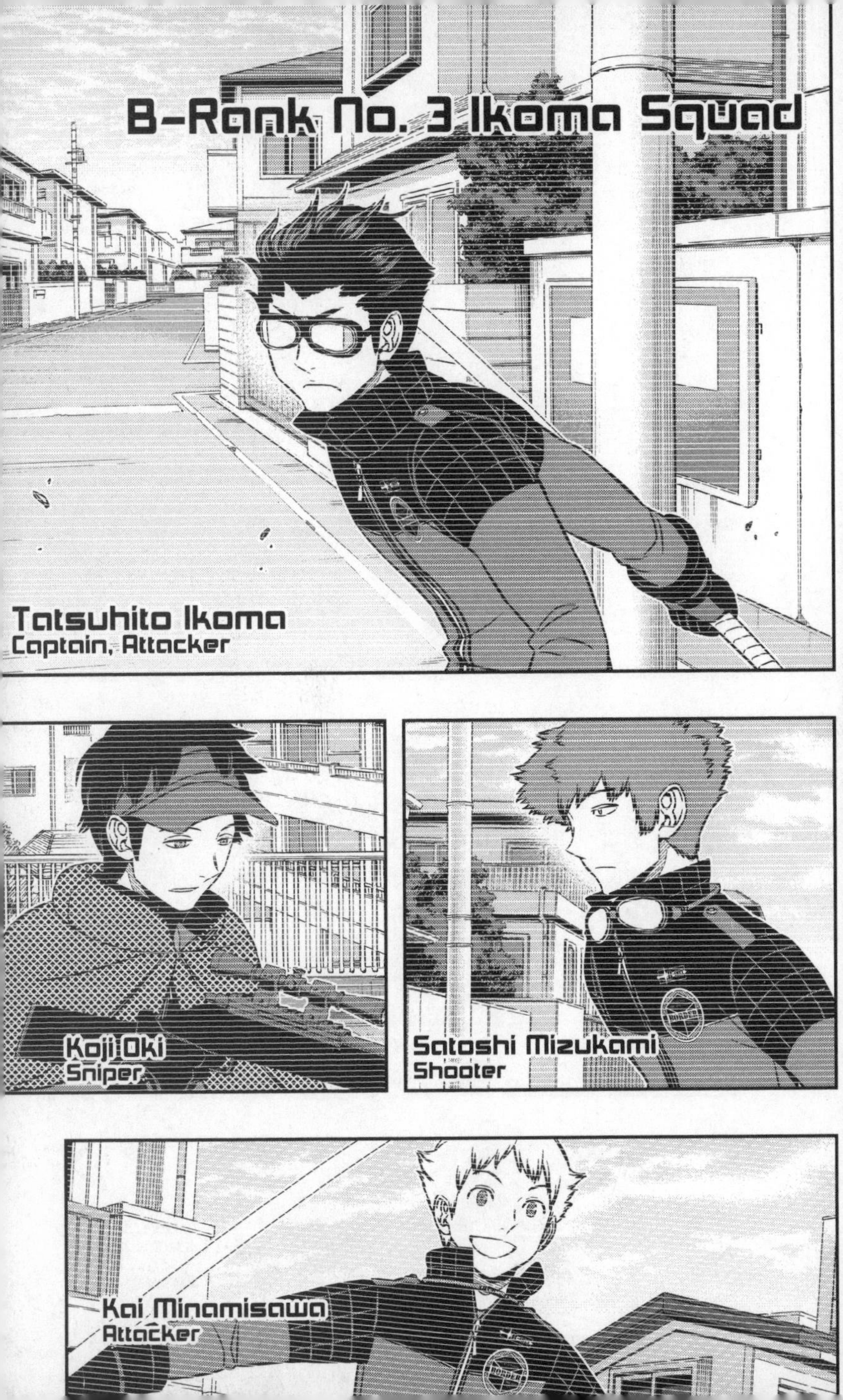
B-Rank No. 3 Ikoma Squad
Tatsuhito Ikoma
Captain, Attacker
Satoshi Mizukami
Shooter
Koji Oki
Sniper
Kai Minamisawa
Attacker

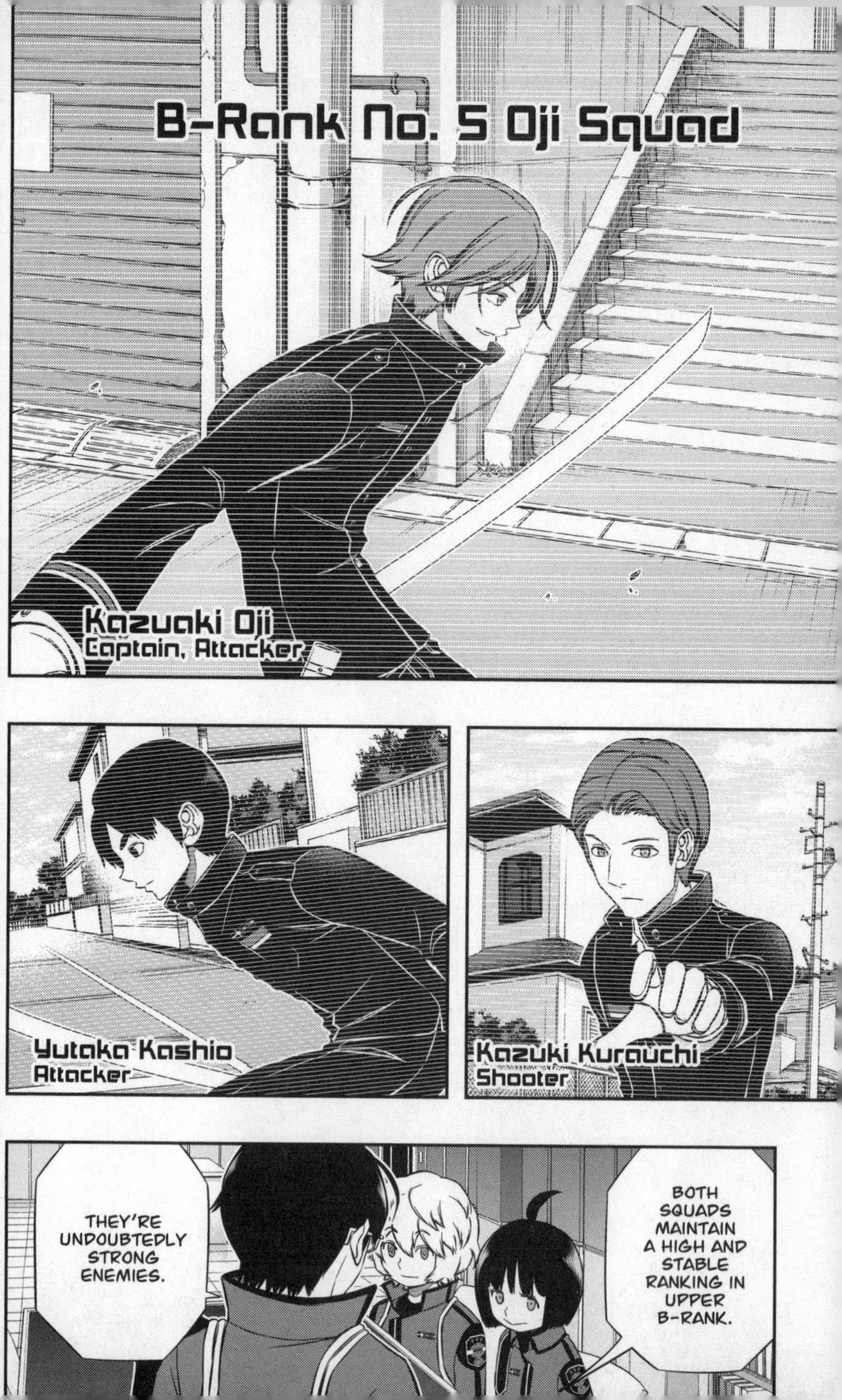
B-Rank No. 5 Oji Squad
Kazuaki Oji
Captain, Attacker
Kazuki Kurauchi
Shooter
Yutaka Kashio
Attacker
BOTH SQUADS MAINTAIN A HIGH AND STABLE RANKING IN UPPER B-RANK.
THEY'RE UNDOUBTEDLY STRONG ENEMIES.

THEY BOTH HAVE A SIMILAR FORMATION.

TWO ATTACKERS COVERED BY ONE SHOOTER.

IKOMA SQUAD ALSO HAS ONE SNIPER FOR COVER.

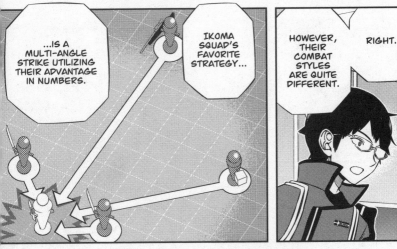

RIGHT.

HOWEVER, THEIR COMBAT STYLES ARE QUITE DIFFERENT.

IKOMA SQUAD'S FAVORITE STRATEGY...

...IS A MULTI-ANGLE STRIKE UTILIZING THEIR ADVANTAGE IN NUMBERS.

WE'VE GOT TO BE CAUTIOUS OF THEIR KOGETSU USER, CAPTAIN IKOMA.

AND OKI, THEIR MOBILE SNIPER WHO'S EQUIPPED WITH A GRASSHOPPER.

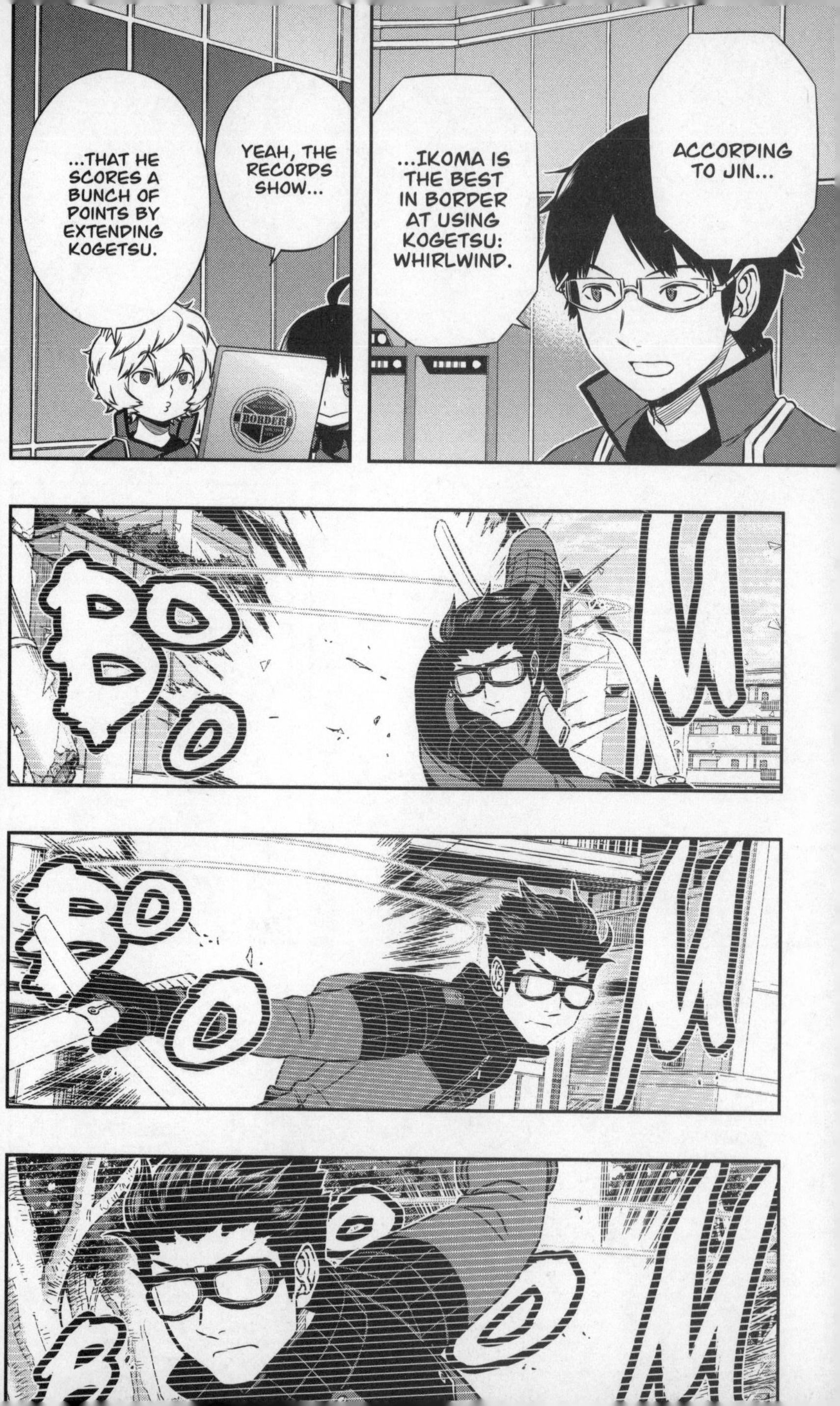
ACCORDING TO JIN...
...IKOMA IS THE BEST IN BORDER AT USING KOGETSU: WHIRLWIND.
YEAH, THE RECORDS SHOW...
...THAT HE SCORES A BUNCH OF POINTS BY EXTENDING KOGETSU.
BOOM
BOOM
BOOM

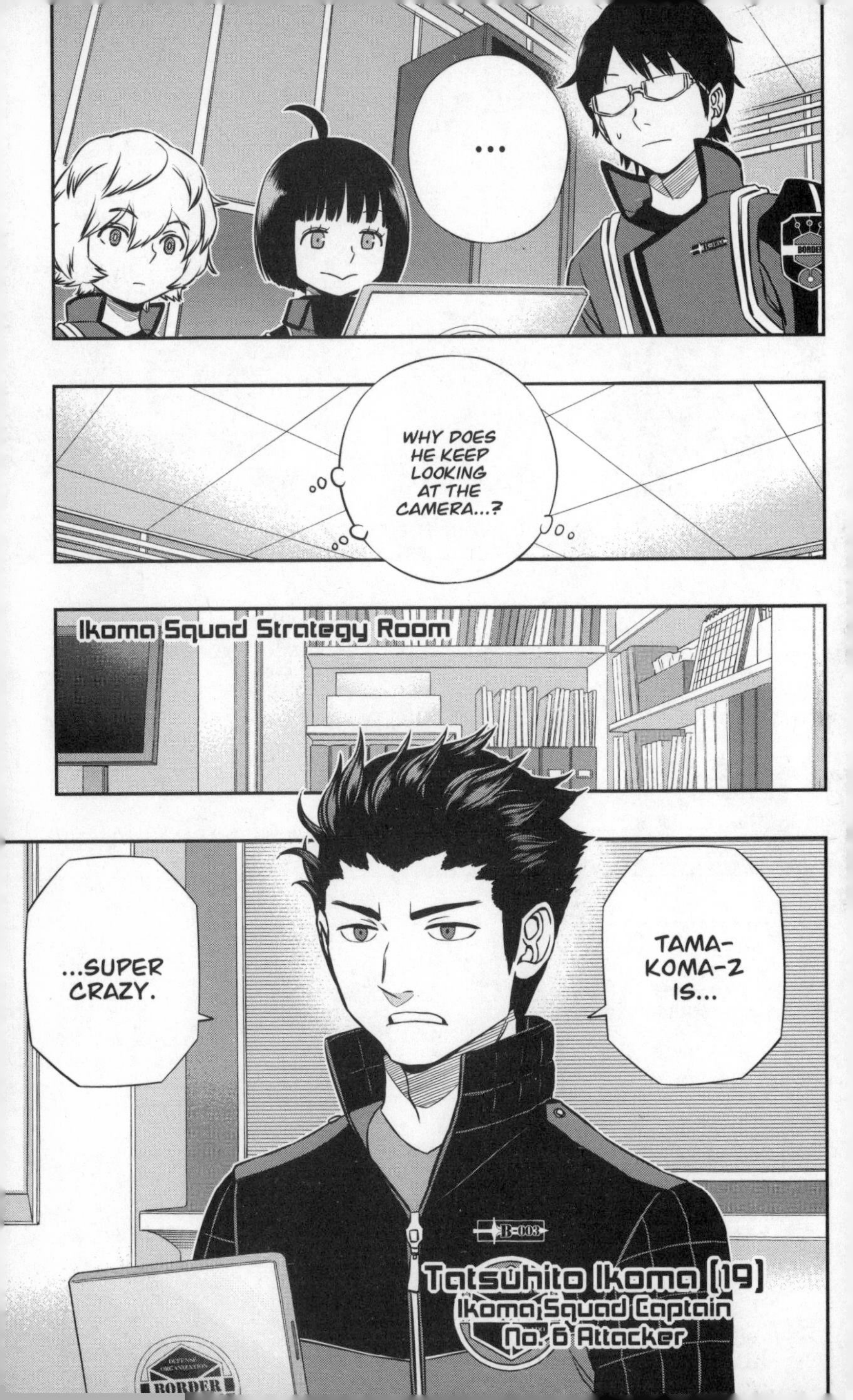
...
WHY DOES HE KEEP LOOKING AT THE CAMERA...?
Ikoma Squad Strategy Room
TAMA-KOMA-2 IS...
...SUPER CRAZY.
Tatsuhito Ikoma (19)
Ikoma Squad Captain
No. 6 Attacker

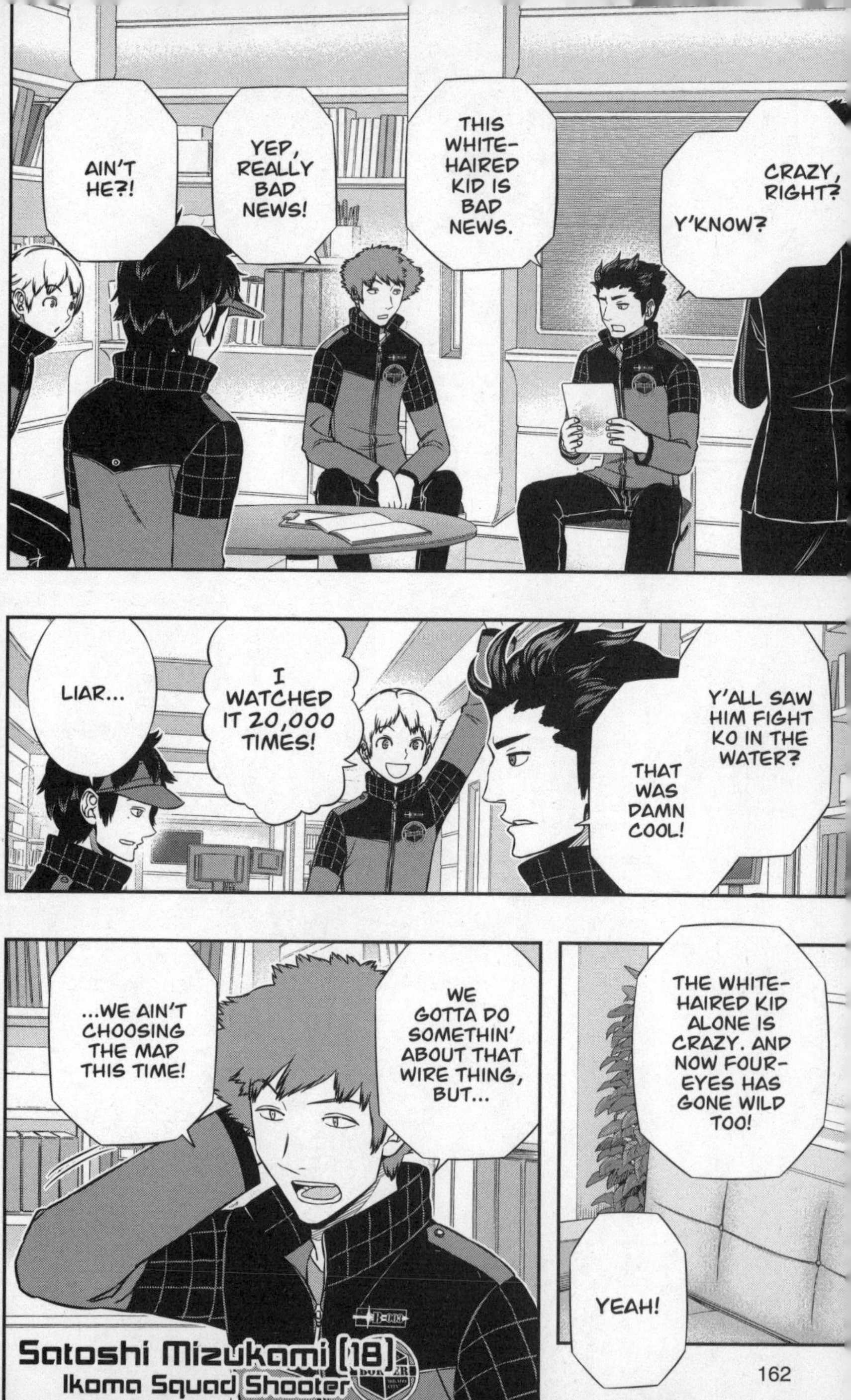
CRAZY, RIGHT?
Y'KNOW?
THIS WHITE-HAIRED KID IS BAD NEWS.
YEP, REALLY BAD NEWS!
AIN'T HE?!
Y'ALL SAW HIM FIGHT KO IN THE WATER?
THAT WAS DAMN COOL!
I WATCHED IT 20,000 TIMES!
LIAR...
THE WHITE-HAIRED KID ALONE IS CRAZY. AND NOW FOUR-EYES HAS GONE WILD TOO!
YEAH!
WE GOTTA DO SOMETHIN' ABOUT THAT WIRE THING, BUT...
...WE AIN'T CHOOSING THE MAP THIS TIME!
Satoshi Mizukami (18)
Ikoma Squad Shooter

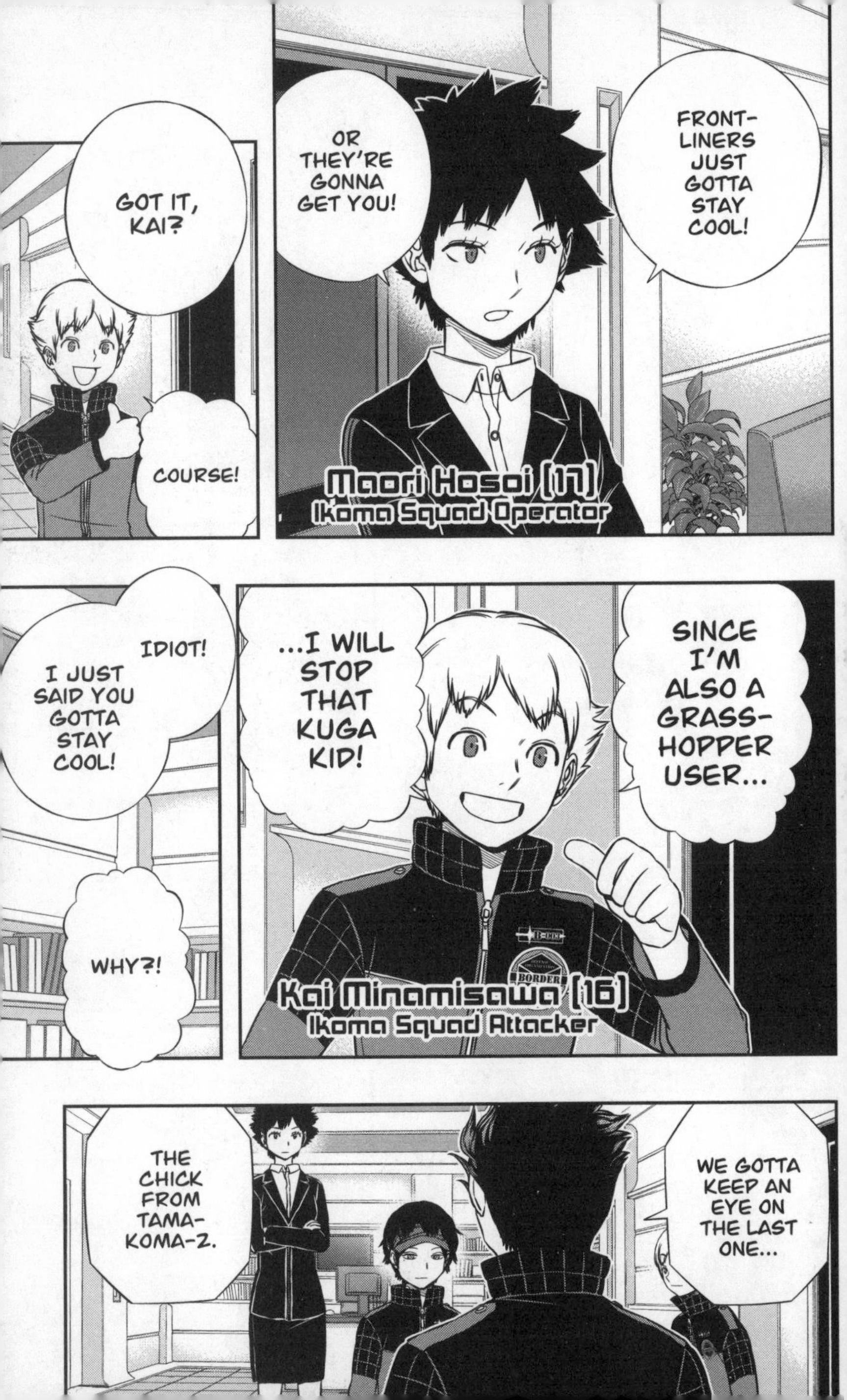
FRONT-LINERS JUST GOTTA STAY COOL!
OR THEY'RE GONNA GET YOU!
Maori Hosoi (17)
Ikoma Squad Operator
GOT IT, KAI?
COURSE!
SINCE I'M ALSO A GRASS-HOPPER USER...
...I WILL STOP THAT KUGA KID!
Kai Minamisawa (16)
Ikoma Squad Attacker
IDIOT! I JUST SAID YOU GOTTA STAY COOL!
WHY?!
WE GOTTA KEEP AN EYE ON THE LAST ONE...
THE CHICK FROM TAMA-KOMA-2.

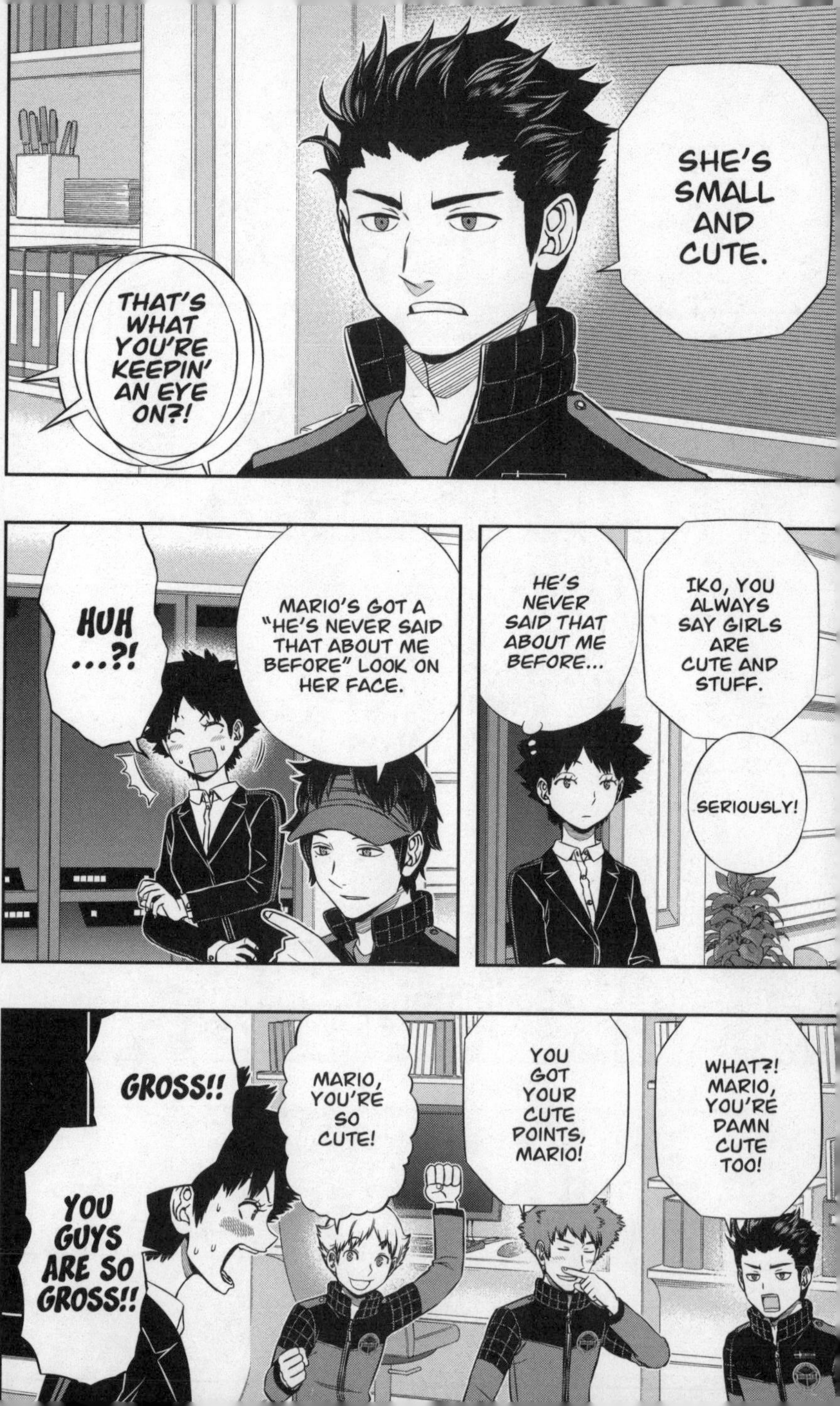
SHE'S SMALL AND CUTE.
THAT'S WHAT YOU'RE KEEPIN' AN EYE ON?!
IKO, YOU ALWAYS SAY GIRLS ARE CUTE AND STUFF.
HE'S NEVER SAID THAT ABOUT ME BEFORE...
SERIOUSLY!
MARIO'S GOT A "HE'S NEVER SAID THAT ABOUT ME BEFORE" LOOK ON HER FACE.
HUH ...?!
WHAT?! MARIO, YOU'RE DAMN CUTE TOO!
YOU GOT YOUR CUTE POINTS, MARIO!
MARIO, YOU'RE SO CUTE!
GROSS!!
YOU GUYS ARE SO GROSS!!

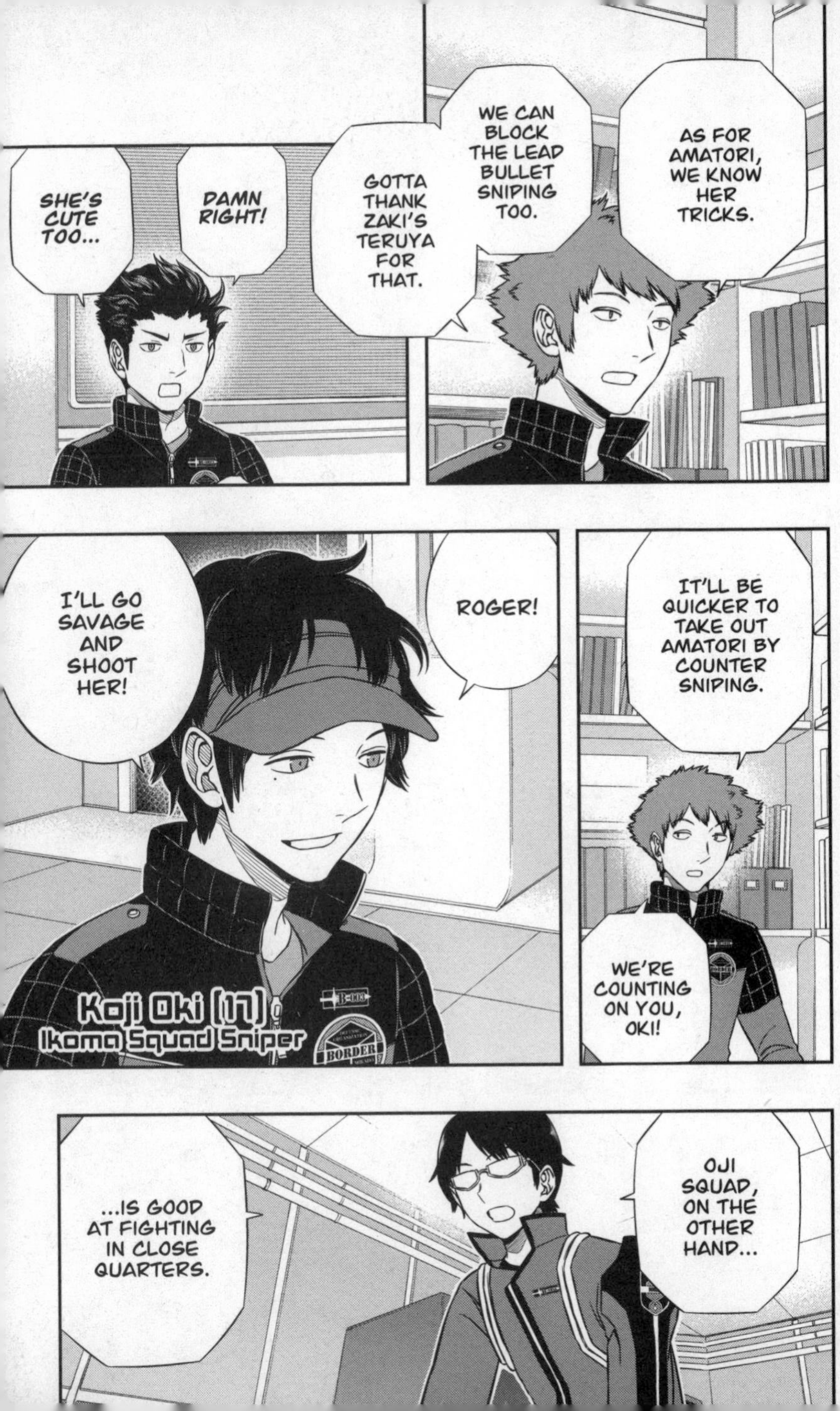
AS FOR AMATORI, WE KNOW HER TRICKS.
WE CAN BLOCK THE LEAD BULLET SNIPING TOO.
GOTTA THANK ZAKI'S TERUYA FOR THAT.
DAMN RIGHT!
SHE'S CUTE TOO...
IT'LL BE QUICKER TO TAKE OUT AMATORI BY COUNTER SNIPING.
WE'RE COUNTING ON YOU, OKI!
ROGER!
I'LL GO SAVAGE AND SHOOT HER!
Koji Oki (17)
Ikoma Squad Sniper
OJI SQUAD, ON THE OTHER HAND...
...IS GOOD AT FIGHTING IN CLOSE QUARTERS.

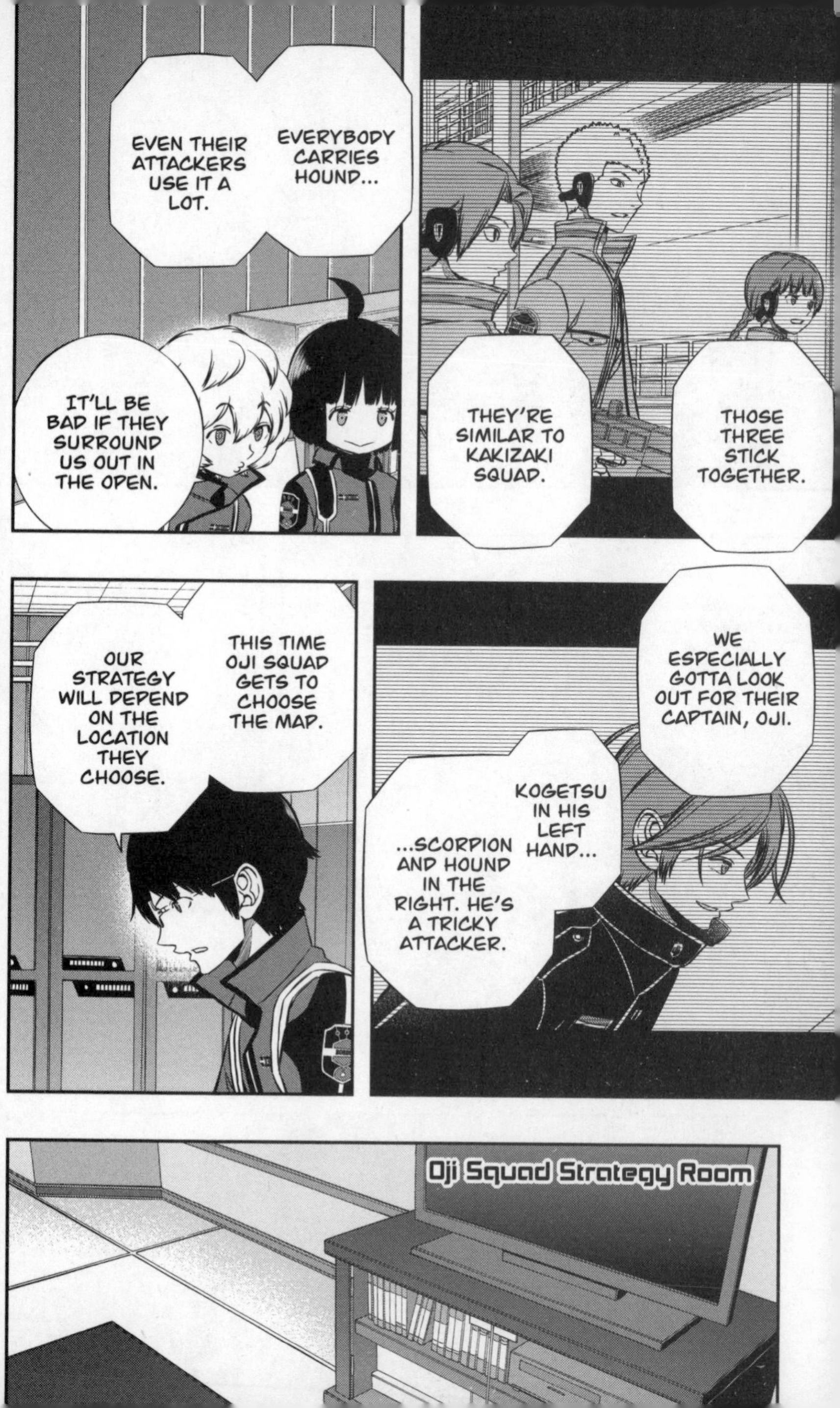
THOSE THREE STICK TOGETHER.
THEY'RE SIMILAR TO KAKIZAKI SQUAD.
EVERYBODY CARRIES HOUND...
EVEN THEIR ATTACKERS USE IT A LOT.
IT'LL BE BAD IF THEY SURROUND US OUT IN THE OPEN.
WE ESPECIALLY GOTTA LOOK OUT FOR THEIR CAPTAIN, OJI.
KOGETSU IN HIS LEFT HAND...
...SCORPION AND HOUND IN THE RIGHT. HE'S A TRICKY ATTACKER.
THIS TIME OJI SQUAD GETS TO CHOOSE THE MAP.
OUR STRATEGY WILL DEPEND ON THE LOCATION THEY CHOOSE.
Oji Squad Strategy Room

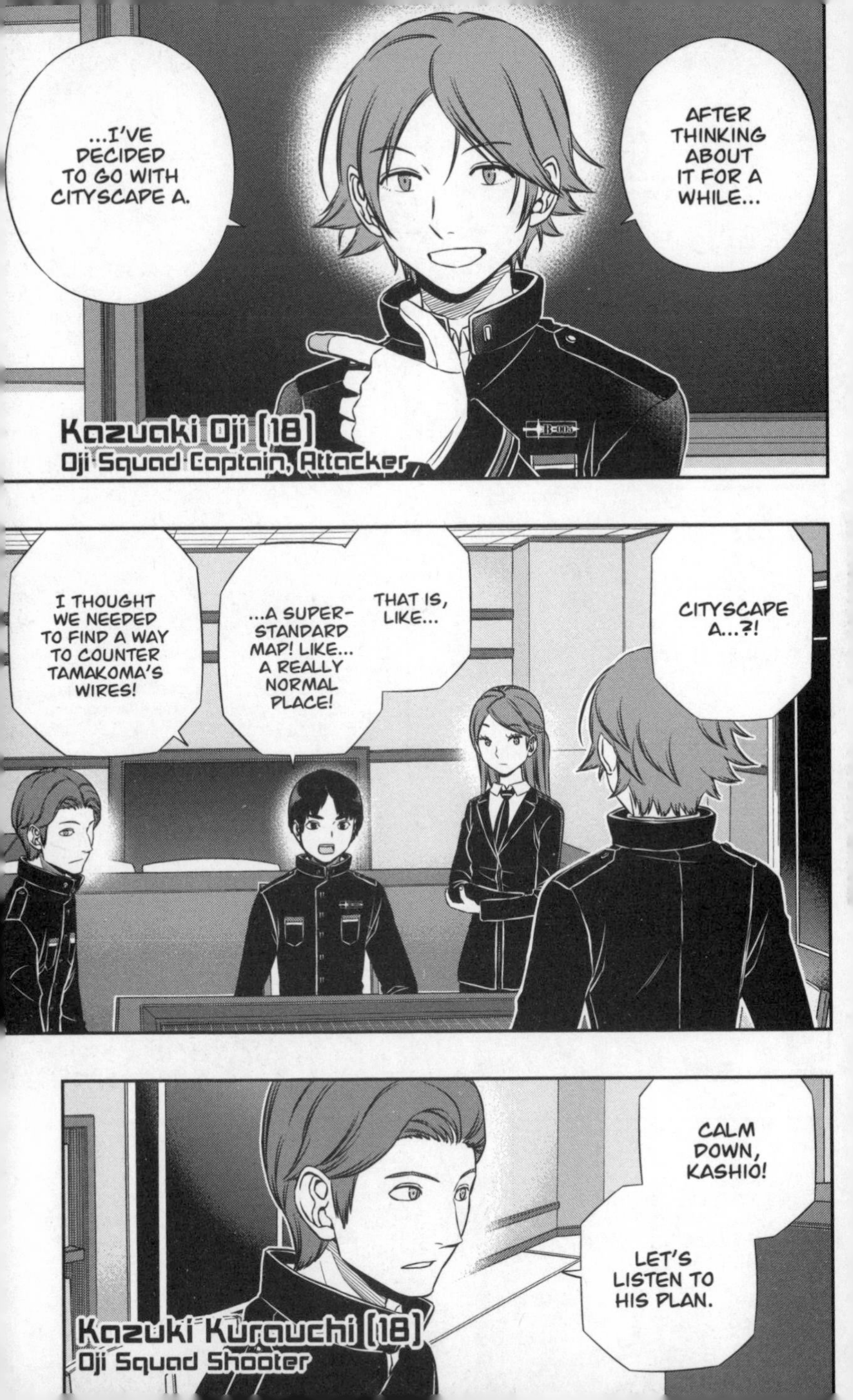
AFTER THINKING ABOUT IT FOR A WHILE...
...I'VE DECIDED TO GO WITH CITYSCAPE A.
Kazuaki Oji (18)
Oji Squad Captain, Attacker
CITYSCAPE A...?!
THAT IS, LIKE...
...A SUPER-STANDARD MAP! LIKE... A REALLY NORMAL PLACE!
I THOUGHT WE NEEDED TO FIND A WAY TO COUNTER TAMAKOMA'S WIRES!
CALM DOWN, KASHIO!
LET'S LISTEN TO HIS PLAN.
Kazuki Kurauchi (18)
Oji Squad Shooter

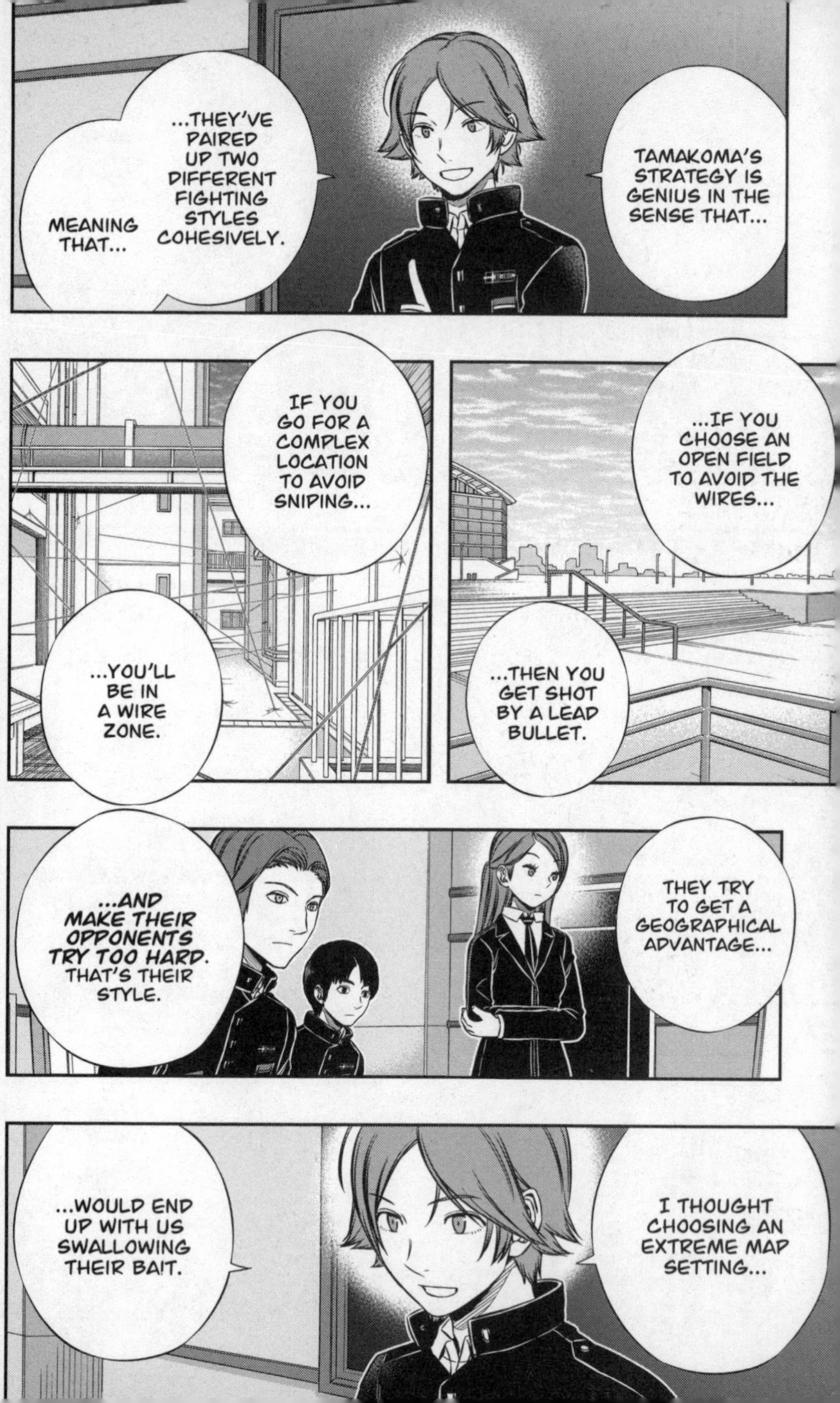
TAMAKOMA'S STRATEGY IS GENIUS IN THE SENSE THAT...
...THEY'VE PAIRED UP TWO DIFFERENT FIGHTING STYLES COHESIVELY.
MEANING THAT...
...IF YOU CHOOSE AN OPEN FIELD TO AVOID THE WIRES...
...THEN YOU GET SHOT BY A LEAD BULLET.
IF YOU GO FOR A COMPLEX LOCATION TO AVOID SNIPING...
...YOU'LL BE IN A WIRE ZONE.
THEY TRY TO GET A GEOGRAPHICAL ADVANTAGE...
...AND MAKE THEIR OPPONENTS TRY TOO HARD. THAT'S THEIR STYLE.
I THOUGHT CHOOSING AN EXTREME MAP SETTING...
...WOULD END UP WITH US SWALLOWING THEIR BAIT.

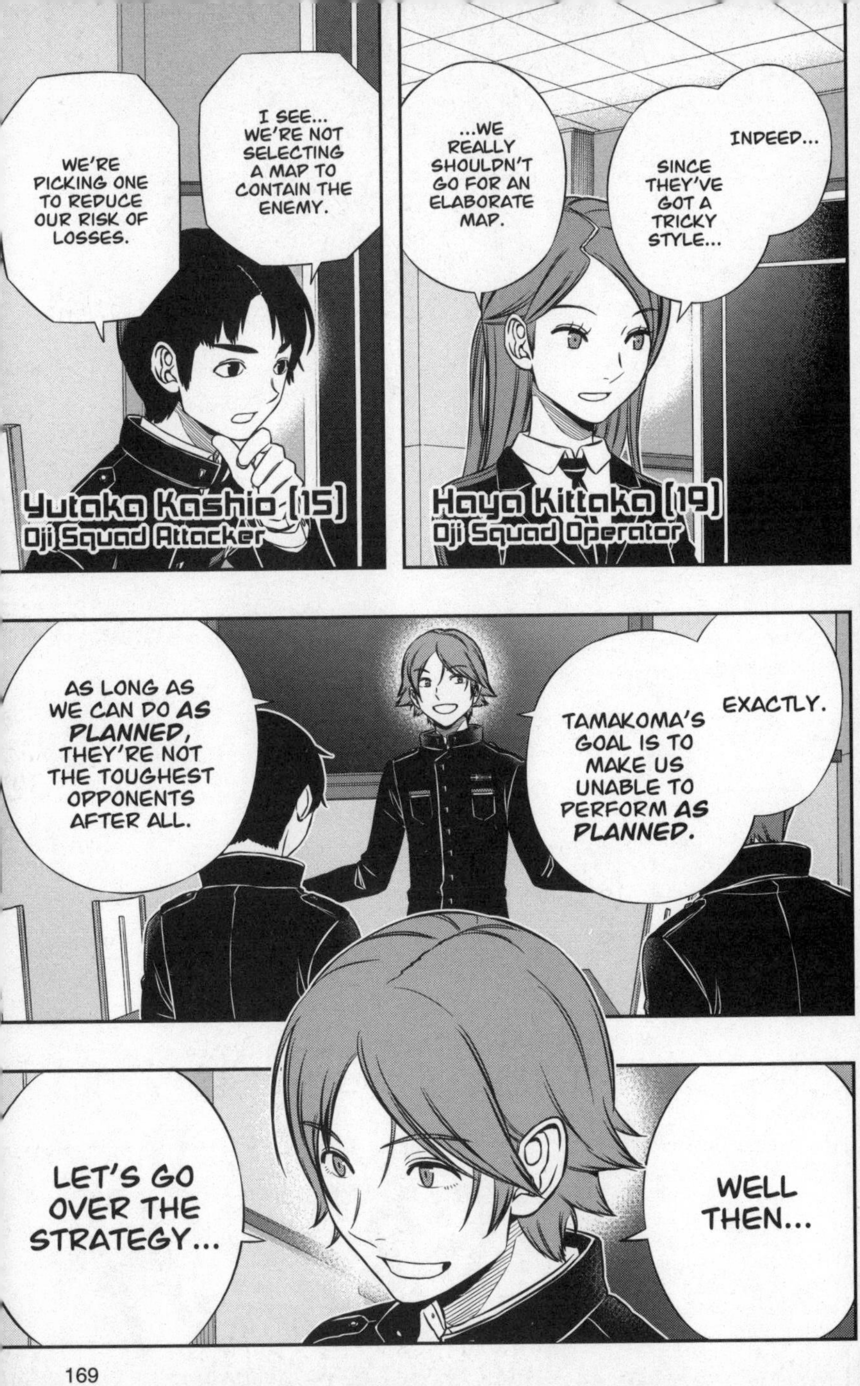
INDEED...
SINCE THEY'VE GOT A TRICKY STYLE...
...WE REALLY SHOULDN'T GO FOR AN ELABORATE MAP.
Haya Kittaka (19)
Oji Squad Operator
I SEE... WE'RE NOT SELECTING A MAP TO CONTAIN THE ENEMY.
WE'RE PICKING ONE TO REDUCE OUR RISK OF LOSSES.
Yutaka Kashio (15)
Oji Squad Attacker
EXACTLY.
TAMAKOMA'S GOAL IS TO MAKE US UNABLE TO PERFORM AS PLANNED.
AS LONG AS WE CAN DO AS PLANNED, THEY'RE NOT THE TOUGHEST OPPONENTS AFTER ALL.
WELL THEN...
LET'S GO OVER THE STRATEGY...

WORLD TRIGGER

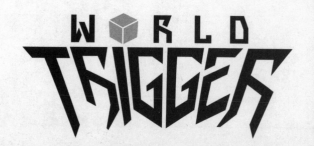

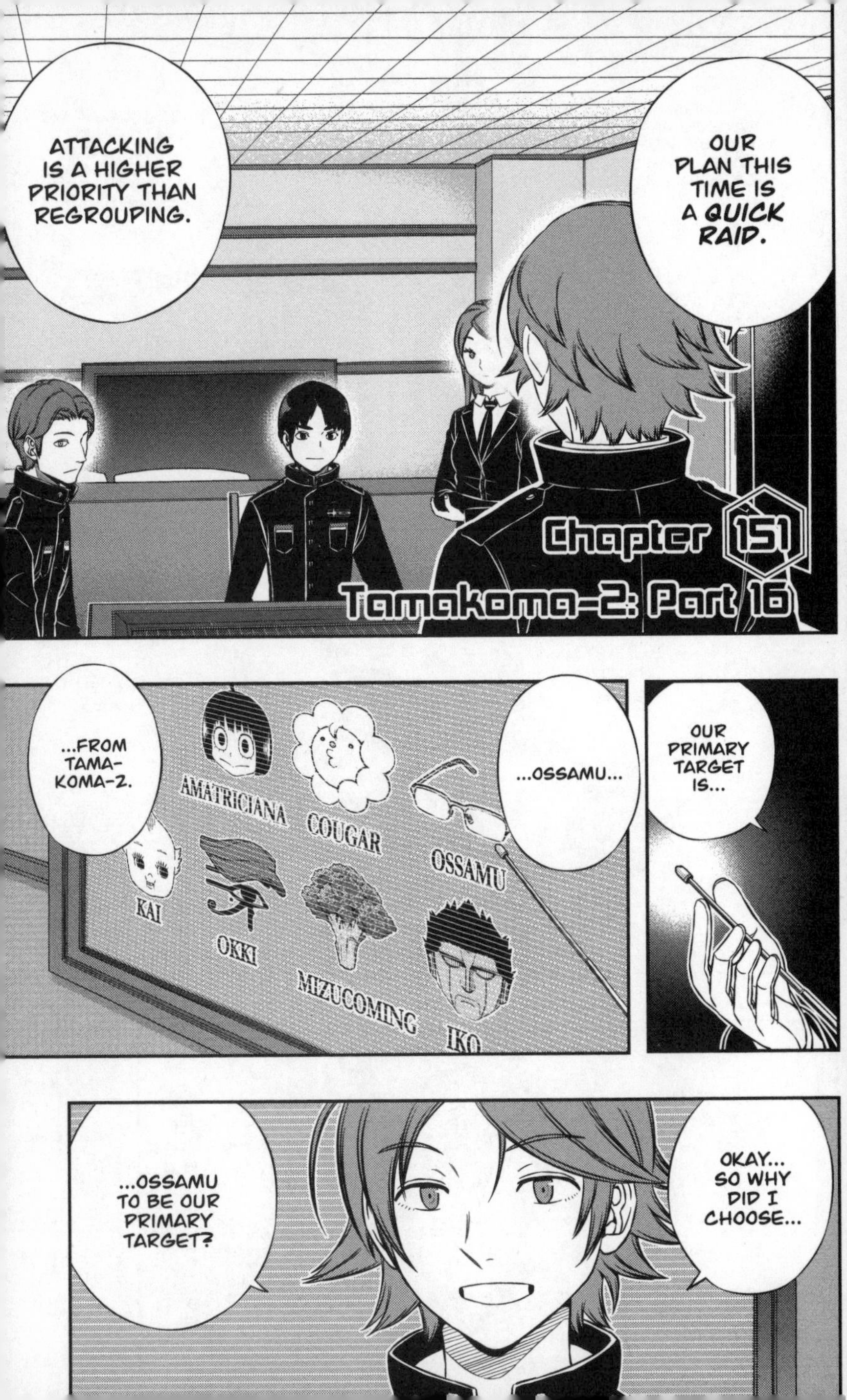
OUR PLAN THIS TIME IS A QUICK RAID.
ATTACKING IS A HIGHER PRIORITY THAN REGROUPING.
Chapter 151
Tamakoma-2: Part 16
OUR PRIMARY TARGET IS...
...OSSAMU...
...FROM TAMA-KOMA-2.
AMATRICIANA
COUGAR
OSSAMU
KAI
OKKI
MIZUCOMING
IKO
OKAY... SO WHY DID I CHOOSE...
...OSSAMU TO BE OUR PRIMARY TARGET?

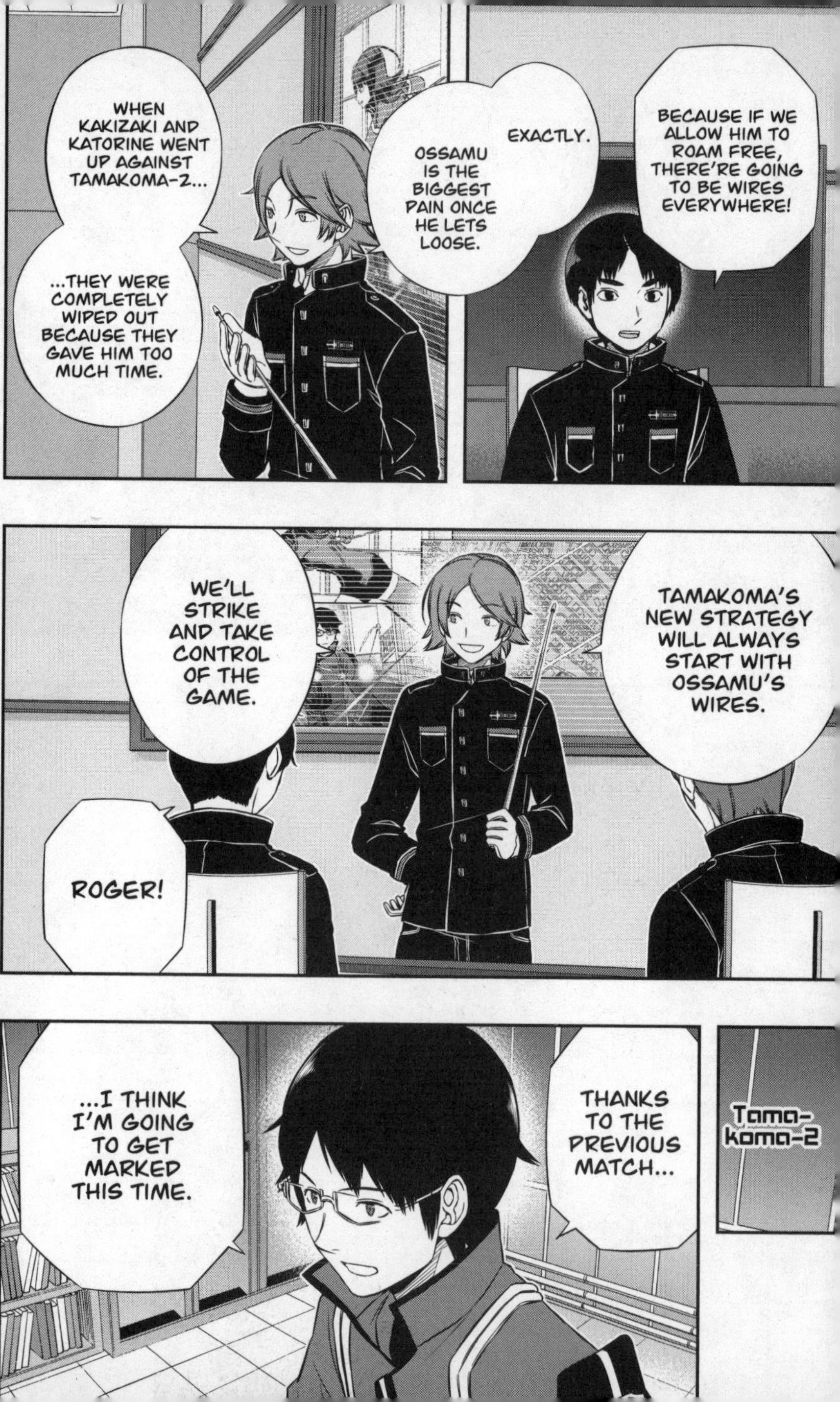
BECAUSE IF WE ALLOW HIM TO ROAM FREE, THERE'RE GOING TO BE WIRES EVERYWHERE!
EXACTLY.
OSSAMU IS THE BIGGEST PAIN ONCE HE LETS LOOSE.
WHEN KAKIZAKI AND KATORINE WENT UP AGAINST TAMAKOMA-2...
...THEY WERE COMPLETELY WIPED OUT BECAUSE THEY GAVE HIM TOO MUCH TIME.
TAMAKOMA'S NEW STRATEGY WILL ALWAYS START WITH OSSAMU'S WIRES.
WE'LL STRIKE AND TAKE CONTROL OF THE GAME.
ROGER!
Tama-koma-2
THANKS TO THE PREVIOUS MATCH...
...I THINK I'M GOING TO GET MARKED THIS TIME.

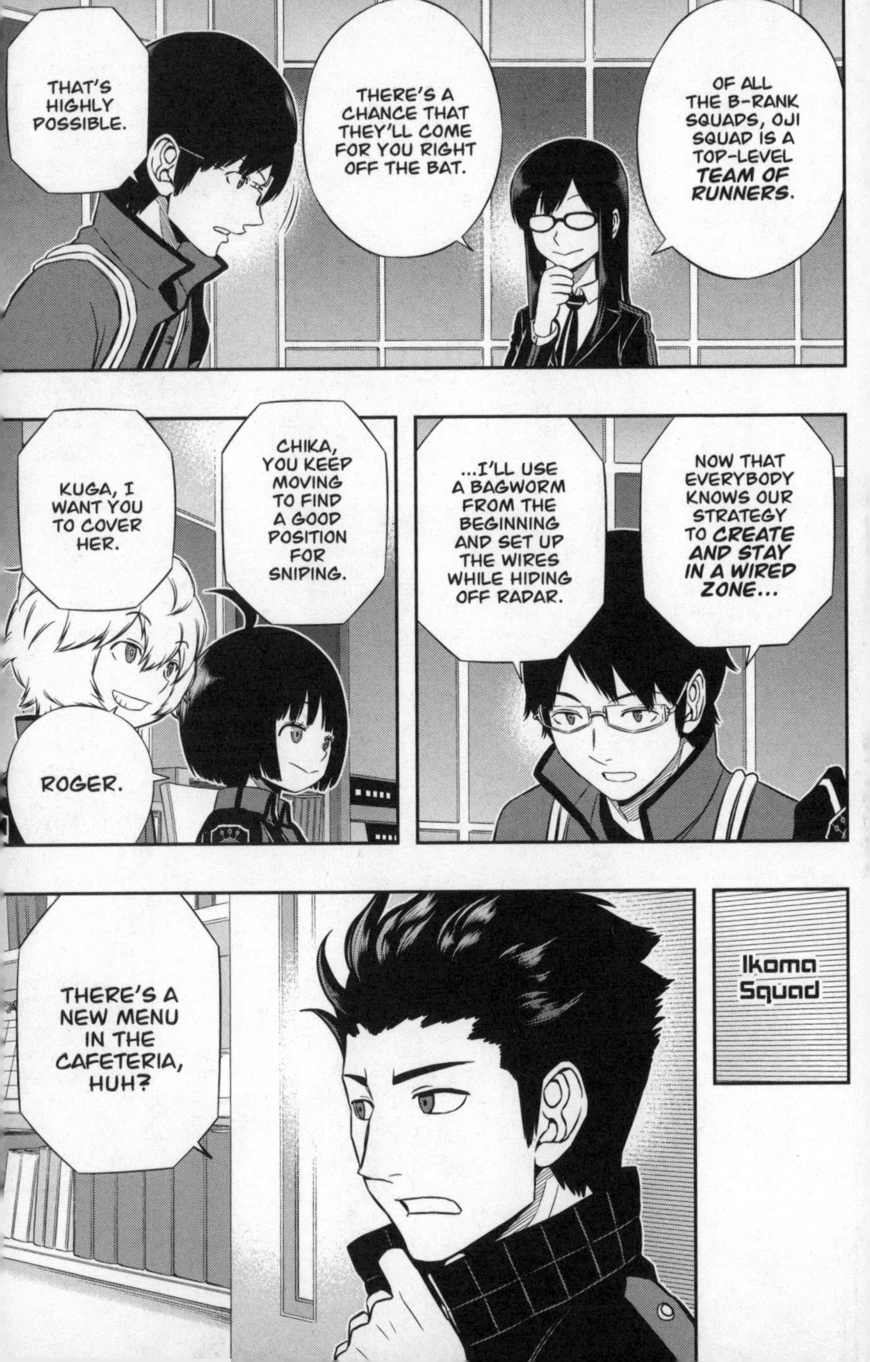
OF ALL THE B-RANK SQUADS, OJI SQUAD IS A TOP-LEVEL TEAM OF RUNNERS.
THERE'S A CHANCE THAT THEY'LL COME FOR YOU RIGHT OFF THE BAT.
THAT'S HIGHLY POSSIBLE.
NOW THAT EVERYBODY KNOWS OUR STRATEGY TO CREATE AND STAY IN A WIRED ZONE...
...I'LL USE A BAGWORM FROM THE BEGINNING AND SET UP THE WIRES WHILE HIDING OFF RADAR.
CHIKA, YOU KEEP MOVING TO FIND A GOOD POSITION FOR SNIPING.
KUGA, I WANT YOU TO COVER HER.
ROGER.
Ikoma Squad
THERE'S A NEW MENU IN THE CAFETERIA, HUH?

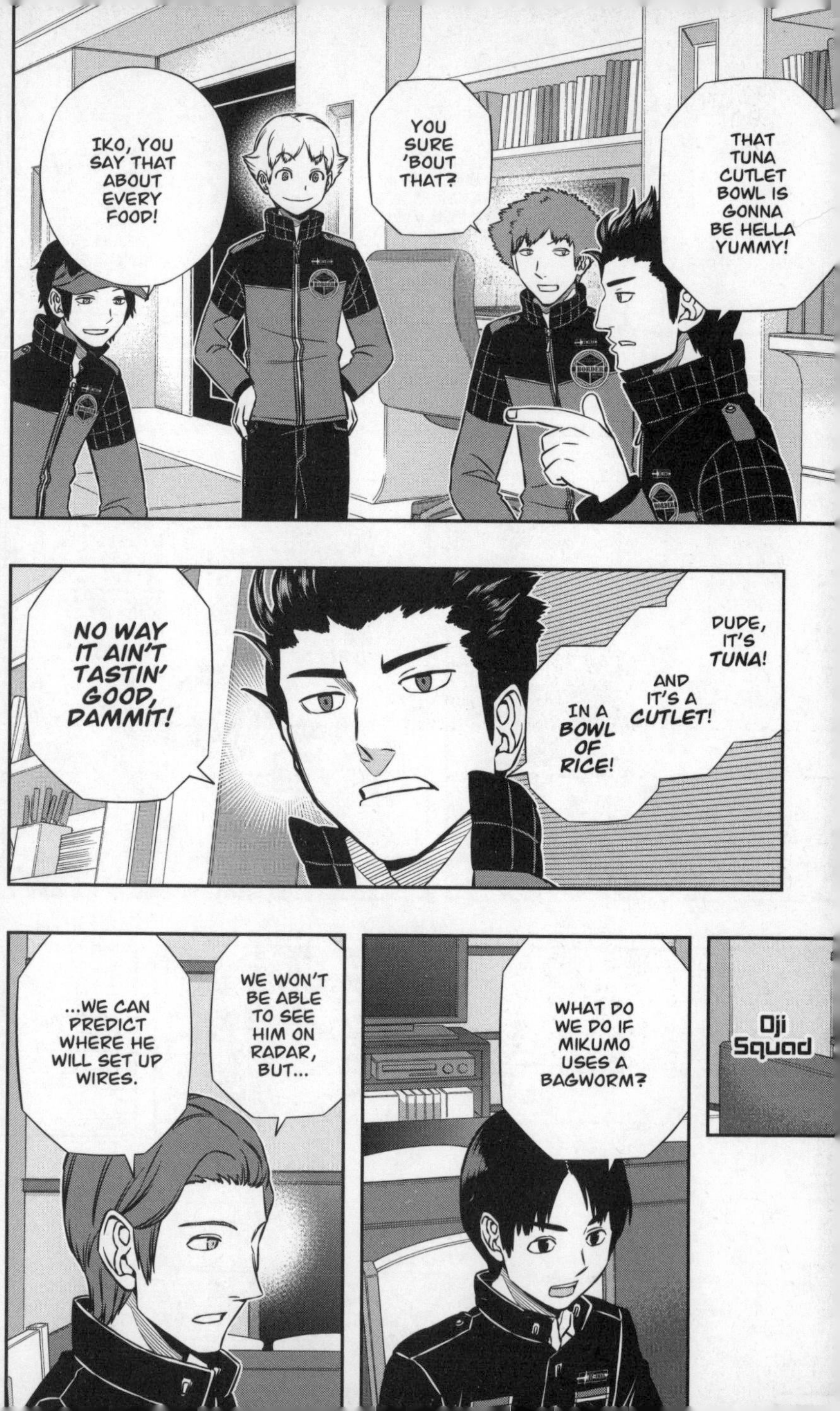
THAT TUNA CUTLET BOWL IS GONNA BE HELLA YUMMY!
YOU SURE 'BOUT THAT?
IKO, YOU SAY THAT ABOUT EVERY FOOD!
DUDE, IT'S TUNA!
AND IT'S A CUTLET!
IN A BOWL OF RICE!
NO WAY IT AIN'T TASTIN' GOOD, DAMMIT!
Oji Squad
WHAT DO WE DO IF MIKUMO USES A BAGWORM?
WE WON'T BE ABLE TO SEE HIM ON RADAR, BUT...
...WE CAN PREDICT WHERE HE WILL SET UP WIRES.

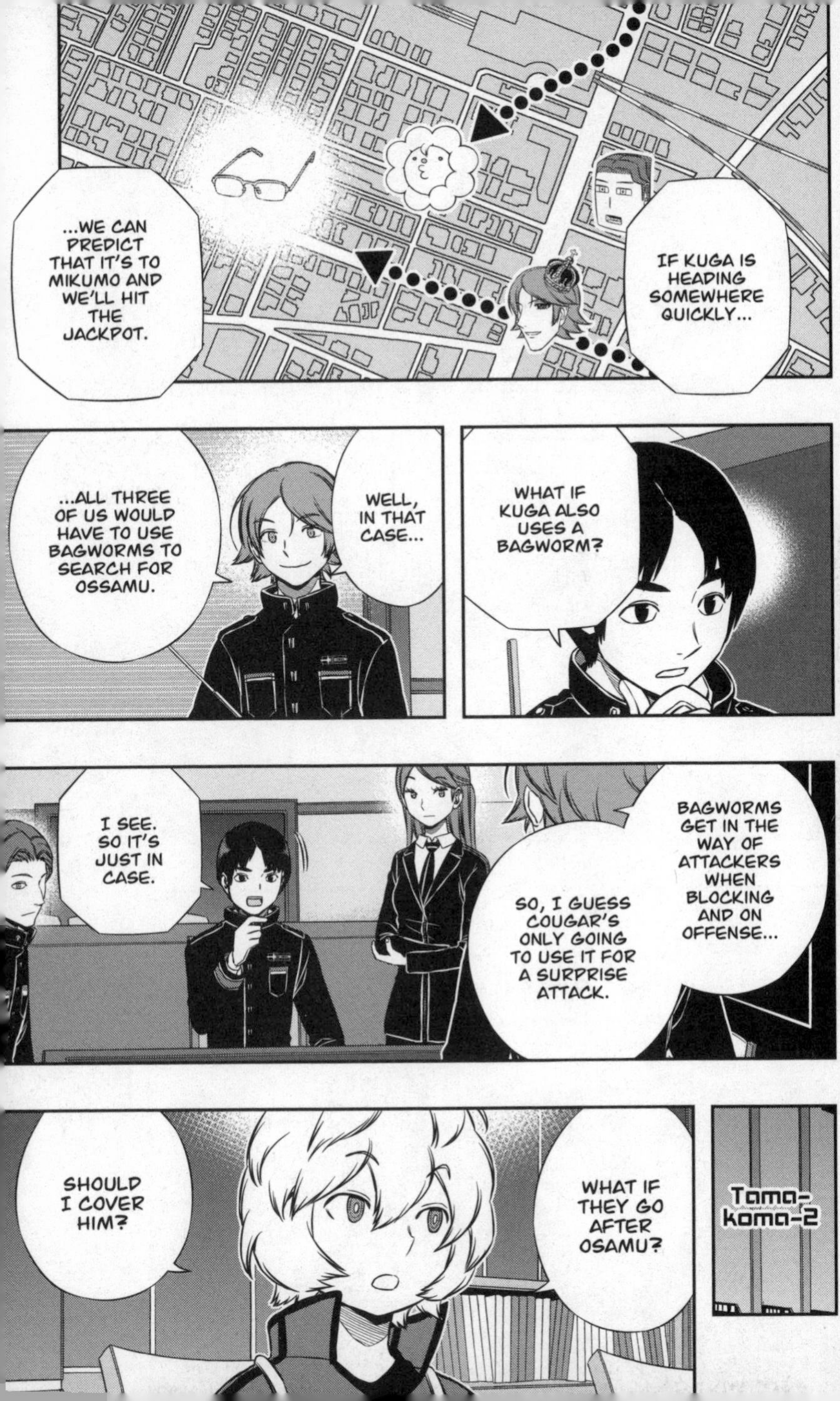
IF KUGA IS HEADING SOMEWHERE QUICKLY...
...WE CAN PREDICT THAT IT'S TO MIKUMO AND WE'LL HIT THE JACKPOT.
WHAT IF KUGA ALSO USES A BAGWORM?
WELL, IN THAT CASE...
...ALL THREE OF US WOULD HAVE TO USE BAGWORMS TO SEARCH FOR OSSAMU.
BAGWORMS GET IN THE WAY OF ATTACKERS WHEN BLOCKING AND ON OFFENSE...
SO, I GUESS COUGAR'S ONLY GOING TO USE IT FOR A SURPRISE ATTACK.
I SEE. SO IT'S JUST IN CASE.
Tama-koma-2
WHAT IF THEY GO AFTER OSAMU?
SHOULD I COVER HIM?

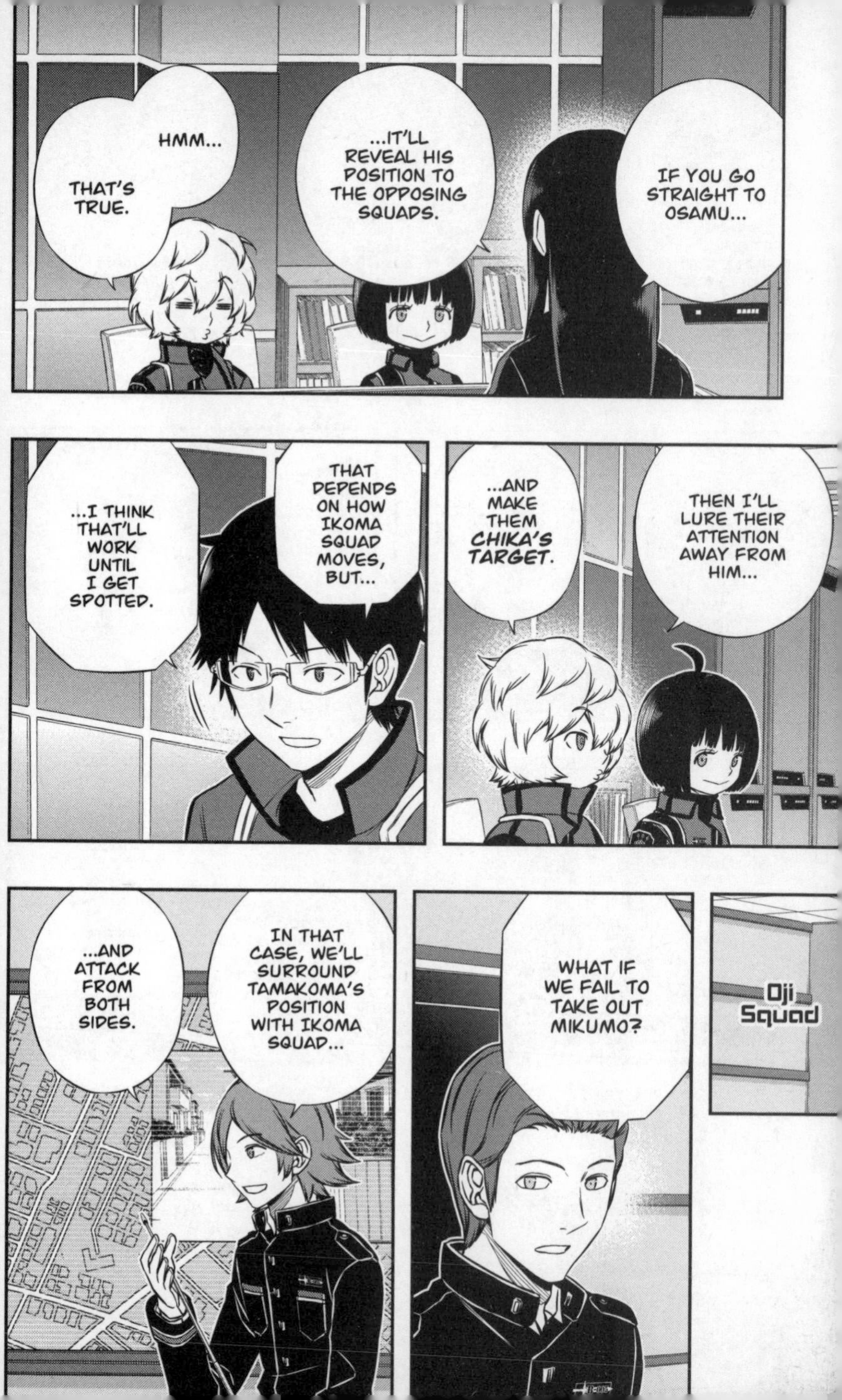
IF YOU GO STRAIGHT TO OSAMU...
...IT'LL REVEAL HIS POSITION TO THE OPPOSING SQUADS.
HMM...
THAT'S TRUE.
THEN I'LL LURE THEIR ATTENTION AWAY FROM HIM...
...AND MAKE THEM CHIKA'S TARGET.
THAT DEPENDS ON HOW IKOMA SQUAD MOVES, BUT...
...I THINK THAT'LL WORK UNTIL I GET SPOTTED.
Oji Squad
WHAT IF WE FAIL TO TAKE OUT MIKUMO?
IN THAT CASE, WE'LL SURROUND TAMAKOMA'S POSITION WITH IKOMA SQUAD...
...AND ATTACK FROM BOTH SIDES.

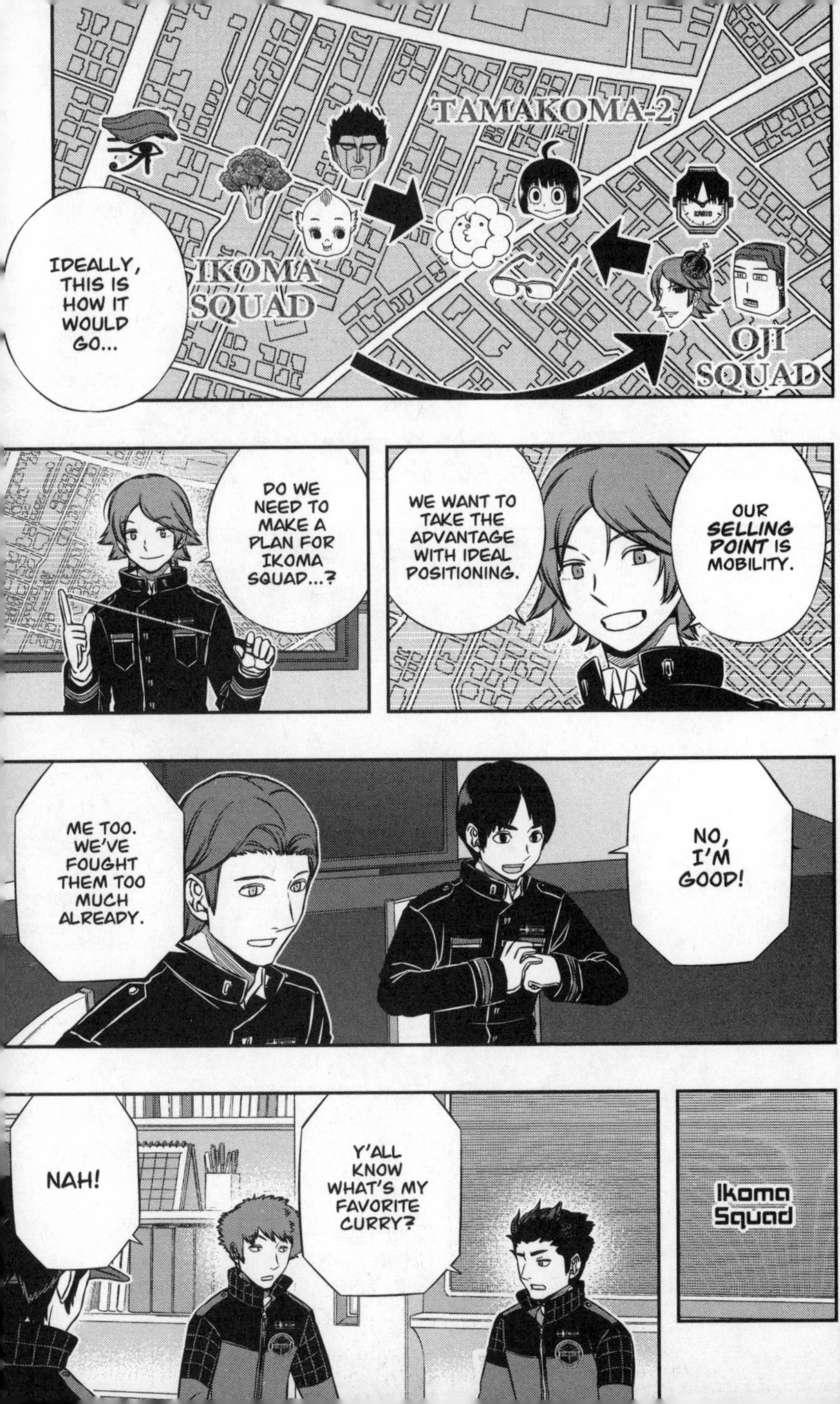
TAMAKOMA-2
OJI SQUAD
IKOMA SQUAD
IDEALLY, THIS IS HOW IT WOULD GO...
OUR SELLING POINT IS MOBILITY.
WE WANT TO TAKE THE ADVANTAGE WITH IDEAL POSITIONING.
DO WE NEED TO MAKE A PLAN FOR IKOMA SQUAD...?
NO, I'M GOOD!
ME TOO. WE'VE FOUGHT THEM TOO MUCH ALREADY.
Ikoma Squad
Y'ALL KNOW WHAT'S MY FAVORITE CURRY?
NAH!

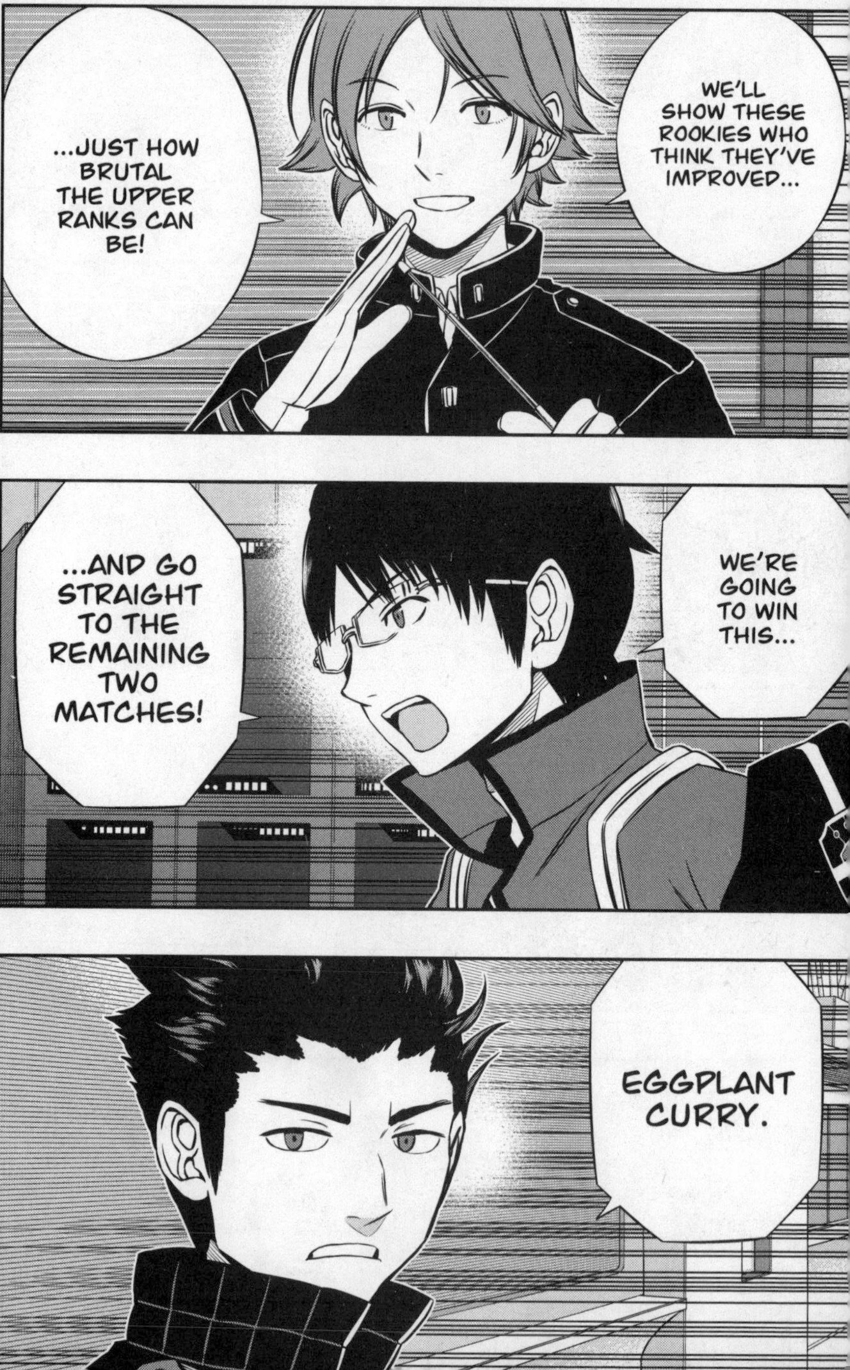
WE'LL SHOW THESE ROOKIES WHO THINK THEY'VE IMPROVED...
...JUST HOW BRUTAL THE UPPER RANKS CAN BE!
WE'RE GOING TO WIN THIS...
...AND GO STRAIGHT TO THE REMAINING TWO MATCHES!
EGGPLANT CURRY.

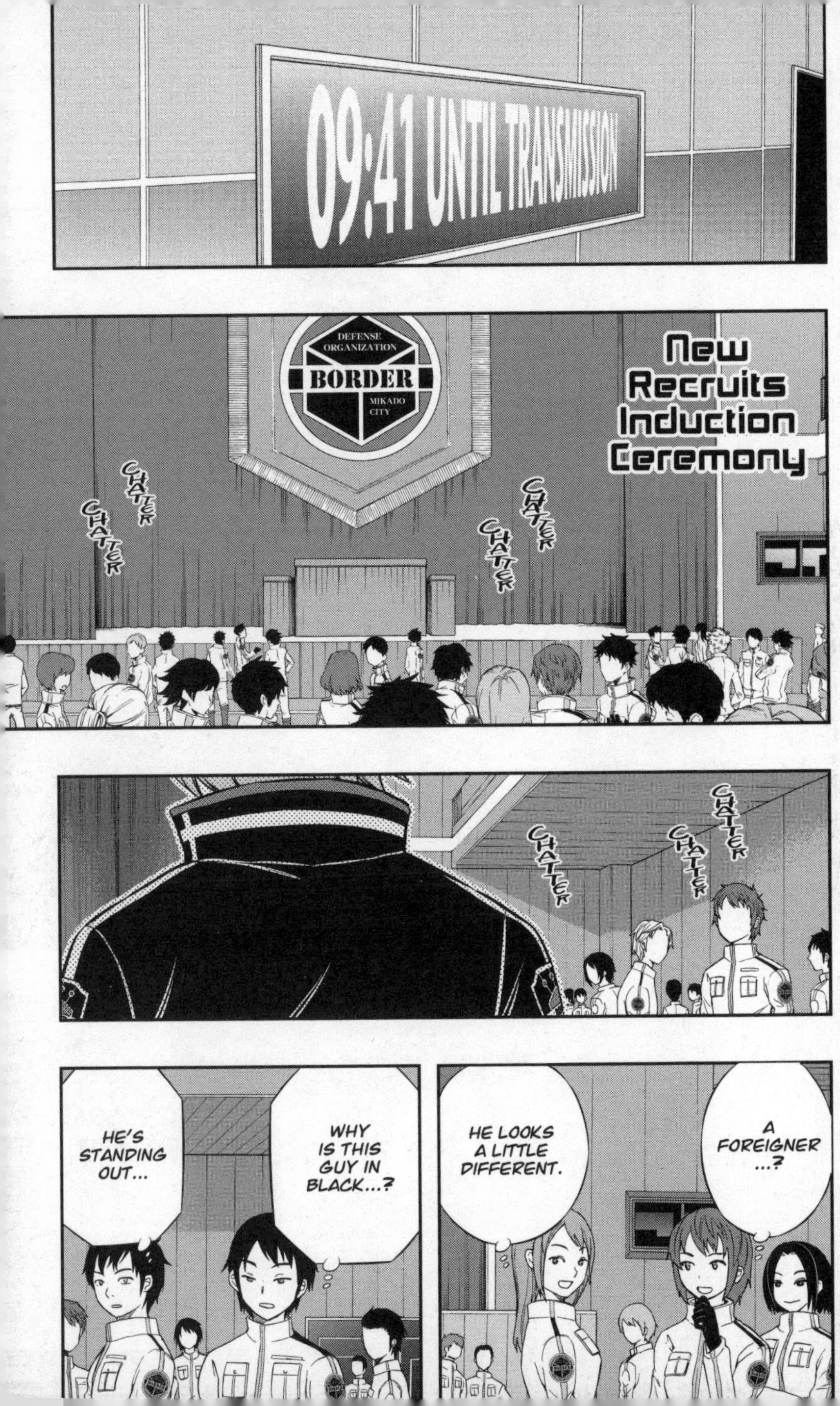
09:41 UNTIL TRANSMISSION
DEFENSE ORGANIZATION
BORDER
MIKADO CITY
New Recruits Induction Ceremony
CHATTER
CHATTER
CHATTER
CHATTER
CHATTER
CHATTER
CHATTER
A FOREIGNER ...?
HE LOOKS A LITTLE DIFFERENT.
WHY IS THIS GUY IN BLACK...?
HE'S STANDING OUT...

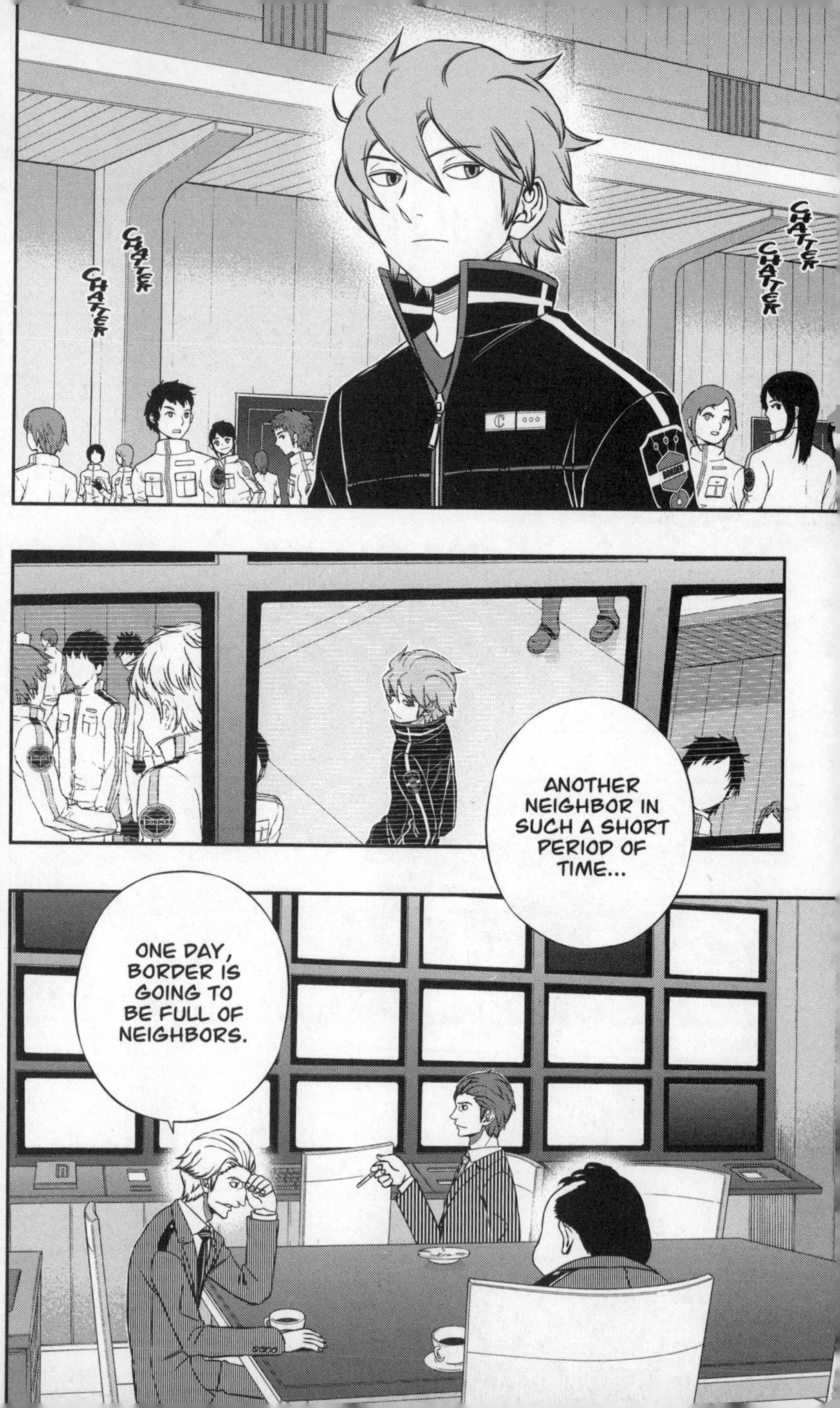
CHATTER
CHATTER
CHATTER
CHATTER
ANOTHER NEIGHBOR IN SUCH A SHORT PERIOD OF TIME...
ONE DAY, BORDER IS GOING TO BE FULL OF NEIGHBORS.

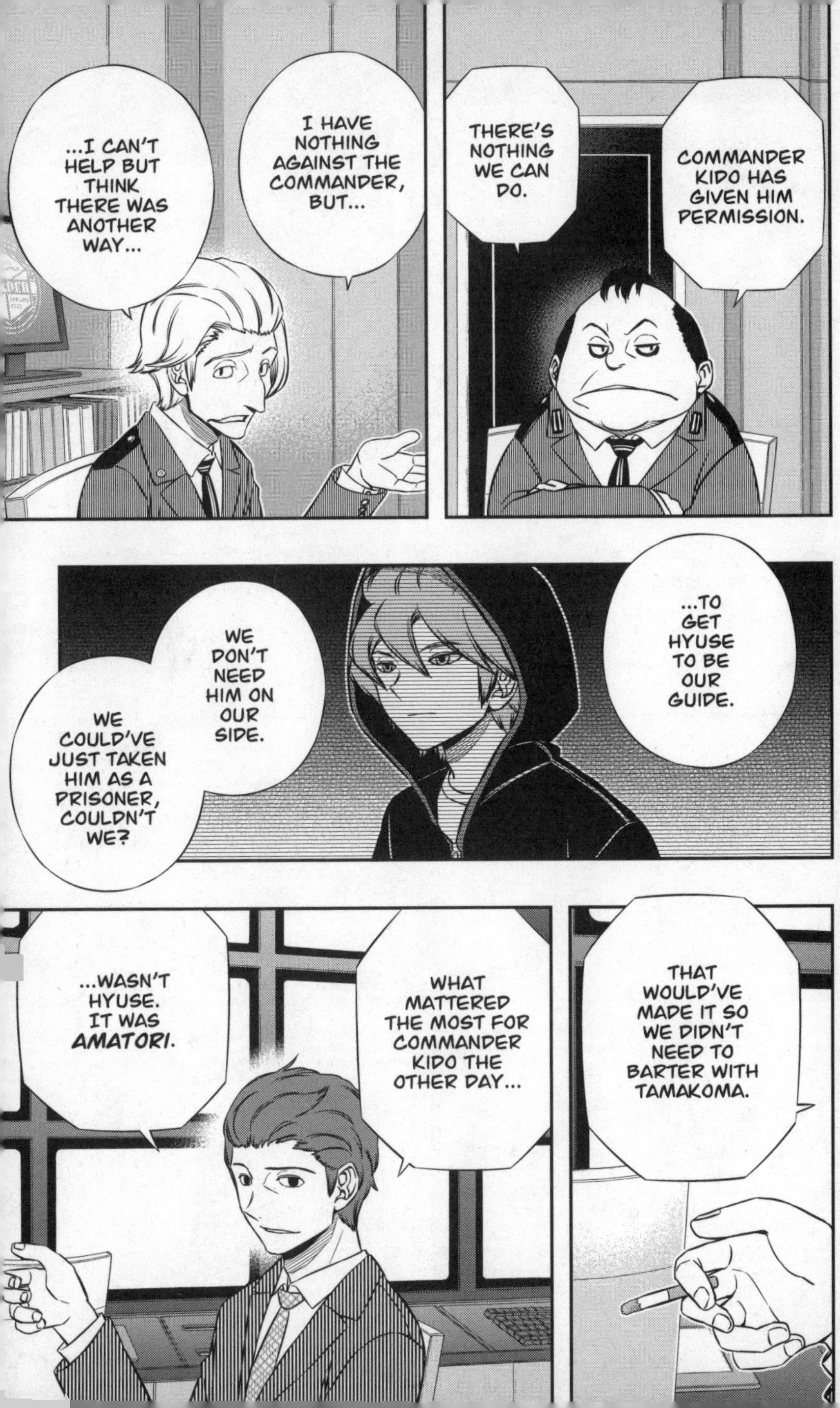
COMMANDER KIDO HAS GIVEN HIM PERMISSION.
THERE'S NOTHING WE CAN DO.
I HAVE NOTHING AGAINST THE COMMANDER, BUT...
...I CAN'T HELP BUT THINK THERE WAS ANOTHER WAY...
...TO GET HYUSE TO BE OUR GUIDE.
WE DON'T NEED HIM ON OUR SIDE.
WE COULD'VE JUST TAKEN HIM AS A PRISONER, COULDN'T WE?
THAT WOULD'VE MADE IT SO WE DIDN'T NEED TO BARTER WITH TAMAKOMA.
WHAT MATTERED THE MOST FOR COMMANDER KIDO THE OTHER DAY...
...WASN'T HYUSE. IT WAS AMATORI.

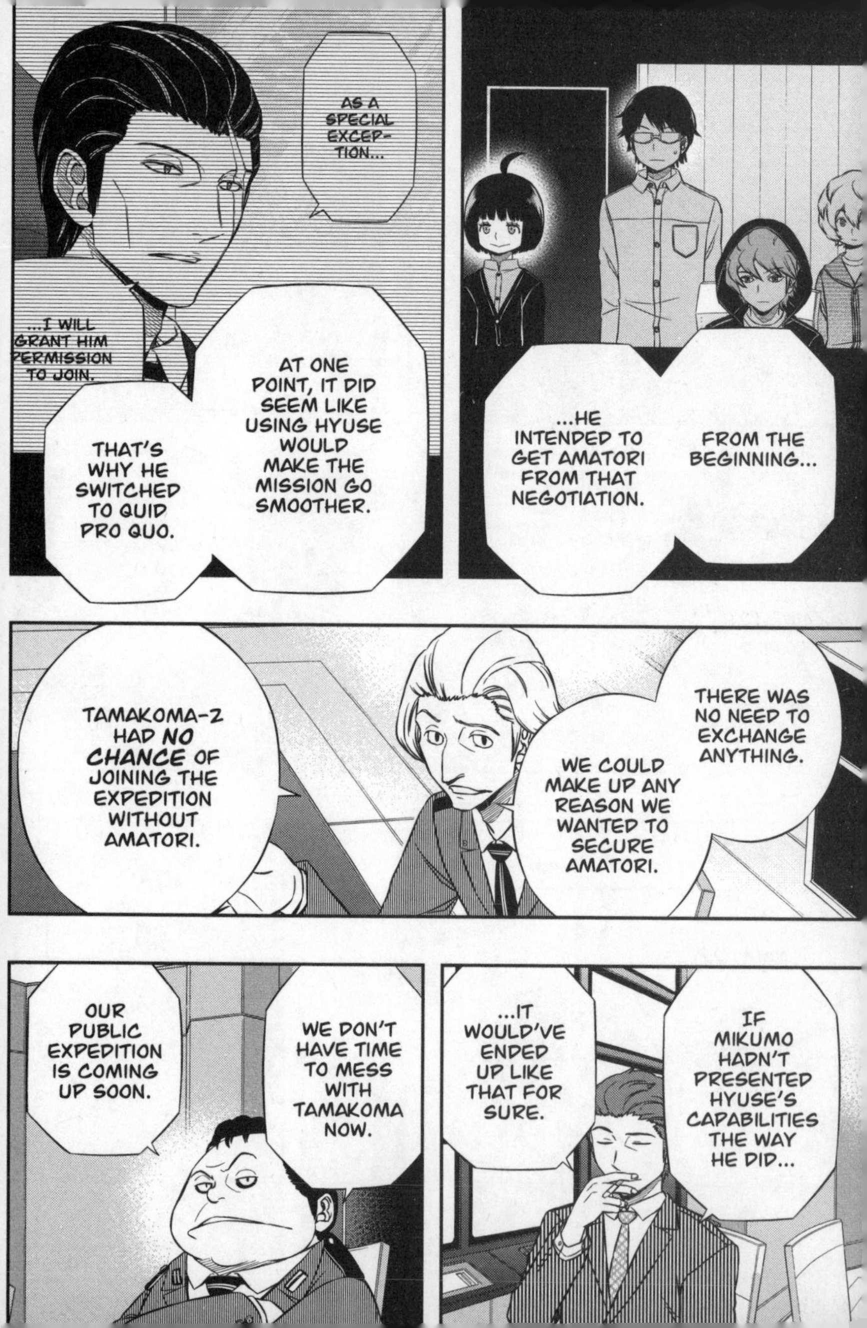
FROM THE BEGINNING...
...HE INTENDED TO GET AMATORI FROM THAT NEGOTIATION.
AS A SPECIAL EXCEPTION...
...I WILL GRANT HIM PERMISSION TO JOIN.
AT ONE POINT, IT DID SEEM LIKE USING HYUSE WOULD MAKE THE MISSION GO SMOOTHER.
THAT'S WHY HE SWITCHED TO QUID PRO QUO.
THERE WAS NO NEED TO EXCHANGE ANYTHING.
WE COULD MAKE UP ANY REASON WE WANTED TO SECURE AMATORI.
TAMAKOMA-2 HAD NO CHANCE OF JOINING THE EXPEDITION WITHOUT AMATORI.
IF MIKUMO HADN'T PRESENTED HYUSE'S CAPABILITIES THE WAY HE DID...
...IT WOULD'VE ENDED UP LIKE THAT FOR SURE.
WE DON'T HAVE TIME TO MESS WITH TAMAKOMA NOW.
OUR PUBLIC EXPEDITION IS COMING UP SOON.

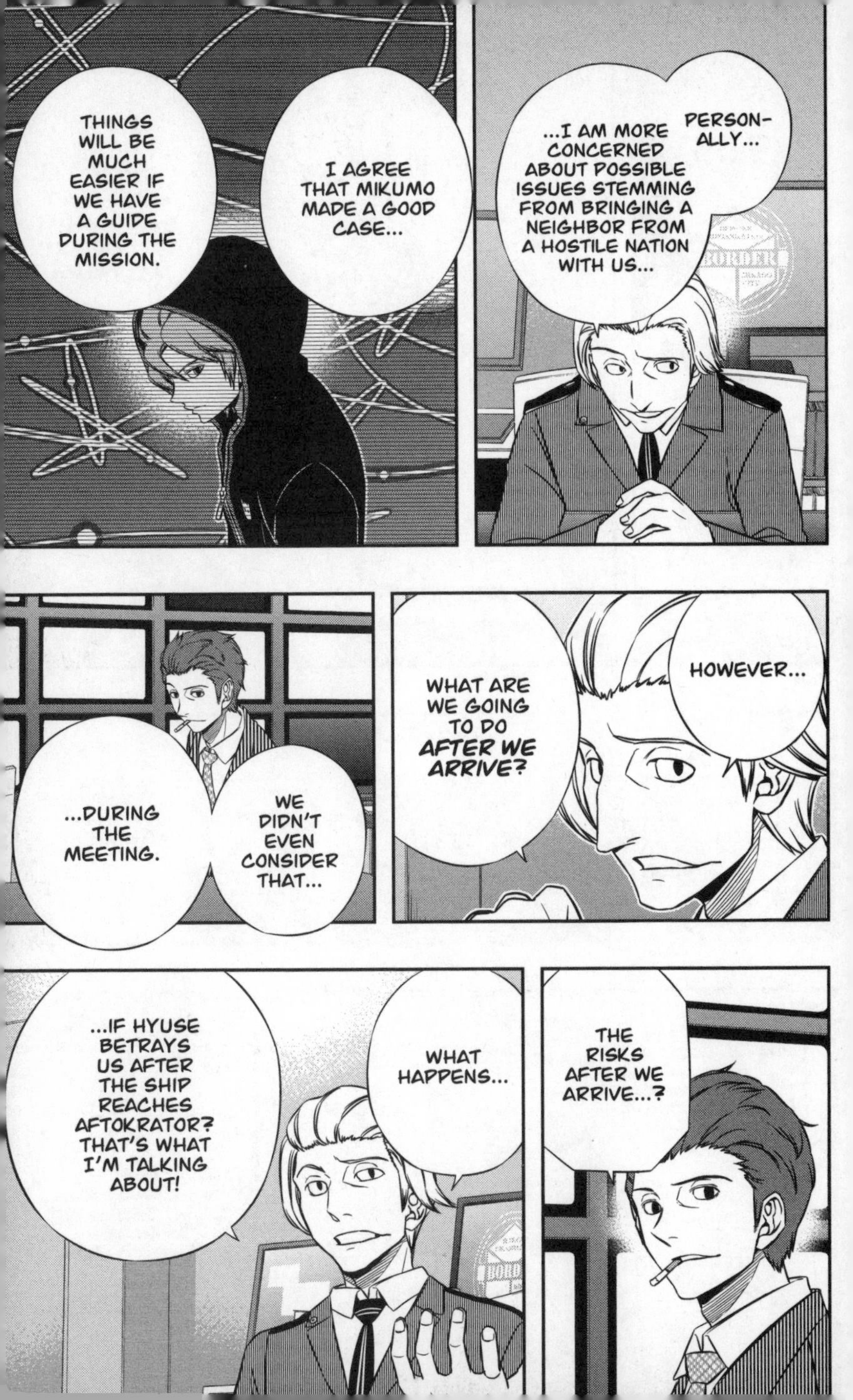
PERSON-ALLY...
...I AM MORE CONCERNED ABOUT POSSIBLE ISSUES STEMMING FROM BRINGING A NEIGHBOR FROM A HOSTILE NATION WITH US...
I AGREE THAT MIKUMO MADE A GOOD CASE...
THINGS WILL BE MUCH EASIER IF WE HAVE A GUIDE DURING THE MISSION.
HOWEVER...
WHAT ARE WE GOING TO DO AFTER WE ARRIVE?
WE DIDN'T EVEN CONSIDER THAT...
...DURING THE MEETING.
THE RISKS AFTER WE ARRIVE...?
WHAT HAPPENS...
...IF HYUSE BETRAYS US AFTER THE SHIP REACHES AFTOKRATOR? THAT'S WHAT I'M TALKING ABOUT!

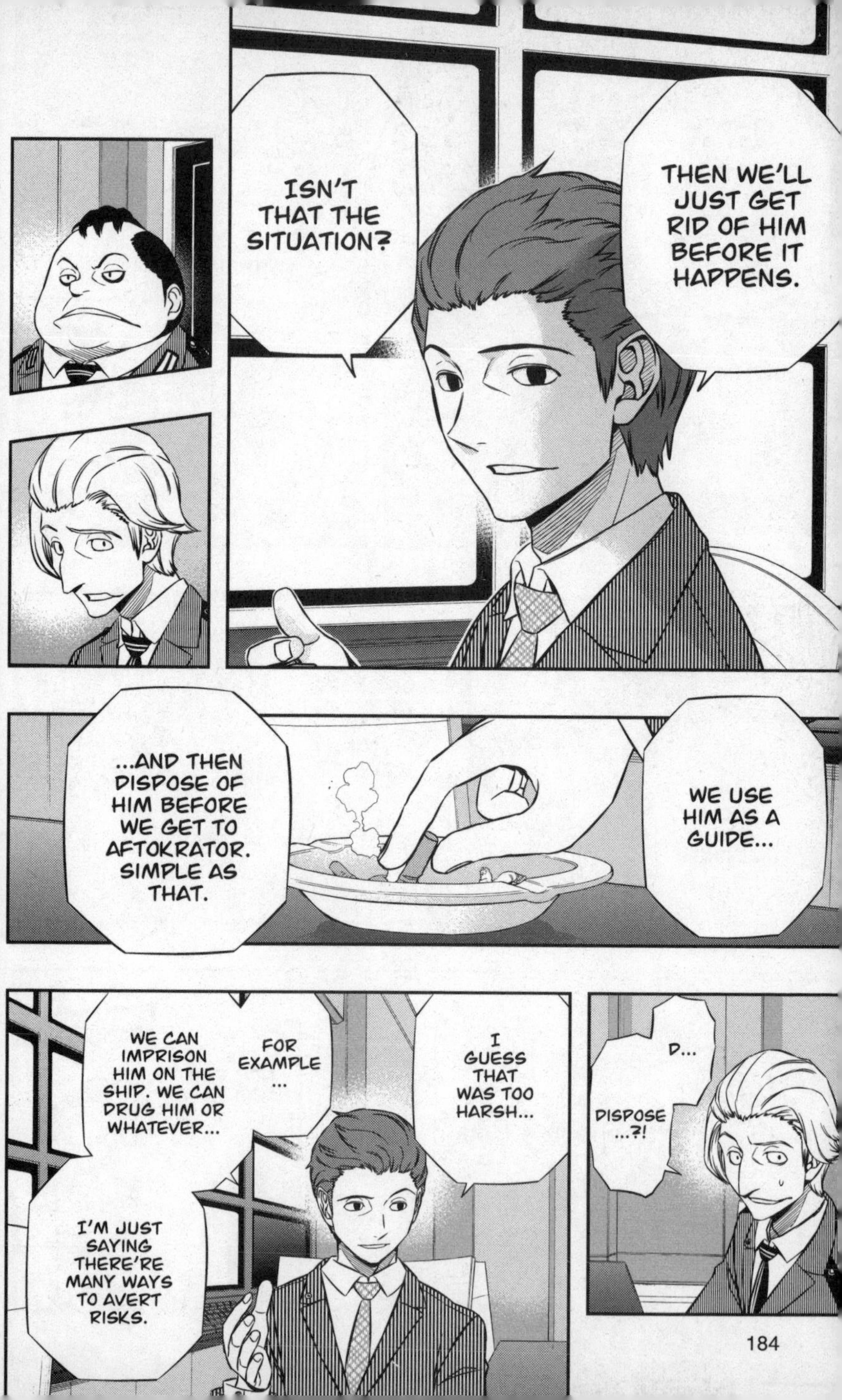
ISN'T THAT THE SITUATION?
THEN WE'LL JUST GET RID OF HIM BEFORE IT HAPPENS.
WE USE HIM AS A GUIDE...
...AND THEN DISPOSE OF HIM BEFORE WE GET TO AFTOKRATOR. SIMPLE AS THAT.
D...
DISPOSE ...?!
I GUESS THAT WAS TOO HARSH...
FOR EXAMPLE ...
WE CAN IMPRISON HIM ON THE SHIP. WE CAN DRUG HIM OR WHATEVER...
I'M JUST SAYING THERE'RE MANY WAYS TO AVERT RISKS.

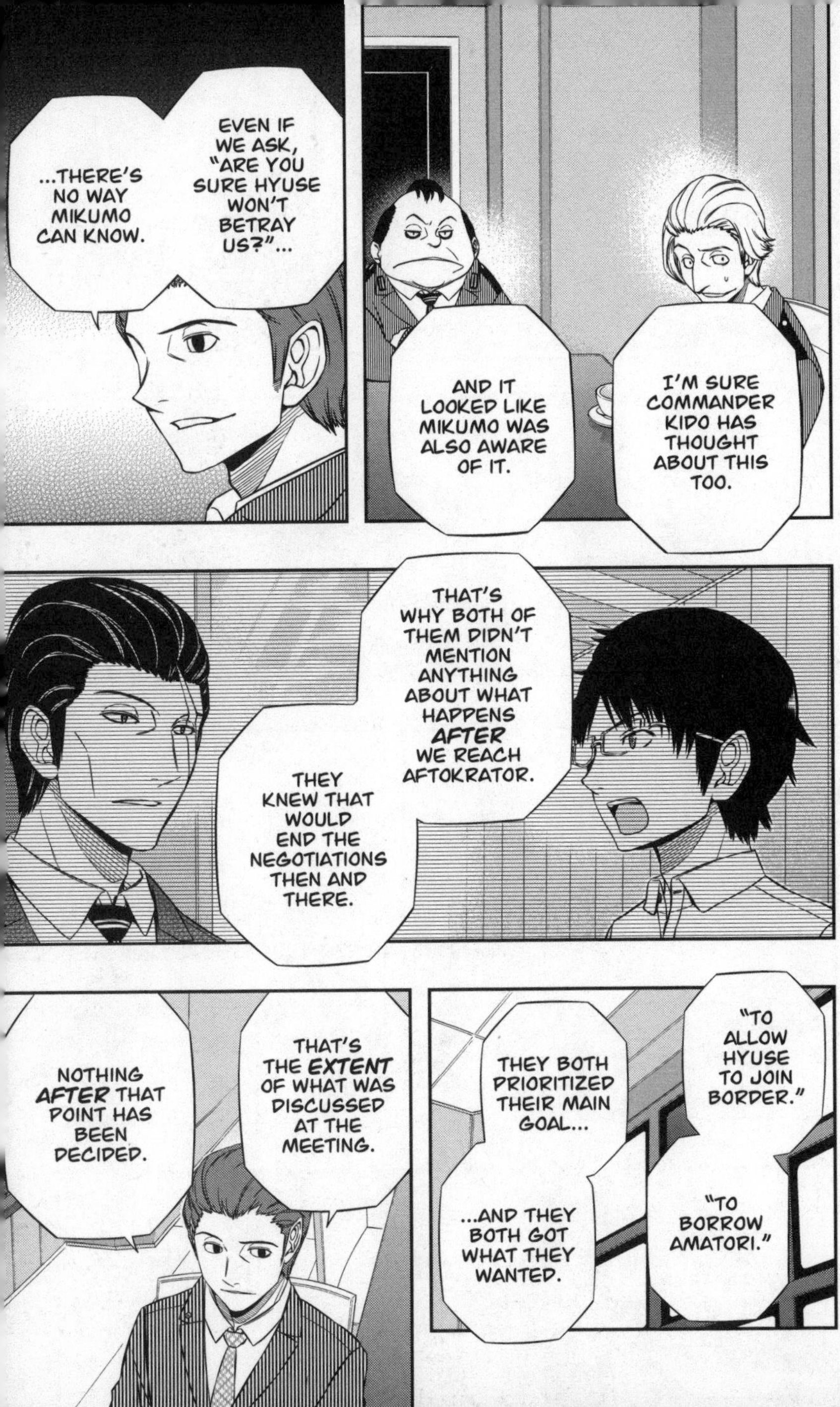
I'M SURE COMMANDER KIDO HAS THOUGHT ABOUT THIS TOO.
AND IT LOOKED LIKE MIKUMO WAS ALSO AWARE OF IT.
EVEN IF WE ASK, "ARE YOU SURE HYUSE WON'T BETRAY US?"...
...THERE'S NO WAY MIKUMO CAN KNOW.
THAT'S WHY BOTH OF THEM DIDN'T MENTION ANYTHING ABOUT WHAT HAPPENS **AFTER** WE REACH AFTOKRATOR.
THEY KNEW THAT WOULD END THE NEGOTIATIONS THEN AND THERE.
"TO ALLOW HYUSE TO JOIN BORDER."
THEY BOTH PRIORITIZED THEIR MAIN GOAL...
"TO BORROW AMATORI."
...AND THEY BOTH GOT WHAT THEY WANTED.
THAT'S THE **EXTENT** OF WHAT WAS DISCUSSED AT THE MEETING.
NOTHING **AFTER** THAT POINT HAS BEEN DECIDED.

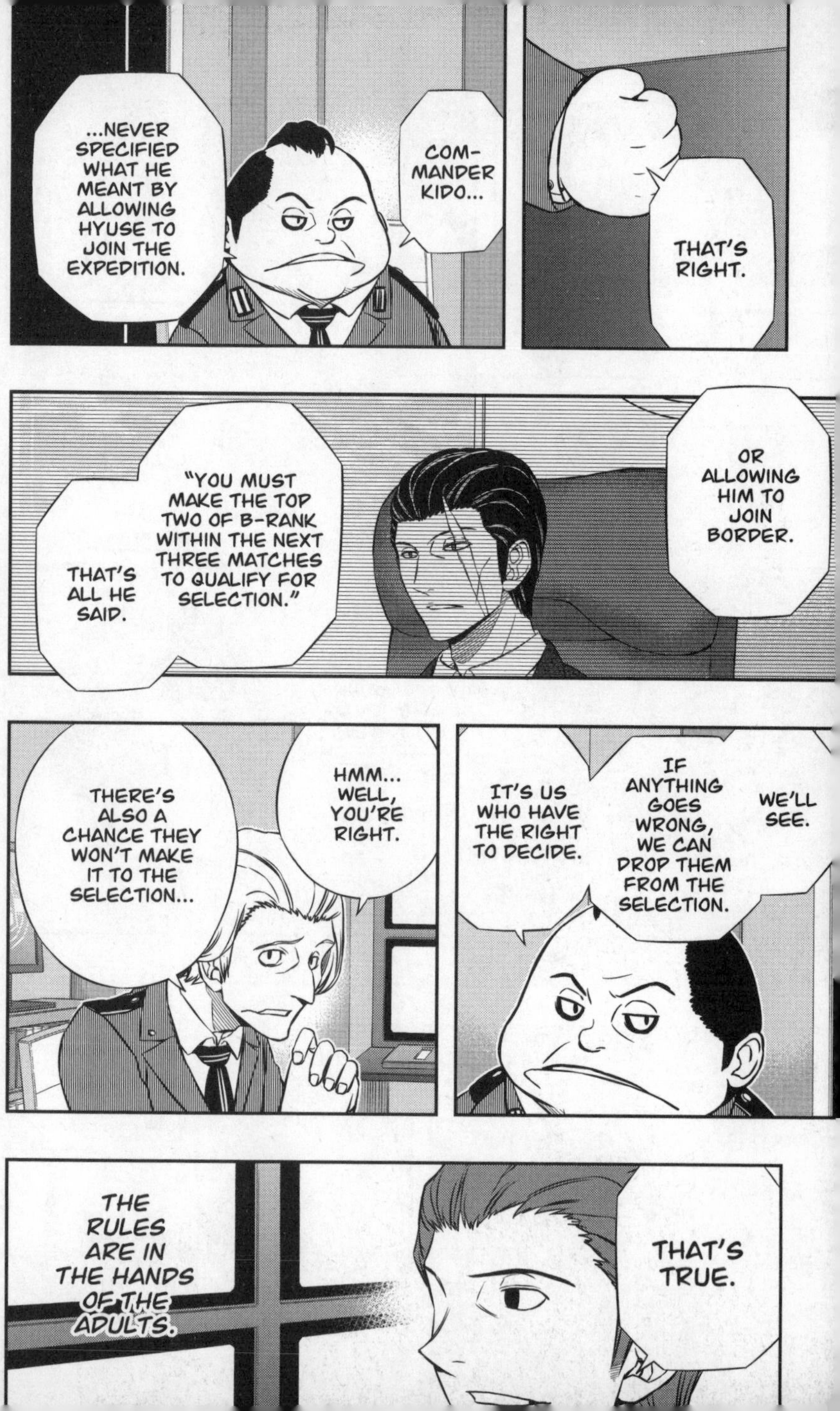
THAT'S RIGHT.
COM-MANDER KIDO...
...NEVER SPECIFIED WHAT HE MEANT BY ALLOWING HYUSE TO JOIN THE EXPEDITION.
OR ALLOWING HIM TO JOIN BORDER.
"YOU MUST MAKE THE TOP TWO OF B-RANK WITHIN THE NEXT THREE MATCHES TO QUALIFY FOR SELECTION."
THAT'S ALL HE SAID.
WE'LL SEE.
IF ANYTHING GOES WRONG, WE CAN DROP THEM FROM THE SELECTION.
IT'S US WHO HAVE THE RIGHT TO DECIDE.
HMM... WELL, YOU'RE RIGHT.
THERE'S ALSO A CHANCE THEY WON'T MAKE IT TO THE SELECTION...
THAT'S TRUE.
THE RULES ARE IN THE HANDS OF THE ADULTS.

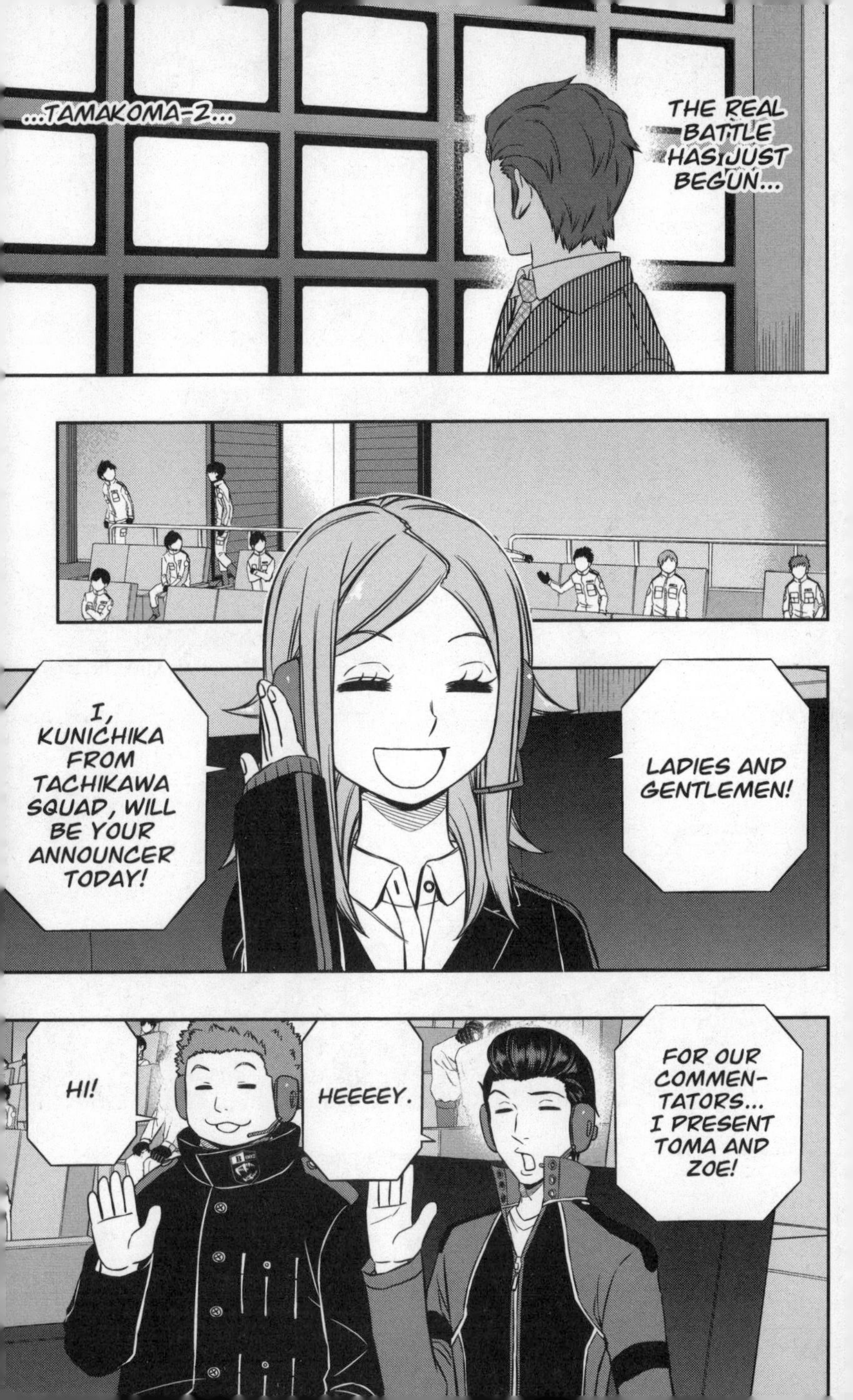
THE REAL BATTLE HAS JUST BEGUN...
...TAMAKOMA-2...
LADIES AND GENTLEMEN!
I, KUNICHIKA FROM TACHIKAWA SQUAD, WILL BE YOUR ANNOUNCER TODAY!
FOR OUR COMMENTATORS... I PRESENT TOMA AND ZOE!
HEEEEY.
HI!

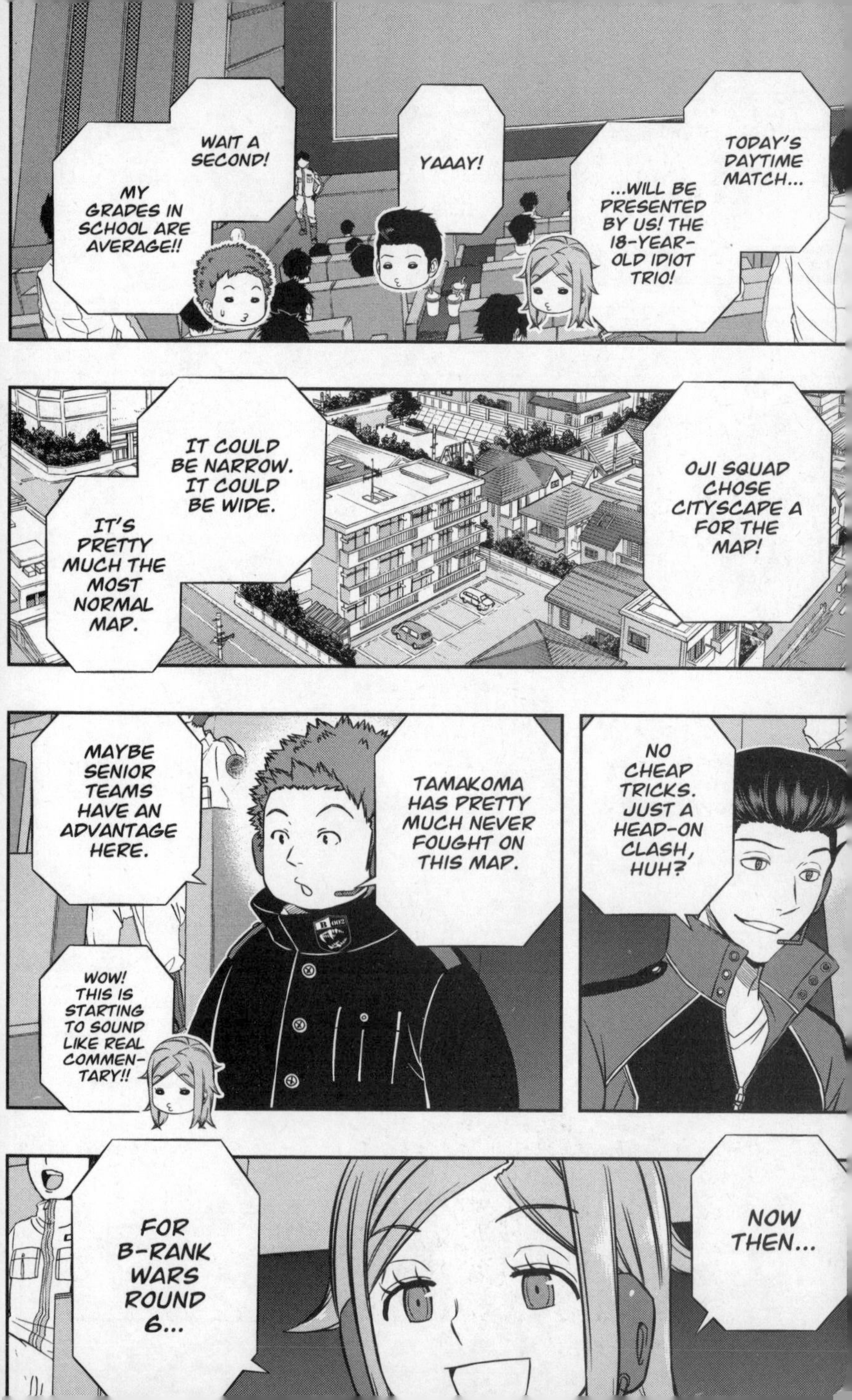
TODAY'S DAYTIME MATCH...
...WILL BE PRESENTED BY US! THE 18-YEAR-OLD IDIOT TRIO!
YAAAY!
WAIT A SECOND!
MY GRADES IN SCHOOL ARE AVERAGE!!
OJI SQUAD CHOSE CITYSCAPE A FOR THE MAP!
IT COULD BE NARROW. IT COULD BE WIDE.
IT'S PRETTY MUCH THE MOST NORMAL MAP.
NO CHEAP TRICKS. JUST A HEAD-ON CLASH, HUH?
TAMAKOMA HAS PRETTY MUCH NEVER FOUGHT ON THIS MAP.
MAYBE SENIOR TEAMS HAVE AN ADVANTAGE HERE.
WOW! THIS IS STARTING TO SOUND LIKE REAL COMMENTARY!!
NOW THEN...
FOR B-RANK WARS ROUND 6...

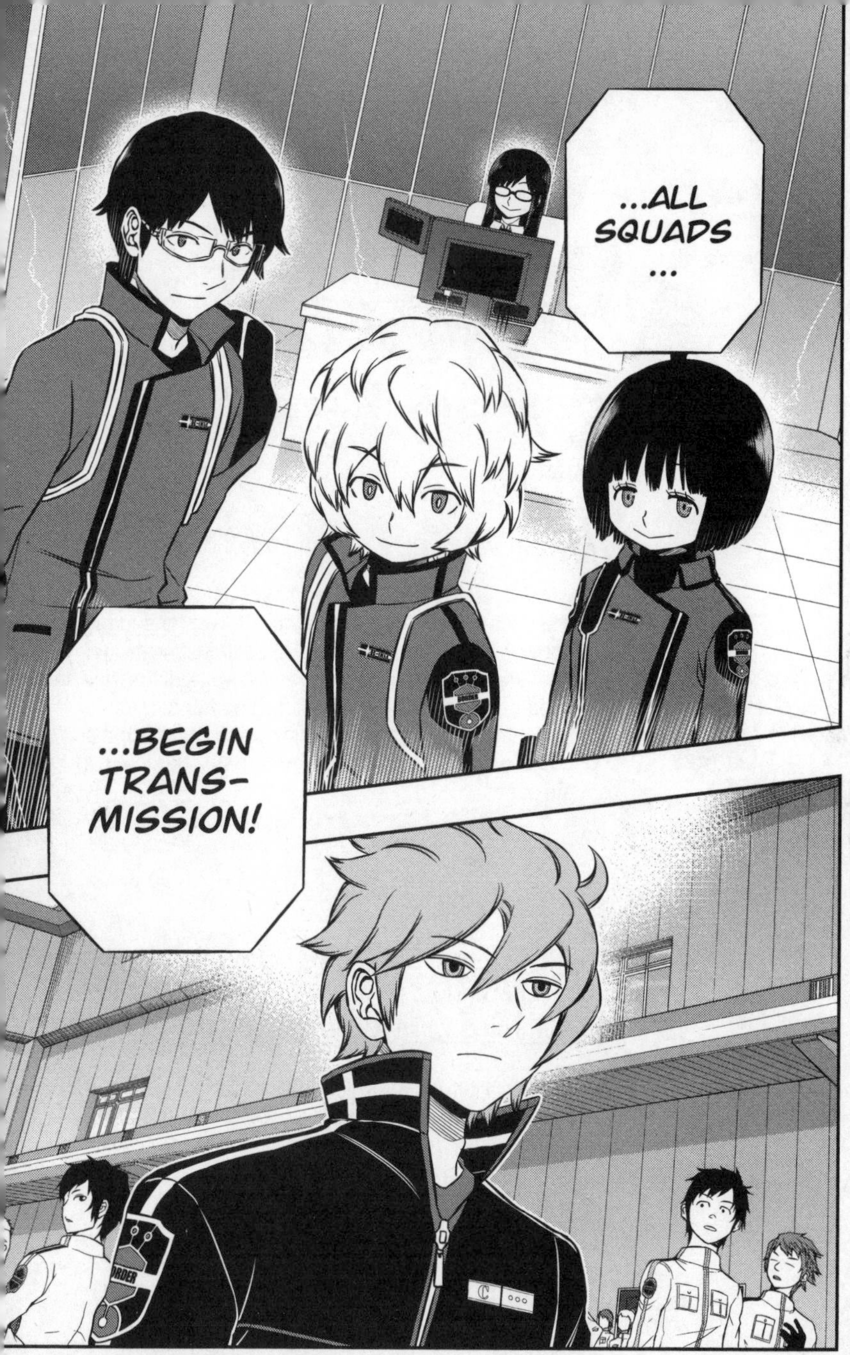
...ALL SQUADS ...
...BEGIN TRANS-MISSION!

To Be Continued In ***World Trigger*** 18!

WORLD TRIGGER

Bonus Character Pages

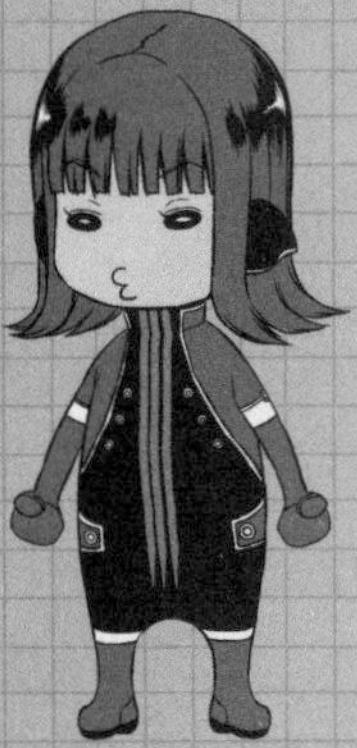

YOKO

Her Boobs Are Probably Fake

Her side effect(?) is increasing her cup size when she uses a Trion Body. She is also known for secretly copying Konami and Nasu Squad's uniforms to increase her own popularity...and it worked! She has a good number of fans who don't mind her bad attitude. Her crush on Torimaru is totally obvious. She's one of my favorite recently introduced female characters in the series.

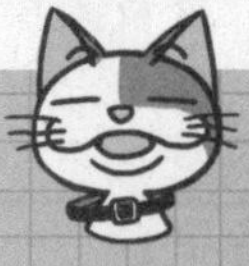

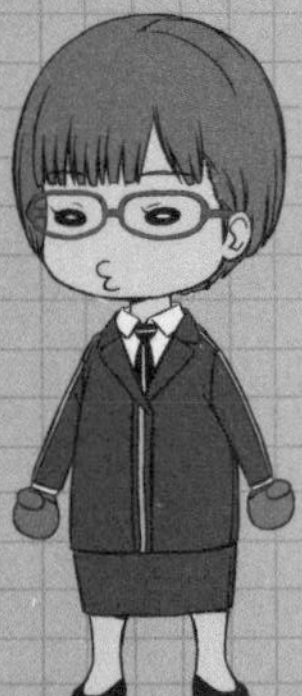

HANA

A Flower That Blooms on the Battlefield

A glove-wearing girl whose past is pretty serious. Until recently, a lot of fans actually theorized she was a germophobe, had a prosthetic, or was even a poison dart-shooting assassin! Yuta is her cousin, though they look nothing alike. After she lost her house, she lived at his place for a while. She's a secret Arashiyama fangirl and enjoys her life at Border.

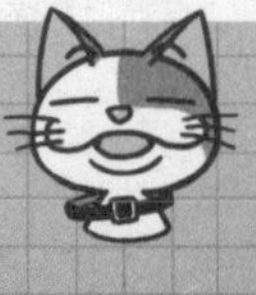

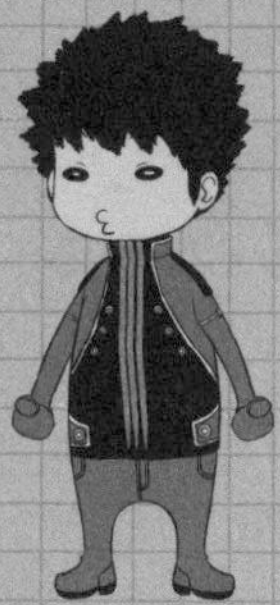

YUTA

Between a Girl and Four-Eyes

A spineless attacker whose catchphrase is, "C'mon, guys!" His current record is repeating it 46 times in one day. He joined Border thanks to his connection to Hana and his crush on Yoko. Even though he's done nothing but kiss up to Yoko, he did manage to man up a bit this volume. He's friends with a lot of the younger Attackers since he's so relaxed and easygoing. With enough funding, he could create his own Kuruma 2.0 slot! I want him to win the lottery.

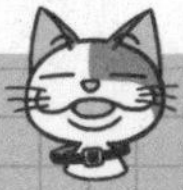

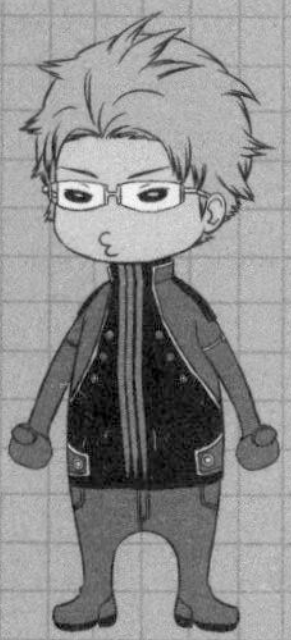

ROKURO

I Wanna Be Master-Class Now!

A tragic hot-blooded four-eyes whose passionate speech landed him a cellphone smashed into his face. He joined the squad because he's friends with Yoko's brother, but now he's just attracted to Hana's cool demeanor. It really just goes to show you we're all attracted to people with things we don't have. I think he's good looking, but his personality is so lame. I expect him to be at least a little popular with the other gunners.

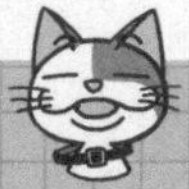

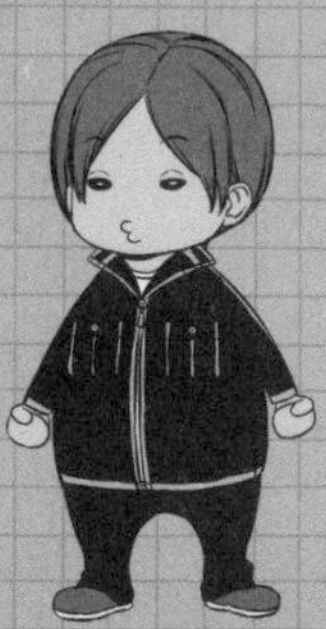

RAIZO

Chubby Thunder

An operator at Border who guards Enedorad. They watch movies at work together like it's no big deal. He specializes in "observation and containment of the shock waves caused by Trion reactions." In addition to the Raygust's Thruster, he's also in charge of finding ways to upgrade Meteor. He's interested in dabbling in Trion Soldier development and seems to be pals with Enedorad both at work and in his private life. He used to be thin but stopped caring about his figure and is now fat.

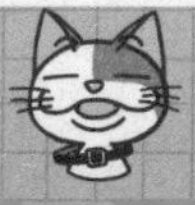

YOU'RE READING THE WRONG WAY!

World Trigger reads from right to left, starting in the upper-right corner. Japanese is read from right to left, meaning that action, sound effects, and word-balloon order are completely reversed from the English order.

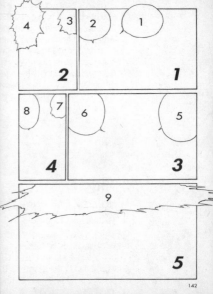

You're Reading in the Wrong Direction!!

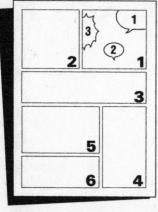

Whoops! Guess what? You're starting at the wrong end of the comic!

...It's true! In keeping with the original Japanese format, **Assassination Classroom** is meant to be read from right to left, starting in the upper-right corner.

Unlike English, which is read from left to right, Japanese is read from right to left, meaning that action, sound effects and word-balloon order are completely reversed... something which can make readers unfamiliar with Japanese feel pretty backwards themselves. For this reason, manga or Japanese comics published in the U.S. in English have sometimes been published "flopped"—that is, printed in exact reverse order, as though seen from the other side of a mirror.

By flopping pages, U.S. publishers can avoid confusing readers, but the compromise is not without its downside. For one thing, a character in a flopped manga series who once wore in the original Japanese version a T-shirt emblazoned with "M A Y" (as in "the merry month of") now wears one which reads "Y A M"! Additionally, many manga creators in Japan are themselves unhappy with the process, as some feel the mirror-imaging of their art skews their original intentions.

We are proud to bring you Yusei Matsui's **Assassination Classroom** in the original unflopped format.
For now, though, turn to the other side of the book and let the adventure begin...!

—Editor

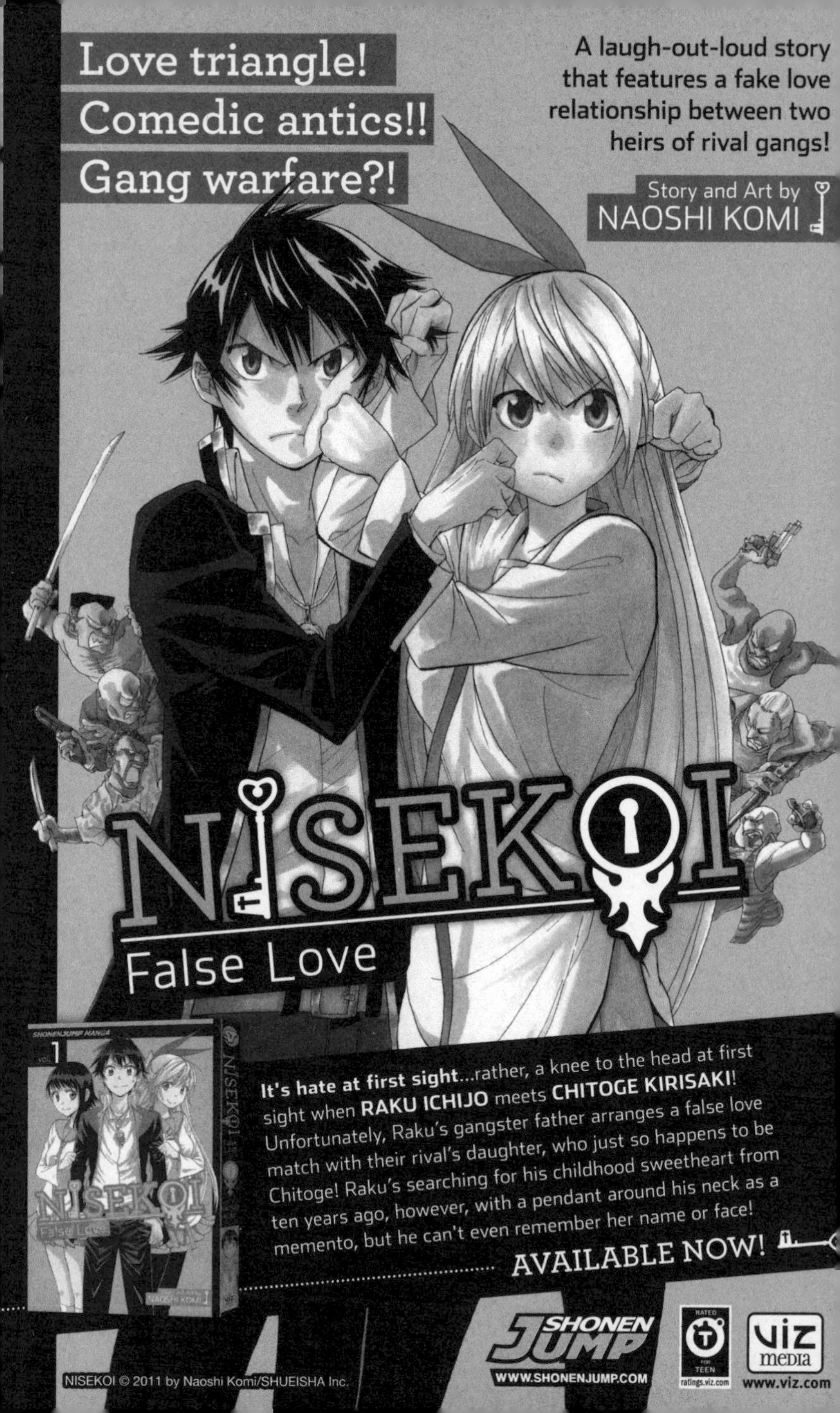
Love triangle!
Comedic antics!!
Gang warfare?!
A laugh-out-loud story that features a fake love relationship between two heirs of rival gangs!
Story and Art by NAOSHI KOMI
NISEKOI
False Love
It's hate at first sight...rather, a knee to the head at first sight when RAKU ICHIJO meets CHITOGE KIRISAKI! Unfortunately, Raku's gangster father arranges a false love match with their rival's daughter, who just so happens to be Chitoge! Raku's searching for his childhood sweetheart from ten years ago, however, with a pendant around his neck as a memento, but he can't even remember her name or face!
AVAILABLE NOW!
SHONEN JUMP
WWW.SHONENJUMP.COM
ratings.viz.com
VIZ media
www.viz.com
NISEKOI © 2011 by Naoshi Komi/SHUEISHA Inc.

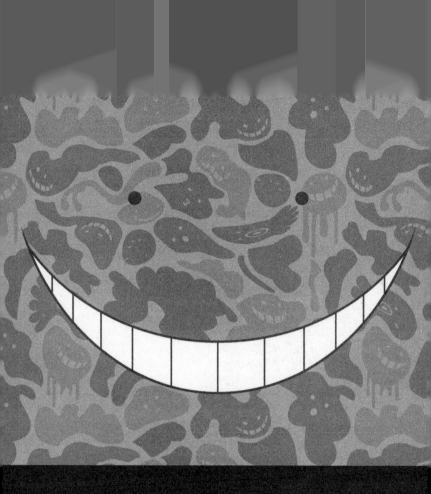

Lowly Class E and elite Class A compete for the most customers at their school festival booths. So far, the students of Class E are holding their own, despite their location on the mountaintop. Then a parade of familiar faces, some welcome and some...not so much...drop by with surprising consequences. Will the principal's son Gakushu be able to maintain his position as the illustrious leader of Class A? Who could possibly replace him in hopes of leading the students to victory and subjugating the weak...?

Available February 2017!

A S S A S S I N A T I O N
CLASSROOM

Volume 13
SHONEN JUMP ADVANCED Manga Edition

Story and Art by YUSEI MATSUI

Translation/Tetsuichiro Miyaki
English Adaptation/Bryant Turnage
Touch-up Art & Lettering/Stephen Dutro
Cover & Interior Design/Sam Elzway
Editor/Annette Roman

Published by VIZ Media, LLC
P.O. Box 77010
San Francisco, CA 94107

10 9 8 7 6 5 4 3 2 1
First printing, December 2016

www.viz.com

www.shonenjump.com

A MOMENT OF TENTACLE ZEN

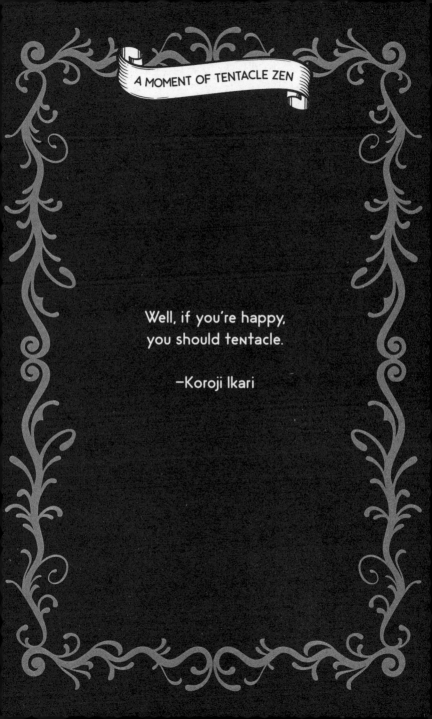

Well, if you're happy,
you should tentacle.

–Koroji Ikari

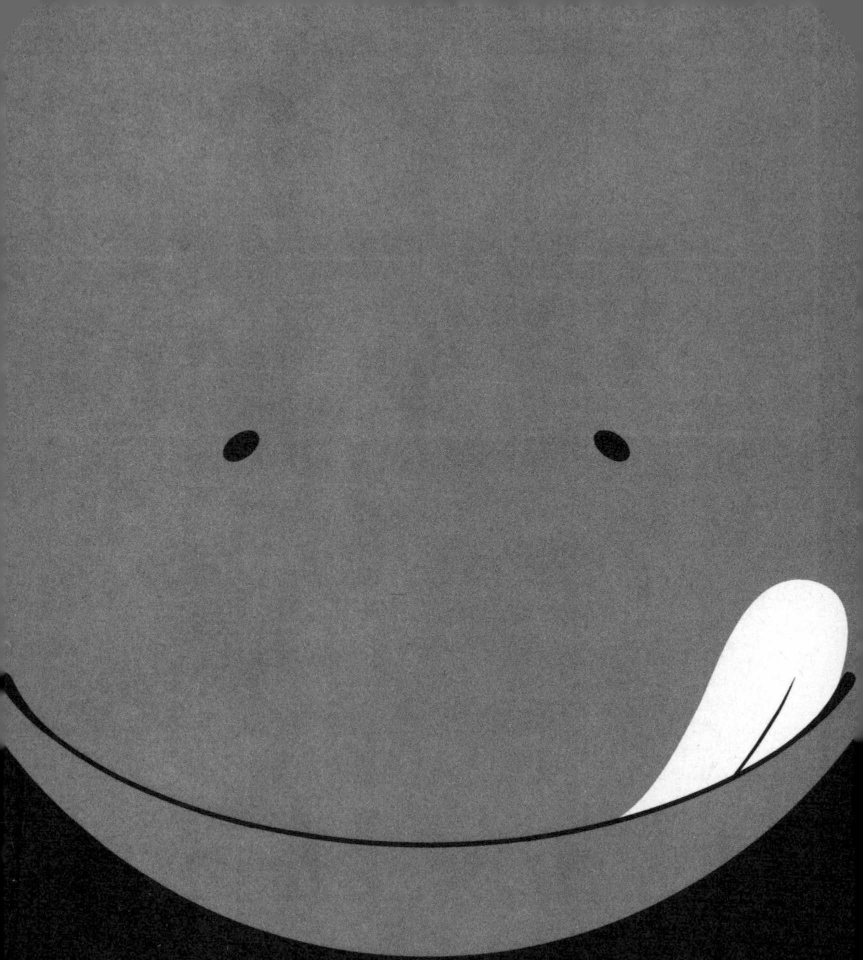

This new pink color appears on Koro Sensei's face when he has the munchies. Now that *Assassination Classroom* is being made into a movie, I've decided to call it "Convenience Store Pink" in hopes that convenience stores will create a collaborative promotional snack using this facial expression and color!

ASSASSINATION CLASSROOM

YUSEI MATSUI

13

TIME FOR A LITTLE CAREER COUNSELING

I'm probably experiencing the busiest days of my life currently.

This manga is getting to the most important part of the story now. Also, I have been photographed, interviewed and have performed various other functions beyond my expertise to promote this manga.

All of these incredible oppourtunities I have right now are the result of your generous support, so I'm putting everything I've got into the work before me.

And when it's all over...

I'll probably return to my days of moving at a slow, sloth-like pace.

—Yusei Matsui

Yusei Matsui was born on the last day of January in Saitama Prefecture, Japan. He has been drawing manga since elementary school. Some of his favorite manga series are *Bobobo-bo Bo-bobo*, *JoJo's Bizarre Adventure* and *Ultimate Muscle*. Matsui learned his trade working as an assistant to manga artist Yoshio Sawai, creator of *Bobobo-bo Bo-bobo*. In 2005, Matsui debuted his original manga *Neuro: Supernatural Detective* in *Weekly Shonen Jump*. In 2007, *Neuro* was adapted into an anime. In 2012, *Assassination Classroom* began serialization in *Weekly Shonen Jump*.

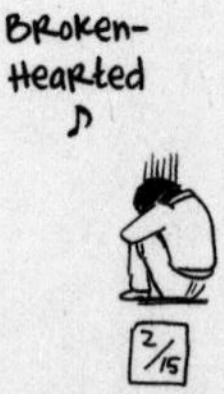
Broken-
Hearted
2/15